Dr Thomas Plume, 1630–1704

His Life and Legacies in Essex, Kent and Cambridge

Dr Thomas Plume, 1630–1704

His Life and Legacies in Essex, Kent and Cambridge

Edited by
R.A. Doe and C.C. Thornton

Essex Publications
an imprint of
UNIVERSITY OF HERTFORDSHIRE PRESS

First published in Great Britain in 2020 by
Essex Publications
an imprint of
University of Hertfordshire Press
College Lane
Hatfield
Hertfordshire
AL10 9AB

© The Trustees of the Plume Library

The right of Robert Anthony Doe and Christopher Thornton to be identified as the editors of this work has been asserted by them in accordance with the Copyright, Designs and Patents Act 1988.

All rights reserved. No part of this book may be reproduced or utilized in any form or by any means, electronic or mechanical, including photocopying, recording or by any information storage and retrieval system, without permission in writing from the publisher.

British Library Cataloguing in publication Data
A catalogue record for this book in available from the British Library

ISBN 978-1-912260-16-4

Design by Arthouse Publishing Solutions
Printed in Great Britain by Hobbs the Printers Ltd

Publication Grants

The editors are grateful for financial support from The Friends of Thomas Plume's Library, The Essex Heritage Trust, The Essex Society for Archaeology and History and The Essex Society for Family History.

This book is dedicated with the greatest respect to the trustees of Dr Plume's charities whose dedication and hard work has secured his legacies for over three centuries.

Contents

List of illustrations	xi
Notes on contributors	xv
List of abbreviations	xvii
Preface and Acknowledgements	xviii

1. Introduction: 'this munificent person' – Dr Thomas Plume and his legacies 1
Christopher Thornton, Robert Anthony Doe, Sue Edward and Helen Kemp

2. The Plume family at Maldon, c.1621–1704 25
J.R. Smith

3. Dr Thomas Plume: 'a man outstanding for his upright character, devotion of life and charity towards the poor' 53
Robert Anthony Doe

4. 'Concerning the trifles of my worldly goods': the making and execution of Dr Thomas Plume's last will and testament 95
Sue Edward

5. Thomas Plume and his Maldon Trust 120
Max Earnshaw and Christopher Thornton

6. Thomas Plume's Library in its seventeenth-century context 155
David Pearson

7. The Plume Building 176
James Bettley

8. 'All my Manuscript-papers of my own hand': Plume's collection of handwritten texts 196
Helen Kemp

9. 'His works do follow him': Dr Thomas Plume and his Kent legacies 225
Catharina Clement

10. 'A studious, and learned Professor of Astronomy and experimentall philosophy': the Plumian professors at Cambridge from 1707 to the present day 249
Mark Hurn

Appendix: Dr Thomas Plume's will 263
Bibliography 283
Index 309

Illustrations

Figures

1.1	Dr Thomas Plume. Untitled and unsigned portrait held in the Moot Hall, Maldon	4
1.2	Dr Thomas Plume's arms	7
1.3	Map of places associated with Dr Thomas Plume and his bequests	8
1.4	Books 'on the railes' at Moorfields, detail from Sutton Nicholls's print of 'The Compleat Auctioneer', c.1700	13
1.5	Postcard of St Peter's Tower (Plume Library building) on the corner of Maldon's High Street and Market Hill, c.1900	15
1.6	Flamsteed House, Greenwich Park, built in 1676 and occupied in the same year by John Flamsteed (1646–1719), the Astronomer Royal (from 1675)	18
2.1	Great Yeldham Hall in north Essex, home of Dr Thomas Plume's forebears	26
2.2	Plume family tree, *temp.* Henry VIII–1704	27
2.3	All Saints' church, Maldon, c.1860, parish church of the Plume family and scene of Plume baptisms, marriages and burials 1623–70	29
2.4	Map of properties in Maldon associated with the Plume family	32
2.5	The Moot Hall, Maldon, home of Maldon's civic government from 1576	37
2.6	Dedication by John Danes to Thomas Plume on flyleaf of his *Paralipomena Orthographiae Etymologiae Prosodiae*, 1639	45
3.1	A pair of silver flagons donated to All Saints church, Maldon, by Thomas Plume, 'in thankful memory of his baptism there'	54
3.2	St Mary's Church, Chelmsford, in 1833, the scene of religious disturbances in 1641–2, probably witnessed by Plume	56
3.3	The frontage to the street of Christ's College, Cambridge, in the nineteenth century	58
3.4	John Hacket (1592–1670), bishop of Lichfield and Coventry	64
3.5	St Alfege's church (detail) and the river Thames from One Tree Hill, Greenwich Park, c.1690	71
3.6	A prospect of Greenwich Hospital from the Thames in 1736	72
3.7	The *Peregrine* and other royal yachts off Greenwich, c.1710	75

3.8	Rochester Cathedral before 1655	78
3.9	St Paul's Cathedral destroyed in the Great Fire of London, 1666	82
3.10	(a) Inside the Royal Exchange before it was destroyed by the Great Fire of London in 1666 (b) The Royal Exchange after it was rebuilt three years later	83
4.1	The first page of Dr Thomas Plume's original will, 1704	95
4.2	Dr Thomas Plume's tomb in the churchyard of St Mary Magdalene, Longfield (Kent)	98
4.3	Extract from page 8 of Dr Thomas Plume's original will, showing the interpolation in another hand of the legacy of £100 to Mrs An[ne?] Beale of Westminster	105
4.4	Engraving of Sir John Comyns, 1744	110
4.5	Plume's Maldon workhouse, built c.1720, but with a frontage transformed by extensive later alterations	112
5.1	The opening entry in the Maldon Trust's first minute book, 12 April 1717	123
5.2	A typical entry from the trust's eighteenth-century minute books recording expenditure	123
5.3	A list of the Plume lecturers for 1767, preserved in the trust's first minute book	126
5.4	A receipt from the sexton of All Saints' church for tolling the bell at Dr Plume's lectures, 1792	127
5.5	Iltney Farm, Mundon, the chief endowment of the Maldon Trust, 1841	133
5.6	A list of 16 poor people attending Dr Plume's lectures, 1848	139
5.7	A receipt from a Maldon watch and clockmaker for the apprenticeship of a Plume charity boy, 1866	141
5.8	The cover of an apprenticeship indenture for one of Dr Plume's charity boys, 1850	142
6.1	A typical example of Plume's inscription in a book, from his later years, together with his 'PL' monogram: flyleaf of *The acts and negotiations* (1698)	163
6.2	The more unusual inscription 'Thomas Plume & Amico[ru]m' ('belonging to Thomas Plume and his friends'), on the flyleaf of J. de Mariana, *Tractatus VII* (1609)	163
6.3	An early example of Plume's inscription, from the flyleaf of *Terence in English* (1641)	164
6.4	Another early Plume inscription, with the name spelt 'Plumme', 1643	164
6.5	Plume's manuscript contents list on the flyleaf of a bound volume of tracts: W. Bishop, *A reformation of a Catholike deformed* (1604; and four others, 1590–1623)	165

ILLUSTRATIONS

6.6	An example of Plume's flyleaf notes in F. Walshingham, *A search made into matters of religion* (1609)	165
6.7	A typical example of Plume's manuscript notebooks, in which he made his reading notes: showing notes on Gassendi's *Institutio Astronomica*	166
6.8	A representative selection of Plume's collection of unbound stitched pamphlets	169
7.1	The location of St Peter's Church and Dr Plume's Library in 1873	177
7.2	The Plume Building, *c.*1840–50	180
7.3	Rules of the Library, 1844, by Robert Nightingale, including miniature portrait of Thomas Plume	182
7.4	Interior of the Library, 1920	183
7.5	Interior of ground floor in use as a Masonic Hall, 1864–99	184
7.6	St Peter's Tower in 1928, showing the iron bands added to the belfry in 1875–6	186
7.7	St Peter's Tower under scaffolding during restoration work in 1930	188
7.8	The Plume Building, 1932, after the completion of repairs	189
8.1	Loose leaf insertions	200
8.2	Side view of TPL showing construction	203
8.3	Address label	205
8.4	Four Evangelists image	209
8.5	Map showing the origins of the manuscripts	213
8.6	Robert Boreman's slip of paper in Edward Hyde's notebook	215
8.7	Inscription in front leaf of TPL	217
9.1	Bromley College, Kent, founded in 1666 by the bishop of Rochester as an almshouse for the widows of clergymen	227
9.2	The Chatham Chest, where funds were kept from 1588 to pay pensions to disabled Royal Navy seamen, and in which Plume had deposited money	230
9.3	Stone Castle, near Gravesend, Kent, bought by Dr Plume in the late seventeenth century	238
10.1	Samuel Vince (1749–1821), Plumian Professor of Astronomy (1796–1821), *c.*1821	253
10.2	Early nineteenth-century print of Cambridge Observatory	254
10.3	Sir George Biddell Airy (1801–1892), Astronomer Royal (1835–81) and Plumian Professor (1828–36), caricatured in *Punch* magazine, May 1883	255
10.4	Revd James Challis, Plumian Professor (1836–82), in 1874	256
10.5	Einstein and Sir Arthur Eddington, Plumian Professor (1913–44), in the garden of the Cambridge Observatory, 1930	257
10.6	Robert C. Kennicutt, Jr, Plumian Professor (2005–17), in 2008	260

Tables

5.1	Plume Trustees in November 1706	122
5.2	Charitable obligations and expenditures of the Plume Trust in 1728	125
5.3	Librarians of Thomas Plume's Library, 1705–2019	130
5.4	Summary of accounts of Dr Plume's Charities, Maldon, Essex, 1845–6	137
6.1	Subject analysis of books in the Plume Library (sample)	159
10.1	The Plumian Professors, 1707–2017	251

Contributors

Dr James Bettley is an architectural historian, whose publications include the Pevsner Architectural Guide to Essex (2007). He received his doctorate from the Courtauld Institute of Art in 1999 and is a Fellow of the Society of Antiquaries. He was chairman of the Plume Library, 2009–19, and remains a trustee; he is also a trustee of the Essex Heritage Trust.

Dr Catharina Clement completed her doctorate in local history at Canterbury Christchurch University in 2013. In the past she has worked as a volunteer on two local Victoria County History EPE projects covering the Medway Towns. She is a member of the Friends of Medway Archives, having contributed a number of articles to their magazine, *The Clocktower,* and has worked at Medway Archives Centre since 2007.

Tony Doe retired in 1995 after 25 years in social work in Essex. Researches in the Plume Library led to studies for the Certificate in Local and Regional History at the University of Essex under the late Dr Philip Hills and Professor John Walter. He gained his MA at the University of Essex in 2006. He is a trustee of the Plume Library and of the Friends of Thomas Plume's Library, and has published articles on the Plume Library and Thomas Plume in the *Essex Journal*.

The late **Max Earnshaw** (1930–2020) retired from his profession of industrial chemist in 1989, having gained his BA at the Open University in 1978. During the 1990s he completed the Certificate in Local and Regional History at the University of Essex under Arthur Brown and Geoffrey Martin. In 1998 he published, privately, *The Church on Market Hill,* a history of Maldon United Reformed Church.

Sue Edward is a history graduate from Southampton University and later studied for the Certificate in Local and Regional History at the University of Essex. After a career in HM Customs and Excise, and latterly HMRC, she retired as a Senior Civil Servant in 2012 and has undertaken several local history projects. She has been a trustee of the Friends of Thomas Plume's Library since 2016.

Mark Hurn is a professional librarian working at the University of Cambridge, Institute of Astronomy. He takes an interest in the history of astronomy, and is a founder member of the Society for the History of Astronomy. He has written biographies for the Biographical Encyclopedia of Astronomers and is a Fellow of the Royal Astronomical Society.

Dr Helen Kemp is Plume Librarian at Thomas Plume's Library, a Community Fellow at the University of Essex and Special Collections Champion at the Albert Sloman Library. Her PhD was about the significance of Plume's manuscript collection and, before starting her current role at the Plume Library, she taught on various history modules at the University of Essex.

Dr David Pearson retired as Director of Culture, Heritage & Libraries for the City of London Corporation in 2017, after a long career managing libraries. He has published and lectured extensively on book history, particularly on ways in which books have been owned and bound. He was Lyell Reader in Bibliography at Oxford in 2017–18, and is a Past President of the Bibliographical Society.

J. R. Smith studied for his M.Phil. degree in the Department of English Local History, University of Leicester. Since retirement from a senior post in the Essex Record Office he has divided his time between his own research and writing, and work as archivist to Lord Rayleigh. His books include *The Borough of Maldon 1688-1800: a Golden Age* (2013). He is a Fellow of the Royal Historical Society.

Dr Christopher Thornton is a graduate of the University of Kent (BA) and the Centre for English Local History, University of Leicester (PhD). After holding research posts at the University of Leicester and Hertford College, Oxford, he joined the Victoria County History of Essex in 1992 and has been county editor since 2003. He is Chairman of the Friends of Historic Essex and a Vice-President of the Essex Society for Archaeology and History.

Abbreviations

BL	British Library
Cal. S.P. Dom.	*Calendar of State Papers Domestic* (HMSO)
Compact DNB	*Compact Dictionary of National Biography* (London, 1975)
Concise DNB	*Concise Dictionary of National Biography*, 3 vols (Oxford, 1992)
CUL	Cambridge University Library
DAC	Dartford Almshouse Charity
DD	Doctor of Divinity
DNB	*Dictionary of National Biography* (1921–2; condensed edition, 1975)
ER	*Essex Review*
ERO	Essex Record Office
GHC	Greenwich Heritage Centre
HMSO	Her/His Majesty's Stationery Office
KHLC	Kent History and Library Centre
LMA	London Metropolitan Archive
MAC	Medway Archives Centre
NPG	National Portrait Gallery
ODNB	*Oxford Dictionary of National Biography* (Oxford, 2004); online version (2008): http://www.oxforddnb.com/
OS	Ordnance Survey
RGO	Royal Greenwich Observatory
SPAB	Society for the Protection of Ancient Buildings
SRO	Suffolk Record Office
SCT	Stone Castle Trust
TNA	The National Archives
TPL	Thomas Plume's Library
Uncat.	Uncatalogued
VCH	*Victoria County History*

Preface and acknowledgements

The idea for this book originated in conversations between the editors in 2012, initially about finding a way to publish Robert Anthony (Tony) Doe's University of Essex MA thesis 'The Churchmanship of Dr Thomas Plume (1630–1704). A Study of a Career in the Restoration Church of England' (2005). We soon came to the conclusion that the full range of Dr Plume's life and legacies, many aspects of which were known only in outline, was deserving of far wider study and appreciation. This feeling was evidently shared, as we received an enthusiastic response whenever we approached other historians to contribute to a larger work, and a project team was rapidly assembled. It met to discuss the development of the essays for the first time in May 2014.

We were also extremely fortunate that the trustees of Thomas Plume's Library kindly agreed to adopt the project in February 2013. They have subsequently overseen the project's development, administered its funding through a management committee and given it their full support. All the contributors, including the editors, have waived their right to royalties in favour of Thomas Plume's Library, to whom any profits will accrue. Two of the trustees, James Bettley and Tony Doe, have contributed chapters to the book.

The project team remained intact until this year, when we lost Max Earnshaw (1930–2020) to a long-standing illness. He was the initiator and co-author of Chapter 5, 'Thomas Plume and his Maldon Trust'. Max was uniquely qualified to do this, having researched the Plume Library's archives for over 30 years while his wife Olive was, first, assistant librarian and then librarian. His meticulous work formed the backbone of Chapter 5 and he was a keen project team member, much valued for his insights and wit. He is greatly missed. The editors would like to thank his daughter Ruth Earnshaw for a generous grant towards the indexing costs of this volume in memory of Max.

The project was also supported by the Centre for Bibliographical History at the University of Essex, which hosted two workshops in September 2015 and June 2016 at which both project contributors and external specialists contributed papers before a specially invited audience. We would like to thank Dr David Rundle, Professor James Raven, other University of Essex staff and all those involved in the workshops for their enthusiastic support and for the additional impetus and lines of enquiry suggested.

PREFACE AND ACKNOWLEDGEMENTS

We are also enormously grateful to the following institutions, which have contributed financially to the project and to its publication: The Friends of Thomas Plume's Library; The Essex Society for Archaeology and History; The Essex Heritage Trust; The Essex Society for Family History.

Further encouragement and assistance has been received from many quarters during the course of the project. The editors and authors would particularly like to thank the recently retired Librarian of Thomas Plume's Library, Erica Wylie, and her staff for their unstinting and patient help with enquiries about the Plume Library collections and for hosting at the library the regular meetings of the contributors between 2014 and 2016. The original research for the project has created an extra workload in the library; their efforts to meet this extra demand are much appreciated. Other individuals who have provided encouragement, support and advice include Ian Kidman, David Foster, Andrew Doe, Chris Manning-Press, Patricia Herrmann and the late Frank Herrmann. We also thank the staff of the University of Hertfordshire Press and their anonymous reviewer, whose questions and suggestions have removed some errors and made for many improvements.

We would also like to express our sincere thanks to the trustees, councillors, archivists, librarians and other individuals at the following institutions and repositories for their assistance with research enquiries: Albert Sloman Library, University of Essex; Cambridge University Library; Christ's College, Cambridge; Dartford Almshouse Charity (Stone Castle Trust); Essex Record Office; Greenwich Heritage Centre; Historic England/NMR; Kent Archive and History Centre; Lichfield Cathedral; London Metropolitan Archive (Guildhall Library); Maldon Masonic Hall; Maldon Town Council; Medway Archive Centre; National Maritime Museum (Greenwich); Royal Greenwich Observatory; Society for the Protection of Ancient Buildings; The National Archives; Trinity College, Cambridge.

The publisher, editors and authors would also like to thank the following for their kind permission to reproduce illustrations: British Museum (Fig. 1.4); Essex Record Office (Fig. 7.2); B. Gunn (Fig. 3.4, photograph); Historic England (Fig. 7.4); Lichfield Cathedral (Fig. 3.4); London Metropolitan Archives (Figs 3.6, 3.9, 3.10(a) and (b)); Maldon Masonic Hall (Brethren of the Lodge of St Peter, number 1024 in the Province of Essex) (Fig. 7.5); Maldon Town Council (Cover image; Fig. 1.1); National Maritime Museum, Greenwich (Figs 3.5, 3.7, 9.2); National Portrait Gallery (Fig. 4.4); The National Archives (Figs 4.1, 4.3, 5.5, 7.6); Thomas Plume's Library (Figs 1.2, 2.6, 5.1, 5.2, 5.3, 5.4, 5.6, 5.7, 5.8, 6.1, 6.2, 6.3, 6.4, 6.5, 6.6, 6.7, 6.8, 7.3, 8.1, 8.2, 8.3, 8.4, 8.6 and 8.7); L. Raymond (Fig. 2.5, photograph); K. Russell (Fig. 3.1, photograph); SciencePhotoLibrary (Figs 10.3 and 10.5); A. Smith (Fig. 10.6, photograph); Society for the Protection of Ancient Buildings (Figs 7.7 and 7.8); University of

Cambridge, Institute of Astronomy (Figs 10.1, 10.2, 10.4 and 10.6); Vicar and Parochial Church Council of All Saints with St Peter (Fig. 3.1). Figure 1.2 was kindly researched and drawn by David Truzzi Franconi, and Figures 1.3, 2.2, 2.4 and 8.5 were kindly drawn by Catherine D'Alton.

Chapter 1

Introduction: 'this munificent person' – Dr Thomas Plume and his legacies

*Christopher Thornton, Robert Anthony Doe,
Sue Edward and Helen Kemp*

Dr Thomas Plume (1630–1704), the younger son of Thomas Plume senior, a wealthy merchant and prominent member of the Maldon Corporation, was born in the small borough and port of Maldon, on the Blackwater estuary in Essex. Plume was educated at Chelmsford School and Christ's College, Cambridge, and probably determined upon a church career at an early date with his father's support. He began his education at a time of acute religious dissension following on from the Reformation initiated by Henry VIII. The religious changes developed further under Edward VI, turning England from a Catholic into a Protestant country. Despite Mary's attempts to reverse the changes, by the reign of Elizabeth I the Church of England was established as the national church with the monarch as Supreme Governor. From the late 1550s until the 1630s there was a working consensus around Calvinist theology and practices, especially in parish life. Jean Calvin (1509–64) taught the doctrine of predestination in which some are destined for eternal life (they were known as the 'elect'), others to eternal damnation.[1]

Although Elizabeth's successor, James I, also supported Calvinism, his son Charles I instead held to the rival Arminian theology and practice taught very forcibly by William Laud (1573–1645), and thus subsequently labelled Laudianism. Jacobus Arminius (1560–1609) had taught that 'predestination is based on foreseen faith, that the human will is not completely bound by sin, that grace may be resisted and that even the elect may fall from grace'.[2] Charles made Laud bishop of London and, later, archbishop of Canterbury and, in addition to theological alterations, Laud enforced extensive changes in church practice affecting church furnishings, clerical dress and the liturgy. These changes were widely distrusted and feared by many congregations, who could not differentiate between them and the 'popery' that they had been taught to abhor for many years. Lay resistance to Laud's 'innovations' spread, being seen for example in Chelmsford from the 1630s, and escalated into full-blown violent iconoclasm following the promulgation of the Root and Branch Petition of December 1640 by the Long Parliament.[3] It is widely held that these religious differences contributed in large part to the Civil Wars of the 1640s between the king and parliament. By the time these wars ended there had been enormous loss of life, families had been torn apart and Laud and Charles I had both been executed by parliament (in 1645 and 1649 respectively). The Long Parliament, in its attempt to impose on the nation a Presbyterian church governed by elders, abolished the episcopacy and its associated posts and replaced the Book of Common Prayer with the Directory for Public Worship.

Following the collapse of the Cromwellian regime in 1658, Charles II returned at the request of parliament in 1660. Initially, the king and others hoped to create an inclusive church but instead 'the restored Anglican Church was narrow in its boundaries, and conservative, perhaps even Laudian, in its nature'.[4] More than 1,900 dissenting Protestant ministers and their many followers were forced out of the church by the prescriptive demands of the Act of Uniformity in 1662, leading to the founding of a number of nonconforming churches.[5] Although the Church of England retained its formal position as the state church, it 'was no longer a national church' because not everyone conformed or belonged to it.[6]

Tracing Thomas Plume's career through these troubled times is by no means a straightforward task, as the surviving documentary evidence for parts of his life is sparse. While his personal religious belief was influenced by his family background and his hometown, which were distinctly Puritan or Presbyterian in outlook, the violence and turmoil of the Civil War period appear to have encouraged in Plume an innate royalism and support for the established church. Notably, Thomas Plume owned portraits of both Charles I and William Laud, which are now preserved in his library at Maldon.[7] He therefore found himself at odds with the prevailing political and religious sentiment by the late 1640s. His moves immediately after graduation from Cambridge are unclear, but he is found living near the village of Cheam in Surrey by 1651. There he became an informal student under the tutelage of the vicar, John Hacket, who, after the Restoration, went on to become bishop of Coventry and Lichfield. Through the contacts of his mentor Plume successfully obtained episcopal ordination at an unknown date, but he did not receive clerical advancement until the winds of change were in the air in 1658, in the final days of the Cromwellian regime, when he was inducted as vicar of Greenwich. He soon gained a solid reputation as a churchman and preacher, conformed in 1662 and used Laudian practices, and by 1679 had risen to become the archdeacon of Rochester and a prebendary of Rochester Cathedral. His progression from the Presbyterian outlook of his family and childhood to the Laudianism he demonstrated after 1662 is a key aspect of his life.

Because he remained unmarried and had no close relatives, Plume planned upon his death to bequeath most of his considerable fortune to good causes, leaving about one-fifth only of his cash and stock, as well as a house, shop and land in Maldon, to family members, friends and servants. His will was long and complex, comprising 19 pages in its original form and with 76 bequests.[8] It disposed of cash and stock worth about £7,270 (equivalent to about £1,101,000 today), plus a considerable amount of real estate in Essex and Kent.[9] A comparison with his archidiaconal peers and more senior bishops and archbishops during this period demonstrates that the scale of Plume's philanthropic giving was exceptional, even allowing that he was a single man with no immediate family requiring support.[10] Several trusts were set up by his will, the largest of which are still in existence today, their work extending across several counties in south-east England. Most of the bequests were associated with Maldon, Cambridge or Kent, the scenes of his childhood, education and life's work respectively.

Numerous benefactions were made to his home town, many of which were incorporated into his Maldon Trust, the modern successor to which is the charity known as Thomas Plume's Library.[11] Indeed, the gift to Maldon of his library, comprising around 7,400 publications, as well as his manuscripts,[12] to be housed in the redundant church of St Peter (which he adapted and rebuilt in his lifetime for that purpose), was one of his chief bequests. Other legacies for Maldon included support for the town's grammar school (later Maldon Grammar School and now the Plume School) and a workhouse for the poor of Maldon, Mundon and neighbouring parishes. In Kent, where Plume had spent his professional life, many of his benefactions were combined into the Stone Castle Charity (named after his country estate near Dartford), the most important of which is the fund for poor clergy in the Diocese of Rochester, which still operates as Dr Plumes Trust.[13] Finally, Plume's financial legacies have probably had their widest impact – indeed, international renown – in his endowment creating the Plumian Professorship of Astronomy at Cambridge University. Yet, notably, Plume was very different from the majority of benefactors in that he consistently sought anonymity, whereas it was customary for benefactors to require that their name be perpetuated.[14] His tombstone does not bear his name, reading instead: 'Beneath here lies the Archdeacon of Rochester …'.[15] Similarly, his almshouses at Deptford in Kent were to be called the 'Archdeacons Poor Almes-Houses'. He forbade his unnamed portrait to be brought into his library and it remains to this day in the Moot Hall at Maldon (Figure 1.1).[16]

The extraordinary extent of Plume's philanthropy was recognised by contemporaries. Leading churchmen, townsmen, academics and other

DR THOMAS PLUME, 1630–1704

1.1 Dr Thomas Plume. Untitled and unsigned portrait held in the Moot Hall, Maldon. In his will, ll. 135 and 136, he forbade his picture 'now in Mr Pond's house' ever to be brought into his library (Maldon Town Council).

INTRODUCTION

influential persons gave their agreement to be drawn into the creation and administration of his trusts. Thomas Cox's *Magna Britannia* (1720s) and Nathaniel Salmon's history of the county of Essex (early 1740s) both included a brief account of Plume's benefactions to Maldon, while the Revd Philip Morant's county history (1768) described in more detail the extensive gifts of 'this munificent person'.[17] However, Plume's name and bequests later appear to have fallen into semi-oblivion. They were first rescued in a series of articles in the *Essex Review* by Revd Andrew Clark, vicar of Great Leighs, Essex. In 1903 he surveyed Plume's pamphlet collection and in 1904 his recently rediscovered loose manuscript papers,[18] and in 1905–6 he published studies of three of Plume's notebooks in the Plume Library, named by him 'Dr Plume as a Cambridge Undergraduate', 'Dr Plume's Pocketbook' and 'Dr Plume's Notebook'.[19] Plume was considered significant enough for a short, but informative, article by Charlotte Fell Smith in the first edition of the *Dictionary of National Biography* (1921–2); this has since been updated by Professor Henry French in the *New (Oxford) Dictionary of National Biography* (2004).[20] In between, the most significant published contribution to understanding Plume appeared in Dr W.J. Petchey's pamphlet *The Intentions of Thomas Plume*, first issued in 1985, which placed Plume more firmly in the society and, to some extent, the history of his own day.[21] Subsequently, R.A. Doe's University of Essex MA thesis built upon the work of Clark and Petchey, looking in some detail at Plume's historical context over the whole of his life, with particular emphasis on the development of his religious practice and belief.[22]

It is now well over 300 years since Dr Plume planned his many benefactions, and almost all were subsequently put into effect. His intentions were complex and varied, being inevitably tied into the historical context of the time but also intimately revealing of his personal attitudes and beliefs. The current work has been planned as the first comprehensive overview of the whole of Plume's life and the subsequent history of his legacies, achieved through a series of articles commissioned from historians with specialist knowledge of their fields. It begins with an examination of his family background, from the extended family in north Essex to his nuclear family in Maldon, including a consideration of his father's role as one of the most senior members of Maldon Corporation through the tumultuous years of the mid-seventeenth century (J.R. Smith, Chapter 2). There then follows a thorough chronological account of Plume's life, religious beliefs and career in the church (Tony Doe, Chapter 3). Plume's will has been forensically examined and contextualised by Sue Edward in Chapter 4, including an account of how, and to what extent, Plume's instructions were followed and his legacies have survived. Both this article and many others in the book have benefited from Edward's recent discovery of Plume's original will in The National Archives (hitherto only the registered probate copy having been known), and a transcript is provided in an Appendix to this book.

It is perhaps in the Plume Library at Maldon that we come closest to the man himself, as it contains his own library in the building that he constructed to house it with the intention of providing a permanent educational resource for the local community. Articles that explore aspects of the library include accounts of the Maldon Trust and its administration, income, activities and survival (Max Earnshaw, Chapter 5) and of the Plume Library building and its contents (James Bettley, Chapter 7), an analysis of the scale and nature of the library's book collection (David Pearson, Chapter 6) and a comprehensive study of the creation, transmission and use of Plume's manuscripts (Helen Kemp, Chapter 8). Further articles concern individual aspects of Plume's works and enduring legacies, including accounts of the history of Plume's charities in Kent (Catharina Clement, Chapter 9) and of the holders of the Plumian Professorship at Cambridge University (Mark Hurn, Chapter 10).

The remainder of this introduction will now provide an overview of Plume in his contemporary and regional society, followed by contextual discussions of areas of special interest to scholars: the nature and scale of his philanthropy, the establishment of his library and his engagement with science. It will conclude with some remarks on remaining unresolved issues concerning Plume's life and legacies and a description of current and prospective future research.

Dr Thomas Plume's background, status and milieu
By the early sixteenth century Thomas Plume's great-great-grandfather, Robert Plume, was tenant of the earl of Oxford at Great Yeldham Hall in Great Yeldham, an Essex parish about ten miles north of Braintree, near the Suffolk border. The later break-up and sale of the Oxford estate, due to the debts of Edward de Vere, the 17th earl, enabled the Plume family to purchase Great Yeldham Hall in 1584, which was passed to a junior branch.[23] Thus, although Plume's direct ancestors had not benefited from the former monastic or church property that flooded the land market at the Reformation, they were comparable to the many newly established gentry families who were a particular feature of the county in the sixteenth and seventeenth centuries.[24] The family evidently prospered but in a relatively modest manner. It remained at Yeldham, where the house was not rebuilt and where the surviving structure is largely medieval in date, although updated in the seventeenth and eighteenth centuries.[25] While its local status was underpinned by wealth based on landed income, like many such families it also sought to proclaim its new-found position by becoming armigerous (Figure 1.2).[26] Another demonstration of the family's acquired status and cultural world can be seen in the education, from the early seventeenth century, of its children at Christ's College, Cambridge – Dr Thomas Plume being the third to benefit after his father and uncle.

INTRODUCTION

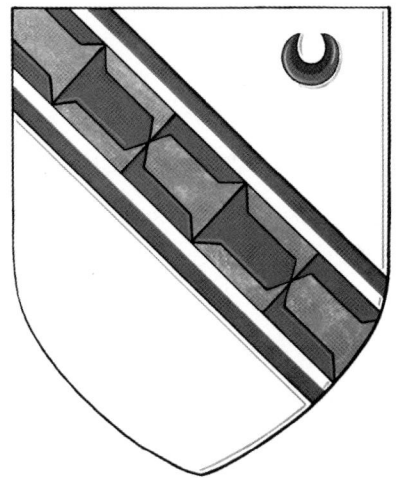

1.2 Dr Thomas Plume's arms, the definitive version devised by T.E. Mathew, Rouge Dragon Pursuivant of Arms. The arms are of the Plume family in Essex but distinguished for Dr Plume by the crescent (repeated) for a second son (research and drawing by David Truzzi Franconi).

Describing the Plume family members is not always easy, as they preferred the names Samuel and Thomas over many generations, as demonstrated by the family tree (below, Figure 2.2, p. 27). Dr Thomas Plume's great grandfather, Robert Plume, had three sons, Samuel, Thomas and Edmund. Robert was succeeded at Yeldham Hall by Thomas, who was succeeded by his own son Samuel. That Samuel's younger brother, Thomas, was followed in turn by his own son called Samuel, whose younger brother was another Thomas (later Dr Plume). The subject of this book therefore began life as the youngest son of a younger son from a relatively recently established junior branch of an Essex gentry family, a position that certainly did not guarantee maintenance of high social position. Many such children, supported by their families, were destined for legal or clerical professions or mercantile careers and must have merged into the growing numbers of the 'middling sort' as society became progressively more commercialised.[27] Thomas Plume, snr (Dr Plume's father, d. by 1658) was more successful, however, as he was able to migrate sometime in the early 1620s to Maldon, presumably supported by the £500 left to him in his

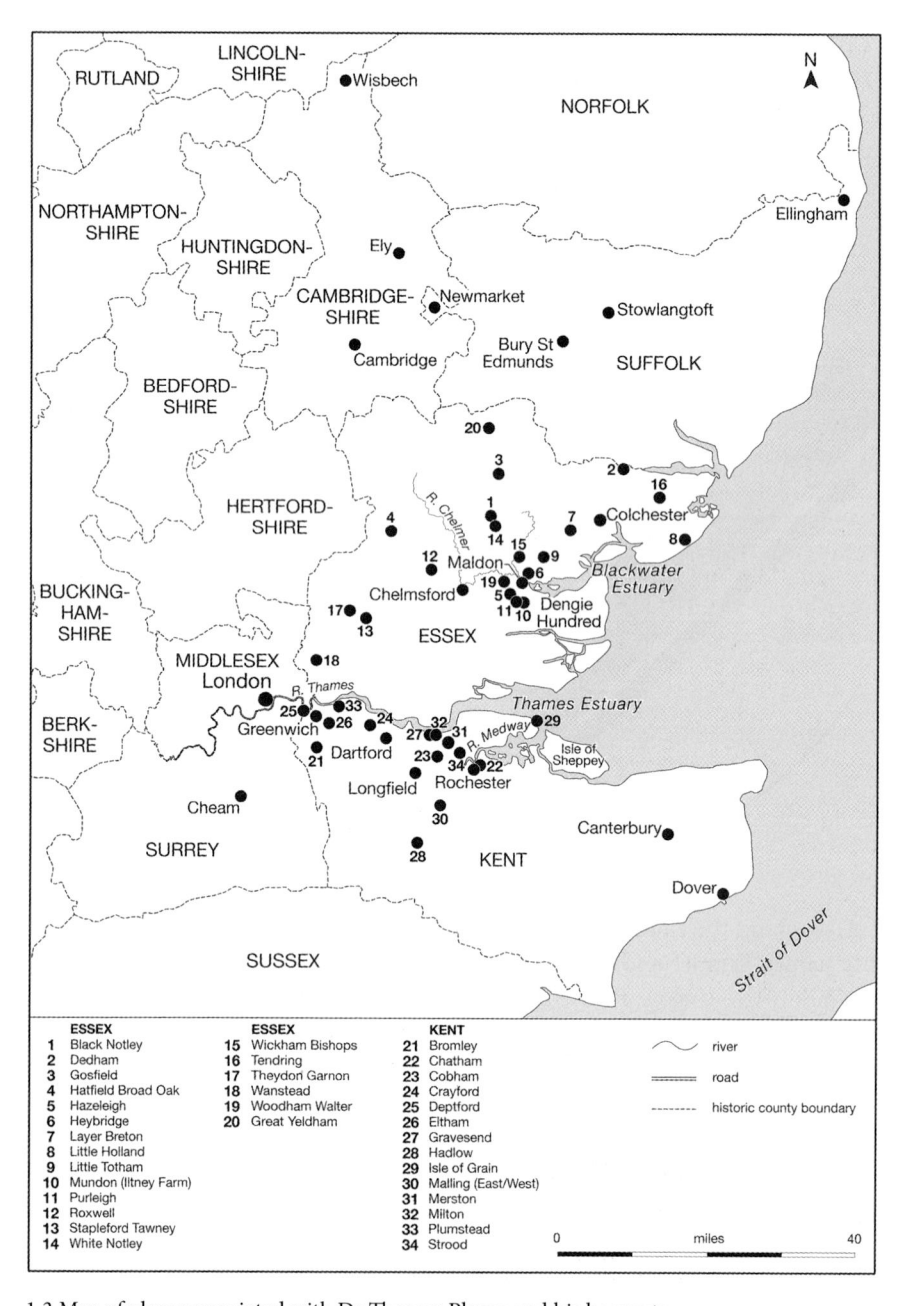

1.3 Map of places associated with Dr Thomas Plume and his bequests.

INTRODUCTION

father's will. Thereafter he rapidly became established as a leading inhabitant, merchant and property owner. Indeed, as Smith demonstrates in Chapter 2, he was both an able and an ambitious man, becoming an important figure in the borough's government and effectively the leader of the Corporation during the disruptions of the Civil War and Protectorate. Although engaged in trade as a merchant, Thomas Plume's family background, combined with his own economic success and political achievements, provided him with considerable social status as a gentleman.

Dr Plume's own professional and personal life, as far as we can reconstruct the latter, remained firmly rooted in the regional society of south-east England, specifically the counties of Essex and Kent and the capital city of London (Figure 1.3). His home town of Maldon was in a state of some overall decline during the sixteenth and seventeenth centuries by comparison with many other small towns. For example, when measured for the purposes of taxation and comparison of the number of occupied households, it had slipped from ranking third in Essex after Colchester and Saffron Walden in the Lay Subsidy returns of 1524/5 to 14th as revealed by the Hearth Tax returns of 1671. Its population had remained stable, whereas there had been significant increases in population among the other towns of the county. On the other hand, the number of the recorded admissions of freemen increased over the period 1515 to 1641 by more than those lost to death and migration.[28] The trade of Maldon apparently revived from the 1630s and Thomas Plume, snr, therefore migrated to the town at a time of economic growth and apparently benefited from it.[29] His elder son Samuel (d. 1670) followed him as an alderman and prominent figure in the borough's government, while his younger son Dr Thomas Plume left substantial bequests to the town, with many trustees to his legacies being connected to the Corporation.

While Dr Plume retained strong links and interests in Maldon, his professional career developed in Kent. His first preferment, in 1658, was as vicar of St Alfege's church, Greenwich, where he resided in the vicarage. Later in his life he also invested in the purchase of a country estate at Stone Castle, near Dartford, but the house there was not his principal residence. Greenwich's peculiarities as a town may have had important consequences for the young clergyman. Its development had been marked by riverside industry and the presence there of the royal palace of Placentia (also known as Greenwich Palace), built by Henry VII in 1500. Henry VIII had favoured this palace, but it was razed in the seventeenth century after long periods of neglect and disuse, to be partly replaced by the Queen's House (1637). Charles II began building another palace on the site of Placentia in 1665 and this building was extended to form the Seamen's Hospital (1694), later the Royal Naval Hospital. The Royal Observatory was also established by Charles II in Greenwich Park in 1675.[30]

Greenwich's population grew from 2,000 at the start of the seventeenth century to 5,000 by the end of it. By that time the town had private docks, a small arms manufactory, copperas works and limekilns. As a result of the spells when Queen Henrietta Maria held court in the Queen's House, courtiers built themselves good houses around the Park. During the Interregnum 'waste' land between the park wall and road was sold by the crown for the erection of houses. These sales were cancelled at the Restoration and the owners had to buy the land again if they wished to retain their properties. In spite of the losses of the Civil Wars and later the Great Fire of 1666, London continued to grow, and there emerged a leisured class who could afford to move out of the noisy, dirty and congested city, some of whom moved to Greenwich to enjoy the peace and quiet of the country with, from the higher ground, excellent views of the river and, some five miles off, the City. For a time, it became a fashionable place of residence for London merchants and lawyers, government officials in the Navy Department and retired people.[31] One such was Sir William Boreman, a senior member of the royal household, who founded with others the John Roan (Grey Coat) School in Greenwich for 20 poor boys in 1677, of which Plume was also a founding member and the first chair of trustees (as vicar of Greenwich).[32] Sir William was connected to Plume through his younger brother, Dr Robert Boreman (d. 1675), who was a major contributor to Plume's manuscript collection.[33] Yet by the time of Plume's death in 1704 Greenwich had begun to decay. Plume's church, St Alfege's, was badly damaged in a storm in 1710 and in a plea for funding for rebuilding the people of Greenwich 'claimed that the town had long been deserted by its richer inhabitants and the largest houses were empty'.[34]

Plume's associations with Kent were strengthened in 1679 when he was appointed as archdeacon of Rochester and installed as a prebendary at the cathedral. He thereby acquired the archdeacon's house in the cathedral close and the manor and Court Lodge (known as Longfield Court) at Longfield, Kent, which was also allocated to the archdeaconry. The Longfield estate was apparently leased, but Plume may have used its residence as a 'house of retirement', as Hasted puts it, because he chose to be buried in the adjacent churchyard.[35] The diocese of Rochester had been founded by Augustine in 604 (only seven years after the foundation of Canterbury) and for many years it 'occupied an intimate and dependent position in relation to Canterbury'.[36] Rochester was the smallest diocese in the Church of England, having only 94 benefices in 1835 compared, for example, with Lincoln, the largest, with 1,234 benefices, or Canterbury, with 343.[37] It was also one of the least endowed in the Church, at only £600 p.a. in 1792. Locally, it was very much the poor relation, lying between London, worth £4,000 and Canterbury, worth £7,000.[38] As little changed in the organisation of the Church of England's dioceses between Henry

INTRODUCTION

VIII's reforms and the later 1830s, in spite of the intervention of the Interregnum, when bishops and chapters were abolished by parliament, the above figures can be used with some confidence, at least in the relative proportions.

The cathedral and its associated offices were, however, very important in the development of the city of Rochester. In the Middle Ages it had been the second largest urban centre in Kent after Canterbury, but thereafter its relative importance declined; in 1664 it had about 3,000 inhabitants and in 1700 still had significantly fewer than 5,000, having been outstripped by Greenwich and the nearby naval dockyard town of Chatham.[39] Rochester was located where Watling Street, also known as the Dover Road, crossed the river Medway, the ancient route ending at London Bridge. Described as 'the most frequented road in England', it carried mail, bullion and light goods, whereas bulky goods went by water.[40] Indeed, Rochester was also a busy port, handling both coastal and overseas cargoes, although the international aspect of its trade declined over the seventeenth century as London became ever more dominant. Increasingly, goods from abroad were shipped first to London and then offloaded to coastal vessels for distribution to the ports of Kent.[41] Rochester's significant coastwise trade included, for example, Kentish timber of various types and paper and pasteboard (manufactured around Maidstone) exported to London, fuller's earth exported to the cloth-producing region of Essex and East Anglia, including the Essex towns of Colchester and Maldon, coal imported from Sunderland and Newcastle in north-east England and timber and other goods imported through Rochester destined for the naval dockyards at Chatham.[42] Communications with the capital were therefore well developed; Watling Street must have facilitated Dr Plume's journeys to his parish at Greenwich, but he may well also have travelled between Rochester and London, and to and from Greenwich and Maldon in Essex, by boat, using the Medway and Thames estuaries.

All the towns with which Plume was associated – Maldon, Greenwich and Rochester – lay in the orbit of London. The influence of the capital city grew powerfully in the sixteenth and seventeenth centuries, as its population grew dramatically from an estimated 55,000 in the 1520s to 475,000 by 1670 and to more than half a million by the end of the seventeenth century.[43] The growth of London had a particularly significant impact on north-western Kent, and Plume would have been well aware of these changes and seems to have taken advantage of the commercial opportunities they brought. As already described, he had easy access to London either along Watling Street or by water, a journey which could be very convenient if tide and wind were favourable.[44] The river took him to the stairs at London Bridge and thence immediately into the heart of the City, where he could buy and sell stocks and shares at the Royal Exchange or in Exchange Alley, or possibly in noted coffee houses such as Jonathan's or Garraway's. From there he could walk to his bankers, Messrs Hoare and Co. in Fleet Street.[45]

Plume made many of his thousands of purchases of secondhand and new books at shops and auctions in and around the City of London, especially in St Paul's churchyard and its associated alleyways, and also, probably, in the open-air market in Moorfields to the north (Figure 1.4) or in Fleet Street to the west.[46] In the seventeenth century booksellers were also publishers employing both printers and binders. They were also, increasingly, auctioneers, as the practice of selling off whole libraries grew steadily during the latter part of the century, following the adoption of the practice from Holland.[47] We also know that Plume visited the west of London to carry out his duties as chaplain in ordinary to the king, probably at Whitehall Palace. He may have visited, on one occasion at least, Mary, Lady Armine (1594–1676), notable for her close association with the parliamentarian cause, in St Martin's Lane 'in-the-Fields', as mail was sent there for him.[48] If he travelled by water, alighting at Westminster stairs, he would have passed Old Palace Yard, home of Mrs Audrey (or possibly Anne) Beale, who was known to him through her connection to the Boreman family in Greenwich.[49]

Dr Plume's philanthropy: the church, education and the poor

Dr Plume's philanthropic interests fell broadly into three categories– supporting the Church, advancing education and relief of the poor – although in many cases these objectives were combined in the form of bequests. His overall intention seems to have been to address problems he had encountered in his clerical career. He planned a large number of interventions and, as they will be discussed in detail in Chapter 4 and other chapters of this book, only the general pattern is addressed here. As might be expected of a clergyman, he made a number of gifts that benefited the Church of England and related charities. Plume had both witnessed and suffered from the tumultuous and damaging decades of the mid-seventeenth century, and evidently wished to contribute to the restoration of the Church. His bequests, however, focused very closely on improving the financial lot of the parish clergy and their education, rather than, for example, the maintenance of church buildings. Examples of the former were his gifts of £400 to augment the income of All Saints' vicarage, Maldon, and £1,000 to purchase tithes for small livings worth under £100 a year in the diocese of Rochester, and the founding of the public lecture in Maldon and another in Dartford or Gravesend.[50] After acquiring and then allocating Iltney Farm in Mundon, near Maldon, as the main endowment for his Maldon Trust, Plume commented that it was former chantry land, which, while inaccurate, was again indicative of his drive to restore the Church.[51]

Plume seems also to have been very aware that an unintended consequence of the Reformation and the dissolution of the monasteries had been disruption of society's structures for social welfare.[52] His second area of interest was therefore

INTRODUCTION

1.4 Books 'on the railes' at Moorfields, detail from Sutton Nicholls's print of 'The Compleat Auctioneer', *c.*1700 (© Trustees of the British Museum).

to assist the poor, although with an emphasis on measures that might enable social improvement or betterment rather than outright gifts to relieve poverty. Among his major benefactions were £2,000 in East India Company stock and other assets to establish a workhouse in Maldon and four properties to create almshouses at Deptford, although the latter was one of the few of his bequests which apparently failed to be implemented.[53] Plume also made provision for payments to the poor who most diligently attended the public lectures, further demonstrating the indivisibility of his interests in religion, education and the relief of poverty.[54]

Finally, Plume made bequests that reflected his belief in the value of education. The largest was nearly £2,000 to erect an observatory and to endow a professorship of astronomy at Cambridge. The intentions behind this bequest have been described as obscure, but it is clear that he had a close association with John Flamsteed, the Royal Astronomer at Greenwich, who was possibly the prime mover behind the bequest.[55] In Kent Plume left four bequests to support the schooling of the poor, including an endowment of property for the clothing and education of two poor boys at the Grey Coat School in Greenwich.[56] Along similar lines but on a larger scale, Plume provided for the education of six (amended to ten) poor Maldon and Mundon boys at that town's existing grammar school (or for them to be put out as apprentices), with a generous provision for their distinctive uniform.[57] As described in Chapters 5 and 7, he had already incurred major costs before his death by reconstructing St Peter's church (Figure 1.5) to house the school on the ground floor and his library above, and must have regarded these developments as a coherent whole. It is possible that Plume supported the provision of 'free' places at the grammar school to enable talented boys of humble origin to achieve a university scholarship and advance themselves through a career in the Church or professions, but if that was the intention the Maldon school produced disappointingly few matriculants before 1850.[58]

While Plume was not a member of the Society for Promoting Christian Knowledge (SPCK),[59] his educational bequest at Maldon was probably influenced by the charity or 'free' school movement and the school's form was quite typical for its time.[60] His will and other actions imply that the teaching of the poor boys was to be combined with that of the fee-paying grammar school boys, entailing a compromise between practical education (in reading, writing and casting accounts) and classical instruction in Latin. Not long afterwards, a similar compromise was more clearly and deliberately set out at Palmer's School in Grays Thurrock (Essex), a free or charity school founded by William Palmer in 1706 and further endowed under his will of 1709.[61] The historian of that school suggested the combination resulted from Palmer's 'common sense and business acumen' and an inability to conceive of education

1.5 Postcard of St Peter's Tower on the corner of Maldon's High Street and Market Hill, c.1900. Plume's library building incorporated the medieval tower of the former parish church of St Peter.

'totally divorced from classical learning', comments that might equally apply to Plume.[62] At Maldon the lack of a strong financial endowment for the whole school, combined with the tension between providing the classical education demanded for the sons of gentlemen and a more general education, desired locally, to prepare children for apprenticeship, seem to have undermined Plume's intentions.[63] Like many small or under-endowed Essex grammar schools it struggled to survive in the eighteenth and nineteenth centuries, interest in teaching classics dwindled further and confusion arose over the distribution of the funds payable by Plume's Maldon Trust.[64] Ultimately the teaching roles and endowments were divided between a new National School and the grammar school. The modern Plume School, successor to the grammar school, has only a slight association with the Plume's benefactions, but these still operate through the Plume Educational Trust.[65]

The Plume Library in context
Between 1680 and 1720 160 libraries were established in the smaller towns and villages of Great Britain.[66] The benefactors ranged across wealthy merchants, gentry and members of the professions. Several reasons have been offered for so many libraries being established in this period, including the availability of books, a drive to raise the clergy's educational standards and increased literacy and interest on the part of the public.[67] At the same time, many gentlemen and

members of the professions felt that it was a responsibility, by virtue of their position in society, to act in a charitable and philanthropic manner for the benefit of the public.[68]

It has been suggested that Plume could have been motivated to bequeath his library by the formation of Archbishop Tenison's Library in London, both libraries being examples of the very few established in purpose-built locations.[69] John Evelyn documented conversations with Thomas Tenison about his library and recorded hearing Plume preach on several occasions, so it is possible that they all knew one another at the time that Tenison's library was being built in 1684. It is also possible that Plume was influenced by Humphrey Chetham's library in Manchester, since that bequest was also discussed and praised publicly by, for example, Thomas Fuller (1608–61), whom Plume admired.[70] Both Tenison's and Chetham's library schemes were well publicised, but, rather than just being inspired by specific individuals, it is likely that Plume was also conscious of the widespread interest in this type of benefaction.

In general, there was a perception that a library represented the focus of a public spirit of knowledge dissemination, which could be acquired from both existing and newly printed books.[71] Therefore, as well as providing a place to store books, libraries facilitated the movement of knowledge out into the communities.[72] At the same time, a 'new associated philanthropy' had emerged towards the end of the seventeenth century,[73] where benefactors donated libraries or single books either through pious religious sentiment or a more socially based view of charity.[74] This can be seen in both Tenison and Plume deciding to make their books available to a wider audience than just the clergy, with Archbishop Tenison's Library stated as being 'for publicke use' (meaning suitably educated persons) and Plume's for 'any Gentleman, or Schollar'.[75] There is a sense that these benefactors wanted to guide the degree to which members of the local community had access to knowledge and that it was their duty to facilitate this as educated and responsible citizens.

The increasing foundation of endowed libraries between 1680 and 1720 was influenced by the 'new spirit of piety' manifesting itself in the late seventeenth century in the formation of religious societies, notably in the work of Revd Thomas Bray and the SPCK.[76] In the 1690s Bray was appointed to oversee the organisation of the Church of England in the colony of Maryland and to provide well-stocked libraries for the clergy there, but shortly afterwards he decided to extend his scheme to include poor clergy in England and Wales.[77] Bray's intention was to help the clergy to improve their knowledge and as a result become better equipped for their role in the community.[78] In particular, he thought that the conformist clergy needed to be able to answer difficult questions from those holding opposing views. Through increased opportunities for learning, Bray hoped to counteract the generally uncertain and apathetic religious climate, which was, he said, 'lukewarm in religion' and 'the worst of ages'.[79] Although the libraries were to be primarily for the poorer clergy, he emphasised that physicians, lawyers and gentlemen would also find the scheme of benefit, and they were encouraged to promote it.[80]

It was therefore within this culture of library provision in both urban and rural locations that Thomas Plume, motivated by the actions and ideas of his contemporaries, combined with his position as a wealthy and unmarried member of one of the professions, decided to donate his library and to provide a new building for Maldon's grammar school. His legacy coincided with Thomas Bray's scheme to improve the educational provision for the clergy and, while Plume had a specific interest in assisting the clergy in Maldon and the neighbouring Dengie hundred, there is a sense that he was taking part in a wider cultural movement to improve access to knowledge.

Plume and science

As will be seen in Chapter 6, David Pearson estimates that Plume's collection of books on science, mathematics, natural history, contemporary experimentation, medicine, astronomy and related matters amounts to nearly 10 per cent of the total, or some 800 books. This is a significant number even when it is considered that Plume was accumulating his library during the latter stages of the scientific revolution, a movement that lasted from 1500 to 1700 and which established science as one of the most dominant forces in the world. Dr W.J. Petchey 'suspected' that the Plume Library 'was a deliberately constructed museum of European intellectual history of the 16th and 17th centuries'.[81] It is possible to take issue with this statement because the information in many of these books was still current at the time of the Plume Library's establishment in 1704. It is now, of course, a museum of thought, but it contains books that are still being actively studied today. For example, the index of Margaret Osler's *Rethinking the Scientific Revolution* contains no fewer than 108 names of pre-1700 authors with books in Plume's original collection.[82]

It is also notable that Plume included 52 books on astronomy in his library.[83] His collection on this topic seems to have been inspired by the establishment of the Royal Observatory by Charles II in 1675 in Greenwich Park, in Plume's own parish. The first Astronomer Royal was John Flamsteed, who counted Plume a friend as well as a neighbour. As described more fully in Chapter 10, it is clear that the development of Plume's interest in astronomy and his decision to set up a Professorship of Astronomy and Experimental Philosophy was influenced by his relationship with Flamsteed.

In spite of his in many ways comprehensive collection, Plume apparently did not place a copy of Isaac Newton's *Philosophiae Naturalis Principia Mathematica* (London, 1687), or any of Newton's other books, in his library. The *Principia*

1.6 Flamsteed House, Greenwich Park, built by Sir Christopher Wren on the site of Duke Humphrey's Tower in 1676 and occupied in the same year by John Flamsteed (1646–1719), the Astronomer Royal (from 1675). Flamsteed was a neighbour and friend of Dr Thomas Plume.

was one of the most seminal works of the scientific revolution and as it was already famous in Plume's day it is not easy to explain its absence. Is it possible that a reason may be found in Newton's religious beliefs. At this time all fellows of university colleges were required to be ordained priests, but Newton was never ordained and he avoided making a conventional acceptance of the teachings of the Church of England. As a senior member of the Church, Plume may have profoundly disagreed with Newton over his stance on religion, which was highly unorthodox, although, presumably for self-preservation, Newton never published his true views.[84]

Nonetheless, Plume did not hesitate to seek to use Newton's talents when setting up his professorship, as in his will he asked his Cambridge trustees to solicit Newton's advice. The scientist was noted for his difficult character, having had violent disagreements with Flamsteed over the 'observations' of the moon, so Plume was probably aware that his collaboration with the trustees could

INTRODUCTION

elonging to the Kings Profesor of Astronimy

not be guaranteed.[85] In the event Dr Richard Bentley (1662–1742), Master of Trinity College from 1700, determined 'to run roughshod over the plans of the Astronomer Royal for the disposal of the endowment of Thomas Plume'. Bentley had decided Trinity College should be the home of the observatory and that his protégé Roger Cotes (1682–1716) should be the first Plumian professor, and this he achieved.[86]

This book has been conceived as a rounded picture of Dr Plume's life and legacies, partly because such a long-awaited project is crucial to greater understanding of this notable individual and partly in response to W.J. Petchey's observation that Plume was 'not to be found in his books'.[87] To remedy the many gaps in our knowledge about Plume, his concerns during his life's work and the motivations behind his legacies, the contributors to this book have applied a combination of diverse approaches to research: intellectual, social, cultural and economic history; architectural, ecclesiastical and bibliographical history; the history of science; and family and local history. By examining all of Plume's legacies together, guided by his will, a much more holistic view of

Plume's life has been gained than that which was achieved in previous studies. Although Plume stands out as a remarkable figure among his middle-status clergy contemporaries for his wealth and the range of his philanthropic vision, his life and legacies are also an important example of the concerns and ambitions of this group of educated professionals who lived through the changing political and religious culture of seventeenth-century England. Thus, as well as highlighting the ongoing impact of Plume's bequests over the three centuries since his death, we expect this book to be of interest to a wide range of scholarly and more general audiences concerned with understanding the professions, philanthropy and knowledge in the early modern period.

Notwithstanding the considerable advancement we have made in our overall understanding of Plume's life and legacies during this project, there remain a number of unresolved issues and much scope for future research. Our knowledge of Dr Plume's social relationships continues to be limited, principally because of a lack of sources such as correspondence. It is certainly possible that material may come to light in the future, perhaps in collections relating to other family members or social and professional contacts. As described in Chapters 3 and 4, lack of sufficient evidence has meant that his precise family relationship to his executor James Plume remains unknown, as does the nature of his friendship with Mrs Audrey (or Anne) Beale, who was present at his deathbed along with Plume's servants, and who was later accused of tampering with Plume's will. A plot against Dr Plume was uncovered in 1695 that involved an attempt to forge his will and poison him (see Chapter 4). The context is again obscure, but it may suggest that the wealthy but ageing archdeacon had been identified as a vulnerable figure. The full sources of Plume's wealth have as yet proved difficult to explain satisfactorily, with the balance between his professional income, inherited wealth and property and his business and commercial acumen remaining opaque (see Chapter 3).

With regard to the book, pamphlet and manuscript collections at the Plume Library in Maldon there are a number of current and future lines of enquiry. One significant avenue for future research is the form and content of Plume's notable collection of some 1,600 unbound pamphlets (see Chapter 6). Funded by the Bibliographical Society, Anna Reynolds is surveying the waste paper and parchment in the library's collection of unbound pamphlets, many of which are in stab-stitched waste covers, as well as many original bindings containing waste. In addition to producing a case study of the bindings of a seventeenth-century clergyman, the work will inform the chapter 'Waste' in *The Oxford Handbook to the History of the Book in Early Modern England* (OUP, forthcoming 2021).[88] In another project, a team of trained volunteers have been working on a conservation programme that involves fitting 'shoes' to the larger folios to support the weight of the spines. At the same time, they have been noting which books contain Plume's monogram and which have fore-edge titles, so that this information is easily accessible for future researchers.[89] Helen Kemp has also been recataloguing Plume's manuscripts, which will lead to a new version of the online catalogue and subsequent publications. In addition, information about the sermons found in the manuscripts are being added to the open-access, fully searchable, online database for the Gateway to Early Modern Manuscript Sermons (GEMMS) project, funded by the Social Sciences and Humanities Research Council of Canada.[90] Documents forming the early archives of the Plume Trustees have been recently accessioned to Thomas Plume's Library's online catalogue. These projects all speak to the continued value and use of the Library's collections many centuries after its original foundation.

Notes

1. S. Doran and C. Durston, *Princes, Pastors and People, The Church and Religion in England, 1500–1700* (2nd edn, Abingdon, 2003), p. 13.
2. M. Todd, 'England after 1558', in A. Pettegree (ed.), *The Reformation World* (London and New York, 2000), p. 380.
3. See below, pp. 55–7; S.R. Gardiner (ed.), *The Constitutional Documents of the Puritan Revolution 1625–1660* (3rd edn, Oxford, 1906), pp. 137, 140–1; Doran and Durston, *Princes, Pastors and People*, pp. 30, 57.
4. Doran and Durston, *Princes, Pastors and People*, p. 6.
5. B. Coward, *The Stuart Age, England, 1603–1714* (2nd edn, London and New York, 1994), p. 294.
6. Doran and Durston, *Princes, Pastors and People*, p. 6.
7. See below, p. 184.
8. TNA, PROB 10/1387. For a transcription of Plume's original will see the appendix. The will, and its contents, is more fully discussed in Chapter 4.
9. Figure based on the change in RPI as measured by the Economic History Association, 'Measuring Worth' calculator: https://eh.net/howmuchisthat/.
10. Chapter 4, pp. 114–15.
11. Registered Charity No. 310661; http://www.thomasplumeslibrary.co.uk/.
12. See Chapters 6 and 8.
13. Registered Charity No. 254048.
14. P.A. Slack, *Poverty and Policy in Tudor and Stuart England* (London, 1988), p. 165.
15. Appendix: Dr Thomas Plume's will, l. 26.
16. Ibid., ll. 50–1 and 135–6; The Public Foundation Catalogue, *Oil Paintings in Public Ownership in Essex* (London, 2006), p. 214; below, Figure 1.1.
17. T. Cox, *Magna Britannia, Antiqua & Nova: or, A new, exact, and comprehensive survey of the ancient and present state of Great-Britain* (London, 1738 edn), vol. 1, p. 691; N. Salmon, *The History and Antiquities of Essex. From the Collections of Thomas Jekyll of Bocking, Esq.* (London, 1740–2), p. 241; P. Morant, *The History and Antiquities of the County of Essex*, vol. 1 (London, 1768), pp. 337–8.
18. A. Clark, 'The Plume Pamphlets', *ER*, xii (1903), pp. 159–65; idem, 'Plume MS papers', *ER*, xiii (1904), pp. 30–3.

19 A. Clark, 'Dr Plume's Pocketbook', *ER*, xiv (1905), pp. 9–20, 65–72; idem, 'Dr Plume as a Cambridge Undergraduate', *ER*, xiv (1905), pp. 147–8; idem, 'Dr Plume's Notebook', *ER*, xiv (1905), pp. 152–63, 213–20; xv (1906), 8–24.
20 C. Fell Smith, 'Plume, Thomas (1630–1704)', *DNB* (1921–2; compact edn (1975)), vol. 2, pp. 1146–7; H.R. French, 'Plume, Thomas (bap. 1630, d. 1704)', *ODNB* (Oxford, 2004); online version: www.oxforddnb.com (2008).
21 W.J. Petchey, *The Intentions of Thomas Plume* (Maldon, 1985).
22 R.A. Doe, 'The Churchmanship of Thomas Plume (1630–1704): a study of a career in the Restoration Church of England', MA dissertation (University of Essex, 2005).
23 Chapter 2, p. 25.
24 G. Mingay, *The Gentry: The Rise and Fall of a Ruling Class* (London, 1976), pp. 44–8; H. French, '"Gentlemen": Remaking the English Ruling Class', in K. Wrightson (ed.), *A Social History of England* (Cambridge, 2017), pp. 273–4.
25 J. Bettley and N. Pevsner, *The Buildings of England. Essex* (New Haven, CT, and London, 2007), p. 433; National Heritage List 1338030.
26 Below, Figure 1.2; French, '"Gentlemen"', p. 272; Letter to the Plume Library dated 7 Mar. 1975, from T.E. Mathew, Rouge Dragon Pursuivant of Arms, The College of Arms, London, E.C.4, giving accurate and definitive details of Dr Plume's arms.
27 For a review of the rise of the 'Middling Sort': C. Muldrew, 'The "Middling Sort": An Emergent Cultural Identity', in K. Wrightson (ed.), *A Social History of England* (Cambridge, 2017), pp. 291–309.
28 W.J. Petchey, *A Prospect of Maldon 1500–1689* (Chelmsford, 1991), pp. 10–16 (quotation p. 16).
29 J.R. Smith, *The Borough of Maldon 1688–1800: A Golden Age* (Studley, 2013), p. 31.
30 The account of Greenwich in this paragraph and the next based on: C. Aslet, *The Story of Greenwich* (London, 1999), pp. 107, 123; C. Chalklin, *Seventeenth Century Kent* (London, 1965), pp. 106, 138.
31 Chalklin, *Seventeenth Century Kent*, p. 31.
32 The name derives from the bequest of John Roan (d. after 10 Oct. 1644). See J.W. Kirby, *History of the Roan School (The Greycoat School) and its Founder* (London, 1929), pp. 34, 36–7. See also Chapter 3, p. 82.
33 Chapter 8, pp. 202–3.
34 Aslet, *The Story of Greenwich*, p. 123.
35 E. Hasted, *The History and Topographical Survey of the County of Kent*, vol. 2 (Canterbury, 1797), pp. 440–4; Chapter 3, p. 76.
36 S. Ollard (ed.), assisted by G. Crosse, *A Dictionary of English Church History* (London, 1912), p. 520.
37 A.J. Christopher, 'Bishops, Dioceses and Cathedrals: The Changing Territorial Organisation of the Church of England', *Geojournal*, 67/2 (2006), pp. 126, 127.
38 J. Gregory and J.S. Chamberlain (eds), *The National Church in Local Perspective: The Church of England and its Regions, 1660–1800* (Woodbridge, 2003), p. xii.
39 Chalklin, *Seventeenth Century Kent*, p. 31.
40 *Ibid.*, pp. 89, 90, 147, 164.
41 *Ibid.*, p. 182.
42 *Ibid.*, pp. 145, 179, 180–1.
43 P. Griffiths, J. Landers, M. Pelling and R. Tyson, 'Population and Disease, Estrangement and Belonging', in P. Clark (ed.), *The Cambridge Urban History of Britain 1540–1840*, vol. 2 (Cambridge, 2000), p. 197.
44 8.6 kms or 2 hrs 14 minutes from Greenwich to London, according to Travel in Times, at https://www.travelintimes.org/#9/51.3769/-0.6812/bartholomew (accessed 25 October 2018). See also Chalklin, *Seventeenth Century Kent*, p. 31.
45 Chapter 3, pp. 81, 84.

INTRODUCTION

46   J. Raven, *The Business of Books* (New Haven, CT, and London, 2007), pp. 91, 106, 114, 117; Chapter 3, p. 82.
47   F. Herrmann, unpublished text of his 1990 Plume Lecture, 'The Importance of Books to Dr Plume', pp. 22–6; Chapter 6, pp. 161–3.
48   J. Eales, 'Mary, Lady Armine', *ODNB* (Oxford, 2009); https://www.british-history.ac.uk/survey-london/vol20/pt3/pp.115-122. The lane stretched between the parishes of St Martin's-in-the-Fields and St Giles-in-the-Fields.
49   Chapter 3, pp. 81–2.
50   Appendix: will, ll. 175–91, 254–7, 271–83, 537–9.
51   *Ibid.*, ll. 171–2.
52   See A. Ryrie, 'Reformations', in K. Wrightson (ed.), *A Social History of England* (Cambridge, 2017), p. 110.
53   Appendix: will, ll. 46–53, 116–23, 433–9; Chapter 4, pp. 109, 111–13; Chapter 9, p. 228.
54   Appendix: will, ll. 189–91, 278–81.
55   French, 'Plume, Thomas (bap. 1630, d. 1704)', *ODNB*; Chapter 10, pp. 249–50.
56   Chapter 9, p. 232.
57   Appendix: will, ll. 192–7, 508–10.
58   A. Fox, 'Words, Words, Words: Education, Literacy and Print', in K. Wrightson (ed.), *A Social History of England* (Cambridge, 2017), p. 132; J. Cannon, *Schooling in England 1660 to 1850, Part II. The Gazetteer of English Schools* (List and Index Soc., Special Series 55, 2016), p. 65.
59   However, Plume was a member of, and left a bequest to, the Society for the Propagation of the Gospel (SPG); see Chapter 4, p. 107.
60   Fox, 'Words, Words, Words', p. 135; Cannon, *Schooling in England 1660 to 1850, Part I – 'A Noiseless Revolution*', pp. 15–16, 45.
61   M. McGinley, 'Palmer's School and the Changing Educational Needs of the Nineteenth Century', *Panorama. The Journal of the Thurrock Local History Society*, 20 (Winter 1976/7), pp. 11–12.
62   *Ibid.*, p. 12.
63   W.J. Petchey, *Maldon Grammar School 1608–1958* (Maldon, 1958), 22–3; Smith, *The Borough of Maldon 1688–1800*, pp. 387–8.
64   Cannon, *Schooling in England 1660 to 1850, Part I*, pp. 22–3; idem., *Schooling in England 1660 to 1850, Part II*, pp. 65–6.
65   Reg. Char. 310924; Chapter 5, pp. 135, 140, 144, 147.
66   For a fuller discussion of the context of seventeenth-century libraries, see H. Kemp, 'Collecting, Communicating, and Commemorating: The Significance of Thomas Plume's Manuscript Collection, left to his Library in Maldon, est. 1704', PhD thesis (University of Essex, 2017). The information here has been adapted from Chapter 3. See also T. Kelly, *Early Public Libraries: A History of Public Libraries in Great Britain before 1850* (The Library Association, London, 1966), p. 69.
67   W.M. Jacob, 'Libraries for the Parish: Individual Donors and Charitable Societies', in G. Mandelbrote and K.A. Manley (eds), *The Cambridge History of Libraries in Britain and Ireland, Volume II 1640–1850* (Cambridge, 2006), p. 66.
68   Kelly, *Early Public Libraries*, pp. 118–19; R. O'Day, *The Professions in Early Modern England: 1450–1800: Servants of the Commonweal* (London, 2000), p. 28.
69   Thomas Tenison (1636–1715) was archbishop of Canterbury from 1694 until his death. M. Powell, 'Endowed Libraries for Towns', in Mandelbrote and Manley (eds), *Cambridge History of Libraries in Britain and Ireland, Volume II 1640–1850*, p. 85.
70   Humphrey Chetham (c.1580–1653) was a financier and philanthropist. See further A. Crosby, 'Chetham, Humphrey (bap. 1580, d. 1653), financier and philanthropist', *ODNB* (Oxford, 2004); C. Hartwell, *The History and Architecture of Chetham's School and Library* (New Haven, CT, 2004),

p. 62. Thomas Fuller was a scholarly clergyman and historian. Plume owned 22 of his publications and made notes from his work: see for example TPL, MA0007, fo. 1v.

71 P.A. Nelles, 'Libraries, Books and Learning, from Bacon to the Enlightenment', in Mandelbrote and Manley (eds), *Cambridge History of Libraries*, Vol. II, p. 27.
72 *Ibid.*, p. 23.
73 G. Best, 'Books and Readers in Certain Eighteenth-Century Parish Libraries', PhD thesis (Loughborough University of Technology, 1985), p. 14.
74 *Ibid.*, p. 243.
75 John Evelyn, *The Diary of John Evelyn*, vol. iv (London, 1955), p. 367; Appendix: will, l. 161.
76 Kelly, *Early Public Libraries*, p. 90.
77 Sir Roger Twysden (d. 1672) first had the idea of putting libraries in poor clergy's livings: see N. Ker (ed.), rev. M. Perkin, *A Directory of the Parochial Libraries of the Church of England and the Church of Wales* (Bibliographical Society, London, 2004), p. 33.
78 Thomas Bray, *Bibliotheca Parochialis, or, A scheme of such theological heads both general and particular, as are more peculiarly requisite to be well studied by every pastor of a parish together with a catalogue of books which may be read upon each of those points* (London, 1697), Epistle Dedicatory.
79 Bray, *Bibliotheca parochialis*, Epistle Dedicatory.
80 Thomas Bray, *An Essay Towards Promoting all Useful Knowledge both Divine and Human, in all Parts of His Majesty's Dominions, Both at Home and Abroad* (London, 1697 [1698]), Preface.
81 Petchey, *Intentions of Thomas Plume*, pp. 19–20.
82 M. Osler (ed.), *Rethinking the Scientific Revolution* (Cambridge, 2000), index, pp. 333–40.
83 Online catalogue of the Plume Library, http://library.thomasplumeslibrary.co.uk (accessed 11 January 2017).
84 R. Westfall, 'Newton, Sir Isaac 1642–1727', *ODNB* (Oxford, 2009).
85 *Ibid.*; Appendix: will, l. 406.
86 V. Morgan, *A History of the University of Cambridge*, vol. 2 (Cambridge, 2004), pp. 519–20; J. Gascoigne, *Cambridge in the Age of the Enlightenment: Science, Religion and Politics from the Restoration to the French Revolution* (Cambridge, 1989), p. 150.
87 Petchey, *Intentions of Thomas Plume*, p. 11.
88 Pers. comm. A. Reynolds, 21 November 2018.
89 In the sixteenth century it had been customary to shelve books with their fore edge outward, so a book's title was written on its fore edge to identify it.
90 http://gemmsproject.blogspot.com/p/about-gemms.html (accessed 29 October 2018).

Chapter 2

The Plume family at Maldon, c.1621–1704
J.R. Smith

This chapter is primarily concerned with the Plume family's activities in the seventeenth century at Maldon, a small Essex parliamentary borough, market and port town. While containing information about Dr Thomas Plume it concentrates chiefly on other and much less well-remembered family members, two of whom – Dr Plume's elder brother, Samuel, and his father, Thomas Plume – were merchants and leading members of Maldon's community. All this provides contextual information on Dr Plume's background and the possible influence on him of factors such as commerce, wealth, religion and status in the local community.

Family origins at Great Yeldham
In the 1760s the antiquary Philip Morant observed that the Plume family 'was for a while considerable' in several places in Essex and other counties.[1] The earliest documented evidence of the family's presence in Essex dates from *temp.* Henry VIII, when Robert Plume was tenant of the Great Yeldham Hall estate in the north Essex parish of Great Yeldham, between Castle Hedingham and the Essex–Suffolk boundary, which then formed part of the huge estate of the de Vere family, earls of Oxford. His son Robert married Elizabeth Purchas of Great Yeldham, by whom he had three sons, Samuel, Thomas and Edmund, and in 1584 purchased the Yeldham Hall estate, including the manor and advowson of Great Yeldham, for his two younger sons, Thomas and Edmund, both probably under the age of 21.[2] Thomas lived at Great Yeldham Hall (Figure 2.1), married Mary Hamond from Ellingham, Suffolk, and by her had at least eight children: four sons, Samuel, Thomas (in 1630 to become father to Thomas Plume, subject of this book), John (who appears to have died a minor) and Robert, and four daughters (Figure 2.2).[3] He was already 'sicke in bodye' when

2.1 Great Yeldham Hall in north Essex, home of Dr Thomas Plume's forebears, including his great-great-grandfather (Robert Plume, *temp*. Henry VIII), great-grandfather (Robert Plume, *fl.* 1584) and grandfather (Thomas Plume, d. 1615). The Georgian façade masks a fine early sixteenth-century timber-framed house.

he made his will in February 1615 and was dead by 24 May, when probate was granted to his eldest son, Samuel. Substantial bequests were made to his wife, sons Samuel (Great Yeldham Hall estate), Thomas (£10 immediately and £500 payable out of the Yeldham Hall estate upon attaining the age of 25) and Robert (real estate in the neighbouring parishes of Belchamp St Paul, Belchamp Otten and Belchamp Walter upon attaining the age of 25), and all four daughters (a total of £1,500).[4]

Education

Three family members were educated at Christ's College, Cambridge. The first was Samuel, eldest son of Thomas Plume of Great Yeldham Hall, who entered in 1605 and was awarded a BA degree in 1609.[5] He was followed in 1607 by his brother Thomas, who appears to have left without graduating.[6] In 1638 Samuel Plume gave £10 in response to an appeal to Christ's men soliciting funds for a new building at the college. Constructed in 1640–2, the building is now known as the Fellows' Building.[7]

The third family member to go to Christ's was Thomas (baptised in Maldon in August 1630, son of Thomas Plume and nephew of Samuel Plume of Great

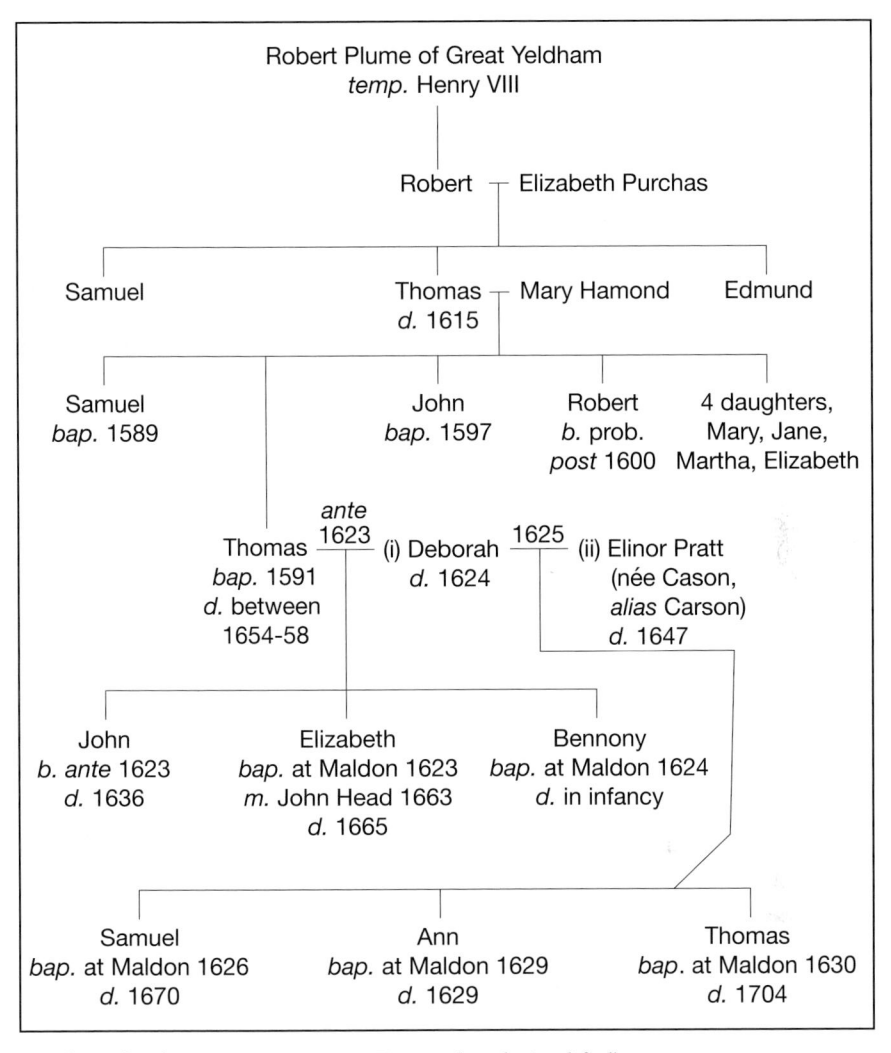

```
                    Robert Plume of Great Yeldham
                         temp. Henry VIII
                                │
                         Robert ─┬─ Elizabeth Purchas
          ┌──────────────────────┼──────────────────────┐
      Samuel               Thomas ─┬─ Mary Hamond    Edmund
                           d. 1615 │
          ┌────────────┬───────────┼───────────┬──────────────┐
      Samuel        John       Robert        4 daughters,
      bap. 1589    bap. 1597   b. prob.      Mary, Jane,
                               post 1600    Martha, Elizabeth
                        ante
                       1623              1625
              Thomas ─┬── (i) Deborah ─┬── (ii) Elinor Pratt
              bap. 1591    d. 1624          (née Cason,
              d. between                     alias Carson)
              1654-58                        d. 1647
       ┌──────────────┬──────────────────┐
     John         Elizabeth           Bennony
    b. ante 1623  bap. at Maldon 1623  bap. at Maldon 1624
    d. 1636       m. John Head 1663    d. in infancy
                  d. 1665
       ┌──────────────┬──────────────────┐
     Samuel           Ann              Thomas
   bap. at Maldon 1626  bap. at Maldon 1629  bap. at Maldon 1630
   d. 1670           d. 1629            d. 1704
```

2.2 Plume family tree, *temp.* Henry VIII–1704 (much simplified).

Yeldham), who was admitted in February 1646, aged 15. He was awarded a BA degree in 1650[8] and went on to become Dr Thomas Plume, vicar of Greenwich, archdeacon of Rochester and Maldon's greatest benefactor. More will be said later in the chapter about the significance of these Cambridge links.

Migration to Maldon, and baptisms, marriages and burials

The earliest evidence of the family's connection with Maldon appears in a statement that Thomas Plume (second son of Thomas Plume of Great Yeldham Hall) purchased in about 1621 a meadow there from Widow Alice Garrington.[9]

Firm evidence of his presence appears in a lease, dated 13 January 1623, describing him as of Maldon and a gentleman; this suggests he had arrived by 1622.[10] The next reference appears in Maldon All Saints' baptismal register, recording on 4 May 1623 the baptism of a daughter, Elizabeth, and naming his wife as Deborah.[11] In December of that year he was described as a gentleman who had been born in Great Yeldham and who had two infant children, John and Elizabeth.[12] It is probable that Elizabeth had been born in Maldon, but it is postulated that John was born and baptised in Yeldham, so that when Thomas migrated to Maldon he was probably accompanied by his wife and infant son. It is likely that John was educated at Maldon's grammar school under the tutelage of his father's friend John Danes, master since 1612. An exercise book bearing his name is preserved in the Plume Library;[13] it contains mercantile accounting exercises by John, indicating he may have been destined to follow his father into trade. Little else is known of John except he was undoubtedly the John Plume buried at All Saints on 3 August 1636.[14] The exercise book was later used by Thomas Plume, his younger half-brother.

A second Plume baptism at All Saints (Figure 2.3) took place on 29 December 1624, this time of Bennony, son of Thomas and Deborah. Thomas was then a widower, for Deborah was buried on the same day.[15] She must have died in or very shortly after childbirth. The choice of the Hebrew name Bennony, 'son of my sorrow', was therefore appropriate and poignant. Nothing more is known of Bennony, who is presumed to have died in early childhood.

Thomas's time as a widower was short, for in July 1625 he married a member of a well-established Maldon family of merchant tailors with which he already had links, and thereby strengthened his standing in the town. His new wife, Elinor, was the widow of Alderman Jeremy (*alias* Jeremiah) Pratt, who had died aged about 33 at the beginning of 1625.[16] She came originally from Little Holland, a parish on the Essex coast near Great Clacton, and generally referred to herself and was addressed not as Elinor but as 'Ellen' or 'Hellen'.[17]

The new marriage was quickly productive, with a son, Samuel, being baptised in All Saints in June 1626.[18] A daughter, Ann, was baptised there on 2 February 1629; she was probably the Ann Plume buried on 10 May 1629.[19] A second son, Thomas (later Dr Thomas Plume), was baptised in All Saints on 18 August 1630.[20]

Elinor Plume died in September 1647.[21] Thomas appears then to have remained a widower. He had moved from Maldon by January 1654[22] and died intestate between 5 June 1654, when he was described as being of Hazeleigh (a small parish adjoining Maldon), and 1 July 1658, when his son Samuel became a freeman and Thomas was described as being deceased.[23] While the exact death date may never be established, it was probably nearer the end of the possible time span than the beginning.[24]

2.3 All Saints' church, Maldon, parish church of the Plume family and scene of Plume baptisms, marriages and burials 1623–70, depicted c.1860 by an unknown artist (possibly the Maldon artist Robert Nightingale). Published by R.J. Bridge.

The family home in Maldon and real estate transactions

Between its arrival in Maldon (about 1621) and 1631 the family lived in the tiny parish of All Saints, though in which house is uncertain; it is postulated it was in Mrs Annastacy Wentworth's house for at least part of the time. This old house stood in High Street, directly opposite the town's seat of government, the Moot Hall, and within All Saints. By 1631 the family was certainly living there.[25] Mrs Wentworth, who lived in London, was the widow of a London lawyer, Henry Wentworth, and daughter of a former Maldon alderman, William Hale (d. 1582).[26] In 1633 Thomas Plume took a 21-year lease at £15 per annum, from which was excluded the 'chamber over the salt shop at the east side of the house', which was reserved for Mrs Wentworth's use.[27] When Annastacy Wentworth died in 1634 ownership passed, under the terms of her will, to Henry Wentworth's grandson Francis Mitchell (son of Mrs Cecily Mitchell, his daughter by a former wife, and her husband Francis Mitchell of Theydon Garnon).[28] In 1637 Mitchell, then described as being of Coopersale, in Theydon Garnon, granted a new 21-year lease to Plume, to run from 29 September, with the annual rent to be paid at the 'hall house of the said messuage'; it included conditions that Plume would supply and plant the yard with fruit trees, and maintain the premises with 'convenient repairs'.[29] Mrs Wentworth's bequest to Mitchell was for the term of his life only, and contained specific remainders, but in April 1641 Mitchell mortgaged the house to Robert Brooke of Woodham Walter, clerk (rector), for £50, and in August forfeited ownership to Brooke by failing to fulfil the mortgage conditions.[30] Plume remained tenant.

At Brooke's death in 1647 ownership passed to his elder son, Edward Brooke, then at Oxford University, who on 5 June 1654 conveyed it to Thomas Plume.[31] The house was described as a capital messuage with an orchard and garden.[32] Plume, however, had already moved to Hazeleigh and the house was now the home of his spinster daughter, Elizabeth, and elder son, Samuel. It seems no monetary transaction was involved. Instead, the conveyance was in recognition 'of the faithful discharge of the especiall trust and confidence ... imposed upon ... Robert Brooke in his lifetime by the said Thomas Plume which the said Robert often signified and declared unto the said Edward'. Exactly what that means is a mystery, although Robert Brooke, in his will of 16 August 1647, referred to Plume as his loving friend and 'brother' and appointed him an executor.[33]

When Plume proved Brooke's will at Maldon, on 23 October 1647, he was appointed guardian of Edward Brooke, then aged 20, for the remainder of his minority. Edward subsequently became curate of his father's parish, Woodham Walter. Later evidence points to a long-standing friendship between the Plume and Brooke families that continued until Dr Thomas Plume's death in 1704; Edward Brooke became vicar of the Kent parish of Hadlow within Plume's archdeaconry of Rochester in 1701[34] and was bequeathed £100 in Plume's will.[35]

Following Thomas Plume's death ownership of the house passed to his clergyman younger son, Thomas. This was because at Maldon the custom of Borough English applied, which meant that in the absence of a will specifying inheritance the deceased's real estate would pass to the younger or youngest son. However, Thomas senior had instructed his son Thomas that the house should pass to Samuel.[36] These instructions were honoured on 9 September 1659 when Thomas, now vicar of Greenwich, transferred ownership to his brother. The conveyance recites that Samuel had been brought up in the house with his father and that he was 'acquainted with the trade and calling of his father'.[37] Ownership remained vested in Samuel until his death in 1670, when it reverted to his brother and the old house ceased to be a Plume family home and was leased to tenants.

Thomas Plume (the father) began dealing in Maldon real estate about the same time as his migration to the town, beginning with the purchase in about 1621 of the meadow next to Ware Pond, already noted. On 13 January 1623 the Corporation, Maldon's governing body, at a meeting convened at the 'ernest sute & Petition of Thomas Plume gent', described as owner of the meadow, agreed to lease to Plume a small piece of land lying between it and the pond, four yards wide and thirty-seven yards long, with permission to fence it in with the meadow. The lease was to run for 21 years from 29 September in return for a fine of 3s 4d and a yearly rent of 12d. An obligation was placed on Plume to clean and scour Ware Pond at his own expense 'from time to time when & so often as neede shalbe or require'.[38] A few years later, at the beginning of 1629, Plume and others sold the meadow, now said to comprise two and a half acres and abut west on land called Gravel Pitts, to Thomas Lawe, a Maldon market gardener, for £48.[39]

In 1620 and 1621 most of Maldon's ancient Butcher Row was demolished as part of a programme of reorganisation by the Corporation of the High Street market place.[40] The site, outside the King's Head and Spread Eagle inns (the site of the latter now occupied by NatWest Bank), henceforth to be used for stalls 'for butchers and Com[m]on victuallers and sellers of fleshe in and upon the m[ar]kett days', was then let on a succession of leases to private individuals, including Thomas Plume by 1623 to about 1640.[41] Plume's next recorded transaction took place in about 1636, when he sold an unidentified tenement in Maldon to Widow Damarys Rice for £20.[42]

For a few years Plume also owned a brewery in Maldon, which he probably leased to a brewer rather than operating himself. The brewery stood on Great Potman Marsh, on the east side of the Causeway and just north of Fullbridge bridge, and included a capital house (Figure 2.4). In 1608 it had been sold to Paul Dewes of Stowlangtoft, Suffolk, a Middle Temple lawyer and government official, who was a freeman of the borough and occasional resident, and in about 1642 Dewes' son, the antiquary and diarist Sir Simonds Dewes, sold it to Plume for a sum reported to have been £200.[43] Plume may have been distantly related to the Dewes family: Sir Simonds Dewes was named after his maternal grandfather Richard Simonds (*alias* Symonds), another Middle Temple lawyer, whose daughter and heir Sissilia (Sir Simonds' mother) married Paul Dewes, while another Richard Symonds, a Court of Chancery official who also had a home in Great Yeldham, married Elizabeth Plume, daughter of Robert Plume of Great Yeldham Hall, in 1580.[44] A few years later, in about 1649, Plume sold the brewery to William Jarman of Maldon for a sum reported to have been £109 10s.[45] At about the same time he leased from the borough a piece of land in Fullbridge Street, a short distance north of the bridge. This probably formed part of the brewery complex, and Jarman later succeeded Plume as tenant.[46]

Thomas Plume's son Dr Thomas Plume (who by the 1650s had already moved away from Maldon) also acquired considerable property in and around the town. For example, in August 1687 he was described as owner of a piece of land near Maldon Hythe.[47] Plots there were in demand by merchants, and it may previously have belonged to his father or brother. Some ten years later, in about

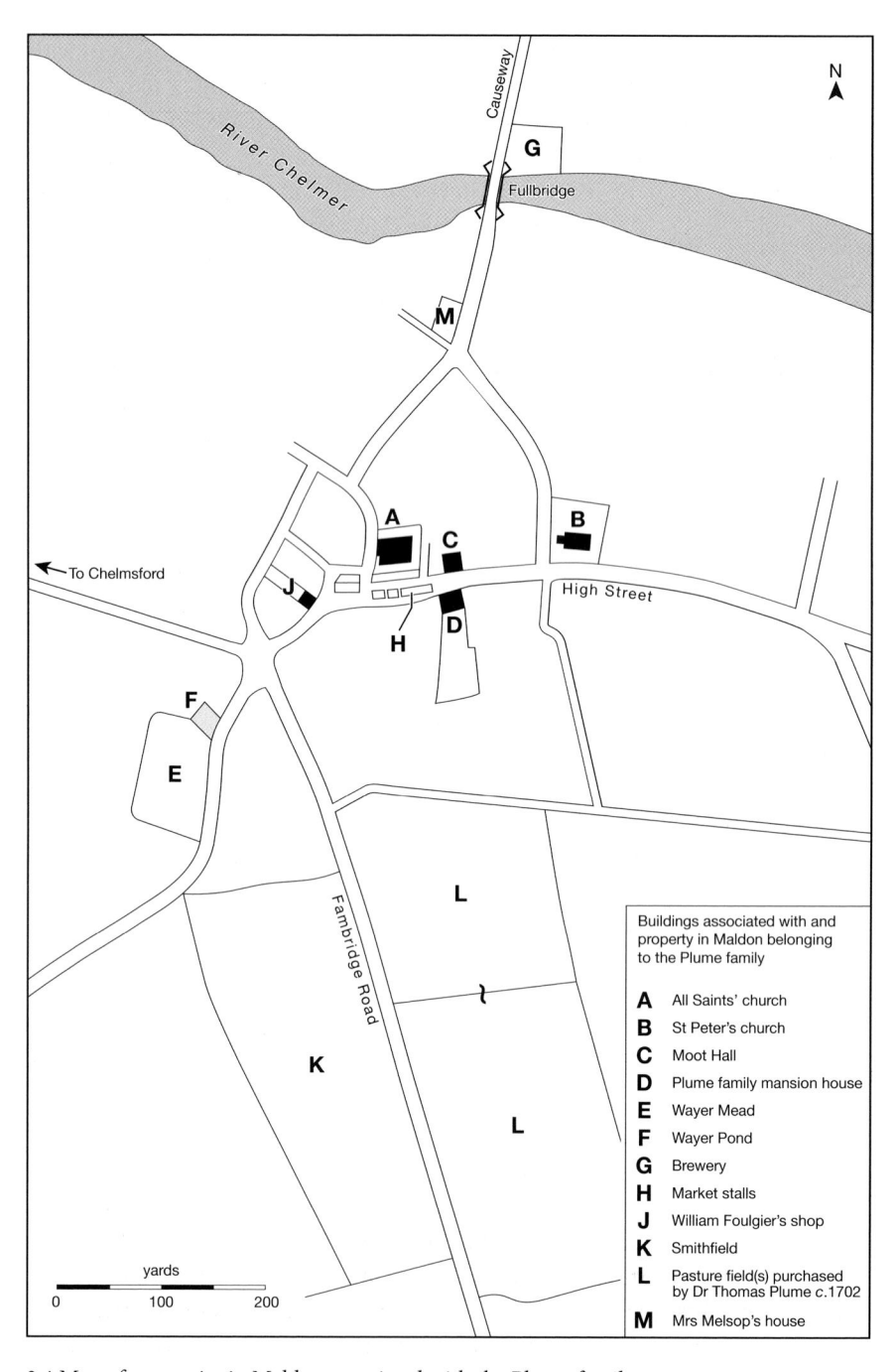

2.4 Map of properties in Maldon associated with the Plume family.

1697, Plume sold a piece of land in St Mary's parish to Thomas Stace, merchant tailor, for £10.[48] Possibly this was the same piece he had owned in 1687.

Another sale by Dr Plume took place in August 1696, this time of Grove Croft near Broad Street Green in the neighbouring parish of Heybridge, to John Waight of Little Totham, yeoman, for £5 10s.[49] The witnesses to the conveyance, Francis Thompson, William Carr and James Taverner, are of particular interest for their connections with Plume. Thompson is undoubtedly to be associated with Dr Francis Thompson (c.1640–1715), beneficiary and trustee in Dr Plume's will, whose nephew, also Francis Thompson, became first Plume Librarian and a Plume Charity trustee (*ex-officio*) early in the eighteenth century, and was master of the grammar school at Maldon from 1716 to 1720 and vicar of Steeple from 1716 to 1742.[50] Carr was town clerk of Maldon and tenant of Plume's High Street house, while Taverner was a Maldon lawyer who in 1702 succeeded Carr as town clerk and also lived in the High Street house.[51]

In probably early 1702 Dr Plume purchased from John Norton and his wife, Mary, for £483 pasture totalling 16 acres on the east side of Fambridge Road in Maldon to provide a rental income to help pay the salary of the librarian at Maldon, to be appointed after his death.[52] This land is now the site of the Upper Plume School and its playing field. At about the same time, in the summer of 1702, he lent £350 to William Carr as part of the purchase price of £756 for land in Maldon called Hawksdown Hills and Clover Field.[53] This and other evidence, including Carr's witnessing of the 1696 conveyance mentioned above, suggests a relationship of trust and friendship between the two men.

In addition, at an unknown date, Plume became mortgagee of a house in Fullbridge Street, described in his will of 1704 as Mrs Melsop's house,[54] which stood on the north-west side of the street where the former town workhouse now stands and abutted to the north-east on premises now 29 Market Hill.[55] The mortgage was bequeathed by Plume for the use of his Maldon workhouse charity (to become operational following his death) and his executor was instructed to pay £10 to Charles Huggett (probably to be associated with the Maldon freeman and mariner of that name [d. August 1718]) in return for his release of a claim of equity of redemption, Plume commenting that 'the House is not worth so much as it owes mee'. This evidence indicates that Plume intended the house should form part or all of the site for the workhouse.[56] The lawyer John Comyns, recorder of the borough of Maldon from 1700 to 1736, an MP for Maldon from 1701 to 1726 and a mutual friend of both Plume and William Carr, may have been privy to this intention: Plume ordered in his will that the workhouse was to be set up in accordance with Comyns' 'direction, & his draught'.[57]

In 1704 Plume bequeathed three Maldon properties to his cousin Nathaniel Plume of Great Yeldham, an attorney 'of very good reputation'.[58] They were, firstly, the High Street house and former family home then occupied by James Taverner and his wife Mary (one of William Carr's daughters, whom Taverner had married in 1703).[59] The second property was about 12 acres of land called Smithfield *alias* Smithfields on the west side of Fambridge Road (and opposite the pasture purchased from John and Mary Norton), leased to John Browne at £14 a year and which, it seems likely, had come into Plume family ownership through Dr Thomas Plume's mother, Elinor Plume (d. 1647).[60] The third was a butcher's shop at the top end of the town, 'wherein Folgier now kills, & uses his trade', already owned by Plume by the 1680s.[61] It was leased to John Wasse until 1687, when William Foulgier succeeded him. Foulgier's rent in 1703 was £4 a year.[62] It is not known how Plume came into possession of the shop. Nathaniel Plume was also bequeathed a mortgage of unidentified property belonging to a Mr Gyon, whose family had been 'wasted by others'.[63]

Thomas Plume's membership of Maldon Corporation
On 1 December 1623 the Corporation voted to make Thomas Plume (Dr Thomas Plume's father) a freeman upon the pledge and undertaking ('manucaproem') of Alderman Jeremy Pratt. When the chamberlains recorded payment of an admission fee of £6 13s 4d (a somewhat higher amount than usual for admission by purchase) it was noted Plume had two children, John and Elizabeth.[64] A few weeks later, on 19 January 1624, he was elected to the Corporation, filling the vacancy created by Headburgess Joseph Pratt, yeoman and a member since 1617, who was retiring on the grounds of old age and infirmity.[65] These weren't to be the only links between Plume and the Pratt family; it has already been noted how, 18 months later, in July 1625, Plume married Jeremy Pratt's widow, Elinor.

At the annual Court of Election of Officers on 7 January 1625, Thomas Plume was elected a justice of the peace of the borough, to hold that office for a year.[66] This is the only instance known of a headburgess being a justice, the office otherwise (under the terms of the borough charter) being reserved to aldermen. On the same day the Corporation agreed unanimously that Plume should be deputy to Thomas Cheese, the town clerk, then aged about 67, who had declined the Corporation's request that he should retire.[67] These appointments suggest that Plume was recognised as a man of exceptional ability. Plume remained deputy town clerk until the beginning of October, by which date Cheese appears to have ceased acting as town clerk and had left the Corporation,[68] and was probably then temporary town clerk for a short period until a new clerk, John Bentley, took up his post.[69] Also in this year Plume lent £10 to the Corporation, 'the boxe being w[i]thout monye'.[70]

Plume remained a headburgess for just two years until, in January 1626, he was fast-tracked to the rank of alderman.[71] Even for Maldon, with its highly transient population and where many newcomers became leading Corporation members, this was rapid promotion, and indicates that Plume had the support of the Corporation's inner ruling group, the eight aldermen. He served his first year as one of the two bailiffs, the 'masters of the town', in 1627, and was to hold that office a further five times, in 1633, 1637, 1641, 1645 and 1649.[72] (The two annual bailiffs were appointed from the eight aldermen every January, in accordance with a four-year cycle.) Following the death in 1636 of John Soan, an alderman for more than 20 years, Plume emerged as 'clear leader', governing behind the scenes in the years when he was not a bailiff and responsible for guiding Maldon through the Civil Wars and the Interregnum until the commencement of Cromwell's Protectorate.[73]

The next evidence outlines Maldon's connection with the Dutch lawyer, scholar and republican Isaac Dorislaus (1595–1649) and perhaps throws light on the political sympathies of Corporation members in the late 1620s and 1630s. In 1622 Dorislaus married in Leiden, Elizabeth Pope from Maldon. The couple then lived in Leiden until 1627, when he was appointed lecturer in Roman History at Cambridge University and moved to England in October. They made their home in Elizabeth's father's house in Maldon, and a series of family baptisms and burials took place at All Saints' church during the period from November 1627 to September 1633.[74] Dorislaus gave just two lectures at Cambridge before Matthew Wren, master of Peterhouse, led a successful movement to silence him as a danger to monarchical government and on suspicion of espousing republican theories of sovereignty. This, however, seems not to have been a problem for Maldon Corporation, which gave support by employing him as clerk to the borough Court of Admiralty. The Elizabeth 'Dorsley' buried at All Saints on 2 September 1633 was probably his wife;[75] Dorislaus then moved to London in about 1634. His final year of employment by Maldon Corporation appears to have been 1638, when he made three visits from London to attend the court, in May, September and December, and was paid a total of £9 4s 6d, most being personally authorised by the bailiffs.[76] Ten years later parliament employed him to assist in drafting the prosecution case for the trial of Charles I, and he was present at the trial. He was to pay a heavy price for his republicanism; in May 1649, while on a diplomatic mission at The Hague, he was assassinated by a gang of English royalists.[77]

In 1638 Plume, acting in his capacity of alderman and justice *ex-officio*, was one of the three members who, at the Moot Hall on 29 March, witnessed the Oath of Supremacy by four men about to migrate, with their families, to New England, where they founded the settlement of Malden, Massachusetts. The four were Thomas Ruck, Joseph Hills and their two servants.[78] Both Ruck and Hills were aldermen, well known to Plume; Ruck and Plume had served together as bailiffs the previous year.[79] The other two witnesses were the borough bailiffs, and the additional participation by Plume perhaps indicates his support for the migration.

Although there was no armed conflict at Maldon during the Civil Wars, it was nevertheless a time of great tension and dissension, and a few examples of how the Corporation (guided by its *de facto* leader Thomas Plume) responded are given here. In 1642 a 'watch house' was erected at the top end of the town; ammunition, including 'great bullets', was imported by ship and stored at the Moot Hall (Figure 2.5); 'Popishe' books and pictures were burned.[80] In 1643 Headburgess George Gifford, a saddler, was ejected from the Corporation. He had been arrested in August not, it seems, in Maldon, and brought to the town by 'a troop'. His place was taken by John Jennings, cooper. W.J. Petchey observed that Gifford had been 'at the least suspected of disloyalty to the Parliamentarian cause' and 'must have been a royalist in his sympathies'.[81] In 1647, with the Second Civil War looming, existing ramparts were strengthened with ironwork and carriages provided for 'great guns'. In the following year, 1648, the ramparts were further strengthened with timber and iron, timber was purchased to make wheels and carriages for 'great guns' and 2s 4d was paid for wine for Colonel Thomas Pride.[82] The extent to which these responses may have resulted from pressure from Essex's chief families, most of whom supported parliament, and from the County Committee and borough's two MPs, remains open to conjecture. There is also evidence that some of Plume's colleagues on the Corporation were very active in their support for the parliamentarian cause, and had actually fought against Prince Charles at the 1651 battle of Worcester 'and elsewhere'.[83]

Towards the end of Plume's membership there is evidence hinting at dissension within the Corporation. In January 1653 elections were held to fill the vacancy caused by the removal from office of Alderman Thomas Langdell (*alias* Langdale), who had left Maldon. Two headburgesses, Isaac Robject and Thomas Francis, were in turn elected, but refused to accept office and were fined. The third elected was John Jennings, who accepted office.[84]

A year later, on 9 January 1654, Plume resigned. His resignation took place immediately before the opening of the annual Court of Election of Officers, and had he not resigned he would almost certainly have become one of the two bailiffs, which office required daily attention to a myriad of tasks associated with the administration of the borough. He was described as the 'eldest and most auncient Alderman' and, like Thomas Langdell, had already left Maldon. It was his 'earnest desire' to stand down, giving as his reason 'his age disability of body and because he hath removed his habitation out of this Burrough'. His request was accepted by the members present in the Moot Hall, but it was not a unanimous decision.[85] His resignation also came just three weeks after the installation of Cromwell as Lord Protector. This may have

2.5 The Moot Hall, Maldon, home of Maldon's civic government from 1576. This was a building very familiar to Thomas Plume and his son Samuel (respectively, the father and brother of Dr Thomas Plume), both leading Corporation members.

been no more than coincidence, but it is tempting to see it as stemming from Plume's disapproval of Cromwell's elevation and the increasing concentration of power into his hands.

Thomas Plume's links with education in Maldon

By his will, made 28 February 1609, Ralph Breeder, a wealthy Maldon alderman, haberdasher, farmer and merchant, bequeathed funds for the purchase of real estate to provide a rental income for the maintenance of 'a Schoolemaster within the Towne of Maldon to teach a grammar schoole'.[86] Breeder died very shortly afterwards and his will was proved in March.[87] The school was closely associated with and controlled by the senior members of the Corporation, for the trustees of Breeder's charity were the aldermen and bailiffs, and so when Plume became an alderman in January 1626 he also became, *ex-officio*, a trustee.[88] In March 1650 Plume played an active role when he was one of three trustees (all described as 'the surviving feoffess') who leased two of the Breeder charity properties, Maldon houses called Schoolmasters, to John Jennings.[89]

Thomas Plume was also a founding trustee of the Annastacy Wentworth Charity, being appointed in 1631 by Wentworth's will, in which he was described as one of her 'trustie friends'.[90] His connection with Mrs Wentworth (d. 1634), as tenant of her High Street mansion house, has already been described. The Maldon charity founded by the will (proved in June 1634) included provision of £3 a year for the education in 'the Grammar Schoole of Maldon' of three poor children born in All Saints' parish, 'capable of and to be disposed in that course'. In the event of unavailability of All Saints' children then children of the other two Maldon parishes could be sent.

In addition to these trusteeships Plume had a close friendship with John Danes, master of the grammar school from 1611 until his death in 1639. The friendship is described more fully near the end of this chapter.

A few years after Ralph Breeder's death, Alderman Benjamin King, one of Breeder's 'loving friends' and an executor of his will, made provision for improved accommodation for the school, then housed in the town's ruinous 'middle church', St Peter's. King set out the scheme in his will, made in November 1613, in which he recalled 'the benivolents and guifte' of Ralph Breeder for the 'Continuannce of a Grammer Schole' in Maldon. A 'fitt and Convenient howse' for the school was to be provided, to the minimum value of £40, by either the purchase of an existing house or the construction of a new house. The money was to be raised from the rents and profits of Asheldham Hall Farm and, following notice in writing, was to be paid to Alderman John Soan at his house in Maldon. King died in January 1614 and his will was proved in the same month, but no action is known to have been taken to provide a new schoolhouse, and it seems likely that the scheme finally foundered in 1636 with Soan's death.[91] The school remained in St Peter's church until the end of the century, when Plume's son Dr Thomas Plume provided a purpose-built schoolroom on the site of the nave and chancel (below the library room). The gift of the schoolroom and the educational charities founded by Dr Plume, including one at Maldon, are described elsewhere in this book.

Thomas Plume and the Heybridge tolls prosecution (1631) and ship seizure (1641)

Since the Middle Ages Maldon had claimed the right to charge tolls on cargoes imported and exported at the small neighbouring port of Heybridge, because those cargoes passed through waters belonging to the borough. By 1600 traders from various parts of Essex had begun challenging the custom, claiming that the borough had no right to charge them for use of port facilities at Heybridge. In response the Corporation issued a new bye-law in 1611 setting out the tolls payable to the borough water bailiff for every vessel that loaded or unloaded cargo at Heybridge, 'before the same vessel goeth away'. This was followed in 1618 by drastic action to prevent vessels going up to Heybridge without paying a toll: the blocking of the entrance to Heybridge Creek (the one-mile section of the river Blackwater from its confluence with the river Chelmer at Maldon upriver to Heybridge bridge) with a chain fastened to posts on either side. Heybridge parish responded by suing the borough in the High Court of Admiralty and the case dragged on into 1619 with substantial legal costs. Although Maldon eventually won the case, several merchants importing coal and iron at Heybridge were by the mid-1620s once again evading payment.[92]

It was at this point that Thomas Plume became involved in the borough's maritime affairs. In 1626, newly promoted to the rank of alderman, he accompanied Bailiff Thomas Wells to Ipswich 'abowt the Towne busynes in avoyding the Charge of Shippinge', and also joined Wells on Goodman Dowsett's boat to witness the laying of a new buoy at Rhebank in the Blackwater estuary, marking the seaward limit of Maldon's jurisdiction.[93] At the same time he became involved in a scheme to bring a collusive lawsuit in the Court of Exchequer to establish beyond all doubt the Corporation's right to levy tolls on goods imported and exported at Heybridge. The scheme was probably devised by the aldermen, with legal advice from the town clerk and the borough recorder, and possibly also the high steward, and knowledge of it may have remained confined to that small group for the next few years. Plume joined the merchants at Heybridge by setting up a wharf there and importing coal, fuller's earth and other goods; like them, he did not pay tolls. It seems likely that the other merchants were probably led to believe that Plume was really acting in his own interest. This remained the situation until 1631, when the Corporation, now having accumulated from its water bailiff (and doubtless also from Plume) a mass of evidence of toll evasion, commenced legal proceedings in the Court of Exchequer against Plume and three others who had 'plotted together' to avoid payment.[94] Plume did not defend the case, and the water bailiff in his evidence to the court stated that since September 1630 he had 'received of Thos Plume & his servant many times … tolls for fulling earth & sea coles landed at Heybridge which have been demanded by him'.[95] This was crucial evidence, for it constituted a tacit acknowledgement by Plume in his role of one of the men being prosecuted over the Corporation's right to levy tolls. The court found for the Corporation, going even further in defence of Maldon's rights by ruling 'noe wharffes to be made at Heibridge to the pre[ju]dice of the said Corporation', and ruled that 'neyther the Defendant nor anie oth[er] p[er]sonne or personnes shall passe or sayle with anie ship or shipps boates or other vessels to or from … Heybridge aforesaid to lade or unlade there w[it]howt the lycence of the said Corporation and paying reasonable fines'.[96] Having won the case the Corporation in 1632 ordered that all vessels passing to Heybridge to load or unload should have a licence from the Corporation and pay 'reasonable Fines for the same'.[97]

Plume continued to be an active defender of Maldon's maritime rights and seaborne trade, as is illustrated by an extraordinary incident in 1641. For several years a merchant named William Slater had been selling coal and iron ore at Heybridge, importing 662 chaldrons of coal (about 1,400 tons by the Newcastle measure) in the four years 1638 to 1641 and dutifully paying tolls. But in 1641 Maldon Corporation not only raised the tolls but also acted to enforce a demand from Maldon freemen, probably merchants, for complete monopoly of the coal trade, and Slater's vessel was seized for a short while by order of the bailiffs, one of whom was Plume.[98]

Israel Hewitt's ministry, 1620–49

In October 1619 the living of the united Maldon parishes of All Saints and St Peter became vacant upon the death of the vicar, Ralph Hawdon, a moderate Puritan.[99] Shortly afterwards, at the beginning of November, the Corporation asked the patron, Richard Frank of Hatfield Broad Oak, to nominate a minister, but Frank delegated the choice to the Corporation and early in 1620 the Corporation chose Israel Hewitt as Hawdon's successor in preference (by 18 votes to six) to a rival older and much more prominent candidate, John Rogers, lecturer of Dedham, one of the most powerful of all Puritan preachers, who had long-standing connections with Maldon.[100] At the time of appointment Hewitt was a Fellow of Christ's College, Cambridge. He had entered the college in 1602 and was awarded an MA degree in 1609 and a fellowship in 1610.[101] During his 29-year Maldon incumbency Hewitt benefited from the Corporation's support and in return provided a safe pair of hands, helping to ensure that the religious strife that had beset the town in the later years of Elizabeth's reign did not resurface.[102] He became a freeman on 12 January 1624, by Corporation vote and with no fee payable.[103] This was just a few weeks after Plume's admission the previous December.

An event that occurred in 1638 involving Thomas Plume, now an alderman and justice, and the Corporation's *de facto* leader, provides evidence of a readiness to clamp down on religious extremism threatening to stir up dissension and to protect Hewitt's pastorate. In July Enoch Grey, rector of Wickham Bishops, a parish about four miles north-west of Maldon, came to the town to preach, but before he could do so he was arrested on orders from Plume and the two bailiffs. Grey was accused of sedition, refused bail and imprisoned. Proceedings against him were commenced before the commissary of the bishop of London, and when he managed to escape from the town gaol a warrant was obtained from the Lord Chief Justice for his apprehension as a felon and traitor.[104]

The Corporation's support for Hewitt also took the form of monetary payments. This occurred throughout his long ministry and helped supplement his stipend, which remained at £50 until 1646, when the Committee for Sequestrations increased it by £40.[105] For example, in 1623 he was given £5; in 1633 he was given £5 'towards the weekly Wednesday lecture'; in 1635, 1636 and 1638 he received 2s a week to help pay for his food; in 1641 he was given £3 2s 6d 'in consideration of his great pains and [in] token of their great loves and good affection towards him'; and in 1644 he was given £10 for his series of sermons known as the Saturday Lectures.[106] Hewitt, however, was probably not poor, for in 1638 he purchased for £50 a house on the east side of the street now known as Silver Street, close to All Saints' church and vicarage.[107]

Further evidence of a close relationship between Hewitt and Plume was demonstrated by an incident during divine service in All Saints' church, probably in the first half of 1639, when Hewitt came 'out of the [altar] rayle to administer the Com[munio]n to Thomas Plume Gent.' This special treatment for Plume and breach of church protocol resulted in Hewitt appearing before an archdeaconry court in July 1639 and being fined 2s 8d.[108]

When in 1648 the Presbyterian-dominated parliament replaced the episcopacy in England and Wales by dividing the counties into Presbyterian *classes*, Maldon was included in the Dengie Hundred Classis, and was represented, as minister, by Hewitt, and by eight elders whose number included Corporation members Thomas Plume, John Jennings and Thomas Langdell.[109]

Hewitt's tenure at Maldon ended in a somewhat unsatisfactory manner. The Parliamentary Committee for Plundered Ministers considered him too old to give sufficient pastoral value for the extra annual income of £40 granted in 1646 by the Committee for Sequestrations and wanted a new vicar and town lecturer to be appointed. Hewitt, probably under pressure, resigned his Maldon living in 1649 and moved to Tendring as rector. His successor at Maldon, Thomas Horrocks, rector since 1646 of Stapleford Tawney, near Romford, and the Parliamentary Committee's nominee, was appointed by the patron, Richard Ingram, in 1650.[110]

Samuel Plume: Corporation membership

Samuel Plume, Thomas Plume's elder son by his second marriage, became a freeman on 1 July 1658, shortly after the probable date of his father's death. He was aged about 32 and without children. By 4 October Samuel had joined the Corporation as a headburgess;[111] it seems plausible that he became a freeman specifically to be eligible and expecting to join at an early opportunity. He was quickly appointed to a position of responsibility, becoming in January 1660 one of the two chamberlains, managers of the borough's finances.[112]

The Restoration (29 May 1660) impacted on parliamentary boroughs not least because four-fifths of members of the Commons were returned by those boroughs and the restored government wanted to exclude political opponents, notably Presbyterians, from places on the corporations. The first impact at Maldon came on 2 July 1660 when a royal writ restored George Gifford to his place and removed Alderman John Jennings, who had taken Gifford's place as headburgess in 1643.[113] Jennings had also, in 1648, served with Thomas Plume as an elder of Dengie Hundred Classis. His place as alderman was taken on the same day by Samuel Plume by a majority vote of bailiffs and headburgesses, even though most other headburgesses, from whose number the eight aldermen were elected, had served for much longer.[114] Fourteen months later, in September 1661, another royal writ removed Maldon's high steward, Sir Henry Mildmay of Wanstead (c.1594–1668), 'whoe stands convicted of that black & horrid murther of our Late Soveraigne Lord King Charles'.[115] Mildmay had additionally been an MP for Maldon in 1621–2 and 1625, and from 1640 to 1660, and was a major figure in Essex and national politics. He had been favoured with office and fortune by James I and Charles I, but sided with parliament during the Civil War and participated in the trial of Charles, although he was not a signatory to the king's death warrant.[116]

At about the same time a petition to Charles II by 'diverse of the Aldermen and Freeburgesses', one of whom may have been Samuel Plume, complained that the Corporation was still in the hands of men disloyal to the king, 'for ye most part members of Schismaticall Congregations' who neglected to administer the Oath of Allegiance (revived in July 1660), and that 'some' of them had fought against him at the battle of Worcester.[117]

The year 1662, in which Samuel Plume served his first term as a bailiff, was a dramatic one for the Corporation. In August the town was visited by 14 commissioners appointed by the 1661 Corporation Act, whose number included Maldon's new high steward, the lawyer Sir John Bramston (1611–1700) of Skreens, Roxwell, who had replaced Henry Mildmay, and who thought Mildmay should have been executed for his treason.[118] The Act required, among other things, that Corporation members should take communion according to the rites of the Anglican Church and renounce the

Solemn League and Covenant, and was therefore aimed particularly against Presbyterian members such as those at Maldon, where they formed a majority. A meeting of Corporation and commissioners took place on 11 August. Nine members renounced, including Bailiff Samuel Plume and two aldermen, one of whom was John Jennings, who had been restored to the Corporation by a vote of the House on 2 December 1661. But 15, including Plume's fellow bailiff, John Harrison and four other aldermen, refused and were immediately deposed and replaced.[119] In the space of one day Maldon Corporation had been purged of its Presbyterian members. Plume's survival suggests that he probably shared the same political and religious convictions as his younger brother, a royalist and Anglican, or was an opportunist. He now emerged as one of the leaders of the Corporation.

Samuel Plume and the persecution of Thomas Horrocks
From late 1662 to the summer of 1663 Samuel Plume, in his capacity as alderman, bailiff (until early January 1663) and justice, was involved in the persecution of Thomas Horrocks, vicar of All Saints' and St Peter's since 1650, town preacher and a Presbyterian, the circumstances of whose appointment to Maldon have already been described. The Corporation had agreed on 30 September 1650 to pay for the removal of his household to Maldon and for repairs to the vicarage house in advance of his arrival, to a maximum total cost of £14, and made him a freeman in January 1651 without fee.[120] He was described by Edmund Calamy as 'a diligent and painful preacher … instrumental in converting many souls' and as 'much respected' by the earl of Warwick, Sir Thomas Honywood, and many other Essex noblemen and gentlemen.[121] In 1662 he refused to subscribe to the Act of Uniformity, enacted in May, and was ejected from his living. A new vicar, John Head, was instituted on 26 November, and Samuel Plume and his fellow bailiff Henry Symond ordered the cost of transporting Head's household goods to the town (£1 1s 6d) be met from Corporation funds.[122]

In early December 1662 Horrocks surrendered church plate into Plume's hands, 'for the benefit of the town,'[123] but he had many loyal followers and remained in Maldon. He moved from All Saints' to the parish of St Mary, which belonged to the dean and chapter of Westminster and was therefore outside the control of Essex ecclesiastical jurisdictions, and continued to preach. He may, however, have underestimated the vindictiveness of the newly-purged Corporation. In March 1663 he was arrested for refusing to attend church and for holding religious assemblies in his house. Declining to find sureties for his good behaviour he was committed on 9 March to the town gaol, where he remained for ten days. His offence was presented at county assizes later in the month and was found a true bill, but no trial followed. In July, still in Maldon, he and 19 others were summoned to explain their absence from church, and in the trial that followed he was accused of all manner of crimes, was called a heretic, schismatic and traitor, was assaulted by Alderman John Hart (a butcher who had been appointed to the Corporation in August 1662 by the 1661 Corporation Act Commissioners), and was fined and told he must leave the town. He was put on a horse and escorted by the two borough sergeants-at-mace 'thro' all the towns like a criminal' to London, where in March–July 1663 he was prosecuted by John Hart, now a bailiff.[124]

In May 1663, during the course of this persecution, 'Mistress' Elizabeth Plume, half-sister of Alderman Samuel and Dr Thomas, married John Head, thereby strengthening the new vicar's standing in the town.[125] On 31 March 1665, two years after the marriage, Head baptised a daughter, Elizabeth, and on the same day buried his wife.[126]

As well as being aldermen and leading figures in Horrocks' persecution, Samuel Plume and John Hart were linked in other ways. Both were 'loving' friends of John Green of Hazeleigh Hall, gentleman: Plume was a beneficiary and executor of Green's will, made in 1665, while Hart was a beneficiary, witness and overseer. Additionally, Green's friends had included Reuben Robinson, another Maldon alderman, who in 1663 had been one of the two Maldon bailiffs, the other being Hart.[127] Robinson, 'Professor of Physick', died in April 1665 and his eldest daughter, Mary, married in c.1680 William Carr, town clerk.[128] Until the first decade of the eighteenth century the Carr family lived in the High Street mansion house ownership of which had reverted to Dr Thomas Plume in 1670.[129]

Samuel Plume's death

Samuel Plume was a bailiff again in 1666 and 1670, but did not complete his third term, for he died, aged about 44, at an unknown date between 14 November 1670, when he was present at the Court of the Clerk of the Market, and 5 December 1670, when his death was reported.[130] It is impossible to be more precise; in 1670 burials of All Saints' parishioners were entered in the St Peter's register, but Plume's name does not appear.[131] He seems not to have married, and to have died intestate and without issue.

An inventory of his goods and chattels made for probate purposes on 10 December 1670 provides a glimpse of his lifestyle and business activities. The High Street house comprised a hall (living room), a parlour, seven chambers (bedrooms), a garret, kitchen, buttery and two stairways, plus two shops, one described as 'the little shop'. The house seems to have been furnished in a restrained manner: just one looking glass was noted, carpets were noted as being in two rooms only, and no wall hangings or pictures were listed. Outside were a yard and a stable. Plume also had workshops, but their location was not

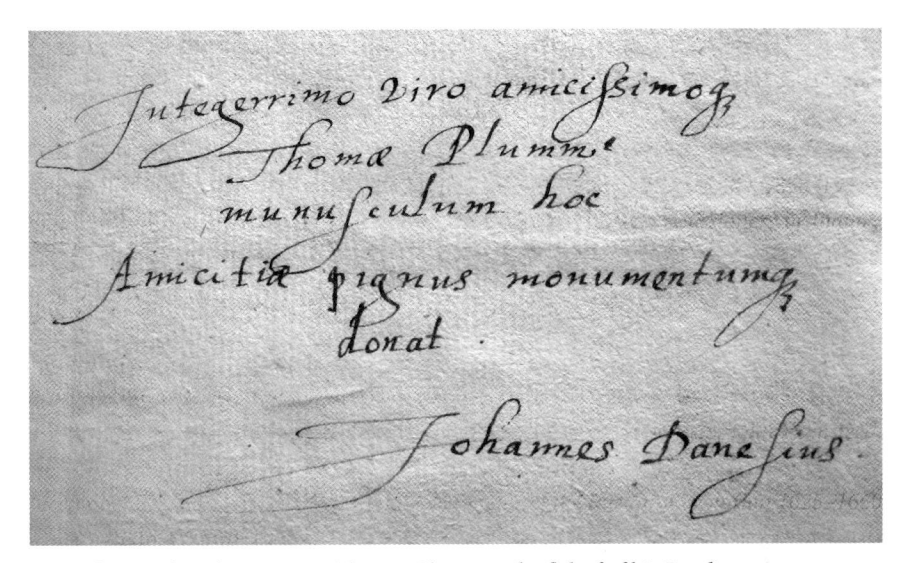

2.6 Dedication by John Danes to Thomas Plume on the flyleaf of his *Paralipomena Orthographiae Etymologiae Prosodiae*, 1639 (TPL, B04640).

stated. Stock-in-trade comprised cloth, groceries, candles, iron, fuller's earth and coal. The total value of his estate was assessed at £1,691 12s 0d, of which £1,200 was money owed to him.[132]

Thomas Plume's migration to Maldon: a possible explanation
It has already been noted that two of Alderman Thomas Plume's brothers, Samuel and Robert, inherited from their father landed estates, but that Thomas was bequeathed money – a total of £510 – but no land. There may, of course, have been a separate arrangement or settlement for Thomas, but there is no evidence to support that proposition. What he did in the years after leaving Cambridge without a degree, and then in the interval between his father's death in 1615 and the move to Maldon, other than marrying and beginning a family of his own, is unknown. Because he seems to have inherited no land it seems reasonable to suggest that Plume chose to support himself and his family by means other than agriculture, and so became a merchant at Maldon, a town particularly well situated for importing and exporting goods, where enterprising men with some capital could establish businesses and accumulate fortunes.[133]

But Maldon may have had an additional attraction for Thomas Plume: the presence of two men who, like him, were migrants, and with whom friendship very possibly originated at Cambridge. One was Israel Hewitt, who was at Christ's College when Thomas Plume was an undergraduate there, and whose association with Plume it seems reasonable to surmise began at that time. Furthermore, Hewitt's Maldon ministry commenced at almost the same time as Thomas Plume's migration to the town. This may have been coincidental, but it is tempting to conjecture there may have been a link.

The other was John Danes, with whom Plume seems to have been especially close. Danes was at Cambridge from 1605 to 1611, at Caius and Emmanuel Colleges, and so it is possible that he, too, became acquainted with Plume at Cambridge. In 1611 he became curate of Mundon, a marshland parish adjoining Maldon, but lived in Maldon, and in the following year became master of the town's grammar school, where for the next 28 years he taught with great success.[134] Danes clearly had considerable confidence in Plume, for in August 1638 he bequeathed £50 to him in trust for his unmarried daughter Ursula, and the witnesses to his will were none other than Thomas Plume and Israel Hewitt.[135] In 1639 Danes published a book of Latin grammar, the Latin title of which translates as 'Outlines of Spelling, Word-Construction and Scansion'.[136] One copy, now preserved in the Plume Library, he gave 'to that most honest man and greatest of friends, Thomas Plumme, as a token and a memorial of friendship' (Figure 2.6).[137]

In its 50 years of residence at Maldon the Plume family prospered through trade and played a prominent role in the turbulent years of the Civil Wars and Restoration. The prosperity enabled the youngest member, Thomas, to receive a good education and to follow in the footsteps of his uncle Samuel Plume by graduating at Christ's College, Cambridge. This, in turn, provided the foundation for his successful career as an Anglican clergyman in Kent. Although Alderman Samuel Plume's death in 1670 marked the end of Plume residence at Maldon, Thomas Plume, who inherited the family's mansion house there, maintained close links with the town and its leading inhabitants, notably William Carr, town clerk from 1675 to 1702, accumulated more Maldon real estate and lent money on the security of mortgages. Some of those property dealings were in connection with the Maldon charities to be set up at his death.

Notes

1. P. Morant, *The History and Antiquities of the County of Essex*, vol. ii (London, 1768), p. 300.
2. *Ibid.* Elizabeth was possibly the Elizabeth Plume buried 25 June 1596 (ERO, D/P 275/1/1). For further evidence of the purchase see final concord, 1584, catalogued in F.G. Emmison (ed.), *Feet of Fines for Essex*, vol. vi (Oxford, 1993), p. 23.
3. ERO, D/P 275/1/1; TNA, PROB 11/125/553, will of Thomas Plume made 9 February 1615, proved 24 May 1615; Morant, *History of Essex*, vol. ii, p. 300.
4. TNA, PROB 11/125/553. The testator described himself as a yeoman.
5. J. Peile, *Biographical Register of Christ's College, 1505–1905*, vol. i (Cambridge, 1910), p. 252. Plume matriculated as a pensioner in July 1605.
6. Peile, *Biographical Register*, vol. i, p. 263. He matriculated as a pensioner in July 1607. The statement in W.J. Petchey, *The Intentions of Thomas Plume* (Maldon, 1985; tercentenary edition, 2004), p. 6, that Thomas Plume graduated from Christ's is incorrect. Petchey cites as his source

Peile, *Biographical Register*, but the entry in Peile (vol. i, p. 263) does not mention the award of a degree. Thirty years earlier Petchey stated Plume 'took no degree': W.J. Petchey, *Maldon Grammar School 1608-1958* (Maldon, 1958), p. 14.

7   A.H. Lloyd, 'The Benefactors to Fellows' Building', *Christ's College Magazine*, 38/119 (1929), pp. 26-37; J. Peile, *Christ's College* (Cambridge, 1900), p. 36. The statement in Petchey, *Intentions of Thomas Plume*, p. 20, that Thomas Plume was a benefactor appears to be erroneous.

8   Peile, *Biographical Register*, vol. i, p. 503. As with his father and uncle Plume was admitted as a pensioner.

9   ERO, D/B 3/3/293, borough chamberlains' account for 1623 recording Plume's payment of Landcheap tax on his purchase made 'about Twoe yeres past'.

10 ERO, D/B 3/1/19, court book containing copy of lease of land adjoining Ware Pond and Ware Mead, Maldon Corporation to Plume. No evidence has been found to substantiate the statement in W.J. Petchey, *A Prospect of Maldon 1500-1689* (Chelmsford, 1991), p. 156, that Plume migrated from Danbury. Elsewhere, however, Petchey described Plume as an immigrant from Great Yeldham: W.J. Petchey, 'The Borough of Maldon, Essex, 1500-1688', PhD thesis (Leicester University, 1972), pp. 122, 196.

11 ERO, D/P 201/1/1.

12 ERO, D/B 3/1/19, court book containing record of admission of Thomas Plume to freedom of borough of Maldon.

13 TPL, MA0007.

14 ERO, D/P 201/1/1.

15 *Ibid.*

16 *Ibid.* Pratt was buried at All Saints on 9 January 1625. W.J. Petchey incorrectly named the new wife as Elizabeth (Petchey, *Prospect of Maldon*, p. 243), thereby perpetuating an error by the genealogist and transcriber R.H. Brown who in the 1890s incorrectly read the bride's name as Elizabeth (transcript by Brown in custody of All Saints with St Peter Parochial Church Council). Jeremy (*alias* Jeremiah) Pratt, baptised in All Saints in February 1593, was son of (Alderman) John Pratt (ERO, D/P 201/1/1).

17 She is described in Peile, *Biographical Register*, vol. i, p. 503, as 'Ellen', daughter of Philip Cason or Carson of Little Holland. See also conveyance (in Latin) of Wayer Mead, 1629, in which she is named 'Helonam' (copy in ERO, D/B 3/1/19).

18 ERO, D/P 201/1/1.

19 *Ibid.*

20 *Ibid.*

21 *Ibid.*: Pratt was buried at All Saints on 22 September.

22 ERO, D/B 3/1/20, court book containing statement by Plume to his fellow Corporation members, 9 January 1654.

23 ERO, D/DWd 13; D/B 3/1/20. The Hazeleigh parish register (ERO, D/P 123/1/1) contains no burial entries for those years. The Hazeleigh connection continued after Thomas Plume's death. In 1666 John Green of Hazeleigh, gentleman, made his 'loving friend' Samuel Plume of Maldon a beneficiary and executor of his will and a guardian of his nephew John Green: TNA, PROB 11/319/164.

24 This is because ownership of the family house in Maldon (vested in Thomas Plume until his death) was transferred by Dr Thomas Plume to his brother Samuel in July 1659, in fulfilment of instructions given to Dr Thomas by his father. Fuller information on this matter appears in the next section of this chapter.

25 TNA, PROB 11/165/637, Annastacy Wentworth's will, made 13 February 1631, proved 14 June 1634, which contains the statement that the house was 'in the occupation of Mr Thomas Plumbe Alderman of … Maldon'.

26 ERO, D/ABW 19/74, William Hale's will, made 24 March 1582, proved 15 November 1582, containing information on Hale family relationships. Hale was buried at All Saints on 21 May 1582: ERO, D/P 201/1/1.
27 ERO, D/DWd 8, lease, 15 May 1633, to run from 25 March.
28 TNA, PROB 11/165/637. See also TNA, PROB 11/123/117, Henry Wentworth's will, made 10 November 1613, proved 8 February 1614, in which he described Francis Mitchell of Theydon Garnon as his son-in-law. Annastacy Wentworth was interred on 8 June 1634 in All Saints' church (ERO, D/P 201/1/1), where she and her husband Henry are commemorated by a wall tablet.
29 ERO, D/DWd 9.
30 ERO, D/DWd 10–12, and recitals in D/DWd 17.
31 Edward Brooke was also 'cosen' of John Soan of Maldon, gentleman (d. 1656) and a beneficiary under his will made 1656, in which he was described as being 'late of Oxford, clerk': TNA, PROB 11/260/616.
32 ERO, D/DWd 13.
33 ERO, D/ABW 59/47. 'Brother' in this context probably denotes a close male friend or a fellow member of the Christian church rather than a family relationship. Brooke was well connected at Maldon. His 'Cozen' John Stevens, overseer of the will and one of two witnesses to a codicil (19 August 1647), was an alderman for 20 years (1642–62) and fellow member with Plume in 1648 of the Dengie Classis (see below). Town Clerk Nowell Hammond witnessed both the will and codicil. John Soan (d. 1656) was another 'brother'; he was son of Alderman John Soan (d. 1636) and 'cosen' of Edward Brooke (see TNA, PROB 11/260/616). There is little doubt that Brooke was the Robert Brooke referred to in the will of Alderman John Soan (undated; proved 10 October 1636) as 'my sonne in Lawe' (ERO, D/ABW 53/184). In 1628 Brooke and (Alderman) John Soan were appointed joint overseers of the will of John Turnidge, a Maldon linen-draper and kinsman of John Stevens (ERO, D/ABW 49/83).
34 C.H. Fielding, *The Records of Rochester Diocese* (Dartford, 1910), p. 127. I am grateful to Dr Catharina Clement for this reference. It is postulated that Edward Brooke is to be associated with the Edward Brookes 'minister of Walsoken', Norfolk, who in 1677 was a beneficiary of the will of John Stevens of Maldon, gentleman (TNA, PROB 11/354/546). Dr Thomas Plume was another beneficiary of the will, in which he was described as 'loving friend'.
35 TNA, PROB 10/1387; below, Appendix: Dr Thomas Plume's will, l. 124.
36 ERO, D/DWd 16 recital in conveyance to Samuel Plume, 1659.
37 *Ibid.*
38 ERO, D/B 3/1/19, court book containing copy of lease.
39 ERO, D/B 3/1/34, court book containing copy of conveyance, 4 January 1629; D/B 3/3/298, borough chamberlains' account for 1629 recording payment of Landcheap tax by the purchaser and naming Thomas Plume as vendor.
40 ERO, D/B 3/3/289; D/B 3/3/393/25. See also J.R. Smith, 'Maldon's Old Moot Hall and Market Place: A Reinterpretation', *Essex Archaeology and History*, 4th ser., 7 (2017), pp. 104–13 (especially 108).
41 ERO, D/B 3/3/293, chamberlains' account for 1623, entry referring to 'grant of the new lease' to Plume; D/B 3/1/3, fos 105–7. See also Smith, 'Maldon's Old Moot Hall', p. 108.
42 ERO, D/B 3/3/301, entry in chamberlains' account for 1636 recording payment of Landcheap tax by the purchaser, then newly remarried as Mrs Damarys Merrills.
43 ERO, D/B 3/3/306, entry in chamberlains' account for 1642 recording Plume's payment of Landcheap tax on the purchase. Evidence of Plume's ownership also appears in ERO, D/B 3/1/35, court book containing a copy of a conveyance of 16 October 1672, reciting that it had formerly belonged to Plume, and before him to 'Sir Symon D'Ewes'.
44 Morant, *History of Essex*, vol. ii, p. 300. Paul Dewes' will, made January 1630, does not mention property in Maldon or members of the Plume family: TNA, PROB 11/159/401.

45 ERO, D/B 3/3/493, entry in chamberlains' account for 1649 recording Jarman's payment of Landcheap tax on the purchase.
46 ERO, D/B 3/3/98. The chamberlains' account for 1649 (ERO, D/B 3/3/493) records a payment of 4s 'for making Mr Plumes lease'. For more information on the brewery see Petchey, *Prospect of Maldon*, p. 117.
47 ERO, D/DHt T174/11.
48 ERO, D/B 3/3/319, chamberlains' account for 1697 recording Stace's payment of Landcheap tax on the purchase.
49 ERO, D/B 3/11/13, conveyance, 25 August 1696.
50 For much fuller information on Dr Francis Thompson see below, Chapter 4, pp. 99–100, 111.
51 For information on Carr and Taverner see J.R. Smith, *The Borough of Maldon 1688–1800: A Golden Age* (Studley, 2013), pp. 180–2.
52 ERO, D/B 3/3/501, entry in chamberlains' account for 1702 of payment by Plume of Landcheap tax on his purchase; bequest by Plume to 'the Library keeper' of, *inter alia*, £23 a year 'out of ye lands in Maldon lately purchased of Mr Norton' (below, Appendix: will, ll. 226–7). A final concord was levied in Trinity Term 1702 (recited in ERO, D/DCf B10/40, p. 5). For further discussion of the librarian's salary, see below Chapter 5, pp. 125 (Table 5.2), 129, 132, 135, 137 (Table 5.4), 145.
53 ERO, D/ABW 77/136, statement in codicil, 5 August 1702, to Carr's will.
54 Below, Appendix: will, ll. 122–3. Mrs Melsop, *alias* Millsop, is probably to be associated with the Mrs Catherine Melsoph, widow, buried 16 December 1708 at St Mary's, Maldon (ERO, D/P 132/1/2).
55 The location of Mrs Melsop's house has been determined from analysis of conveyances of 29 Market Hill, 1685, 1698 and 1720 in ERO, D/DB T610; Smith, *Borough of Maldon*, p. 288.
56 Below, Appendix: will, ll. 132–3. For information on the workhouse, built in 1716–19, see Smith, *Borough of Maldon*, pp. 362–5.
57 Below, Appendix: will, l. 119. Carr refers in his will, 1702, to his 'worthy friend John Comyns': ERO, D/ABW 77/136. For further information on Comyns (*c*.1667–1740) see *ODNB* and Smith, *Borough of Maldon*, pp. 64–5.
58 Below, Appendix: will, ll. 91–9. The quotation is from Morant, *History of Essex*, vol. ii, p. 300.
59 For later history of the house (rebuilt between 1749 and 1754) see Smith, *Borough of Maldon*, pp. 180–2, 207–8. It is now 40 and 42 High Street and used as a Marks & Spencer store.
60 Smithfield abutted south on land called Portlands; see copy of conveyance of Portlands, May 1762, in ERO, D/B 3/1/36. Elinor Plume was formerly wife of Alderman Jeremy Pratt (d. 1625). Shortly before his death Jeremy Pratt purchased the reversion and inheritance of 'Smithfields', paying Landcheap tax on his purchase in 1624 (ERO, D/B 3/3/108, chamberlains' account for 1624). Nathaniel Plume sold it in about 1715 to Richard Potter, a Maldon grocer, for £215, when it comprised two closes (entry for Potter's payment of Landcheap tax in chamberlains' account for 1715, ERO, D/B 3/3/502). See also Smith, *Borough of Maldon*, pp. 40, 213, 218.
61 The quotation is from Plume's will, below, Appendix: will, l. 93.
62 ERO, D/B 3/3/183, borough rental, 1687. For information on Foulgier see Smith, *Borough of Maldon*, pp. 217–19, Appendix 1 (p. 468), Appendix 6 (p. 473).
63 Below, Appendix: will, ll. 97–9.
64 ERO, D/B 3/1/19; D/B 3/3/293, chamberlains' account for 1623.
65 ERO, D/B 3/1/19. Membership of the Corporation comprised 18 headburgesses and eight aldermen. The aldermen were elected from the headburgesses, and the two annual bailiffs were drawn from the aldermen on a four-year cycle.
66 ERO, D/B 3/1/19.
67 *Ibid*. Evidence of his age appears in a statement made by Cheese in September 1611 that he was 'aged 54 years or thereabouts' (TNA, E 134/9JasI/Mich38). For further information on Cheese see Petchey, *Prospect of Maldon*, pp. 163, 238–9, 259.

68 ERO, D/B 3/1/19. Cheese died on 17 November (memorandum in same source) and was buried at St Peter's on 19 November (ERO, D/P 201/1/3).
69 ERO, D/B 3/1/19. Bentley had commenced his clerkship by early January 1626.
70 ERO, D/B 3/3/294, chamberlains' account for 1625.
71 ERO, D/B 3/1/19. He replaced Alderman Thomas Hutt, who had died in December 1625, and was buried at St Mary's on 26 December: ERO, D/P 132/1/1.
72 Annual Courts of Election recorded in ERO, D/B 3/1/19, 20.
73 Petchey, *Prospect of Maldon*, p. 162.
74 ERO, D/P 201/1/1, parish register (the parish clerk spelling the surname throughout as 'Dorsley'). Entries include those for a son, John, born 20 November 1627, baptised nine days later and buried 4 January 1632 (see also inscription on a gravestone, now wall-mounted in the church, and transcript thereof in L. Hughes, *A Guide to the Church of All Saints, Maldon* (Maldon and London, 1909), Appendix IX, p. xxx, and giving 4 January as date of death).
75 ERO, D/P 201/1/1.
76 ERO, D/B 3/3/302, chamberlains' account for 1638.
77 For other information on Dorislaus see *ODNB*; Petchey, *Prospect of Maldon*, p. 57; C. Spencer, *Killers of the King: The Men Who Dared to Execute Charles I* (London, 2014), pp. 32, 33, 37, 61–7, 88, 127, 210.
78 ERO, D/B 3/1/20.
79 *Ibid.*
80 ERO, D/B 3/3/306, chamberlains' account for 1642.
81 ERO, D/B 3/1/20; D/B 3/3/308, chamberlains' account for 1644; Petchey, *Borough of Maldon*, pp. 243–4.
82 ERO, D/B 3/3/310, D/B 3/3/81, chamberlains' accounts for 1647 and 1648.
83 ERO, D/B 3/12/2.
84 ERO, D/B 3/1/20. In 1648 Langdell and Jennings had been appointed, together with Plume and five others, as elders representing Maldon on the Dengie Hundred Classis: T.W. Davids, *Annals of Evangelical Nonconformity in the County of Essex* (London, 1863), p. 271.
85 ERO, D/B 3/1/20.
86 TNA, PROB 11/113/233. For further information about the school history and later relationship with the Maldon Plume Charity, below Chapter 5, pp. 127–8, 134–5, 140, 144, 147.
87 Breeder was interred in All Saints' church on 4 March and his will was proved on 9 March: ERO, D/P 201/1/1; TNA, PROB 11/113/233; Petchey, *Maldon Grammar School*, p. 11.
88 The founding trustees included, in addition to the bailiffs and aldermen, Sir William Harris of Maldon, Raphe (*alias* Ralph) Hawdon, vicar of All Saints', and John Pratt, headburgess: TNA, PROB 11/113/233 (Breeder's will).
89 ERO, D/B 3/3/410, lease for 11 years from 24 June 1650 at an annual rent of £7 for the first four years and £8 for the remaining years. One of the houses was occupied by Jennings, the other by John Chambers, glazier. Samuel Plume was a witness. For further information about Schoolmasters see Petchey, *Maldon Grammar School*, p. 11; Smith, *Borough of Maldon*, p. 266, endnote 78.
90 TNA, PROB 11/165/637, will made 13 February 1631. The other founding trustees were Mr Bachelor, Mr William Legge and Mr Tucher Castell. In 1602 a Tucher Castle was the vendor of two properties in Maldon: TNA, C 108/15.
91 ERO, D/P 201/1/1, burial of King at All Saints, Maldon, on 16 January 1614. For a probate (29 January 1614) copy of his will see TNA, PROB 11/123/64. John Soan died on 7 September 1636 aged 62 (inscription in gravestone in All Saints' church recited in Hughes, *Guide to the Church of All Saints*, Appendix IX, pp. xxx–xxxi).
92 These events are set out in more detail in Petchey, *Prospect of Maldon*, pp. 143–4.

93 ERO, D/B 3/3/295. For further information on the Rhebank boundary see Smith, *Borough of Maldon*, pp. 60, 62, 257. Maldon was a 'creek' or member port of the headport of Ipswich for customs purposes (*ibid.*, p. 340).
94 ERO, D/B 3/3/664/1, depositions, 1 February 1631 (copies, 1819).
95 *Ibid.* (deposition by Francis Tunbridge, water bailiff).
96 ERO, D/B 3/3/664/1; TNA, E 134/6and7ChasI/Hil10, papers in case Maldon Corporation *v.* Thomas Plume, 1631, 1632.
97 ERO, D/B 3/3/578/24, copy, *c.*1840, of proceedings and decree in Court of Record, 1632.
98 ERO, D/B 3/3/302-5, chamberlains' accounts for 1638-41 giving details of Slater's imports. See also Petchey, 'The Borough of Maldon', pp. 290-2.
99 ERO, D/P 201/1/1. Hawdon was buried at Maldon on 23 October 1619.
100 ERO, D/B 3/3/393/3, poll for new vicar; D/B 3/3/159, minute of assembly 4 November 1619; Hughes, *Guide to the Church of All Saints*, p. 19. Rogers had preached at Maldon in 1606 and 1613 by invitation of the bailiffs (Petchey, 'The Borough of Maldon', p. 219). His candidacy may also have owed something to his family connection with Alderman Edward Hastler (d. 1622) whose first wife was daughter of Rogers' kinsman Richard Rogers, lecturer at Wethersfield from *c.*1577 to his death in 1618. See Hastler's will, 1622 (TNA, PROB 11/140/281) and J.R. Smith, *Pilgrims and Adventurers: Essex (England) and the Making of the United States of America* (Chelmsford, 1992), pp. 11, 12, 35, 39.
101 Peile, *Biographical Register*, vol. i, p. 240.
102 For a discussion of religious changes and dissention during the period *c.*1530-1642 see Petchey, *Prospect of Maldon*, pp. 187-245.
103 ERO, D/B 3/1/19.
104 These events are described in detail in Petchey, *Prospect of Maldon*, pp. 244-5.
105 Hughes, *Guide to the Church of All Saints*, p. 30; Davids, *Annals*, p. 424.
106 Entries in chamberlains' accounts for those years: ERO, D/B 3/3/80, 293, 300, 301, 302, 305, 308.
107 ERO, D/B 3/1/34 (enrolled conveyance). See also ERO, D/B 3/3/302, chamberlains' account for 1638 recording Hewitt's payment of Landcheap tax on his purchase. The house, which had formerly belonged to the Guild of St Katherine, is probably to be associated with the present-day 4 Silver Street, but it may possibly have been a house to the north demolished in 1757 (see ERO, T/B 288/14), which stood on the present-day garden fronting the street between numbers 4 and 6 Silver Street.
108 ERO, D/AEA 42. For an explanation of this incident, see Chapter 3, p. 56.
109 For details of the Essex *classes* see Davids, *Annals*, pp. 214-16, 255-306.
110 Davids, *Annals*, pp. 422-4; Petchey, *Prospect of Maldon*, p. 233 (where the naming of Horrocks as 'John' is clearly an error); Hughes, *Guide to the Church of All Saints*, Appendix XV, pp. xlvi. The orders and papers of the Committee for Plundered Ministers, 1642-50, are TNA, SP 22. Hewitt died at Tendring in 1663.
111 ERO, D/B 3/1/20.
112 *Ibid.*
113 ERO, D/B 3/1/20, fo. 268v. Jennings had become an alderman on 10 January 1653.
114 ERO, D/B 3/1/20.
115 *Ibid.*
116 See article by A. Thrush, 'MILDMAY, Sir Henry (*c.*1594-1668), of Wanstead, Essex and Twyford, Hants', in A. Thrush and J.P. Ferris (eds), *The History of Parliament: The House of Commons 1604-1629* (Cambridge, 2010; online edition www.historyofparliamentonline.org (accessed 24 June 2020)); Spencer, *Killers of the King*, pp. 34-5, 40, 113-14, 245-6; *ODNB*.
117 ERO, D/B 3/12/2.
118 ERO, D/B 3/1/20. Bramston was high steward from 1661 to his death in 1700. He was also an MP for Maldon, 1679, 1685-9. For further information see Smith, *Borough of Maldon*, pp. 63-4, 111,

112, and article by M.W. Helms and G Hampson, 'BRAMSTON, John (1611–1700), of Skreens, Roxwell, Essex', in B.D. Henning (ed.), *The History of Parliament: The House of Commons 1660–1690* (London, 1983; online edition www.historyofparliamentonline.org (accessed 24 June 2020)).
119 ERO, D/B 3/1/20.
120 Davids, *Annals*, pp. 422–3; ERO, D/B 3/1/20.
121 Quoted in Davids, *Annals*, p. 424.
122 ERO, D/B 3/3/311, chamberlains' account for 1662.
123 ERO, D/B 3/1/20.
124 N. McNeil O'Farrell, comp., 'Calendar of Essex Assize Files in the Public Record Office', vol. iv, presentment 23 March 1663 in assize file 35/104/1, no. 21 (typescript in ERO library); ERO, D/B 3/1/20, minutes of committal and summons, March and July 1663; Hughes, *Guide to the Church of All Saints*, Appendix VI, pp. xxi–ii; E. Calamy, *The Nonconformist's Memorial*, 2nd edition by S. Palmer, vol. I (London, 1778), pp. 510–12; Davids, *Annals*, pp. 424–5; Petchey, 'The Borough of Maldon', pp. 307–8; Petchey, *Prospect of Maldon*, pp. 252–4. For Hart's appointment see ERO, D/B 3/1/20.
125 ERO, D/P 201/1/1.
126 *Ibid*. Daughter Elizabeth Head was buried at All Saints three years later on 24 February 1668.
127 TNA, PROB 11/319/164; ERO, D/B 3/1/20.
128 ERO, D/P 201/1/1; Smith, *Borough of Maldon*, pp. 180–1.
129 Smith, *Borough of Maldon*, p. 180. Dr Plume's relationship with Carr is described earlier in this chapter in section 'The family home in Maldon and real estate transactions'.
130 ERO, D/B 3/1/21.
131 ERO, D/P 201/1/3, St Peter's parish register.
132 TNA, PROB 6/45. The three assessors were John Stevens, Edmund Whitefoot and Thomas Hutt, substantial Maldon tradesmen.
133 For general discussions of Maldon's economy at this period see Petchey, *Prospect of Maldon*, and Smith, *Borough of Maldon*.
134 Petchey, *Maldon Grammar School*, pp. 12–16 and Appendix 1 (p. 30); Petchey, 'The Borough of Maldon', p. 144.
135 ERO, D/ABW 56/143, will made 18 August 1638, proved 20 December 1639. Ursula Danes was baptised on 14 October 1618 (ERO, D/P 201/1/1).
136 The title is *Paralipomena Orthographiae, Etymologiae, Prosodiae, …. Distributa* (London, 1639).
137 The quotation is a translation of the Latin dedication on the fly-leaf.

Chapter 3

Dr Thomas Plume: 'a man outstanding for his upright character, devotion of life and charity towards the poor'

Robert Anthony Doe

The Revd Max Buck's sermon, preached on 30 January 1702, on the anniversary of the martyrdom of King Charles I 'of blessed memory', was dedicated to Dr Plume in the glowing terms repeated in the title of this chapter just two years before Plume's death.[1] Buck was the vicar of Seale in Kent, in Plume's archdeaconry. One wonders if Plume heard this sermon being preached? He would certainly have celebrated this anniversary as a holy day because of his devotion to Charles I, as we will see. In his will of 1704 Plume left Buck £20 as a 'poor divine'.[2] So, who was this paragon to whom Buck referred?

Education in Maldon and Chelmsford

Plume's ancestry and parentage have already been considered in Chapter 2, the first record of him being his baptism in All Saints Church, Maldon, on 18 August 1630 (Figure 3.1).[3] The next formal mention of him is in the Cambridge University records, which reveal that he went to Chelmsford School.[4] Why was he not educated in Maldon? We know that his father, also named Thomas Plume, and John Danes, master of Maldon School, were very good friends from the note Danes placed in his newly published textbook, *Paralipomena* ... (London, 1639), 'to that most honest man and greatest of friends, Thomas Plumme as a token and memorial of friendship'.[5] Plume the elder passed this book on to his son, who put it in his library, where it remains. Sadly, a few months after his gift, Danes together with his daughter and a son died, probably of bubonic plague, and they were all buried at All Saints church, Maldon on 13 December 1639.[6]

3.1 A pair of silver flagons donated to All Saints church, Maldon, by Thomas Plume, 'in thankful memory of his baptism there' (by kind permission of the Vicar and Parochial Church Council of All Saints with St Peter, Maldon).

With the death of its master, Maldon School closed and Thomas the younger was sent to Chelmsford School at about nine years of age. By this date he would have learned to read and write, had some Latin and have known his catechism. Maldon is ten miles from Chelmsford, so he would have been a boarder, possibly with the headmaster Daniell Peake, who had been appointed in 1633. Peake had attended St John's College, Cambridge (DD 1645) and he remained at Chelmsford until his death in 1668. His will shows his devotion to education, demonstrating the seriousness with which he would have educated Plume, as well as – by referring to the articles of his faith – his devotion to the Church of England.[7]

Plume would have spent long periods away from his family, as school holidays amounted to only five to eight weeks a year. During the six-day week, hours of study were long and discipline at Chelmsford School was severe, even by the standards of the day. The curriculum may have been based around Latin taught from Lily's *Latin Grammar* and the regular daily and seasonal ritual of the Church of England. Teaching was mainly by rote, but the more able pupils were encouraged to use a notebook to record Latin phrases that caught their attention. Plume started just such a book while at Chelmsford, but made only a few entries for this purpose. He went on to use the largely empty pages for quite different purposes when he got to Cambridge, as will be seen.[8] He was also required to make written notes of some of the sermons he heard and these have survived in three notebooks. We know that he heard Israel Hewitt, vicar of Maldon, preach on one unknown date and once on 29 June 1645.[9] He also heard Mark Mott, vicar of Chelmsford, preach on a Sunday in 1645.[10] (We will see that Mark Mott, who was the curate at Chelmsford when Plume first arrived, went on to become vicar after the settled incumbent, John Michaelson, was forced out by violent religious opposition.) These sermons were thoroughly Puritan, with a strong emphasis on sin (being like a 'gangraene' [sic])[11] and how very full preparation before taking the sacraments was essential. Failure to do this was like 'sheathing a keen sword in Christ's wounds'.[12]

Chelmsford was going through a period of religious turmoil when the young Plume arrived. The forces unleashed by the Puritans' continuing reformation were hard at work and, whereas the Church could control its ministers, some elements of their congregations were very much out of control. The appointment of Thomas Hooker (1586?–1647), a noted nonconformist of considerable powers as a preacher, to the town lectureship in 1625 created great difficulties with the Church authorities, even at the most senior levels. He was silenced by 1630 but his departure from the town completely failed to resolve its religious tensions, which continued to underlie the civil and religious strife occurring when Plume took up his place at Chelmsford School.[13]

A series of incidents in Chelmsford parish church in the 1630s and 1640s attracted the attention of the Church authorities, including the purchase of a scarlet hood in 1640, which was rejected by the parish as being papist, the presentation of a man for refusing to stand up for the reading of the creed in 1635 and, in 1639, the presentation of a man 'learning his dog to fetch and carry his glove' in church. As Hilda Grieve summarises: 'by 1636 a small but coherent group of religious zealots was active in the town'.[14]

Beginning with the first Bishop's War in 1638, and continuing through the Civil Wars, both the king and, subsequently, parliament billeted troops in Chelmsford. Billeting was a severe imposition on local people and the forces of unrest against the Church were encouraged by the profoundly disaffected soldiers' behaviour, which supported the inhabitants' attitudes. On 29 July 1640 'drunken soldiers billeted at Braintree (15 miles away) tore out the communion rails in Bocking church and burned them', and on 2 February 1641 'helly' women of Sandon (two miles away) similarly destroyed the rails from their church (communion rails around the altar were one of Laud's most hated innovations).[15] Grieve's account of these events acknowledges that local people were involved as well as 'drunken soldiers', but so colours the report that these attacks on altar rails seem to be simply the irrational behaviour of a mob, or the 'many headed monster'. John Walter argues instead that a 'thickened' account of this destruction characterises it as a series of ritual acts that were meaningful

3.2 St Mary's Church, Chelmsford, in 1833. The church was the scene of religious disturbances in 1641–2, probably witnessed by Plume (published by G. Virtue in T. Wright, *The History and Topography of the County of Essex* (London, 1833), drawn by W. Bartlett, engraved by W. Watkins).

for the deeply held beliefs of those carrying out the iconoclasm. He also finds that, while some of those involved had separatist sentiments, others might have been committed Presbyterians, intent on remaining within the Church.[16]

To the extent that the young Plume might have been aware, at some level, of Presbyterian involvement in these acts, so might the seeds of his aversion to grass-roots Presbyterianism have been sown at this time. Indeed, Plume may well have already had some experience of the discord that railed altars could bring. In July 1639 the vicar of All Saints, Maldon, Israel Hewitt, had been reported to the archdeacon of Essex for 'comeing out of the rayle to administer the Com[munio]n to Thomas Plume Gent'. For Hewitt to have behaved in this way was a clear sign of his opposition to the Laudian practice of communicants kneeling at the altar rail and of Thomas Plume senior's status in expecting the vicar to come out of the rails to give him communion. For this Hewitt was fined 2s 8d.[17] If he was aware of this incident, it may have been Plume's first encounter with the tensions existing within the church between those who were content with the status quo of the last three or four generations, such as his father and the vicar, Israel Hewitt, and the reforms being imposed by the bishop of London, William Laud, and his officers. These reforms, later to be known as 'Laudianism', are discussed more fully later in this chapter.

In August 1641 parliament required 'scandalous pictures' to be removed from churches and in Chelmsford limited steps were taken to comply with this order, the pictures of the Virgin Mary and Christ on the cross being removed from the great east window. This was not enough for the more radical section of the population, however, and on 5 November a mob headed by a glazier attacked and destroyed what was left of the glass in the east window (Figure 3.2).[18] On the next Sunday, 10 November 1641, the rector, John Michaelson, wearing the surplice and scarlet hood, preached against the extremists, declaring that reformation, even when well-intended, 'casts out one devil with another'.[19] Very soon after this a carbine was discharged into his room (thankfully unoccupied at the time). On Sunday 24 November he was attacked in church by a group of youths led by a clothier; he was caught by the throat and an attempt was made to tear off his surplice. Services were regularly interrupted at this time.[20] Further serious attacks on Michaelson, this time by soldiers, took place following the formal outbreak of the Civil War on 22 August 1642, when the king raised his standard at Nottingham. The soldiers forbade Michaelson to pray for the bishops or to use the Book of Common Prayer. Initially defiant, he was ultimately silenced and his prayer book was destroyed and defiled. On 30 January 1643, when parliament abolished the episcopate, bonfires were lit using the rector's own wood; he was attacked again and an attempt was made to throw him into the flames. He was saved by the company commanders and fled for his life. After this his family were held at gunpoint while he was being sought.[21] He was succeeded in the post of vicar of Chelmsford by Mark Mott, who had formerly been his curate. Following a parliamentary ordinance later in the year the church was whitened, a cross was removed, the angels from the nave roof were taken down and burned and the 'pictures' on the font were painted over.[22]

From 1643 on Chelmsford gradually recovered from these years of disorder and, by the time Plume went up to Cambridge late in 1645, order had been restored. Nonetheless, Plume spent his most formative years in a town that experienced extreme stresses and strains caused by the religious conflicts of his day and the war for which those religious movements were in some large measure responsible. Plume's reaction, as will be further discussed below, was to support the king and to turn against the religious opposition to the established church. During his time in Chelmsford he had the guidance and example of his headmaster, Daniell Peake, who was devoted to the established church, but who seems to have been able to keep his peace during these violent times.[23]

Christ's College, Cambridge
Plume was admitted pensioner (i.e. a commoner or paying student) to Christ's College, Cambridge, on 24 February 1646 at the age of 15 years and six months (Figure 3.3).[24] He joined a student body of about 265 in his college

3.3 The frontage to the street of Christ's College, Cambridge, in the nineteenth century. Plume was admitted to the college in February 1646 (chromo-lithograph from *Views of Cambridge*, published in the nineteenth century by T. Nelson and Sons).

and over 2,000 in the university as a whole.[25] He brought with him his little-used notebook of Latin phrases and, apparently, ample funds, according to the accounts he kept.[26] What was the religious teaching of the college to which he was admitted? Petchey saw it as 'one of the principal nurseries of Anglican Puritanism',[27] but Peile maintains that by 1642 Christ's was notable in not taking sides: 'It was not devotedly loyal – it sent neither plate nor money to Charles in 1642; neither was it distinctively Puritan; among the fellows the balance inclined to the royalist side.'[28] Plume's tutor was William More or Moore, who had conformed in 1644 during the earl of Manchester's purge of the university of those who were considered to be scandalous in their manner of living or who refused to obey parliamentary ordinances or deserted their places for any reason other than serving the parliamentary cause.[29]

Christ's anticipated to some extent the ritual changes that were underway when parliament began to oppose Charles I, because it seems to have changed its altar and accoutrements by 1641. However, when the college was visited by the iconoclast William Dowsing in December 1643 'pictures and angells' were removed and the master agreed to take down the steps, presumably at the east end of the chapel, which were another of Laud's innovations.[30] The changes to college chapels were not the only physical alterations brought about by religious upheaval and the Civil War. From 1642 soldiers were billeted in some colleges and they caused damage in a number of places. Victualling the soldiers was a burden and they caused damage by taking doors and boards for firewood, and by some acts of iconoclasm. This damage was not very serious, but it was disruptive and psychologically harmful.[31]

Such, then, was the scene that greeted Plume on his arrival in Cambridge in 1646. He had moved from one scenario of violent change to another. The purge of the heads of colleges was complete and they had been replaced by men who opposed prelacy and Arminianism but were 'essentially moderate, orthodox Presbyterians, with no leanings towards some of the schemes for religious renewal which were gaining ground at that time'.[32] As John Twigg observes, 'They believed Parliament was justified in taking up arms against the King but were not against the monarchy itself'.[33] To the extent that Plume was aware of their views he would have profoundly disagreed with them: he began his account book at Cambridge with a strongly royalist poem:

> Up up wrong'd Charles his friends!
> What can you ly Thus mantled in a stupid lethargy
> When all the worldes in arms … [34]

and so on for a further 23 lines.

This book, together with an inserted sheet, continues until the midsummer quarter 1650 and is, therefore, a reasonably complete account of his income and expenditure while at Cambridge. The accounts show that a total of £128 was expended over four and a quarter years, or £30 per annum on average, demonstrating that Plume was quite well off. He was absent from Cambridge for the first half of 1648. In his first two years most of the funds went through his tutor, William More, and he received only 10s a quarter for himself, but in 1649 he had £10 to spend and in one quarter in 1650 he had £6. Plume wrote down a detailed expenditure only for his final quarter (on a separate sheet inserted in the account book), showing, for example, that £1 5s 6d was paid to the cook, 2s for mending clothes, 1s 4d for shoes, 8s for 'Rhegius Philosophy', 1s for candles, 2s 6d for the barber and 9s for laundry and cleaning.[35]

The other Cambridge notebook, begun as a Latin phrasebook (probably in Chelmsford), consists mainly of verses and anecdotes with no scholastic content apart from short notes of one sermon.[36] We do know, however, that his education was based on lectures, formal disputations between students and declamations (which were dialectical in nature). This latter activity may have led to Plume so faithfully collecting books that gave 'an answer to an answer of an answer' on numerous specific topics when he assembled his library.[37] The curriculum consisted of logic, rhetoric and ethics, known collectively as the arts, and metaphysics, physics, mathematics and cosmography, known as the sciences. Theology was accounted a science. The mornings were given over to the study of physics, metaphysics, logic and ethics to inculcate the student into the world of scholasticism. In the afternoons students studied poetry, rhetoric, grammar, classical oratory and history, which were intended to enable them to express themselves accurately and forcefully. This scheme of studies was devised by Richard Holdsworth (1590–1649), who was master of Emmanuel College until he was sequestrated and imprisoned in 1643.[38]

Apart from one short set of religious notes, which will be discussed below, the only indications of Plume's formal education are the textbooks that he owned while at Cambridge and the fact that he graduated BA in 1649/50. In the Library there are five books signed in Plume's juvenile hand. There is a book of speeches in Latin, and one each on the Greek language, rhetoric, science and philosophy. The prices paid range from 8s to 1s 4d, but it is not known when they were purchased.

In the absence of a scholastic record, Plume left a quite extensive legacy of his stay in Cambridge in his informal writings in two notebooks, neither of which he signed but which are identified as being his on the basis of internal evidence.[39] First, the handwriting can clearly be related to his early hand, as demonstrated in the books that he owned at Cambridge and which he signed (see above). Second is the clear evidence of the development of the hand, maturing over a period of some five years. Third, the account book gives exactly the same admission date as is independently recorded.[40]

The first notebook consists of 45 unnumbered leaves, mostly covered in writing.[41] The book contains six pages of religious notes, some 245 anecdotes and 15 poems (or verses, as Clark describes them), many of them revealing royalist feeling. One of Plume's 'royalist' poems has been found in The Loyal Garland, a collection of songs of the seventeenth century.[42] The following is Plume's text:

(Verse 1)
Fair Fidelia tempt no more
Grant they beauty now adore
Nor offer to thy shrine
I serve a mistress divine
And brighter far than thine
Heark ye trumpets sound away
I must go lest a foe
Take ye field, and win the day
March bravely on
We will charge them in ye Van
Oure cause Gods is, but ye odd is
Ten times ten to one

(Verse 2)
One kiss more, & so farewell
Yes No now no more
I pray thee fool give ore
Why clouds thou thus thy beams
I see by thy extremes
A woman's heaven on hell
I pray ye King may have his owne
That ye Queen may be seen
W[i]th her babes on Englands throne
Cavaliers bee bold
Loose none of yo[ur]e holds
O[ur]e Cause Gods is
But ye odds is
Ten times ten to one.[43]

Detailed comparison with the Loyal Garden version shows that it has three verses compared with Plume's two and is titled 'The Soldier's Delight', whereas Plume gives no title. Many of the lines are similar and some are virtually identical. Most of the second verse of the Loyal Garland version is missing from Plume's version, except for one line. Plume does not record this as a song, as does the Loyal Garland, but it seems that Plume may have heard this sung, possibly more than once, and may have written down the above from memory, with some improvements of his own. Another explanation may lie in the time span; Plume probably made this note in the 1640s, whereas the Loyal Garland version is from the fifth edition of 1686. The words may well have evolved over time. This remains the only poem of Plume's that has been identified elsewhere.

Five more of the poems can be dated by internal evidence. 'The w[or]lds down, since Char. is dead' is clearly post-January 1649; 'Ye one-eyed gunner in ye Town' references, in the scatological verses, the siege of Colchester in 1648; and 'An Epithalmy to his friend J [?] composed Aug 19 – 49' speaks for itself, as does that dated 1649 ('Woe be to Gregory').[44] Finally there is a reference to 'Colonell le Strange imprizoned by ye P[ar]liament'.[45] This is a reference to Sir Roger L'Estrange (1616–1704), who was imprisoned by parliament from 1644 to 1648 and went on to play a leading role in a royalist rising in Kent, after which he had to flee to Holland. All the poems are fair copies with the exception of 'An Epithalmy', which contains two deletions and corresponding substitutions that appear to be evidence of composition. The author of these poems or verses is not known, but as none of them have as yet been found elsewhere Plume may have composed them, or at least 'An Epithalmy'.[46]

The poems are on a variety of subjects. There are six amours – three romantic, two comedic and one lewd (the 'Epithalmy') – and three royalist poems. There are two poems of imprisonment, one of a madman and the other of 'Colonell le Strange'. There is a brief poem on death, a comic one on being a soldier ('A Braggadocian'), an extremely scatological poem 'Upon a gentlewoman yt had 500 stooles by one purge' of 116 lines, and 'Woe be to Gregory' on a feast at Stourbridge Fair (comedic).[47] Whether or not he was the author, the writing-up of these verses portrays Plume as a young man of lively and varied interests, particularly in the more sensational side of life. He also had a keen interest in the opposite sex, which manifested itself in different ways. At times he is romantic, putting women 'on a pedestal'. In 'An Epithalmy' he is sexually frank when he prepares a bashful friend for marriage, using a military analogy and urging him: 'Coward now Cock thy peece, prime thy pan, Make ready, present, prove thyself a man, Discharg, give Fire: ....'[48] There is, however, misogyny in the scatological poem, with its 'theme of unveiling the nasty core of a woman's body'.[49]

The 245 anecdotes are too numerous to be analysed in detail here, but they are extremely diverse, referring as they do to no fewer than 31 topics. It was not possible to classify 39 of the anecdotes and sayings because the 'point' of them seems to have evaporated over the centuries. As might be expected from a young man, humour (61 jokes), bawdry (17 anecdotes) and romance (12 anecdotes) are well represented, but there are also ten moralistic sayings. The law comes in for much criticism in seven anecdotes, while the aristocracy and royalty (always King James) are quite favourably treated in 22 anecdotes. Tensions between Town and Gown are evident in several anecdotes, with the scholar usually but not always besting the townsman or alehouse-keeper. In spite of strict rules confining them to their colleges, students seem to have moved freely in the town, as the reference to Stourbridge fair above suggests. They not infrequently got into fights and committed other misdemeanours.[50] Reflecting Plume's royalism are anecdotes praising one college don for his stand in refusing the Covenant and another for condemning parliament in front of 500 soldiers.[51]

Sixteen anecdotes are anti-papistical and anti-Puritan, showing that such antagonisms were common enough to form the stuff of anecdote and revealing Plume to be a proto-Anglican. Parliament is the subject of criticism in three anecdotes, as is Hugh Peter (or Peters, 1598–1660). In the late 1640s Peters was at the height of his fame for the role he had played in raising recruits for parliamentary army with his fiery preaching. He was later accused of having instigated the trial of King Charles, but always denied this. Plume has a long anecdote concerning Peters preaching at Whitehall to the soldiers after the death of the king, showing how he justified the king's death with a piece of specious logic. The other two anecdotes about Peters are not about politics but are more concerned to show his supposed venality and his ability to chop logic. Peters was executed as one of the regicides in 1660.[52]

The second notebook contains six pages of notes, made in some haste, apparently of a sermon because they contain much repetition in a rhetorical style and have later been amended here and there in a different coloured ink. The subject of the sermon is the body and blood of Christ at the time of holy communion. Plume clearly took it very seriously and was in accord with the preacher's conclusion, which understood the topic at a mid-point between the Puritan and Catholic views of this hotly disputed area of theology. Repeatedly in later life Plume was able to find a path between two extremes.[53]

Graduation, Nonsuch and Cheam
We now turn to a period of Plume's life for which there is no formal knowledge: from his graduation BA from Christ's College in 1649/50 to his appointment as vicar of Greenwich in 1658. The evidence that survives from this period is contained in two notebooks and his memoir of his friend and mentor, Dr John Hacket (Figure 3.4).[54] Because of the lack of information during this period Petchey speculated that Plume might have gone with his tutor, William More, when he left his fellowship at Christ's in 1649 and 'probably' went into residence at the college living of Kegworth in Leicestershire. Some students apparently went with their tutors as pupils or curates.[55] There is no evidence that this happened. However, Plume did begin a new notebook bearing the date 1 January 1651 near the beginning and 'Finis Nonsuch September 20 1656' near the end.[56] Why did he go to the disused royal palace of Nonsuch? It may be significant that it was just two miles south of the village of Malden in Surrey (now known as Old Malden). In this notebook Plume made notes and paraphrases from a succession of books and pamphlets (and also recorded a number of anecdotes), giving the strong impression that he was following a course of study, possibly in the earlier stages under the guidance of William More but definitely in the later part of this period under John Hacket (1590–1670), rector of Cheam and later to become bishop of Lichfield.[57]

As noted above, parts of the new notebook were written at Nonsuch, the disused royal palace only one mile from the village of Cheam, where Dr Hacket was rector. He was 38 years older than Plume and had been a highly esteemed student both at Westminster School and Trinity College, Cambridge. Subsequently he had risen quickly through the ranks of the Church of England, aided by his patron, John Williams (1582–1650), lord keeper, bishop of Lincoln and archbishop of York. Hacket was a firm adherent of the episcopacy and monarchy and suffered accordingly during the 1640s, when the king was defeated and then executed and parliament abolished the bishops together with their deans and chapters. Hacket lost all his preferments with the exception of

3.4 John Hacket (1592–1670), bishop of Lichfield and Coventry, who was Plume's patron from the 1650s (portrait in J. Hacket, *A Century of Sermons* (London 1675) by kind permission of Lichfield Cathedral).

the rectory of Cheam, to which he retired in 1643 and where he lived in some seclusion until the Restoration in 1660.[58]

A close relationship developed between Hacket and Plume in the 1650s, and Hacket's influence on Plume's life continued for many years thereafter. In 1675 Plume wrote of the early days of their relationship and how Hacket had helped him, a poor scholar, in spite of being in straitened circumstances himself: 'In bad times, when he had lost his best income and, like the Widow of Sarepta, had but an handful of meal and Cruze of Oyl for himself and his family, yet he then … has given a distressed Friend twenty pounds at a time … '.[59] The reason for Plume's financial distress at this time remains uncertain. As has been seen, Plume had been well supported by his father while at Cambridge, but thereafter there is no record of his receiving funds until his father transferred ownership of the family home in Maldon to him. His father had retired from Maldon Corporation in 1653 on the grounds of extreme old age and ill health, and the transfer took place on a date unknown but between 6 June 1654 and his death before 9 September 1659.[60] It therefore seems possible that Plume may have fallen out with his father as a result of their acute differences over religion and politics at around the time that his formal education ceased.[61] Perhaps Plume senior stopped his son's allowance at this time and Plume may have felt unable to return home. He may have been attracted to Malden (Surrey) because of the sentiment of the name or perhaps he was already aware of Hacket's presence in the vicinity and was drawn to him because of what he knew of his life and beliefs.

Material in the Plume Library sheds some light on his relationship with Hacket. MS MA0029 is an unbound, unpaginated quarto of 93 leaves closely covered in a fine hand. It bears no signature, but the hand is clearly that of the writer of the second Cambridge notebook, where a firm attribution to Plume has been made. The attribution to Plume of MS MA0029 is based on the hand, the placing of the author at Nonsuch and the mention of Dr Hacket and 'Dr H.' In this notebook Plume made notes on the works of 20 identifiable authors, some of whom are discussed below, but there are also large areas of script that still await analysis. It must be admitted that there is a difficulty with this material. Some of it is merely copied from printed books and it can, therefore, be argued that it reveals nothing of Plume's own opinions and beliefs. I have taken the view, however, that these notes are Plume's own selections and they were made over a period of no fewer than six years.

It is not known when Plume and Hacket first met, but there are numerous references in MS MA0029 to 'Dr H.' Plume also made notes: 'Out of Dr Hacketts ψυχολογια', a work that has not been traced.[62] The title translates as *Psychologia*, the study of the mind, or the soul or breath. Unfortunately, owing to the extremely truncated notes that Plume made of this work, it has not been possible to reconstruct Hacket's text or argument. The following gives a flavour of some of the anecdotes that Plume recorded as having been told to him by Dr Hacket:

Dr H[acket] told me that B[isho]p Buckridg[63] (who I think p[rea]ch[e]d B[isho]p Andr[ewes][64] fun[eral] ser[vice]) told him he never drunk wine till he was 85 y[ea]rs old – unl[ess] ho[wev]er at a Com[m]un[ion] but then he began to find a coldn[ess] in his stom[ach] and was advis[ed] to drink wine – w[hi]ch when he had once begun he ... [?] go bib and bib that eu [every] afternoon he w[ou]ld fox himb [himself] alone. B[isho]p Laud[65] would be extr[emely] round and severe with him for it – need to beware of Infirm[ities] in old age.[66]

Dr H[acket] ackn[owledged] he c[ou]ld nev[er] imit[ate] Mr Hawksw[or]th for poesy – my L[or]d St Albans[67] for an Engl[ish] style nor B[isho]p Brownrig[68] for p[re]aching.[69]

It is remarkable that, out of the 20 authors identified in MS MA0029, only three are not royalists or defenders of episcopacy or Arminians. The followers of Jacob Arminius (d.1609) maintained that good works were essential to salvation, not faith alone, and as such were opposed to Calvinism, the dominant theology of Puritanism. By this period (i.e. the 1650s) the word 'Arminian' was used to describe not only theology but high church ritual as well.[70] This belief system has been referred to as 'Laudianism' by Fincham and Tyacke.[71]

Plume's studies as revealed by MS MA0029 show that he was identifying authors who preached a real and deep toleration, a desire to be peaceable and a desire not to take sides in the Civil Wars. He also recorded a failed attempt to convert Charles I to Roman Catholicism, and the views of a Presbyterian who advocated episcopacy without the government of the presbyters.[72] Another theme that the notes suggest is that of a middle way, neither papist or Puritan, and it may be significant that it is right at the start of the manuscript.[73]

It must be noted, however, there are limits to the toleration expressed above. These limits apply to both Presbyterianism and the Roman Catholic church. In regard to Presbyterianism, for example:

> Classical resolutions of the Brethren are so magisterially delivered ... that they annex unto their pens and pulpits Infallibility of Judgem[ent] as well as the Pope to his chair ... our puritanicall parochiall who would be Popes over Kings and Kesars [sic] and all that are called Gods ... I will not be putt over unto Classical decisions ... nor ... unto any propheticall determinable in private Conventi[cles] after lectures.[74]

In these passages the word 'classical' refers to the district assemblies or classes that represented congregations within the Presbyterian system of church government and the final phrase refers to the practice of the godly meeting to discuss sermons or lectures after divine service. These passages are unattributable owing to the damage to the manuscript, but the Puritan John Saltmarsh is clear that presbytery does not constitute an office in the Church. He states that it is not found in scripture and that it is nothing more than another name for an elder or senior person. This was written at a time when parliament had abolished the episcopacy and was attempting to implement a Presbyterian form of church government.[75] Plume's father was one of the three elders of the Dengie classis, of which Maldon was the chief town.[76] His was clearly a Presbyterian role and, therefore, diametrically opposed to the position his son was taking. As already noted above, it is possible that these opposed religious views may have affected their personal relationship.

Plume's notes show that he is prepared to consider the limitations of the Calvinist doctrine of 'election' by recording that salvation comes from obedience to God, not from being a member of the elect.[77] Similarly, the doctrine of justification by faith is heavily qualified, even to the point of introducing the concept of justification by works, a much more Arminian position. After pointing out that justification is not only before God but before men, Plume's note concludes: 'Until I may perceive that you shew forth your faith by your works and manifest your belief by reall practice you must give me leave to think you dissemble in the point and would perswade men of a case of necessity that yourselves may feed fatt upon their folly ... '.[78]

Just as Plume's notes reveal a bias against the more extreme Puritan positions on various issues, so they also show a clear bias against the Roman Catholic church. Papal infallibility is seen as worse than heresy and Plume believed that, even though the Catholic Church damns people for heresy, they are not damned by God.[79] Rome is also attacked for the execution of thousands of those it deemed heretics. Plume wrote further: 'You make ign[orant] souls believe you can fish Friends out of Purgatory with a silver hook',[80] referring to the widespread practice of the selling of indulgences by the priesthood to reduce the length of time spent by the soul in purgatory. Plume studied one work of philosophy, Thomas Hobbes' *Leviathan* (London, 1651), among other works which are noted by Helen Kemp in Chapter 8 of this volume.[81]

Another of Plume's manuscripts in use during the time of his association with Hacket was that named by Andrew Clark as 'Dr Plume's Pocket-book'. Clark transcribed this manuscript fully and published it in a series of articles in the *Essex Review*.[82] It consists of 272 pages and begins: 'London, St Martins Day 1657: I began to note this book upon Whitsun Tuesday, May'. The book is not signed, but detailed and careful analysis of the hand(s) and content led Clark to conclude that it is Plume's work. He finds that many of the notes are 'of no value'. There are many anecdotes and comments on William Laud, Charles I, Oliver Cromwell, John Warner (bishop of Rochester), John Hacket and many other senior clergymen and it can be concluded from these, as has already been found elsewhere, that Plume was a royalist and an anti-Presbyterian. Using the material in the pocket-book to attempt to build up a picture of Plume, Clark described him as:

> a theologian, with special interest in the Cambridge divinity disputations and in the eccentricities of successive Cambridge Professors of Divinity; a Royalist, with pronounced dislike to Scots and Irish; a Churchman very antagonistic to Presbyterianism; a bachelor deeply convinced of the burdens incidental to the state of matrimony ... .[83]

Petchey challenged this summary, stating that the material in the pocket-book was not Plume's but was very probably from Dr Hacket and two of his friends, Robert Boreman[84] and Dr Edward Hyde.[85] It is the case that Plume collected many manuscripts by Boreman and Hyde (analysed by Helen Kemp in Chapter 8), and in his will Plume clearly states his approval of marriage, so Clark's assessment cannot be supported.[86] However, this being so, why did he never marry? His juvenile poems referred to above indicate a very clear heterosexuality, so his sexuality does not seem to have been a bar. Clerical celibacy was much discussed in this period and Plume placed two books on the subject in his library, one by his friend Edward Hyde. These both conclude that celibacy is not enjoined on Church of England clergy; on the contrary, they are required to abide by Article 32 of the 39 Articles of Religion, the founding principles of the Restoration Church, which presented no obstacles to the conformist Plume:

Of the marriage of Priests.

Bishops, Priests and Deacons are not commanded by God's Law either to vow the estate of single life, or to abstain from marriage: therefore it is lawful for them, as for all other Christian men, to marry at their own discretion, as they shall judge the same to serve better to godliness.

Having a free choice in the matter, Plume may have chosen not to marry, the better to exercise his ministry, and he may have been following the example of his friend and mentor Robert Boreman, who never married but, according to Anthony Wood, 'spent his time in celibacy'. It may be, of course, that he simply never met the right marriage partner.[87]

During his stay in or around Nonsuch, Plume was neighbour to two senior parliamentarian military commanders, both named as regicides. Such was their eminence that he must have been aware of this. It is a deep irony that Hacket and Plume, with their devotion to the memory of Charles I and abhorrence of the sacrilege of his execution, should find two men deeply involved in his execution as owners of nearby property sequestrated from the crown. Col. Thomas Pride, the 'purger' of parliament and veteran of such battles as Naseby, Dunbar and Worcester, bought Nonsuch Great Park, including the Keeper's House, on 12 May 1652. Pride spent quite a lot of time on his estate, living at Worcester House, as the Keeper's House became known. He died there and was buried at Nonsuch on 2 November 1658, just six weeks after Plume's institution at East Greenwich.[88] Nonsuch Palace and the Little Park were conveyed to Major-General John Lambert on 31 October 1654. Lambert had been one of Oliver Cromwell's most distinguished commanders. He had led the armies at Dunbar and Worcester and held very senior posts in the governments of both Oliver and Richard Cromwell. He owned the former queen Henrietta Maria's very fine house at nearby Wimbledon, but there are no surviving records of his use of the palace or the park. All these properties reverted to the crown at the Restoration in 1660.[89]

Greenwich and Rochester

During the Interregnum the bishops had been deprived of all their temporal powers and most of their income, their response to which was to retire to country livings and keep a low profile. However, they made a crucial contribution to the Church in that they continued to ordain. Parliament made arrangements for ordination by the Presbyterian classes, but during the years 1642–9 the great majority of new ministers received Episcopal ordination. There is no record of Plume's ordination but, given his views on the Church and the king, Presbyterian ordination would not have been open to him. At this time, Brian Duppa, bishop of Salisbury (1558–1662), was living at Richmond, only seven miles from Cheam. In 1659 he ordained Thomas Tenison, the future archbishop, so it is possible that he also ordained Plume upon Hacket's recommendation. Duppa's portrait is in the Plume Library.[90]

Petchey speculates that Hacket may have been able to use his 'reviving influence' to secure the desirable benefice of Greenwich for Plume, the patron of which was Richard Cromwell, newly made Lord Protector.[91] Cromwell presented Plume to St Alfege's parish in East Greenwich on 22 September 1658 only 19 days after the death of his father, Oliver Cromwell. The royal patronage of this parish had passed to Oliver Cromwell and on his death on 3 September 1658 to his son. It is not known how Plume's name came before Oliver Cromwell (it is very likely that he was living when Plume's name was first put forward), but I speculate that Plume may have been known to John Thurloe (1616–68), who was Oliver Cromwell's Secretary of State and intimate friend. Thurloe was similarly close to Richard Cromwell at the start of his brief rule. We know that Plume donated a book on the prerogatives and privileges of cathedral churches, *De Ecclesiis Cathedralibus Erumque Privilegiis et Praerogativus Tractus* ... by Michael Antonius Frances de Urrutigoyti (Lyons, 1665), to Wisbech town library around the time that the bishop of Ely was seeking to have Wisbech Castle restored to him.[92] During the Interregnum this valuable property had been acquired by Thurloe and he had had a large house built there. It is possible, therefore, that Hacket had recommended Plume to Thurloe for this living and that subsequently Thurloe had learnt of Plume's expertise in buying books. Might Thurloe, having helped Plume to obtain the living of Greenwich, called in a favour by asking Plume to obtain the book for him?[93]

The relationship between Plume and Hacket continued to flourish. Hacket had come to have an aversion to London as the city where Charles I had been executed (or martyred, in Hacket's eyes) and he would not go there. He still needed books, however, and, in buying them for Hacket, Plume began his long association with the London book trade. Plume continued to buy books and transact other business for Hacket in London after he became bishop of Coventry and Lichfield in 1661. Plume was admitted BD *per literas regis* (by royal mandate) in 1661 and DD in 1673. Hacket, as bishop of Lichfield, would have been able to recommend him for the BD without the need for Plume to have followed a formal course of study to achieve this highly desirable second degree. In 1667 Hacket recorded his 'promise of the next prebend that shall be void if I live so long, to Mr Plume of Greenwich who is of great merit'.[94] This did not happen, but upon his death in 1670 he left Plume £10 and two books of manuscript sermons. These Plume published in 1675 as *A Century of Sermons upon Several Remarkable Subjects* under Hacket's name, with a 54-page memoir of him.[95] There is elsewhere some evidence that Plume may have had a hand in publishing Hacket's biography of his own patron Archbishop John Williams.[96]

Plume's memoir of Hacket gives a very clear picture of his mentor's churchmanship, and he at no point indicates that his own views were any different. On the contrary, he writes approvingly and, indeed, affectionately of this much older and more senior man. It is clear that, although Plume is writing about Hacket, many of the general views expressed apply equally to Plume. At the outset Plume claims that this memoir is 'from his Lordships most intimate acquaintance, and for the most part from his reports'.[97] Further on, Plume describes the pleasant relationship between them: 'After he was made Bishop, it made no change of his former sweetness and affability, *still he knew us*'.[98] The memoir is laudatory but quite well rounded, referring as it does to Hacket as having a very sharp temper, although one that quickly subsided.[99] The memoir shows Hacket as deeply committed to the Church of England as a reformed church by law established:

> and accordingly he would often render hearty thanks to God that his birth and breeding was in a Reformed Church and of all others the most prudent and exact according to the doctrine of Holy Scripture and Primitive Pattern; that would neither continue in the Fulsom superstitions of the Roman Church, nor in Reforming be born down with the violent torrent as some others were.[100]

Hacket opposed separation and blamed Puritan corporations and their conventicles for fomenting war against the king. This point would have had particular resonance for Plume, as his father had been a leading member of just such a corporation at Maldon. As reported by Plume, Hacket had no quarrel with moderate Arminians; even Arminius himself had approved of the moderation of the Church of England. Plume reported also that '[Hacket was] a great enemy to sharpnes and violence in the matters of religion'.[101]

Plume referred to the civil war period as a dark and gloomy time that would never be forgotten. During the Interregnum Hacket was under great constraint at Cheam, but he regularly used the Prayer Book until he was barred from doing so by the Committee of Surrey. On one occasion a soldier entered his church, presented a pistol at his breast and ordered him to stop. Hacket replied that he would do what became a divine, let the other do what became a soldier, and continued the service.[102] Even after this he managed to use parts of the Book of Common Prayer, including the Creed and the Ten Commandments,

3.5 St Alfege's church and the river Thames from One Tree Hill, Greenwich Park (detail), c.1690 by Jan Griffier the Elder. The medieval tower survived the collapse of the nave in 1710, but was rebuilt by 1718 (© National Maritime Museum, Greenwich, BHC1833).

saying the rest of the service at home. As will be seen, Plume began his clerical career by using the Prayer Book. Hacket told Plume that 'the Church of England was still in being, and not destroyed, rather refined by her sufferings'.[103] Plume maintained that Hacket did not hold 'private and singular opinions', but was a firm adherent to the 'Articles of the Church of England'.[104]

Plume surely drew on his own education when he stated the need for the clergy to be educated:

> such preaching being oftentimes so poor and easie, that every Justice of Peace his clerk thought he could perform as well as his minister; whereas a good preacher had need be skill'd in the whole Encyclopedy of Arts and Sciences, Logick to divide the word aright, Rhetorick to perswade, School Divinity to convince Gainsayers, knowledge of many tongues to understand originals and learned authors … .[105]

He also expressed his own devotion to the Church of England: 'And though I am likely to do all this [i.e. write this memoir] with very small acumen and judgement, yet I hope with true zeal, and sincere affection to the glory of God and honour of the Church of England'.[106] And Plume's relationship with Hacket continued to the end in 1670: 'when he was first taken sick he did not conceive it to be mortal, and therefore he sent the week before he died to a Friend in London to send him down the new books from abroad or at home'.[107]

When Plume began his ministry at St Alfege's Church, Greenwich (Figure 3.5), in 1658, the use of the Book of Common Prayer was still forbidden by parliament, having been replaced by the Directory for Public Worship in 1645. Petchey maintains that, in spite of this ban, Plume used the Prayer Book from the start of his ministry, citing the record of the diarist John Evelyn receiving Holy Communion from Plume's hands at Easter 1659: as Evelyn sought out the proscribed services, this would have been according to the Prayer Book rite. It has not proved possible to confirm this from other sources, but both Morrill and Spaeth are clear that large numbers of parishioners ('village Anglicans', as Spaeth calls them) were deeply loyal to the Prayer Book, were resistant to the use of the Directory and welcomed the return of the Prayer Book in 1660. Plume subscribed to the Act of Uniformity on 28 July 1662. As a royalist having episcopal ordination, subscription would not have presented him with any problems.[108]

Both Evelyn, living at Deptford, and Samuel Pepys, living in Greenwich during the Great Plague of London, recorded visiting St Alfege's church on separate occasions during September 1665. The devout Evelyn commented on September 10 that Plume had shown 'how our sins had drawn God's Judgements'.[109] The more worldly Pepys remarked on 1 September: 'To Church where a company of fine people, and a fine church, and a very good sermon, Mr Plume being a very excellent scholar and preacher'.[110] Evelyn was there again just a year later, immediately after the Great Fire of London (16 September 1666): 'I went to Greenwich church where Mr Plume preached very well on II

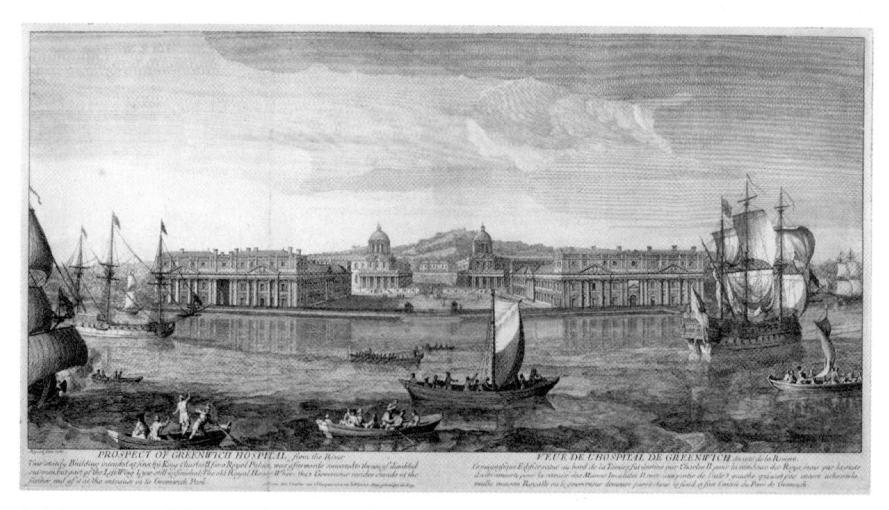

3.6 A prospect of Greenwich Hospital from the Thames in 1736. The buildings were originally begun in 1663 as a royal palace for Charles II, but made into a hospital for disabled sailors by Queen Mary II: work began in 1692 and Plume subscribed £20 in 1695. In the foreground can be seen shipping and a number of small passenger boats of the type Plume would have engaged to visit the City when he travelled by water (LMA, Collage no. 22638).

Peter, chapter III verses 11 and 12 ... taking occasion from the late unparalleled Conflagration to mind us how we ought to walk more holily in all manner of conversation'.[111] Plume clearly believed in God's judgement on a sinful nation[112] but, despite his numerous sermon notes, their sparsity, Plume's partial use of code and his mature hand, which is extremely difficult to decipher, mean that so far it has not been possible to reconstruct his argument.[113]

Evelyn also noted that Plume allowed French refugees to use his church, writing on 1 April 1687: 'the congregation consisting of about 100 French Protestant refugees from the Persecution of which Monsieur de Rouvigny (present) was the chief and had obtained the use of the church after the parish had ended their service'.[114] This arrangement was a part of a long-standing connection between the parish, Plume and a leading French minister, Peter Allix (1641–1717). It was a similar story at the Roan School, Greenwich, of which Plume was the chairman of the feoffees for 25 years; on 1 November 1699, with Plume present, the board gave the following instruction: 'Ordered that the Ministers of the French Congregation be civilly admonished to take some Effectuall care that the Schoole room may be kept clean and left in decent order for the reception of Schollers every Monday morning and that Mr Watson lett him know it'.[115] In his will of 1704 Plume left £100 to be paid to Mr Allix 'aboute the Charterhouse' for 'poore French protestant ministers or other French laymen',[116] and to 'thank him for his Translation of Nectarius'.[117] Nektarios (or Nectarius) (1605–c.1680) attacked both the Roman church and the Calvinists. Allix's gift of this book indicates his appreciation of Plume's generosity in helping the French congregation and his scholarship. Allix had left his native France in 1685 at the revocation of the edict of Nantes and obtained a royal patent to establish a new French church conforming to the Anglican rite in Aldersgate in July 1686. Plume and Allix shared a common devotion to the Church of England; the latter stated in his will: 'I have always wished for the welfare of this Nation and the Church of England'.[118]

Another minister in difficult circumstances and helped by Plume was John Sidway, who converted from Roman Catholicism to the Church of England some time before 1681. He wrote about his experiences and concluded his book, on a separate page, after 'Finis':

> Advertisement. I am informed by too many hands since my writing this piece, how that the Reverend Dr Plume of Greenwich has been aspersed for entertaining me some days in his house, and permitting me to Preach in his Church. I assure all people upon the faith of a Christian, That I had been received into the Church of England by the Bishop of London about a Twelvemonth before that time, and brought the Dr. the certificates of the Deans of Canterbury and Chichester and other Reverend Divines to witness it.
>
> John Sidway.[119]

It has not proved possible to uncover anything else about Sidway, but it may be that his 'Advertisement' was written at Plume's behest.

Church income, household expenditure and royal patronage

In spite of Plume's 46 years as their vicar, there is little trace of him in the parish records of St Alfege's church, Greenwich. He made no personal entry in the parish registers of baptism, marriage and burial, and the churchwardens' accounts for the period have been largely lost. He is mentioned in the overseers' accounts as having paid an annual rate of £2 to £3 on the vicarage house from 1691–1703 at a time when some rates were as low as two shillings and the average was about six shillings.[120]

Plume's income from the church was never high, even when he became archdeacon. The tithes due to Plume from the parish of East Greenwich were £21 p.a. less tenths of £2 2s, leaving him with £18 18s. In addition, he received £5 2 6d as a tithe from the attached park, and the tithes of rods and reeds, of all fruits, and of herbage or pasture ground. Plume was appointed to the sinecure living of Merston, Kent, in 1662, where there was no church or inhabitants, for which the tithes were £14 less tenths of £1 8s, leaving him with £12 12s.[121] Although it has been stated that Plume also held the living of Little Easton in Essex, this cannot be substantiated, as can be seen by reference to Newcourt.[122]

In 1679 Plume was made archdeacon for the diocese of Rochester with a salary of £42 and no fines, and in the same year he was granted the 6th prebend of Rochester cathedral, always reserved for the archdeacon, worth £20 p.a.[123] It can be seen that Plume's income from the church (apart from the chaplain's groats discussed immediately below) was only £24 0s 6d for his first four years, rising to £36 12s 6d for the next 17 years and only then reaching £98 12s 6d, at which level it persisted until his death 25 years later. As there are no surviving records, it is not known if the fines levied by the archdeacon's court sufficed to pay its expenses. After his death Rochester Cathedral paid £30 to his executor, James Plume, being 'the Testators salary', but no other details regarding this payment are given in the accounts produced by the executor to defend himself in Chancery.[124]

Plume clearly thought his remuneration from the Church was inadequate and he approached the king: on 8 March 1670 is recorded 'another [request for an order] for Thos. Plume, vicar of Greenwich, for groats due to him from his Majesty's yachts lying before Greenwich from 1663 to 1670'.[125] Charles II was a very keen yachtsman, and it seems from Plume's petition that the king had his yachts moored at Greenwich (Figure 3.7). Plume was claiming the chaplain's groats, which would have been collected by the master of each yacht, amounting to one groat or fourpence per month from each seaman. These yachts were substantial vessels, having up to 30 crew, and during his reign Charles had 27 of them at different times.[126] There are no surviving records of these payments,

3.7 The *Peregrine* and other royal yachts off Greenwich c.1710, by Jan Griffier the Elder (© National Maritime Museum, Greenwich, BHC1821).

but it seems that his application was successful for a time; however, much later, on 5 November 1700, Plume petitioned the crown again at Whitehall to the effect that he had 'enjoyed' the benefice of East Greenwich in the king's gift for many years at 'a very great charge'; because the tithes were only £60 p.a. this had been augmented with the monthly groats from the king's yachts, but he lost these seven years ago 'to a minister that does no duty for them'. He requested the king to restore them to him because of his 'conscientious discharge of his duties'. His petition was referred to the Admiralty, but there is no record of the outcome.[127] The sums involved might well have been significant; for example, during the period 1736–9 chaplain's groats amounting to £198 14s were collected from 'sundry yachts' in the Thames (but not necessarily from vessels moored at Greenwich).[128]

In 1678 Plume again petitioned the king, this time for the rectory of Llanrhaeadr, Wales, 'when it shall become vacant on the grounds that this rectory is likely to become void by the death of the present incumbent, the petitioner having diligently discharged his duty as vicar of Greenwich and having once presented his Majesty with a dedication of a bishop's works, when his Majesty promised to confer some token of favour on him'. On the back of this petition is written: 'Aug 2nd Memorandum the Mr Secretary moving the King on this petition, he granted it'.[129] It seems that Plume sought this post because of it being of much higher value than Greenwich, but was forestalled in this move by being offered the archdeaconry of Rochester.

Before concluding this account of Plume's income from the church, mention must be made of how little we know of his household expenditure. Included in the manuscripts are records of his household accounts from 1698 to 1703, approximately. The accounts and their dates are somewhat vague and rudimentary, but they indicate expenditure on household items such as food, clothing, candles, fuel, postage, services of watermen and so on, amounting to about £11 per annum over about five years. Considering that Plume's household consisted of two maids and a coachman (whose wages are not included in these accounts), his regular expenses amounted to nearly half of the tithes he received from Greenwich. His income from the church had been somewhat augmented when he became archdeacon, but he paid very high rates on the vicarage house and even in 1700 he was clearly conscious that the parish was a 'very great charge' on him.[130]

Plume's petitions were not his only connection with the king: on 5 January 1682 he was, for a week, one of the chaplains in ordinary to the royal household (as the king's main residence, and where he died on 16 February 1685, this would have probably been at Whitehall Palace). Chaplains to the royal household were usually doctors in divinity, mostly deans or prebends, and all excellent preachers. Their duties were to wait at court and to preach in the chapel on Sundays and other festivals for the king, and separately to the household. They were also required to read the daily service to the king and to say grace at meals in the absence of the Clerk to the Closet. Plume received no payment for this, only his food, but it was held that this was more than made up for by being near the king, with the opportunities this presented for possible preferment to a wealthier position within the church. However, this did not happen for Plume.[131]

Archdeacon of Rochester
Plume was installed archdeacon of Rochester and prebendary in the sixth stall of Rochester Cathedral in 1679 and in the same year was made a freeman of the City of Rochester.[132] With these preferments came two properties: the prebendal house, or archdeaconry, as it was known, in the precincts of Rochester Cathedral and the manor and court lodge in Longfield, Kent, about 11 miles from Rochester. There is good evidence that Plume lived in the archdeaconry at Rochester, as the canons of the cathedral challenged his claim to this house, but these demands were unsuccessful.[133] His occupation of the archdeaconry house is further supported by Plume's executor, James Plume, who recorded in his accounts that he paid 16s 6d [?] for putting the books at Rochester into casks and transporting them to the waterside.[134] Plume may also have resided at Longfield occasionally because, as Hasted puts it, 'The Court Lodge ... was once probably made use of by the Archdeacons as

a house of retirement'. This may be the reason he chose to be buried in the churchyard there.[135]

Plume was collated to the post of archdeacon by his bishop, John Dolben (1625–86). His appointment may be related to the fact that the Dolben family and John Hacket, Plume's mentor, had a common patron in John Williams (1582–1650), bishop of Lincoln and archbishop of York. Dolben's father William (1588?–1631) married Williams' sister Elizabeth and while Williams was bishop of Lincoln he had appointed his brother-in-law to a prebend there. There may have been some personal sympathy between John Dolben and Plume because Dolben fought on the royalist side in the Civil War and began his clerical career in the late 1650s by holding proscribed Prayer Book services.[136]

The archdeaconry of Rochester was coterminous with the diocese. Plume's role was to induct the ministers and admit the churchwardens to the 99 parishes and to conduct regular visitations. He also had to administer the ecclesiastical property and oversee the archdeacon's courts. In the parishes he was *oculi episcopi* (the eyes of the bishop), all the more necessary as the bishop's palace was at Bromley, in the extreme west of the diocese, some 20 miles from Rochester and just a few miles from Greenwich, where Plume remained vicar.[137]

One of the main duties of archdeacons was to 'visit' – that is to say, to carry out a formal inspection of each parish under their control on a regular basis. The churchwardens and incumbents of every parish were sent the 'articles' of the visitation, setting out in great detail the questions they would be required to answer. In theory this was a highly significant event because there lay behind it the power to present individuals to the archdeacon's court, with potentially serious consequences. By Plume's day, as will be seen, the reality was rather different. The first of four bishops under whom Plume served was John Warner (1637–42 and 1660–66), who was a confirmed Laudian.[138] The history of Laudianism is too extensive to go into here in any detail: suffice it to say that by the 1660s Laudians such as Warner had in common 'an abiding hostility to Puritan non-conformity and proposals for the comprehension of dissenters, strict adherence to the formularies and canons of the church, Arminian views on grace, and the creation of a richly ceremonial setting for divine worship and the celebration of the sacraments'.[139] Warner speedily set about restoring Rochester cathedral (Figure 3.8) and reinstated the altar rails. In the parishes, however, there was so much to be done by way of the repair of churches and reordering of vicarage houses and churchyards that he omitted all mention of the railing of communion tables from his Visitation Articles of 1662.[140] Fincham and Tyacke maintain that another factor in taking matters slowly was that the railing of communion tables was such a contentious issue in theology and practice (and, some argued, of dubious legality) that many

3.8 Rochester Cathedral before 1655 (from Sir William Dugdale, *Monasticon Anglicanum*, vol. 1 (London, 1655), plate between pp. 28–9).

bishops preferred not to confront their parishioners with these issues at their first visitation since the Restoration.[141]

Plume kept his copy of Bishop John Warner's Articles of Visitation of 1662.[142] Also surviving are Archdeacon John Lee Warner's findings from his visitations of 1663 and 1670.[143] It is worth noting that John Lee was nephew to his bishop, John Warner, and assumed his surname upon the bishop's death in 1666. The bishop was childless and John Lee inherited a large fortune. He therefore carried out the 1663 visitations as John Lee and the 1670 visitations as John Lee Warner.

In 1663, as archdeacon, John Lee did address the issues concerning the communion tables, and required three parishes to remove seats from around the communion table and three others to set up the rails once again. These limited numbers suggest that he was responding to requests from people within each parish. The articles of the archdeacon's visitation of 1670 do not survive, but they clearly included the railing of the altars because he required nearly 50 parishes to set up their communion tables 'altarwise' under the east window and to rail them in 'as formerly'.[144] The records for Lee's visitation of Plume's parish of East Greenwich in 1663 do not survive, but in 1670 his parish received a very clean bill of health, except that he had to provide a book of homilies 'and other such books and ornaments for the church as the minister by his discretion shall think fit'. In this visitation of 95 parishes Plume was the only minister to be granted any discretion.

Another sign of the archdeacon's favour was that in 1670 Plume acted as his surrogate in 13 parishes (naturally not including his own), an excellent preparation for his promotion nine years later. Of his various requirements, the following were clearly Laudian: two parishes were to raise the chancel floor, seven to place their communion tables under the east window and ten to provide rails to the communion table as at the cathedral church at Rochester, a fine illustration of its status as exemplar and 'mother' church.[145] Two of these parishes were required to remove seats from under the east window.[146] This list leaves us in no doubt of Plume's conversion to Laudian practice at the parish level, and in this his studies of Arminianism in the 1650s will have prepared the ground for a change of view from his earlier Calvinism.[147] As we shall see, however, when his will is examined, his most personal and private beliefs reflected something of the Puritanism in which he had been brought up.

Also surviving are the citations for Plume's visitations of the Rochester and Malling deaneries of 1704. These are formal documents giving notice to the apparitors (those required to appear before the visitation, chiefly incumbents and churchwardens) of these deaneries of Plume's intention to carry out visitations of them on 11 May 1704 and 16 May 1704 respectively – that is, just six months before his death. No mention is made of Plume appearing in person; instead, in both cases the persons summoned were to appear before a judge sitting in the 'Consistory Court'. This bears out Tarver's conclusion that 'The bishops and archdeacons with ultimate authority over the [church] courts seldom appeared in person, being engaged in a variety of other business, and they both appointed officials to oversee the courts'.[148] In the case of the visitation to the Rochester Deanery, the court was to be held in the parish church of St Nicholas, Rochester, and in the case of the Malling deanery the court was to be held in the parish church of West Malling.[149] There is no mention of the use of the Court Lodge at Longfield for this purpose. The articles for these visitations do not survive, but the churchwardens' presentments made in response to them do not declare any deficiencies in the interiors of their respective churches concerning the communion tables. However, as we do not have Plume's findings it is not possible to ascertain the true state of these matters.

The presentments of 1704 are also notable for their complete failure to present any of the parishioners for immorality, blasphemy or abuse of the Sabbath, although these matters would almost certainly have been in the visitation articles. As late as the 1780s the articles of the visitation of the Archdeaconry of London put these questions in detail.[150] The ecclesiastical courts had ample theoretical authority to take action in such matters and in Elizabethan and early Stuart times had been extremely busy with them. These courts had, however, been suspended during the Interregnum and never fully recovered their prestige and powers following the Restoration. Even so, there were still presentments for these matters until James II's Declaration of Indulgence in 1687 and the Toleration Act 1688. After 1689 churchwardens failed to present and were prepared to risk a possible charge of perjury; in thousands of presentments, they replied as did the churchwardens of All Saints, Rochester in 1704: 'nothing pleadable'.[151]

The failure of the ecclesiastical courts to address the morals of the nation with the attendant danger that it would fall under God's judgement led to demands for a reformation of manners from the churches and William III. The reformation of manners was aimed at controlling the poor, who were much more numerous in the 1690s owing to population growth, rises in bread prices and disruption caused by war, just at a time when the institutions set up for poor relief, the wardmote and the guilds, were in decline. Contemporaries did not recognise these socio-structural factors, but instead blamed individual moral and physical degeneration for the ills of prostitution, beggary, street merchants and 'other loose, idle and disorderly people'.[152]

To combat these ills the Church of England supported the setting up of various voluntary societies, including the Society for the Promotion of Christian Knowledge (SPCK) in 1698 and the Society for the Propagation of the Gospel in Foreign Parts (SPG) in 1701. Plume, as has been seen, was a providentialist preacher and believed that God's judgement on this sinful nation needed to be averted by moral reform. Part of his own response was to join the SPG, and he left it £100 in his will 'to be disposed of by them accordingly'.[153] He also joined the SPCK, but did not pay the membership fee.[154] It is typical of Plume that he would make his formal contribution to the reformation of manners to an exclusively Anglican body. As Isaacs put it:

> The Religious Societies, the SPCK and the SPG did not compete with the Church of England for moral influence over the laity; instead they were extensions of that Church. Any successes they might achieve would only redound to the Church's credit; for that reason the Anglican hierarchy gave them its unreserved support.[155]

Plume served under four bishops of Rochester and the influence of John Warner and John Dolben upon him has already been discussed above. Francis Turner was a notable Laudian and bishop of Rochester from 1683 to 1684. His father had followed Charles I and had been dean of Rochester. Turner was chaplain to James, duke of York, and while in Rochester he implemented weekly communion, indicating that he held a 'high' view of this sacrament. As bishop of Ely he was sent to the Tower with six other bishops for refusing James II's second declaration of indulgence. He refused to take the oath of allegiance to William and Mary. Plume would have been in sympathy with his royalist connections and probably with his 'high' view of the sacredness of his oath of allegiance to James II. He placed a portrait of James II in his library.[156]

Thomas Sprat (bap. 1635–1713) was bishop of Rochester from 1684 to 1713 and is chiefly remembered today for having written *The History of the Royal Society of London* (London, 1667).[157] In April 1688 Sprat complied with the reading of James II's second declaration of indulgence and accommodated himself to the new regime, taking the oath of allegiance and participating in the coronation of William and Mary. In his writing and preaching, Sprat emphasised the primitive quality of the Church of England and frequently attacked 'enthusiasm' much as Plume had done in his studies under Hacket. It seems, however, that Sprat's practice at the time of communion could be decidedly 'low', because at St Margaret's, Westminster (where he was curate and lecturer from 1679), the vestry minutes of 16 May 1683 (the year before he became bishop) required that he and others remain within the rails to administer the bread and wine and not to come out of them except for the infirm. In the politics of the Church, however, Sprat was a member of the 'High Church' party, with which Plume was in sympathy, as will be seen in due course.[158]

Plume in London: book buying, finance and personal relationships
Throughout his adult life Plume visited London frequently to attend to his business affairs in the City of London and to buy books there. As we shall see, he had other contacts further west as well: one in St Martins Lane 'in the Fields' and possibly also one in Westminster. From Greenwich, his parish for 46 years, he could have travelled to London either by water on the Thames or by road. He might well have travelled by boat when the tide served, as did Samuel Pepys on many occasions from the City and Whitehall to Woolwich, Deptford and Greenwich.[159] Plume had Watling Street as an alternative to the Thames: a good, straight road on which he could have travelled by coach. In 1701 one Richard Browne proposed that he and Plume jointly hire a coach to travel from London to Dartford if Plume was not using his own coach.[160] At his death Plume owned 'an old chariott of small value'.[161] The executor used this 'about the management of the Testators Estate'. Additionally, at his death there were in Plume's stables two horses that were returned to their owner, the bishop of Rochester.[162]

There is evidence that post was directed to Plume at the house of Lady Armine in St Martins Lane 'in the Fields'. Lady Mary Armine (1594–1676) was a wealthy widow who had been closely associated with the parliamentarian cause and was very religious. Nothing is known of Plume's relationship with her, but while she was far removed from him in religious sentiments (she was endorsed by Richard Baxter, who was arch-enemy to Plume's friend Robert Boreman[163]), she founded three almshouses just as Plume intended in his will.[164] Plume had another contact in London, Audrey or Anne Beale, who lived at Old Palace Yard in Westminster.[165] She was niece of Dulcibella Boreman, the first wife of Sir William Boreman (1614–86), clerk and clerk comptroller of the Green Cloth, and, as such, a member of the royal household.[166] William Boreman (1564–1646), Sir William Boreman's father, had also lived in East Greenwich and had been a member of the royal households of Elizabeth, James I and Charles I. Sir William Boreman was brother to Robert Boreman (d. 1675), Plume's friend and mentor.[167] Dulcibella Boreman and Robert Boreman both died at Greenwich in 1675 and were buried there. Sir William founded the Greencoat School in Greenwich in 1672 and the Greycoat or Roan School there in 1677. Plume was very closely associated with Sir William in the founding of the Roan School; he helped to fund it and was a feoffee and chairman of it until his death.[168]

As already noted, Plume began buying books for John Hacket in the 1650s and continued to do so until Hacket's death in 1670. Long before, and long after, however, he was also buying on his own account and building up the library of some 7,400 publications that he would eventually donate to Maldon, his birthplace. By 1698 he was making plans for the building of his library and its attached schoolroom and in 1699 he was presented with a gift of wine and

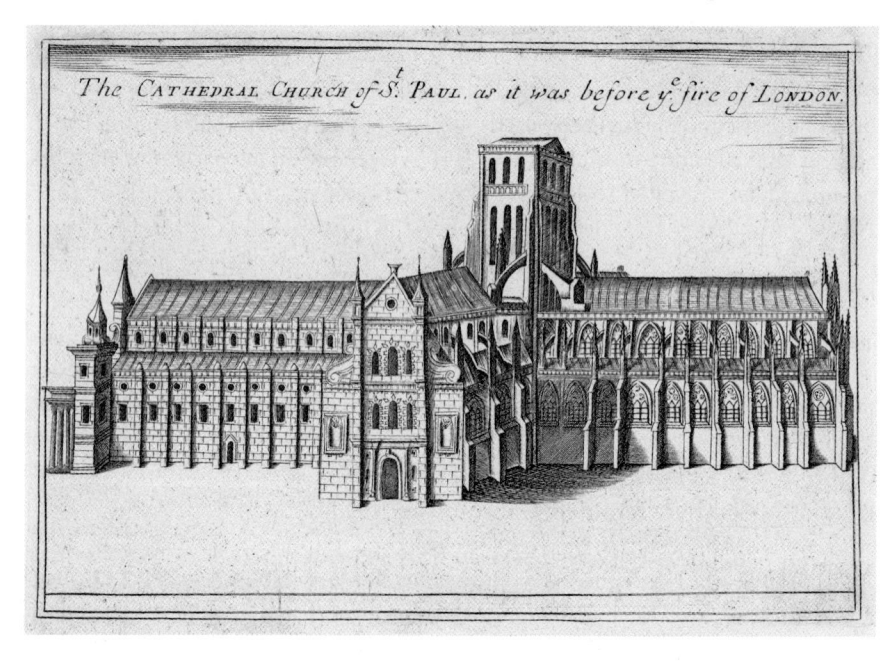

3.9 St Paul's Cathedral, destroyed in the Great Fire of London, 1666. The churchyard housed many printers and book dealers and was frequented by Thomas Plume. As the fire advanced many thousands of books were stored in the crypt for safety: all were destroyed. The present building was not completed until 1708, four years after Plume's death (LMA, Collage no. 5912).

3.10 (a) Inside the Royal Exchange before it was destroyed by the Great Fire of London in 1666 (b) The Royal Exchange after it was rebuilt three years later. Plume would have been familiar with both of these buildings (LMA Collage nos 6019 and 7223).

oysters by the Corporation of Maldon; it may be that this was the occasion when he presented the new building to the town.[169]

The centres of the new and secondhand book trade in London were around St Paul's churchyard (Figure 3.9) and in Fleet Street, and Plume would have spent much time there. Plume was also a man of business, who bought and sold considerable holdings of stocks and bonds, for which he would have had recourse to the Royal Exchange in Threadneedle Street (Figure 3.10) and nearby coffee houses in Exchange Alley, such as Jonathan's and Garraway's, where much business was transacted.[170] He held an account at the bank of C. Hoare and Co. in Fleet Street and the ledger shows that during May–August 1695 he deposited a total of £89 10s, which sum he had withdrawn by October the same year. All the entries are either 'by note' or 'to note' (perhaps indicating written instructions), but give no other details. Similarly, in December 1703 he deposited £80 and withdrew it all the following July. Hoare's also received a deposit of £19 5s 11¼d from Plume for 'ye fire att Newmarket'. Hoare's account for this fire opened in November 1683 and closed in November 1691. The fire occurred on 22 March 1683 and Charles II, who was in Newmarket at the time, issued a fire brief to many towns, which raised some £20,000 for the rebuilding of Newmarket.[171]

Living in Greenwich, Plume would have often seen the large merchant ships of the East India Company in the Thames. From its beginnings in 1600 the East India Company had become very big business indeed by the time of Plume's death in 1704, and he invested heavily in it from time to time.[172] It may be asked whether the trade of the merchant was compatible with the role of the clergyman. There was in fact a well-developed theology of trade to which the Church as a whole subscribed. Furthermore, towards the end of the century stock-holders constituted a very broad cross-section of society, including clergymen, gentlemen, widows, orphans, shop-keepers and many others. Plume was in good company.[173]

The will: personal beliefs and the summation of a life's work

Plume died on 20 November 1704, but the place of his death is unknown. Susan Edward infers from the accounts of his executor James Plume that it may have been in East Greenwich.[174] The following analysis is of the personal and religious content of this very long will of over 5,700 words.[175] The preamble runs as follows:

> Grant, Lord, that the effects [i.e. belongings] which out of your great goodness you have deemed fit to lavish on me may turn, no matter whose hands they come down to, to your glory. God direct me in the making of my last will, as may most make for his Glory, the benefit of his Church, & my owne soul's Good in the day of his great account.

In Nomine Domini Amen. I Thomas Plume of E. Greenwich D.D. Minister tho' most undeserving being in reasonable good temper of body, &, God be praised, of a sound & disposing mind, & memory, doe make this my last Will, & Testament, in manner, & form following. First, I humbly resign my spirit into thy hands, O blessed Jesu, who didst give up thy spirit into ye hands of thy Father, from thy body crucified for my sins, by which passion, I strongly hope, & trust, to have my many sins, (which I heartily repent of) forgiven, & that my soul, & body, shall escape ye due punishment thereof in ye world to come. Amen, Lord Jesu.[176]

The vast majority of will preambles are completely formulaic and tell us little about the testators' beliefs. There are, however, a relatively small proportion that are much more complex. For example, a small group of 'idiosyncratic and strongly flavoured dedicatory clauses' have been identified that do reveal testators' personal convictions.[177] Plume's preamble is clearly complex and idiosyncratic, containing as it does no fewer than 135 words contributing to its religious meaning (the vast majority of will preambles have only a handful of religious words). He mentions Jesus twice and refers to his sins twice and his desires to benefit the Church: that is, the Church of England. Thus, Plume's preamble is not a formula and is clearly an expression of his personal beliefs. It shows that he is very conscious of sin because he described himself as 'most undeserving' and required that on his tombstone should be the phrases 'the greatest of sinners and, I hope, of penitents' and 'you [?] who will restore me once more to the light of day', which is clearly a reference to the resurrection of the body.[178] Further evidence of Plume's devotion to Jesus Christ is to be found in a painting in the Plume Library of Christ as 'Salvator Mundi', showing him holding the world surmounted by an elaborate cross and giving a blessing.[179]

Anne Duffin's study of Cornish gentry wills between 1600 and 1660 led her to identify three types of phrase in will preambles, of which any two were 'indicative of a likely Puritanism': a 'demonstrable confidence in predestination'; 'a stated belief in physical resurrection' and 'emphasis on personal sin'.[180] Although brought up as a Calvinist, Plume seems not to have recorded any belief in predestination, but he clearly believed in physical resurrection and was convinced of his own sinfulness. However, as has been seen above, he was no Puritan, but in religious belief was not very far from some of them. This also demonstrates how individuals' complexity of belief goes beyond the labels many historians are only too ready to attach to them.

Can any more be said regarding Plume's churchmanship? Petchey states that the will and the books hint at High Church beliefs, maintaining that the library building itself makes a statement that access to learning is only via the Church (i.e. the tower) and suggesting that the construction was also symbolic of the relationship between the secular and the spiritual power in the kingdom.[181]

However, no documentary evidence has been traced to support the suggestion. Plume's memoir of Hacket, written five years after his death, takes a very high view of the role and status of bishops from the opening dedication to Charles II: 'Long may your Majesty peaceably retain your rightful jurisdiction over this Church and State. Long may there be in it such Religious and Learned Prelates [as Hacket] placed by your Majesty in Higher Spheres, free from Parity and Poverty.'[182] This is a vision of the bishop as appointed by the king, not elected as a senior presbyter, a prince of the Church, wealthy and powerful. The word 'Higher' in this context suggests a 'high' view of the role of the bishop – that is, as one exercising power by divine right.[183] Spurr identifies a group of biographies written at this time that share a similarly high view of the rank and responsibilities of the bishops, including Hacket's biography of John Williams and Plume's biography of Hacket, to which he gives the term 'patristic fantasies', indicating that the claims contained in them were intended to support this particular view of the episcopacy, which was not shared by all bishops.[184]

The phrase 'High Church' is difficult to define because it has meant different things at different times. From the Elizabethan settlement there were those within the Church who took a 'high' view of the role of bishops, the value of the sacraments and the authority of the Church; Hacket and, through him, Plume inherited this tradition. During the Restoration there were those whom Spurr calls 'high prelatists' but they did not dominate the politics of the Church and they coexisted with those who were 'unable to accept such an elevated view of episcopacy'.[185] However, after 1688, this consensus could no longer be maintained and there emerged the High Church party (one of whose number was Thomas Sprat, bishop of Rochester), who became identified with the emerging Tory opposition. Plume, in the way in which he built his library and schoolroom, shared their vision of the Church and state in harmony, working together to ensure that both religion and the social order were maintained, but there is no evidence that he ever engaged in religious or secular politics.[186]

Plume bequeathed his pictures to his library and by far the largest of these, and evidence of the high regard in which Plume held him, is of William Laud (1573–1645).[187] Laud's career was marked from early on by his high-church views; even in his doctoral thesis he maintained that bishops were superior to presbyters by divine right. Laud was known as the 'English Cyprian', after St Cyprian, bishop of Carthage (d. 258), who was much studied during the Reformation because of his defence of the rights of a bishop against other bishops (especially the bishop of Rome) and against presbyters and the laity. Plume placed three copies of Cyprian's *Opera* (Antwerp 1541, Paris 1616 and Oxford 1682) in his library, as he did Peter Heylyn's biography of Laud entitled *Cyprianus Anglicus* (London, 1668). Cyprian was cited many times by those defending a 'high' view of episcopacy and it can be seen from the books in his library that Plume would have been well aware of this and of Laud's identification as the English Cyprian.[188]

Plume can also be linked to the Anglican view of the death of Charles I as a martyrdom. By Plume's account, Hacket refers to Charles as a martyr and goes on to report that his patron, John Williams, 'from the heavy time of the King's death', prayed every night at midnight on his bare knees: 'The matter of his prayer was principally this; Come Lord Jesus, come quickly, and put an end to these days of Sin and Misery. So much I learnt from himself and so I report it'.[189] Plume adopted the phrase 'Come Lord Jesu, come quickly' as his own and ended both his memoir of Hacket and his will with it. Further evidence of Plume's devotion to the martyred Charles comes in the form of the dedication to him of the book containing a sermon by a vicar of Kent on the anniversary of the martyrdom on 30 January, with which this chapter began.[190]

While this anniversary had begun to be observed from 1650 it was formally placed in the calendar of the Church of England from 1662, when the Office for King Charles the Martyr was included in the Book of Common Prayer. Spurr states that the office 'formed part of the experience of most of the population'. Kishlansky and Morrill go further and maintain that, with the encouragement of the government (because of the preaching against rebellion), these sermons 'became the property of the high Anglicans who renewed and reconfigured the Laudian ideals, and in due course became the defiant rallying cries of high tory clerics and nonjurors'.[191]

We have seen how Plume was born a gentleman; his father was an alderman, a JP and a leading citizen of Maldon for over 30 years. Plume went on to reinforce this status by becoming a senior member of the Church of England and acquiring a circle of friends that included a bishop, a knight of the realm who was also a member of the royal household, a number of senior academics, a judge and a noble lady. Plume indubitably rose higher in status than his father, as his status came from being closer to the centre of power at both diocesan and national level, whereas that of his father arose from his wealth as a merchant who had only local power in a small port town.

Plume's father, as an elder in the Dengie classis, helped to govern the local churches from 1642 until his death in much the same way that his son did in the Church of England from 1679 onwards. However, far from supporting parliament and the Presbyterian system of church organisation, Plume became a royalist and an Episcopalian who left behind his father's Calvinism and Presbyterianism and became, at least publicly, a committed Laudian, thereby opposing all that his father practised. We have no record whatsoever of their personal interactions, but we know that Plume senior died intestate, having transferred ownership of the family house to his younger son before his death between 1653 and 1658. According to the custom of Borough English, which was followed in Maldon at this time, Plume would also have inherited his father's other tenements and land.[192] The evidence of Plume's income and expenditure, as far as the Church is concerned, seems to indicate that he had substantial independent means with which to support his work in the church, and the most likely sources of this wealth were his family and his own business acumen.

Notes

1. M. Buck, *An Anniversary Sermon on the Martyrdom of K. Charles the First, of Blessed Memory. delivered on Jan. 30th 1701/2 by Maximilian Buck* (London, 1702) (TPL, B05871).
2. TNA, PROB 10/1387; transcribed in the Appendix: Dr Thomas Plume's will, l. 532.
3. ERO, D/P 201/1/1. Plume dated his baptism to 7 August 1630, using the Julian calendar.
4. J. Peile, *Biographical Register of Christ's College, 1505–1905* (Cambridge 1910), vol. i, p. 503.
5. TPL, B04640 (translation from the Latin by John Smith).
6. ERO, D/P 201/1/1.
7. ERO, D/ABR 8, f. 248, will of Daniell Peake; Peile, *Biographical Register*, vol. i, p. 503; A. Tuckwell, *That Honourable and Gentlemanlike House* (n.p., 2001), p. 23.
8. H.R. French, 'Plume, Thomas', *ODNB*; J.H. Brown, *Elizabethan Schooldays* (Oxford, 1933), pp. 96, 102, 131; Tuckwell, *Honourable and Gentlemanlike House*, p. 15; TPL, MA0117.
9. TPL, MA0066.
10. TPL, MA0096.
11. TPL, MA0066.
12. TPL, MA0096; Helen Kemp also deals with these early note-books in Chapter 8, pp. 199, 211.
13. H. Grieve, *The Sleepers and the Shadows*, vol. 2 (Chelmsford, 1994), pp. 38–44.
14. *Ibid.*, p. 49.
15. *Ibid.*, p. 55.
16. J. Walter, '"Abolishing Superstition with Sedition"? The Politics of Popular Iconoclasm in England 1640-1642', *Past and Present*, 183 (2004), pp. 82, 122–3.
17. ERO, D/AEA 42.
18. Grieve, *Sleepers and the Shadows*, vol. 2, p. 56
19. See the title of Walter's article at n. 16 above.
20. Grieve, *Sleepers and the Shadows*, vol. 2, pp. 55–6.
21. *Ibid.*, pp. 59–60.
22. *Ibid.*, pp. 60–63.
23. Tuckwell, *Honourable and Gentlemanlike House*, pp. 25–6.
24. Peile, *Biographical Register*, vol. i, p. 503.
25. J. Twigg, *The University of Cambridge and the English Revolution 1625–1688* (Woodbridge, 1990), appendix 1, p. 289. There were 2,091 members of the university in 1641 and 2,848 in 1651: V. Morgan, *A History of the University of Cambridge* (Cambridge, 2004), vol. 2, p. 120, n. 107.
26. TPL, MA0117; MA0118.
27. W.J. Petchey, *The Intentions of Thomas Plume* (Maldon, tercentenary edition, 2004), p. 6.
28. J. Peile, *Christ's College* (Cambridge, 1900), p. 161.
29. Those who conformed were able to retain their college posts, while those who did not were deprived of them. Twigg, *University of Cambridge*, pp. 91, 96.
30. *Ibid.*, pp. 90, 93, 103; Peile, *Christ's College*, pp. 126, 131, 163, 133–4.
31. Twigg, *University of Cambridge*, pp. 144–5; Peile, *Christ's College*, p. 163.

32 Twigg, *University of Cambridge*, p. 105.
33 *Ibid.*
34 TPL, MA0118 (unpaginated, folio nos given by this writer), fo. 1r; A. Clark, 'Dr Plume as a Cambridge Undergraduate', *ER*, xiv (1905), pp. 147–8.
35 TPL, MA0118; 'Rhegius Philosophy' is dealt with in more detail below.
36 TPL, MA0117; A. Clark, 'Dr Plume's Pocketbook', *ER*, xiv (1905), p. 11.
37 W.T. Costello, *The Scholastic Curriculum at Early Seventeenth Century Cambridge* (Cambridge, MA, 1958), pp. 11, 13–15, 31, 32, 35.
38 Costello, *Scholastic Curriculum*, pp. 42–3.
39 TPL, MA0117; MA0118.
40 Peile, *Biographical Register*, vol. i, p. 503; Clark, 'Dr Plume as a Cambridge Undergraduate', p. 147.
41 TPL, MA0117.
42 J.O. Halliwell-Phillips (ed.), *The Loyal Garland: A Collection of some Songs from the Seventeenth Century Reprinted from a Black Letter Copy supposed to be Unique* (London, 1850), pp. 20–1.
43 TPL, MA0117 (unpaginated, folio nos given by this writer), fo. 81r.
44 *Ibid.*, fo. 63r.
45 *Ibid.*, fo. 77r.
46 *Ibid.*, fo. 65r; 'L'Estrange, Roger (1616–1704)', *Concise DNB* (Oxford, 1995), vol. 2, p. 1775.
47 TPL, MA0117, fos. 73r, 79r, 65r, 63r, 75r; P. Morant, *The History and Antiquities of the County of Essex* (London, 1768), vol. i, book 1, p. 65.
48 TPL, MA0117, fo. 65r.
49 Pers. comm. Dr Karen Harvey, Sheffield University, regarding this poem, 8 July 2005.
50 D. Reynolds, *Christ's: A Cambridge College Over Five Centuries* (Basingstoke, 2005), pp. 53–4.
51 TPL, MA0117, fos. 2r–56r.
52 *Ibid.*, generally, but especially fos. 2r–56r; 'Peter, Hugh (1598–1660)', *Concise DNB*, vol. 3, p. 2363.
53 TPL, MA0117, fos. 91v–85v; J. Spurr, *The Restoration Church of England* (New Haven, CT, and London, 1991), p. 345.
54 TPL, MA0029; MA0119; J. Hacket, *A Century of Sermons* (London, 1675), prefixed by a memoir of Hacket by Thomas Plume, passim.
55 Petchey, *Intentions*, p. 7.
56 TPL, MA0029.
57 Petchey, *Intentions*, p. 7; Peile, *Biographical Register*, vol. i, pp. 405, 503; TPL, MA0029, fols. 10r and 82v.
58 B. Quintrell, 'Hacket, John (1592–1670)', *ODNB* (http://www.oxforddnd.com/view/article/11837; accessed 4 October 2004); B. Quintrell, 'Williams John (1582–1650)', *ODNB* (http://www.oxforddnd.com/view/article/29515; accessed 4 October 2004).
59 Hacket, *Century of Sermons*, p. xlviii, as quoted in Petchey, *Intentions*, p. 8.
60 W.J. Petchey, *A Prospect of Maldon 1500–1689* (Chelmsford, 1991), p. 156; see also Chapter 2, pp. 28, 36.
61 See this chapter, p. 66.
62 TPL, MA0029, fo. 67r. The present writer has allocated folio numbers.
63 'Buckeridge, John (1562? – 1631)', bishop of Rochester and Ely, *Concise DNB*, vol. 1, p. 382.
64 'Andrewes, Lancelot (1555–1626)', bishop of Winchester, *ibid.*, vol. 1, p. 54.
65 'Laud, William (1573–1645)', archbishop of Canterbury, *ibid.*, vol. 2, p. 1730.
66 TPL, MA0029, fo. 93v.
67 'Bacon, Francis, (1509–1579)', lord chancellor and philosopher, *Concise DNB*, vol. 1, p. 105.
68 'Brownrig, Ralph (1592–1659)', bishop of Exeter, *ibid.*, vol. l, p. 368.
69 TPL, MA0029, fo. 87r.
70 Twigg, *University of Cambridge*, p. xiii.

71 K. Fincham and N. Tyacke, *Altars Restored. The Changing Face of English Religious Worship, 1547–c.1700* (Oxford, 2007); see also this chapter, p. 77.
72 TPL, MA0029, fos 9v, 21r, 53r, 39r, 48r, 50v, 66r.
73 *Ibid.*, fo.1v.
74 *Ibid.*, fo. 2r.
75 *Ibid.*, fo. 49r, John Saltmarsh; B. Coward, *The Stuart Age, England, 1603-1714* (2nd edn, London and New York, 1994), pp. 266–7; Twigg, *University of Cambridge*, p. xv.
76 T.W. Davids, *Annals of Evangelical Nonconformity in the County of Essex* (London, 1863), p. 271.
77 TPL, MA0029 (unattributable due to damage), fo. 3r.
78 *Ibid.*, fo. 5v (unattributable due to damage).
79 *Ibid.*, fos 4v and 1v (unattributable due to damage), fo. 53r., Lucius Cary.
80 *Ibid.*, fo. 40v., Dr Bayly.
81 *Ibid.*, fo. 62r; Chapter 8, p. 210.
82 TPL, MA0119 (formerly MS 25); Clark, 'Dr Plume's Pocketbook', pp. 9–20, 65–72; idem, 'Dr Plume's Notebook', *ER*, xiv (1905), pp. 152–63, 213–20, xv (1906), pp. 8–24.
83 Clark, 'Dr Plume's Pocketbook', p. 65, quoted by Petchey, *Intentions*, p. 10.
84 Robert Boreman (d. 1675), royalist divine, educated at Westminster School and Trinity College, Cambridge (as was Hacket), published against Richard Baxter, *Concise DNB*, vol. 1, p. 289; S.G. Deed and J. Francis, *Catalogue of the Plume Library at Maldon in Essex* (Maldon, 1959), p. 22.
85 Edward Hyde (1607–59), royalist divine, educated at Westminster School and Trinity College Cambridge, published theological works, *Concise DNB*, vol. 2, p. 1536; Deed and Francis, *Catalogue of the Plume Library*, p. 92.
86 Appendix: will, ll. 67–77.
87 E. Hyde, *A Christian Vindication of Truth against Errour concerning ... 2. Of Priests Marriage ... by Edw Hide ... in Berks* (London 1659); T. Hodges, *A Treatise of Marriage with a Defence of the 32th Article of Religion ... Better to Godliness* (London 1673); *Book of Common Prayer* (London, 1662); J.J. Smith, 'Boreman, Robert (d.1675)', *ODNB* (http://www.oxforddnb.com/view/article/2903; accessed 1 June 2017).
88 J. Dent, *The Quest for Nonsuch* (Sutton, 1970, reprinted 1981), p. 198.
89 *Ibid.*, pp. 197–9.
90 Petchey, *Intentions*, pp. 6–8; P. King, 'The Episcopate during the Civil Wars 1642-1649', *English Historical Review*, 83/328 (1968), pp. 523, 533; J. Morrill, 'The Church in England 1642-9', in J. Morrill (ed.), *Reactions to the English Civil War* (London, 1982), pp. 99–101; 'Duppa, Brian (1558-1662)', *Concise DNB*, vol. l, p. 867; 'Plume, Thomas (1630-1704)', *DNB* XXII Supplement, p. 1146.
91 Petchey, *Intentions*, p. 8.
92 Wisbech & Fenland Museum, Wisbech Town Library A6.17. There is also a copy in the Plume Library: TPL, B00446.
93 T. Venning, 'Thurloe, John (*bap.* 1616, *d.*1668)', *ODNB* (http://www.oxforddnb.com/view/article/27405; accessed 20 July 2016).
94 'Plume, Thomas', *DNB*, XXII Supplement, p. 1146.
95 Hacket, *Century of Sermons*, p. xxvii; Petchey, *Intentions*, pp. 6–9; 'Plume, Thomas', *DNB*, XXII Supplement, p. 1146.
96 T. Doe, 'Thomas Plume was the Author of Two Bishops' Biographies', *Essex Journal*, 54/2 (2019), p. 66.
97 Hacket, *Century of Sermons*, p. ii.
98 Plume's italics. *Ibid.*, p. xlviii.
99 *Ibid.*, p. xlvii.
100 *Ibid.*, p. iv.

101 *Ibid.*, pp. ii, xlviii, xlii, xliii, xliv, xli.
102 *Compact DNB*, vol. 2, p. 2454.
103 Hacket, *Century of Sermons*, pp. xv, xxvi, xxxviii.
104 *Ibid.*, p. xliii.
105 *Ibid.*, p. xxxviii.
106 *Ibid.*, p. ii.
107 *Ibid.*, p. liii. Clearly, the 'Friend' must have been Plume.
108 Petchey, *Intentions*, pp. 6–7, 34 n. 9, 9.1; Morrill, 'The Church in England', p. 114; D.A. Spaeth, 'Common prayer? Popular Observance of the Anglican Liturgy in Restoration Wiltshire', in S.J. Wright (ed.), *Parish, Church and People Local Studies in Lay Religion 1350–1750* (London, 1988), p. 146; 'Evelyn, John, (1620–1706)', *Concise DNB* (Oxford 1992; paperback edn, 1995), vol. 1, pp. 952–3; 'Plume, Thomas', *DNB*, XXII Supplement, p. 1146.
109 Petchey, *Intentions*, p. 34, n. 9.2.
110 *Ibid.*, p. 35, n. 10.1.
111 *Ibid.*, p. 34, n. 9.3.
112 *Ibid.*, p. 34, n. 9, 10.
113 TPL, MA0107, A.21, 23–39; MA0108, B.1–29, 39, 48; MA0109, C. 27–32, 34, 39, 48; MA0110, D.1, 42.
114 Petchey, *Intentions*, p. 34, n. 9.4.
115 LMA/4442/02/01/01/001, Orders of Mr Roanes Schoole, minute no. 48.
116 Appendix, will, ll. 105–6.
117 Nektarios, *Nectarii … Confutatio Imperii Papae in Ecclesiam*, trans. by P. Allix (London, 1702) (copy in TPL, B02626); Appendix: will, ll. 107–8.
118 V. Larminie, 'Allix, Peter (1641–1717)', *ODNB* (http://www.oxforddnb.com/view/article/407; accessed 4 November 2004); F.L. Cross, *Oxford Dictionary of the Christian Church* (Oxford, 1975), p. 943; 'Cross, Nectarius (1605–c.1680)'; Petchey, *Intentions*, p.11.
119 J. Sidway, *The Reasons of the Conversion of Mr John Sidway from the Romish to the Protestant Religion …* (London, 1681), page not numbered.
120 'Plume, Thomas', *DNB*, Supplement XXII, p. 1146; LMA, P78/ALF/001-2, St Alfege, Church Street, Greenwich, parish registers (on microfilm X094/109); GHC, G. 1A/2.1, Greenwich parish churchwardens accounts, 1616–1663; G. 1A/1.1, Greenwich parish overseers accounts, 1690–1703.
121 E. Hasted, *The History and Topographical Survey of the County of Kent*, vol. 1 (Canterbury, 1778), pp. 372–420; vol. 3 (1790), pp. 477–81.
122 'Plume, Thomas', *DNB*, Supplement XXII, p. 1146; H.R French, 'Plume, Thomas (bap.1630, d.1704)', *ODNB* (http://www.oxforddnb.com/view/article/22395; accessed 4 October 2004); R. Newcourt, *Repertorium Ecclesiasticum Parochiale Londinense* (London, 1710), vol. ii, pp. 235–8, 442–4, where the incumbent 1678–87 was recorded as Joseph Plume.
123 *Cal. S.P. Dom.*, 1637/8, p. 6; TNA, SP 28/355/3, accounts of the revenues of Rochester Cathedral, 1644–6; R. Gilbert, *The Clerical Guide and Ecclesiastical Directory* (London, 1836), p. xxxv.
124 TNA, C 6/348/11.
125 *Cal. S.P Dom.*, Charles II, vol. 10, 1670, p. 105.
126 https://en.wikipedia.org/wiki/HMY_Mary (accessed 1 August 2016).
127 *Cal. S.P. Dom.*, William III, vol. 11, 1700, p. 142.
128 *Journals of the House of Commons*, vol. 23 (London, 1803), pp. 18, 422, 591.
129 *Cal. S.P. Dom.*, Charles II, vol., 20, 1678, pp. 333, 339.
130 TPL, MA0111, E.49.
131 E. Chamberlayne, *Angliae Notitia, or the Present State of England … Time, Part 1* (London, 1687), pp. 137–8, 157–8 (TPL, PP1981); R.O. Bucholz, *The Database of Court Officers, 1660–1837*, available online at http://www.courtofficers.ctsdh.luc.edu (accessed 26 July 2016).

132 MAC, DRc/Arb/2, The Red book, Thomas Plume 1679, pp. 86–88a; MAC, RCA/O2/1, Register of Freemen 1663–1711, microfilm 375.
133 MAC, DRc/Ac/2/2, Chapter book 1, No. 2, cited in R. Austin and P. Seary, 'The Old Archdeaconry. The Precincts, Rochester, Kent', unpublished historic buildings appraisal, Canterbury Archaeological Trust (Canterbury, 2011), p. 8.
134 TNA, C 6/348/11.
135 Hasted, *History of Kent*, vol. 1, p. 273; this chapter, p. 79.
136 S. Wright, 'Dolben, William (1588?–1631)', *ODNB* (http://www.oxforddnb.com/view/article/7778; accessed 10 August 2004); A.M. Coleby, 'Dolben, John (1625–86)', *ODNB* (http://www.oxforddnb.com/view/article/7775; accessed 4 November 2004).
137 Cross, *Oxford Dictionary of the Christian Church*, p. 79.
138 I. Green, 'Warner, John (bap. 1581, d. 1666)', *ODNB* (http://www.oxforddnb.com/view/article/28758; accessed 13 October 2004).
139 Fincham and Tyacke, *Altars Restored*, p. 306.
140 *Articles of Visitation and Inquiry Concerning Matters Ecclesiasticall according to the Laws and Canons of the Church of England Exhibited to the Ministers, Church-Wardens and Sidemen of every parish within the Diocese of Rochester, by the Right Reverend Father in God, John, Lord Bishop of Rochester* (1662) (TPL, B01701).
141 Fincham and Tyacke, *Altars Restored*, p. 323.
142 *Articles of visitation* (TPL, B01701).
143 F. Hull (ed.), *Dr John Warner's Visitations of the Diocese of Rochester, 1663 and 1670* (Kent Archaeological Society, new ser., 1, Maidstone, 1991).
144 Fincham and Tyacke, *Altars Restored*, p. 321.
145 *Ibid.*
146 Hull, *Dr John Warner's Visitations*, pp. 134, 155, 125, 130, 137, 149, 153, 187, 126, 158; G.V. Bennett, *The Tory Crisis in Church and State 1688–1730: The Career of Francis Atterbury Bishop of Rochester* (Oxford, 1975), p. 202.
147 See this chapter, p. 65.
148 A. Tarver, *Church Court Records* (Chichester, 1995), p. 3.
149 KHLC, DRa/VpM1, citation for a visitation of the Deanery of Malling, and DRa/VpRl, citation for a visitation of the Deanery of Rochester (both transcribed and translated by Dr P. Franklin).
150 ERO, D/DCm Q1.
151 F.G. Emmison, *Elizabethan Life: Morals and the Church Courts* (Chelmsford, 1973), p. vii; T. Isaacs, 'The Anglican Hierarchy and the Reformation of Manners 1688–1738', *Journal of Ecclesiastical History*, 33/3 (1982), p. 395; KLHC, DRa/VpR 1.
152 R.B. Shoemaker, 'Reforming the City: The Reformation of Manners Campaign in London 1690–1738', in L. Davison, T. Hitchcock, T. Keirn and R.B. Shoemaker (eds), *Stilling the Grumbling Hive* (Stroud, 1992), pp. 99, 100, 114.
153 *A Collection of Papers printed by Order of the Society for the Propagation of the Gospel in Foreign Parts* (London, 1715), p. 76; Appendix: will, ll. 114–15.
154 Chapter 4, pp. 107, 111.
155 Isaacs, 'The Anglican Hierarchy', p. 393.
156 A.I. Pearman, *Diocesan Histories: Rochester* (London, 1897), pp. 293–5.
157 TPL, B01249.
158 J. Morgan, 'Sprat, Thomas (bap.1635, d.1713)', *ODNB* (http://www.oxforddnb.com/view/article/26173; accessed 8 November 2004); TPL, B04512, B05009, B05992, B02875, B02859, B03218, B02521, BO3522, B02471; Spurr, *The Restoration Church*, p. 380. There are nine more of Sprat's books in the Plume Library.
159 C. Tomalin, *Samuel Pepys: The Unequalled Self* (London, 2002), p. 138; above, this chapter Fig. 3.6.

160 TPL, MA0111, Bundle E.11 (11 December 1701).
161 A chariot was a light four-wheeled vehicle with only back seats.
162 TNA, C 6/348/11.
163 R. Boreman, *Hypocrasie Unvailed and Jesuitisme Unmasked* (1662). Not in TPL.
164 TPL, MA0111, E.8 (undated); J. Eales, 'Armine, Mary Lady Armine (1594–1676)', *ODNB* (http://www.oxforddnb.com/view/article/648; accessed 2 September 2016); Appendix: will, ll. 46–53.
165 Chapter 4, pp. 104, 105 for further details.
166 Chamberlayne, *Angliae Notitia*, pp. 167–8.
167 See Chapter 8 regarding his manuscripts collected by Plume.
168 J.J. Smith, 'Boreman, Robert (d.1675)', *ODNB* (http://www.oxforddnb.com/view/article/2903; accessed 1 June 2017); J.W. Kirby, *History of the Roan School (The Greycoat School) and its Founder* (London, 1929), pp. 17, 35–44.
169 Petchey, *Intentions*, pp. 11–12.
170 R.C. Michie, *The London Stock Exchange: A History* (Oxford, 1999), pp. 20, 22.
171 Inf. from P. Hunter, archivist Hoare's Bank, customer ledgers 2, fo. 56, and 5, fo. 340; www.sawstonhistory.org.uk/mar-2015-meetingreport.htm (accessed 17 August 2016).
172 Chapter 4, p. 99.
173 K.N. Chaudhuri, *The English East India Company: The Study of an Early Joint-Stock Company 1600–1640* (London, 1965), p. 49; N. Glaisyer, *The Culture of Commerce in England 1660–1720* (Woodbridge, 2006), p. 69.
174 For full details, see Chapter 4, pp. 97–99.
175 Appendix: will, ll. 11–15.
176 *Ibid.*, ll. 26–9; Latin translation by Andrew Doe.
177 N. Goose and N. Evans, 'Wills as an Historical Source', in T. Arkell, N. Evans and N. Goose (eds), *When Death Do Us Part: Understanding and Interpreting the Probate Records of Early Modern England* (Oxford, 2000), pp. 54–7.
178 Appendix: will, ll. 26–9.
179 TPL, uncat., catalogue of pictures (unpublished), states a sixteenth-century date, follower of Memline.
180 A. Duffin, quoted in Goose and Evans, 'Wills as an Historical Source', p. 57.
181 Petchey, *Intentions*, pp. 12, 31.
182 Hacket, *Century of Sermons*, Epistle Dedicatory.
183 Petchey, *Intentions*, p. 31.
184 Spurr, *The Restoration Church*, p. 161 and n. 228.
185 *Ibid.*, p. 163.
186 *Ibid.*, pp. 380–1.
187 Appendix: will, l. 135.
188 A. Milton, 'Laud, William (1573–1645)' *ODNB* (http://www.oxforddnd.com/view/article/16112; accessed 4 October 2004); Cross, *Oxford Dictionary of the Christian Church*, p. 363; TPL, *Opera*, B06548; *Opera*, B04270; *Opera*, B00616; P. Heylyn, *Cyprianus Anglicus ... till his death* (London, 1668) (TPL, B04068); Spurr, *The Restoration Church*, pp. 130, 153, 159, 161; Petchey, *Intentions*, p. 31.
189 J. Hacket, *Scrinia Reserata: a Memorial off'rd to the Great Deservings of John Williams, DD, who some time held the Places of Ld Keeper of the Great Seal of England, Ld Bishop of Lincoln, and Lord Archbishop of York. Containing a Series of the Most Remarkable Occurrences and Transactions of his Life, in Relation to both Church and State* (London, 1693) (TPL, B00489) (published posthumously), pp. 225, 226.
190 Petchey, *Intentions*, p. 31; Appendix: will, l. 460; Hacket, *Century of Sermons*, p. liv; Buck, *An Anniversary Sermon on the Martyrdom of King Charles First*.

191 A. Lacey, 'The Office for King Charles the Martyr in the Book of Common Prayer, 1662–1685', *Journal of Ecclesiastical History*, 53/3 (2002), pp. 510, 517; Spurr, *The Restoration Church*, pp. 104, 241; M.A. Kishlansky and J. Morrill, 'Charles I (1600–1649)', *ODNB* (http://www.oxforddnb.com/view/article/5143; accessed 26 July 2005). The non-jurors were the six bishops and 400 clergy ejected from the church because they could not swear the Oaths of Allegiance to William and Mary in 1688.

192 Chapter 2, p. 30.

Chapter 4

'Concerning the trifles of my worldly goods': the making and execution of Dr Thomas Plume's last will and testament

Sue Edward

On 2 September 1704, no doubt with the knowledge that his death could not be far off, Dr Thomas Plume signed his will (Figure 4.1).[1] Witnessed by his attorney, Thomas Power, one of his East Greenwich tenants, William Dawes, and Francis Gillett, an East Greenwich parishioner, the original version comprised 19 pages covering 71 bequests. Two codicils were added on 20 October and 4 November, revoking three of the bequests but adding a further eight, bringing the total to 76.

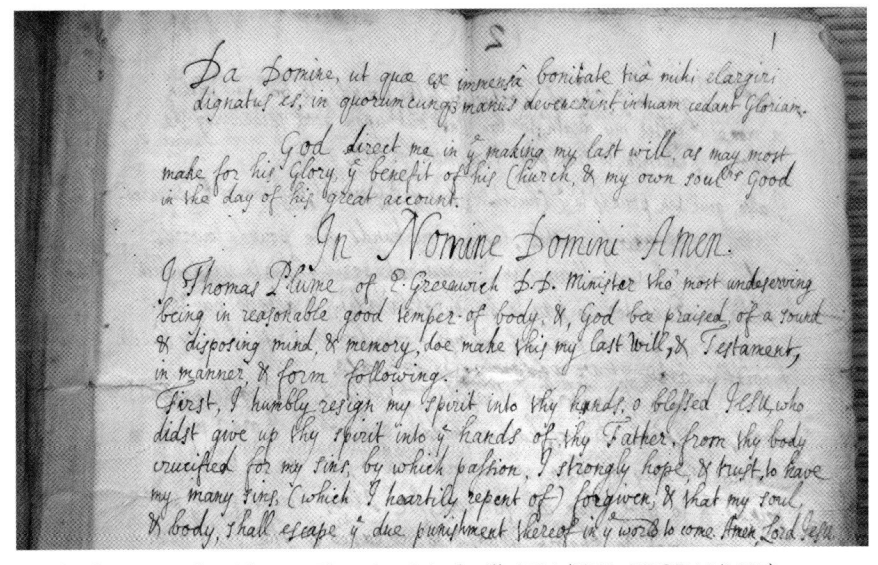

4.1 The first page of Dr Thomas Plume's original will, 1704 (TNA, PROB 10/1387).

This chapter explores the making and execution of Dr Plume's will. First, it examines his choice of executor and trustees, tasked with implementing his wishes, and some of the obstacles they encountered. Then it discusses the many bequests, with particular comment on Plume's legacies for the church, the relief of poverty and the provision of education, where not covered elsewhere in this volume. Finally, a brief summary is given of those bequests that were implemented, flourished and still survive today, those that started but for various reasons failed or have been subsumed into other guises over the last three centuries and those few that never got off the ground.

While this was indeed Dr Plume's last will, several references suggest that a previous version may have existed a decade earlier. An undated draft letter in Plume's hand exists within his archive papers in the Plume Library, which, although difficult to read, appears to refer to an 'att[empt] to rob me of … life and all I have' and makes references also to 'my keys and my will' and to 'Shipsid'.[2] The letter was probably concerned with events that led to the trial on 28 August 1695 of one John Collins, who 'was indicted of a Misdemeanor, for that he, with one George Shipside, not yet taken, did conspire to poison Thomas Plume Dr of Divinity, but it pleased God that it was timely prevented'.[3] Collins was found guilty, fined 100 marks (£66 13s 4d) and ordered to 'stand in the pillory without Temple Bar, at the Maypole in the Strand, and at Charing Cross and to find sureties for his good behaviour and to remain in prison till he pay the same'.

Further research has so far failed to discover more information about this incident. It seems clear, however, that Dr Plume was conscious of the potential for challenge with regard to a previous or a forged will, as he stated in his 1704 will that he renounced 'all other pretended wills, or Deeds of Gift, or bonds, or judgements, which I hear the Shipsides falsely and impudently pretend. Professing before God … I never made them any such, though I have forgiven him an hundred pound bond, or two, made to mee.'[4] Plume was a man of means for the last decades of his life and this was the first of several controversies concerning how he left his estate.

A long and complex will
The length of the will and number of bequests present, at first sight, much confusion, leading the Maldon historian W.J. Petchey to conclude that its 'disorderly composition … shows us a busy man surprised by the imminence of his death and without a clear knowledge of the extent of his possessions'.[5] Certainly the original copy of the will would seem to support this conclusion. It is written in a number of different hands. Two hands (A and B, see Appendix), perhaps of clerks to Plume's attorney Thomas Power, account for the majority of the text, the content of which may have been dictated by Plume in person. A third, unidentified, hand (D) made some minor amendments to the text

written by hand A, some of which are dated 28 December 1703.[6] This all suggests that the will may have been prepared in two main sittings and that Dr Plume had been thinking for some time about what he wanted done with his estate. The second part of the will, written by hand B, refers to investments made in July 1704. It would seem that, while ill health may have prompted him to start the process of composition, the compilation of the text took place over a number of months, possibly even as much as a year or more. A further hand (C) is Dr Plume's own. He clearly went through the text in detail, including the codicils, the second of which was written only two weeks before his death. He made a number of alterations and some extensive additions. Plume's will was in his room when he died, so it is possible that he made additions on an ad hoc, and maybe even unwitnessed, basis.[7]

We know that Dr Plume's plans for the library in Maldon had been underway for some years and his will reflects detailed thinking about the appointment of appropriate trustees and the financing of his trusts.[8] And, before Dr Plume's changes, it had an overall 'shape'. Following the preamble and arrangements for his funeral, the will covers bequests relating to East Greenwich and personal bequests to relatives, friends and servants, before turning to Maldon, and Essex bequests more generally, including detailed instructions concerning the library, the workhouse and various bequests relating to education. These elements are then followed by a series of bequests concerning Kent, some of which, such as the provision of lectures, exactly mirror the provisions for Essex. Finally, there is the section dealing with the setting up of the Cambridge professorship and observatory and a series of bequests to his executor James Plume. This suggests that there was originally a clear, logical sequence of thought. However, as the length of time that the will was in draft extended, Dr Plume seems to have been tempted to tinker with and add to the text, in response either to developments in his thinking or to items he had forgotten. It may have been quite a relief to Mr Power, his attorney, when Dr Plume signed the will in September 1704.

Nonetheless, it seems that even then some matters had been overlooked. The two codicils deal with matters that were clearly afterthoughts, such as the bequest to clothe and teach two boys at the Grey Coat School in Greenwich, where Dr Plume had been chairman of the trustees for over 25 years, but which had not been mentioned previously.[9] The evidence seems to suggest that Dr Plume disposed of his estate according to the overall plans he had been making for several years, although the fine details were still being hammered out in his final weeks of life.

Dr Plume died on Monday 20 November 1704. The place of his death is unknown, although we may infer from his executor James Plume's accounts that it took place in East Greenwich.[10] It is unclear whether James Plume was present at the death, although his accounts show that he paid 16s on that day

4.2 Dr Thomas Plume's tomb in the churchyard of St Mary Magdalene, Longfield (Kent).

for the hire of a coach, presumably to take him to Dr Plume's house, and for other expenses. Certainly present at Dr Plume's deathbed were his servants and Mrs Audrey Beale, as the latter later recalled being in the room with the servants and going into the kitchen after the death to take some refreshments with them.[11]

Naturally James Plume's first priority was to arrange the funeral, which took place on Friday 24 November.[12] In his will Dr Plume stipulated that he should be buried at Longfield, the location of his archdeacon's residence, and James Plume's accounts showed that he travelled there the previous day, paying fees to the minister and parish clerk for the funeral. As James Plume seems to have followed the will's instructions closely, we may imagine the 'small attendance' of neighbouring ministers gathered around the graveside to the south-east of the church.[13] Further bills relating to the funeral were settled on 29 November and over the next six months two additional payments were made for the erection of the brick tomb and the gravestone (Figure 4.2).[14]

Executor and trustees
We know from Mrs Beale that at some point soon after Dr Plume's death his will was read publicly by Dr Francis Thompson.[15] The fate of the assets and real estate that Thomas Plume had accumulated over his long life was now in the hands of his executor and trustees. Dr Plume entrusted the disposal of

his estate to a single executor, James Plume, whom he described as his cousin, although it has not proved possible to establish the exact relationship between the two men.[16] James was baptised on 3 July 1670 at Wandsworth, the son of Nicholas Pluym, scarlet dyer, and it seems likely that they were descendants of the Plume family of Great Yeldham, who had become London woollen drapers and dyers.[17] In the years prior to Dr Plume's death James seems to have had close connections with him. Although resident in Lambeth, James was married, presumably by Dr Plume, to widow Anna Singleton at St Alfege's Church in East Greenwich on 4 June 1702.[18] He had also acted financially on Plume's behalf by making a payment of £1,000 on his account to the United East India Company on 28 July 1704.[19] Both men held accounts at Hoare's Bank.[20]

Like his father, James Plume was a scarlet dyer. Within the dyeing trade scarlet was the brightest, most difficult and among the most expensive colours to create.[21] The inventory taken in October 1728 following James Plume's own death intestate indicates a man of means, occupying a large property in Vauxhall, with a dye house and stock including cochineal, argot, alum, madder and tin.[22] Among his debtors by far the largest was the East India Company, which owed him £1,258 at the time of his death. For some years he had been dyeing cloth for the company, either for export or possibly for uniforms. He was also a man of social status, serving as High Sheriff for Surrey in 1714, and he was a member of the vestry of St Mary's Church, Lambeth.[23]

Aside from James Plume, 66 men were charged with overseeing the disposal of specific bequests and the running of the trusts provided for within the will. Of these, 41 were clergymen, with the remainder being either associated with the church – such as the churchwardens of East Greenwich – or men of standing in the locality where the trust was to be administered. For example, the trustees for the library and workhouse in Maldon included the two borough bailiffs and six leading citizens who at various times served on the Corporation, the town's governing body. The detail of the trustees for the three major trusts – the Library and other Maldon bequests; the Stone Castle Charity; and the Cambridge professorship and observatory – are dealt with elsewhere in this volume, but it is worth noting Dr Plume's careful choice of individuals, geographically and professionally, as being those best placed to carry out his wishes. Although some are referred to by their position – for example, seven out of the 21 trustees for the Stone Castle Charity are described only by the title of their clerical livings – the vast majority are referred to by name and it seems fair to assume that most, if not all, of them would have been known to Plume personally as friends and colleagues of many years' standing.

One individual stands out as playing a significant role in the discharge of Dr Plume's will. Dr Francis Thompson was charged, along with James Plume and Dr Plume's curate Joseph Rawson, with arranging his funeral, carrying out several of his personal bequests and disposing of his household goods. He is named as a trustee for all three trusts set up by the will and, as we have already seen, he read out Plume's will to the assembled company following his death.[24] Dr Plume left Thompson £100,

> for his care, & pains in my affairs, & make him overseer of my Will, & a Trustee, for electing a Library-keeper, & all other Charities given out of my Estate, & desire him to convey all my Manuscript-papers of my own hand, to bee carefully preserved in ye study of the aforesaid Library.[25]

Although no personal correspondence between them has been found, it seems reasonable to conclude that Francis Thompson was a close, trusted friend and colleague of Dr Plume. Born about 1640, he was the son of James Thompson, a merchant of London and Amsterdam. Following admission in 1655 to Caius College, Cambridge, at the age of 16, he seems to have followed a predictable clerical and academic career path, culminating in becoming a Doctor of Divinity in 1680. He was rector of the united parishes of St Matthew Friday Street and St Peter Cheap in London from 1666 until his death in 1715, although this living must at first have been very challenging, as the Friday Street church was destroyed by the Great Fire in 1666 and only rebuilt, to a design by Sir Christopher Wren, in 1685.[26] In 1695 he was president of Sion College, a charitable foundation for the incumbents of City of London parishes, the same institution that Dr Plume charged in his will with approving future keepers of the library in Maldon.[27] Dr Thompson seems to have bequeathed his own books to Dr Plume's library, as a number have been found inscribed with his name. His nephew, another Francis Thompson, became the first library keeper and later schoolmaster at Maldon's grammar school as described in Chapter 5.

Implementation and legal challenges

From accounts prepared by James Plume for the period from Dr Plume's death to October 1707 it is possible to track many of his actions as executor, including his receipt of the grant of probate on 3 March 1705 and the extent to which he involved others named in the will.[28] During this period he gathered in money due to the estate, settled Dr Plume's debts and paid out the majority of individual legacies to family members, servants and friends. He also dealt with the majority of the cash bequests, such as the payment of £10 to the East Greenwich churchwardens for the poor of their parish on 29 November 1704; £20 to poor divines in the deaneries of Tonbridge and Malling in June 1705; £20 for the purchase of two silver flagons for the communion table at All Saints church, Maldon in December 1705; and £100 to the Corporation of the Sons of the Clergy in June 1706.

In the two months after Dr Plume's death James Plume concentrated his efforts on East Greenwich. Between 11 and 18 December he settled debts to local tradesmen, took an account of the goods and books in the vicarage and arranged for the removal of Plume's books, including the purchase of casks for this purpose. He then turned his attention to Rochester, visiting the city between 19 and 22 March 1705 together with Dr Thompson and Thomas Power. Here he again settled debts, paid a £50 legacy for the repair of the cathedral church and arranged for Plume's books at Rochester to be transported to, and warehoused in, London. It was only on 31 July 1705 that James Plume set out on a five-day visit to Maldon, again accompanied by Thompson and Power. The visit seems to have been timed to coincide with the formal setting up of the trust for the Library and Maldon charities, as he records paying £5 7s 6d for a dinner for the trustees at the Star in Maldon, 'where they declared their trust'.[29]

Implementing a will as complex as Dr Plume's was not straightforward and James Plume sought legal help early on. On 29 November, ten days after Plume's death, he paid £1 11s 6d to William Hall, serjeant at law, for advice, and on 5 December a further 4s 'in goeing to Councell ab[ou]t Testators Will'. He was right to do so, because the implementation of the will led to three cases in the Court of Chancery.

The first case was instigated by James Plume himself. Dr Plume had left a house he had purchased in Church Street, East Greenwich, to the trustees for Stone Castle to be used for the benefit of succeeding vicars of St Alfege, presumably by providing rental income. This was on condition that his successors did not sue James Plume for any 'dilapidations' to the East Greenwich vicarage. Dilapidations under ecclesiastical law relate to monies paid at the end of an incumbency by the incumbent, their heirs or executors to make good any damage or wear to the vicarage. But if there were to be any attempt to sue for dilapidations then Dr Plume specified that the house in East Greenwich should be given to James Plume to 'defend himself in law'. He must have thought that such an eventuality would not arise, as he stated that he had made the vicarage 'better than ever. Having laid out above two hundred pounds of my own proper estate to make it habitable, & keep it in sufficient repair'.[30]

On 19 March 1705 James Plume met the new East Greenwich incumbent Dr John Turner and the curate Joseph Rawson about the dilapidations and on 11 July he paid £1 1s 6d to a Dr Loyd for advice about defending himself against Turner.[31] Clearly the new vicar did not agree with Dr Plume's assessment of the state of the property and was prepared to take legal action. According to James Plume's petition to the Court of Chancery dated 20 February 1707, Turner then succeeded in suing him in the ecclesiastical court of Winchester for £103 4s 11d for the dilapidations, plus £10 for costs. In addition, the Stone Castle trustees were insisting that Dr Plume's will left the house in Church Street for the benefit of all successive vicars of East Greenwich, so the disclaimer about the house reverting to James Plume in the case of disagreement about dilapidations would not apply to Turner's successors.[32] How the case was eventually resolved is unclear, but we do know from James Plume's accounts that he paid John Turner the amount ordered by the ecclesiastical court on 15 July 1707 and that the vicarage house was rebuilt in 1708.[33] This would suggest that Chancery upheld the decision of the ecclesiastical court, and it seems that Turner and the trustees had to rescind all claim to the Church Street house, as this was listed in the property assets of James Plume in 1730.[34]

At the same time another more wide-ranging case was playing out in Chancery.[35] It was brought by the combined trustees appointed in the will: that is, those appointed to oversee the setting up of the Cambridge observatory and professorship, to administer the library, workhouse and other bequests in Maldon, and to run the Stone Castle Charity and related Kent bequests. All three sets of trustees made serious accusations against James Plume.

The Cambridge trustees had lost little time since Dr Plume's death in identifying an estate at Balsham, nine miles south-east of the town, on which the observatory could be erected. But when they approached James Plume for the £1,800 needed to purchase the estate he refused, 'until such purchase be approved of by this honourable Court pretending that he doth not understand whether the same be a good purchase or not'. In the meantime, the trustees contended, he was appropriating the interest from the capital for his own use. Following the Attorney General's ruling on the suitability of the estate and that any interest accrued should be paid to the Cambridge trust, James Plume's accounts show that he paid £1,800 for the Balsham estate on 17 January 1706, although no payments in respect of interest are recorded.[36]

The Maldon trustees had two points at issue. First, in his will Dr Plume had directed £400 to be used to purchase impropriate tithes or glebe land (that is, church assets that had passed into lay hands after the Reformation), the profits of which were to be used to augment the living of All Saints Church, Maldon.[37] In common with parishes throughout the country, the living of the united Maldon parishes of All Saints and St Peter had been underfunded since the sixteenth century. The problem had first been addressed in the 1620s, when the Corporation began making one-off payments to assist the incumbent, and in 1646 the Committee for Sequestrations granted £40 a year to augment his stipend.[38] Clearly Plume considered the income still to be inadequate in 1704.

However, the Maldon trustees had found that there were no appropriated tithes or glebe land in or near the town, and they therefore proposed to purchase other land to use for the same purpose. But James Plume contended that only the purchase of impropriate tithes or glebe land fulfilled the terms of the will and, in the meantime, the trustees alleged, he was using the interest from the bequest for his own purposes. Although the Attorney General had already ruled that in the absence of impropriate tithes or glebe the purchase of other land would satisfy Dr Plume's intentions, no payment to the Maldon trustees appears to have been made by the time James Plume's executorship accounts end in October 1707.[39] Subsequently, however, about 42 acres of arable land was purchased spanning the parishes of Tolleshunt Knights and Salcott, about nine miles north-east of Maldon. The rental income was used to supplement the All Saints living until 1886, when the land was sold and the proceeds invested.[40]

Second, and of even more importance to the trustees, must have been the question of the overall funding of all the Maldon charities. The Chancery documents make it clear that the income from Iltney Farm in Mundon, a parish adjoining Maldon, which Dr Plume had intended to fund a number of bequests, would be insufficient to meet the demands to be made on it. Accordingly, the trustees sought a Chancery ruling confirming their right to several of the other bequests in their favour for funding the Maldon charities, the largest of which was £2,000 invested in the East India Company. They also sought to confirm the provision within the will that any residue left from Dr Plume's estate after all debts had been gathered in and all legacies paid, plus any interest that had accrued, should revert to them.[41] How these questions were resolved is again unclear, but a payment by James Plume in October 1707 of £50 to Thomas Power 'on Account of Maldon Charityes depending in Chancery' demonstrates that the matter was still live at that point. The building of the Maldon workhouse does not seem to have got underway until 1716, suggesting that the trustees did not have the confidence to start implementing Dr Plume's bequest for some considerable time and with good reason, as their minutes of 19 August 1717 show them chasing James Plume for payment of £300 due to the builders that they had requested the previous November.[42]

The Stone Castle trustees were concerned with Plume's bequest of £120 to purchase 'some estate of inheritance for setling of five pounds p[er] an[num] for ever, upon the Rector of Longfield, and his successors'.[43] They had found an estate that would provide a yearly income of £6 in Longfield parish, but James Plume had refused to pay over the capital until directed by the Court of Chancery and, in the meantime, they alleged, he was profiting from the interest.[44] It is not known what happened as a result of the Chancery case, but it was not until 1734 that the trustees were able to purchase land and provide the £5 per year augmentation that Plume had wanted.[45]

In his answer to the trustees' allegations James Plume cited the complexity of the will and his need to protect himself in discharging his duties as executor:

'there are severall Clauses so Doubtfull and ambiguous That he could not safely act therein … without the Direccion of this Court and without being saved harmless and imdempnified for soe doing by the Power of this Court'.[46] He denied any use of the estate for his own ends and produced his statement of accounts relating to his executorship from the date of Dr Plume's death.

The combined trustees also seem to have used their Chancery case as an opportunity to quash attempts by members of the wider Plume family to call Dr Plume's will into question. Seven individuals are named, all of whom were descended from Dr Plume's uncle Samuel Plume of Yeldham, plus three spouses. Of these, Thomas Dorrell and Michael Howell had been left legacies of £10 each by Dr Plume. One, Dr Plume's cousin Nathaniel Plume of Yeldham, had been left a house, shop and land in Maldon. The trustees alleged that all ten 'combining and confederating themselves with … James Plume' were claiming title to Dr Plume's estate and 'give itt out in speeches sometimes that [the] said Thomas Plume did never make the said will and codicils and at other times that if any such will or codicils were made that he … was not of a sound and disposing mind and memory'. The trustees asked the court to require an answer from each person regarding their claim and these were provided in December 1706. Whatever the individuals may have alleged previously, all acknowledged the validity of the will.

There is only fragmentary evidence for the final Chancery case arising from Dr Plume's will. Again it was brought by James Plume, but only the answer of the defendant Mrs Audrey Beale, dated 5 June 1710, survives, although a summary of Chancery cases for the period produced in 1740 provides more information.[47] Mrs Beale, already discussed above in Chapter 3, probably became known to Dr Plume because she was the niece by marriage of Sir William Boreman, one of his parishioners, who in turn was the brother of Dr Plume's friend and mentor Robert Boreman.[48] She certainly knew him well enough to visit him in his last illness, as noted above, and was present at his death. James Plume contended that, while left alone in the room with Plume's corpse, she had inserted a legacy in her favour for £100 into the will. Mrs Beale denied this, saying that she left the room with the servants after Dr Plume had died. It was alleged that the legacy was interlined in the will by a different hand. Examination of the original will does seem to bear this out. A number of different hands worked on the will during the period of its drafting, but the writing of this clause is in a hand unlike any of the others (Figure 4.3). The legacy comes at a very odd place in the will, in the middle of a series of bequests concerning Maldon and Essex, evidently where there was some space on the page for an addition.[49] It is also for a large amount when compared, for example, to the legacies that Dr Plume left to family members, typically of £10 each.

4.3 Extract from page 8 of Dr Thomas Plume's original will, showing the interpolation in another hand of the legacy of £100 to Mrs An[ne?] Beale of Westminster (TNA, PROB 10/1387).

In the event the Court's decision, which came only in 1717, did not comment on the likelihood of forgery. It ruled that when the will was proved a reservation should have been made in respect of Mrs Beale's legacy, and the case was dismissed with costs against James Plume, who was told his remedy lay in the court in which the will had been proved, the Prerogative Court of Canterbury. Mrs Beale may have received her £100.

What are we to make of all this litigation? The extent of Dr Plume's personal wealth and the complexity of his will have already been highlighted and there is no doubt that these provided the opportunity for disagreement and dispute. What about the role of James Plume? Was he an executor trying to use his position to his own advantage or simply struggling with the size and complexity of the task? We know that he was involved in a considerable amount of other litigation from about 1700 onwards. There are 14 other Chancery cases on record where he appears either as an appellant or defendant, but this may not have been unusual for a merchant of his means at the time. When he died in 1728 the inventory of his estate showed that his debts amounted to £5,438, as opposed to £2,013 owed to him.[50] His widow and later her executors, following her death in 1747,[51] were still dealing with the creditors of his estate into the 1750s, but this does not necessarily mean that he was in financial difficulties in 1704. Within the list of James Plume's debts at his death is included 'about £700' still outstanding from Dr Plume's will. The Maldon trustees' minutes show that they sent Francis Thompson, the library keeper, to a meeting of James

Plume's creditors in Garraway's Coffee House in London on 2 February 1737 in response to a notice in the *Daily Advertiser*.[52] We will probably never know whether James Plume opportunistically used his position to his own advantage or was trying to do his best in difficult circumstances.

Certainly, the trustees, selected so carefully by Dr Plume, were key players in ensuring that most of his charitable trusts were enacted. They joined together to take prompt action to obtain legal rulings on their respective trusts via Chancery in 1706 and it seems likely that Dr Francis Thompson, as the one common member of all three trusts, must have played a key part in this and the resulting actions. Even so, progress was slow in some areas. For example, the Stone Castle Charity was not set up until 1710 and did not get underway fully for some years,[53] and the Maldon workhouse did not open until 1719. Nevertheless, over time the trustees did acquire the means to fulfil Dr Plume's charitable intentions.

The nature of Dr Plume's bequests

It is not possible to put an overall value on Dr Plume's estate at his death. The very large number of bequests in his will disposed of approximately £7,270 in cash and stock. Additionally, as noted above, he owned land in Essex, both at Iltney Farm in Mundon, on the Dengie hundred peninsula not far from Maldon, and within Maldon itself. In Kent he owned the manor of Stone Castle and the lease of land on the Isle of Grain with related income. In property he possessed eight houses and a shop with related rents and a mortgage. Of the real estate, only the value of Stone Castle is known approximately, as Plume stated in his will that it cost him £1,500 and its rental value was £74 a year. Plume envisaged that the income from Iltney Farm, the Stone Castle estate and, to a lesser extent, other land in Maldon and the Isle of Grain would be used to fund his charities in Essex and Kent. He had also arranged for the former St Peter's church building in Maldon to accommodate his library of approximately 7,400 books and pamphlets, plus the grammar school.

Out of the 76 bequests, 24 were personal gifts to family, friends or servants. These amounted to £1,368, approximately 19 per cent of the total cash bequeathed. James Plume was a major beneficiary, receiving £778 in cash and stock for carrying out the role of executor. Another £60 went to other family members. Only Nathaniel Plume was bequeathed property, all of it in Maldon, being given Plume's own house there, plus a shop with £5 annual rent and lands called Smithfields worth a further £14 a year and money lent out on mortgage.[54] It seems that Dr Plume wanted to continue his family's association with the town.

The vast majority of the estate therefore was left to charitable causes and was targeted on three main areas: the church and religious charities, with special concern for poor livings, poor clergy and their dependants; the poor, with a clear focus on providing means of betterment and rehabilitation; and education, both within the church and at all levels of secular society.

The exact division between locations cannot be determined without a value for the property bequeathed. In very broad terms Cambridge University received about a third of the cash available, to erect an observatory and establish a professor of astronomy and experimental philosophy. The remainder of the estate was distributed, probably not far off equally, between Essex and Kent. In cash terms the Essex bequests totalled £2,740 plus the Iltney Farm estate, further land in Maldon formerly belonging to a Mr Norton, the building for the library and school, the mortgage of 'Mrs Melsop's house', Dr Plume's books and pictures and the residue of his personal estate. Kent's bequests totalled £855 plus the Stone Castle estate bought for £1,500, four houses in 'Dog Kennel Row' and two further houses in Deptford, the lease of land on the Isle of Grain, money in the Chatham Chest of unspecified amount and the value of Dr Plume's household goods, excluding money, plate and books. Additionally, there was the house in Church Street, Greenwich, but as we have seen this was left only on condition that the next incumbent did not sue for dilapidations of the vicarage and it became the property of James Plume. It seems that Dr Plume had determined to benefit more or less equally all those places important in his upbringing, career and education. Only three bequests were made to causes that were not geographically based: for the relief of French Protestant ministers, the Corporation of the Sons of the Clergy and the Society for the Propagation of the Gospel in Foreign Parts.

Religious bequests
Out of the £1,495 in cash left to the church and religious charities only a small proportion, £95, was earmarked for the repair and maintenance of church fabric and only £100 to missionary work via the Society for the Propagation of the Gospel in Foreign Parts. Dr Plume's focus was primarily on addressing clerical education, the underfunding of small livings and the relief of poor clergy and their dependants. Clerical benefices were funded by parishioners' tithe payments. During the medieval period the patronage of many parishes were granted to monasteries, which had to provide for a cleric in the parish but could use any excess income as they pleased. Following the sixteenth-century dissolution of the monasteries the payment of tithes, instead of reverting to the parish clergy, became the income of those who bought former monastic property from the crown. This led to serious underfunding of many livings and clerical poverty, which Plume must have witnessed at first hand during his years as an archdeacon.

The income from the Stone Castle estate and Isle of Grain land were the means by which Dr Plume intended that poor livings in Kent should be augmented and opportunities for education increased. For Essex the income from Iltney Farm and lands was to make reparations to the church. He considered this appropriate, as 'The Farm of Iltny in Munden having been (as I have credibly heard) a Chantry land given to Maldon but alienated by King Henry ye eighth; I now restore, & give for ever to ye Town of Maldon'.[55] Dr Plume asked that any residue from the income from the Iltney estate should be paid by the Maldon trustees to poor ministers and their families in the Dengie hundred. Unfortunately, the income from the farm was rarely sufficient to meet the demands placed upon it and the Maldon trustees were only ever able to make grants to poor clergy for a very short period between 1856 and 1873.[56]

Dr Plume also addressed the relief of clergy dependants. His gift of £100 to Bromley College provided for the maintenance of clergy widows. The Corporation of the Sons of the Clergy, to which he bequeathed a further £100, was by its Royal Charter of 1678 dedicated to the support of clergy widows and children. Neither was the Church of England his sole focus. Poor French Protestant ministers exiled in England following the Revocation of the Edict of Nantes in 1685 were bequeathed £100.[57]

The library in Maldon and the provision of weekly lectures between Lady Day and Michaelmas there, as well as those in Dartford or Gravesend, may similarly be regarded as part of Dr Plume's legacy to the church. Although the library was intended to be available for use by 'any Gentleman or Schollar'[58] it was also available for the clergy both of Maldon and of the 16 Dengie hundred parishes, many of whom lived in the town partly because of the unhealthy nature of the peninsula's marshland. There they would gain access to a wealth of learning, mostly focused on theological issues.

The lectures provided opportunities for clergy to improve their scholarship by preparing their own presentations and by hearing their colleagues preach, but they were also open to the public. Between the Reformation and the Civil War there had developed a tradition of supporting public lectures in many Protestant market towns, with the objective of extending religious instruction and inspiration among the laity as well as promoting social order. These might be delivered in 'combination' by local and visiting clergymen or by public preachers salaried by local magistrates.[59] Additionally, Plume may have been drawing upon the principles underlying the late seventeenth-century 'Reformation of Manners' movement to enforce the moral principles of the Anglican Church. Certainly, the lectures became well established in both Kent and Essex and continue in modified form in the twenty-first century.[60]

How did Dr Plume's giving for religious purposes compare with that of his contemporaries? W.K. Jordan found that over the period 1480 to 1660 amounts given for religious purposes declined dramatically, to be replaced by secular causes such as the poor and education.[61] However, Slack and other critics have cast doubt on this analysis, pointing out that it is anachronistic to separate out lay and religious bequests because religion was an integral part of the early modern world view, with Christian duty being expressed in many areas of life apart from the overtly religious. Piety underlay giving to both, seeking to save the souls of the donors and those receiving their charity.[62] Doubtless these were part of Dr Plume's motivation too, but his religious bequests were more than that. As a professional churchman he focused them specifically on improving the situation and the performance of the clergy, their income and education, and the needs of their dependants and of church officers. Jordan's analysis of charitable giving in ten English counties categorised some 12 per cent of bequests as given to specifically religious causes.[63] In comparison, Plume bequeathed approximately 20 per cent of the total cash he left in his will to the church plus the largest proportion of his real estate. His priorities reflected his life's work and were significantly different from those of his peers.

Bequests for the poor
Within the will were 11 bequests specifically for 'the poor' or the less well-off totalling £2,385, or about 33 per cent of the total cash bequeathed. But of these only three legacies were outright gifts or 'dole' made to the poor of Rochester, East Greenwich and Stone, amounting to only £35, and there was only one other scheme to be set up, the almshouses for East Greenwich, which were for the poor with only the intention of relief. The remainder of the bequests all had some element of social improvement or betterment as part of their objective. For example, the gift of £50 'to bee lent out on good security' to five poor tradesmen in Rochester doubtless had the aim of establishing them more securely in business; the two annual apprenticeships for the poor boys placed at Maldon school would provide a start in a trade; and the gift of £10 each 'to the placing of ten Maids in marriage' would have been a good contribution to enable a couple a respectable start in married life.[64] Dr Plume's attitude to poverty as evidenced by references in his will to the 'most godly and deserving poor' seems to have mirrored that of the majority of his peers in regarding the relief of poverty as a God-given duty, but with discrimination in favour of the 'deserving'.[65]

By far the largest bequest for the poor was directed to the purchasing and provision of materials for a 'Workhouse for the poor of Maldon, Munden & neighbo[u]r Parishes'. For this Dr Plume set aside up to £2,000 from stock held in the East India Company, plus a further £200, the residue of his personal estate and 'the mortgage of Mrs Melsops house'.[66] This was a huge amount, particularly at a time when setting up work for the poor was not a popular cause among benefactors.[67]

According to Petchey, in 1689, when his study of Maldon finishes, poverty was not a pressing problem in the town. However, his conclusion was based

4.4 Engraving of Sir John Comyns, by George Vertue after an unknown artist, 1744. Comyns was borough recorder and MP for Maldon whose ideas for a workhouse in the town were commended by Dr Plume (NPG, D9375).

upon wills and the records of Maldon Corporation, as no records survive that can be used analytically to establish poverty levels.[68] Maldon had a population of about 1,000 in this period and Petchey reasoned that poverty was low because its artisan population was small and immigration was strictly controlled. Yet in the 1690s poverty increased sharply across the country due to bad weather, poor harvests and war with France, so the situation in Maldon may have changed. A clue to Dr Plume's generosity may also lie in his stipulation that the workhouse should be for neighbouring parishes as well as those in Maldon.

Dr Plume specified that the workhouse be set up 'according to Mr Commins's direction, & his draught, sent mee by Doctor Thompson'.[69] In 1704 the lawyer John Comyns was the Maldon borough recorder and an MP for the town (Figure 4.4). He had much in common with Plume, being a zealous Anglican, a member of the Society for Promoting Christian Knowledge, a subscriber of money to support parochial libraries and one of those who drafted the charter of the Society for the Propagation of the Gospel in Foreign Parts.[70] He was later knighted and was the builder of Hylands House near Chelmsford. His 'draught' no longer exists, but it is likely that it would have been based on Sir Matthew Hale's influential 'A discourse touching provision for the poor', which proposed that parishes combine their poor rates to purchase or erect a workhouse, purchase materials to employ the poor and instruct both adults and children in a trade or work.[71] Plume's copy of Hale's 'Discourse' is still held by his library and we can assume that he was familiar with its proposals, particularly as he specified that the scope of the workhouse should cover a number of parishes. Had his bequest been implemented in this way the Maldon workhouse might have been a forerunner of the approximately 600 workhouses established in England and Wales between 1723 and 1750 as a result of the Workhouse Test Act of 1723. This allowed the establishment of workhouses where poor relief would be provided either by an individual parish or by a group of neighbouring parishes acting collectively and sharing the cost. While the setting up of workhouses had increased during the 1690s in some of England's biggest cities, at its foundation the Maldon workhouse and its source of funding were unusual outside a larger urban context.[72]

More than a decade passed between Dr Plume's death and the implementation of his bequest for the workhouse. It was recorded in 1724 that for 'some Reasons, it was not thought proper to demand the Money ... of the Executor, for several Years after the Doctor's Death'.[73] No doubt the Chancery case described earlier in this chapter had some bearing on this delay. The Maldon trustees' minute book shows that a large timber-framed building was erected in Fullbridge Street in Maldon between 1716 and 1719 with payments totalling £908 16s 5¾d (Figure 4.5). This amount included £1 17s 6d for a 'raising dinner'.[74] Thereafter the responsibility for running the workhouse devolved to

4.5 Plume's Maldon workhouse, built *c.*1720, but with a frontage transformed by extensive later alterations.

the three Maldon parishes, All Saints', St Peter's and St Mary's. There was to be no uniting of parishes into a single workhouse authority, as recommended by Sir Matthew Hale and, contrary to Plume's wishes, no extension of the assistance afforded by the workhouse beyond the town of Maldon.

Records for the early years of the workhouse are sparse, as only the accounts of the All Saints vestry survive. Governors were employed to take charge of the workhouse, but they seem to have been a succession of widows employed on short-term contracts.[75] Peggy Edmond has suggested that this indicates that the workhouse was being run 'more like an old-fashioned poor house than what Thomas Plume had envisaged'.[76]

By 1741 the workhouse was in disrepair, with no governor in charge. On 16 November that year the All Saints annual vestry meeting resolved 'to put the Workhouse into Repair in order for the Employment of the Poor … and … provide a Person proper to take Care of & govern' it.[77] In the 1750s major alterations were carried out to the building, which Edmond contends turned it from a poor house into a workhouse, with space for inmates' employment. It is not clear precisely what this employment comprised, although an inventory of the workhouse contents records seven spinning wheels.[78]

By the end of the eighteenth century the average population of the workhouse was about 55 permanent and 125 occasional occupants.[79] In 1800 the governor fed the inmates at four shillings a week per head, while receiving the benefit of the workhouse garden and the profits of any work carried on by the inmates.[80] The cost of clothing the paupers was borne by their parish, but no uniform was imposed, unlike at many other institutions. Later the rising cost of poor relief cut the governor's allowance for feeding the inmates, but even in 1830 the bill of fare included hot meals on Sunday and Wednesday.[81]

Following the passing of the Poor Law Amendment Act in 1834 the Maldon Union Board of Guardians was created and on 10 February 1836 they accepted the valuation put forward by the three Maldon parishes of £840 for the workhouse and premises, plus £550 for other cottages and appurtenances, and forwarded their proposal for purchase to the Poor Law Commissioners for approval. Following outbreaks of serious illness such as cholera and smallpox it was recognised in 1870 that the building could not be adapted to provide isolation wards or comply with the requirements of the Poor Law Board of Commissioners. A new workhouse, now St Peter's Hospital, was built in Spital Road. The workhouse premises bequeathed by Dr Plume were sold in August 1875 and converted to private housing.[82]

Educational bequests

Dr Plume's bequests for educational purposes comprised £2,022, or about 28 per cent of the total cash bequeathed, plus the building for the library and school in Maldon and his books and pictures. The running costs for the library were to be funded by the Iltney estate income. Of the cash bequests by far the most valuable was the £1,902 12s 2d set aside for the building of the Cambridge observatory and the establishment of the professorship of astronomy there.[83]

Additionally, Dr Plume left £100 to his old college, Christ's Cambridge, on condition that they provide an annual exhibition of £6 'towards ye maintenance of one scholar educated at Maldon but if there bee none from thence to bee given to one educated at Chelmsford, & in default of both ... the County of Essex or at Brentwood'.[84] He bequeathed £20 to his old school at Chelmsford to buy books and create a library 'in thankfulness for my education there'.[85] Endowments were to be set up for six poor boys (later amended to ten by a codicil) of Maldon or Mundon to attend Maldon school, of whom two should be 'yearly put out apprentices either by sea, or land'. This also would be funded by Iltney Farm rents.[86] Two houses in Deptford were left to the trustees of the Grey Coat School in Greenwich (also known as the Roan School), where Plume had been the founding chair of trustees for 25 years. Five pounds a year was to come out of the income from his lease of land on the Isle of Grain, Kent, for the education of children there. The library and the lectures to be given in Maldon and in Kent, while intended to contribute to the education of the clergy, as we have seen, were open to all and Plume hoped to encourage attendance at the lectures by making available 'ten shillings at each of ye said two quarter days, to bee divided among ye most Godly indigent Poor of Maldon, that repair to this lecture, prayers, & sermon most constantly'.[87] Dr Plume made provision for education at all levels of society, no doubt seeing it as both a route out of poverty and, in the Puritan tradition of his upbringing, encouraging a learned laity.[88] While Doe points out that there is a clear bias in terms of educational bequests towards the better off, this is heavily skewed by the considerable bequest for the Cambridge professorship.[89] Plume's decision to make provision for the education of poor children may have been influenced by the Society for Promoting Christian Knowledge, under whom many charity schools were founded. Plume was a society member.[90]

The Maldon school, for which Dr Plume made available the ground floor of his library building and which was to educate his poor boys, had been made possible by Ralph Breeder, haberdasher and borough alderman, who left £300 in 1609 to 'maintain a schoolmaster to teach a grammar school' in Maldon. It was founded in 1621 and enjoyed widely fluctuating fortunes during the seventeenth century.[91] Plume himself was not educated there but instead at Chelmsford grammar school. The Maldon school was apparently housed in the converted St Peter's church in Maldon and, as described in Chapter 7, at some point in the late seventeenth century, probably in the 1690s, Dr Plume rebuilt the nave into a two-storey brick building to accommodate his library and the school.[92] His intention seems to have been to reinvigorate the grammar school in his home town and, although the school ran into difficulties in the late eighteenth and nineteenth centuries, it survived to become the modern-day Plume School.[93]

Scope and ambition

The summaries above and elsewhere in this volume attempt to outline the wide range of Dr Plume's charitable bequests, but how did they compare with those of his clerical contemporaries? An analysis of the 35 wills of archdeacons proved in the Prerogative Court of Canterbury between 1680 and 1720 and available for examination shows that 12 contain no bequests to charity at all. Of the remaining 23 wills, 20 contain between one and four bequests only, ranging from very small gifts to the poor of a single parish to larger bequests across several areas including gifts for the church, the poor and educational purposes. While it is very difficult to determine what proportion of each estate was left for charitable purposes, given often unspecified amounts and the problem of valuing property, there can be no doubt that the overall bulk of each archdeacon's estate went to their immediate family and that the percentage given to charity was very small – understandable, given that most were family men. Three wills stand out as different from the rest. The largest part of the estates of Timothy Halton, archdeacon of Oxford and provost of Queen's College (d. 1704), Humphrey Hody, also archdeacon of Oxford (d. 1707), and Edward Waple, archdeacon of Taunton (d. 1712) were left to educational causes, but in each case the majority of these bequests were for their respective Oxford colleges. Halton and Waple were both single men, like Plume, while Hody left a widow but no children.[94]

A further analysis of the wills of bishops and archbishops proved in the Prerogative Court of Canterbury for the same period has yielded similar results, even though the estates of these individuals were usually wealthier. Of the 24 wills available for examination, seven contain no gifts to charity, while 15 contain between one and six charitable bequests across a range of headings including education, the church and the poor. Again, the bulk of these estates was left to close family members, usually widows and children and occasionally siblings, nephews and nieces. The will of Seth Ward, bishop of Salisbury (d. 1689), a single man, has something of the feel of Dr Plume's will, as he left 13 bequests focused mainly on the city of Salisbury and encompassing gifts to the cathedral and its officers, to the poor, including an amount to the workhouse, and to the cathedral close school. The will of Thomas Tenison, archbishop of Canterbury (d. 1715), also contains extensive giving in its 14 charitable bequests. A number are to the same or similar causes as Dr Plume's bequests, such as the widows of Bromley College, poor Protestant refugees, the Corporation of the Sons of the Clergy and the financing of the school for 12 poor girls which he had already set up in Lambeth. Tenison's wife had pre-deceased him and he had no children.[95]

Unlike the majority of these men, Dr Plume was not only unmarried but also had no close family, his nearest relatives being his cousins or their children. In this respect it may not be surprising that he chose to leave the vast majority of his estate to charity, but, even so, compared with his peers and those of higher ecclesiastical office, the scope and ambition of Dr Plume's bequests must surely be seen as exceptional.

A lasting legacy
Despite the complexity of his will, Dr Plume's wishes regarding his earthly possessions seem, to a quite striking degree, to have been implemented by those entrusted by him. We know from James Plume's executorship accounts that almost all the personal bequests and one-off payments had been made by October 1707.[96] Research has identified that of the 76 bequests only four were not implemented at all. Of these the most significant was the bequest to the East Greenwich churchwardens of 'four Brick Houses in Debtford in Dog-kennel-row' to be used as almshouses.[97] This was never achieved and indeed the ownership of the properties by the church seems only to have been rediscovered in 1811, when the parish vestry agreed to apply the rent from the land to the Jubilee almshouses that had been set up in 1809, as being most in keeping with Plume's intentions.[98] There is also no evidence that the charnel house in the East Greenwich churchyard was ever built, even though James Plume paid the churchwardens the money bequeathed for this in June 1706.

There is no indication that Dr Plume's legacy of £5 a year 'to ye Curate of Grain, or any sober man, that shall teach their children at school there' was ever paid out.[99] Possibly the slow start of the Stone Castle trust meant that this was overlooked. Although it was queried with the Stone Castle Charity by local vicars in the nineteenth century their questions appear to have been ignored.[100]

Several undertakings established by the will have been subsumed into other entities and guises in subsequent centuries. The £100 left to Christ's College Cambridge for an annual exhibition for an Essex-based scholar was abolished by a royal commission and statute in 1860, with the annual sum assigned by Dr Plume being distributed among deserving students of the college.[101] As we have seen, the Maldon workhouse was transferred from local parish to Poor Law Union control in 1834, subsequently moved to Spital Road and became an NHS hospital in the twentieth century. The sponsorship of scholars at the grammar school and of apprenticeships has ceased, but the funds have become part of the Plume Educational Trust, which still benefits local students. The school room within the library building in Maldon served its purpose for many years, but it was outgrown and now houses the Maeldune Heritage Centre. Even the lectures to be given at Maldon and in Kent still take place in a residual form.

The main survivors of Dr Plume's legacy are dealt with in detail elsewhere in this volume. The Cambridge Plumian Professorship of Astronomy and Experimental Philosophy has had a long and distinguished history. The Stone Castle Charity continues to support the clergy of Rochester diocese and their families and the Maldon trustees continue to ensure that Thomas Plume's library survives intact and is accessible to both the public and academics, although the funding, scope and governance of both trusts have altered over the years. It is remarkable that the legacy of Dr Thomas Plume has been so long-lasting and is still influencing lives well into the twenty-first century. His bequests have made a positive and lasting contribution to the many localities of his personal knowledge and interest.

Notes

1. TNA, PROB 10/1387 (original will) and PROB 11/481/24 (probate copy). See Appendix: Dr Thomas Plume's will.
2. TPL, MA0113, G.3.
3. www.oldbaileyonline.org, v.7.0, Trial of John Collins, 28 August 1695 (accessed 15 August 2014).
4. Appendix: Dr Thomas Plume's will, ll. 422–7.
5. W.J. Petchey, *The Intentions of Thomas Plume* (Maldon, tercentenary edition, 2004), p. 25.
6. Appendix: will, l. 123.
7. TNA, C 6/362/46, Plume v Beale, 1710; W.P. Williams, *Report of Cases Argued and Determined in the High Court of Chancery*, vol. 1 (London, 1740).

8   Chapter 5, p. 120.
9   Appendix: will, ll. 518–22.
10 TNA, C 6/348/11, Attorney General v Bernard, 1706.
11 TNA, C 6/362/46. For Mrs Beale see Chapter 3, pp. 81–2 and this chapter, pp. 104–5.
12 TNA, C 6/348/11.
13 Appendix: will, ll. 16–29.
14 TNA, C 6/348/11.
15 TNA, C 6/362/46.
16 Appendix: will, ll. 16–17.
17 https://www.ancestry.co.uk: baptism James Pluym, All Saints, Wandsworth, 3 July 1670.
18 https://www.ancestry.co.uk: marriage James Plume to Anna Singleton, St Alfege, Greenwich, 4 June 1702.
19 Appendix: will, ll. 434–6.
20 For Thomas Plume: Hoare's Bank archive, Customer ledger 2, fo. 56; Customer ledger 5, fo. 340; Daily Cash Book (7 July 1684). For James Plume: Customer ledger 3, fo. 245.
21 D. Gerhold, 'Wandsworth's Industrial Transformation c.1634–90', *Surrey Archaeological Collections*, 95 (2010), p. 182.
22 TNA, PROB 3/27/188, Plume, James, Vauxhall, parish of Lambeth, county Surrey, esq. Anne Plume relict and adtrix, 17 October 1728.
23 *London Gazette*, 16 November 1714; 10 September 1715; TNA, C 11/2637/18, Fage v Bishop of Lincoln, 1717.
24 Appendix: will, ll. 17, 56, 84.
25 *Ibid.* 134–45.
26 J.A. Venn (ed.), *Alumni Cantabrigiensis*, vol. iv (Cambridge, 1927), p. 223.
27 Appendix: will, l. 152.
28 TNA, C 6/348/11.
29 *Ibid.*
30 Appendix: will, ll. 320–33.
31 TNA, C 6/348/11.
32 TNA, C 6/550/309, Plume v [unknown], 1706.
33 J. Kimbell, *An Account of the Legacies, Gifts, Rents, Fees & appertaining to the Church and Poor of the Parish of St Alphege, Greenwich in the County of Kent* (Greenwich, 1816), p. 22.
34 TNA, C 11/1486/32, Plume v Fleetwood, 1730.
35 TNA, C 6/348/11.
36 However, in the event, the observatory was not erected there: Chapter 10, p. 250.
37 Appendix: will, ll. 537–9.
38 Chapter 2, p. 41.
39 TNA, C 6/348/11.
40 ERO, D/CT 306A, B; D/CT 365A, B; D/DQs 137/3.
41 TNA, C 6/348/11.
42 TPL, MA0120, 19 August 1717.
43 Appendix: will, ll. 487–91.
44 TNA, C 6/348/11.
45 DAC, SCT, Indenture, the Revd Mr Lamb to the Trustees of Stone Charity, 7 May 1734.
46 TNA, C 6/348/11.
47 TNA, C 6/362/46; Williams, *Report of Cases Argued and Determined*.
48 Chapter 3, pp. 81–2.
49 Appendix: will, l. 239 (TNA, PROB 10/1387, p. 8).
50 TNA, PROB 3/27/188.
51 TNA, PROB 11/762/41, will of Anna Plume, widow of Clapham, Surrey (4 May 1748).

52 TPL, MA0120, 31 January 1737.
53 Chapter 9, pp. 235–6.
54 Appendix: will, ll. 91–6.
55 *Ibid.*, ll. 171–3.
56 TPL, MA0123, January 1856–July 1873.
57 Appendix: will, ll. 105–08, 541–4.
58 *Ibid.*, l. 161.
59 W.J. Petchey, *A Prospect of Maldon 1500–1689* (Chelmsford, 1991), pp. 213, 233–5; P. Collinson, *Birthpangs of Protestant England: Religious and Cultural Change in the 16th and 17th Centuries* (Basingstoke, 1988), pp. 40–7; P. Collinson, 'Lectures by Combination, Structures and Characteristics of Church Life in 17th-Century England', *Bulletin of the Institute of Historical Research*, 48/118 (1975), p. 209.
60 Chapter 5, pp. 124–6, 147; Chapter 9, pp. 232–3.
61 W.K. Jordan, *Philanthropy in England 1480–1660* (London, 1959), pp. 146, 297.
62 P.A. Slack, *The English Poor Law 1531–1782* (Cambridge, 1995), p. 42.
63 Jordan, *Philanthropy in England*, p. 368.
64 Appendix: will, ll. 39, 68–9, 509–10.
65 S. Hindle, *On the Parish? The Micro-politics of Poor Relief in Rural England c.1550–1750* (Oxford, 2004), p. 99.
66 Appendix: will, ll. 116–19, 122–3, 436–9.
67 P.A. Slack, *Poverty and Policy in Tudor and Stuart England* (London, 1988), p. 164.
68 Petchey, *Prospect of Maldon*, pp. 20–1.
69 Appendix: will, l. 119.
70 http://www.historyofparliamentonline.org/volume/1690–1715/member/comyns-john-1667-1740 (accessed 18 September 2015).
71 M. Hale, *A Discourse touching Provision for the Poor* (London, 1683).
72 K. Morrison, *The Workhouse. A Study of Poor-Law Buildings in England* (London, 1999), p. 10.
73 Anon., *Account of Several Workhouses … as also of Several Charity Schools* (2nd edn, 1732), pp. 104, 105. Quoted in J.R. Smith, *The Borough of Maldon 1688–1800: A Golden Age* (Studley, 2013), p. 362.
74 TPL, MA0120, 1716–19.
75 ERO, D/P 201/5/4.
76 P. Edmond, *Maldon Workhouse 1719–1875* (Maldon, 1999), p. 25.
77 ERO, D/P 201/5/4.
78 Edmond, *Maldon Workhouse*, p. 36.
79 M.G.L. Earnshaw, '"Always with you": public and private charity in Maldon and district', unpublished paper for the University of Essex Course EFW 9002 – the origins and development of English towns.
80 ERO, D/P 201/12/1; D/P 201/12/4.
81 Earnshaw, '"Always with you"'.
82 Edmond, *Maldon Workhouse*, pp. 19, 20.
83 Chapter 10, pp. 249–50.
84 Appendix: will, ll. 240–45.
85 *Ibid.*, ll. 209–11.
86 *Ibid.*, ll. 508–10.
87 *Ibid.*, ll. 189–91.
88 Petchey, *Intentions*, p. 26.
89 R.A. Doe, 'The Churchmanship of Thomas Plume (1630–1704): A Study of a Career in the Restoration Church of England', unpublished MA thesis (University of Essex, 2005), p. 66.

90   Petchey, *Intentions*, p. 24.
91   ERO, D/B 3/3/622; Chapter 5, pp. 127–8.
92   Chapter 7, pp. 178–9.
93   For the subsequent implementation of the poor boys' education and apprenticeship bequest by the Maldon Trust, and its interaction with the fortunes of the grammar school, see Chapter 5, pp. 127–8, 134–5, 140–4, 147.
94   TNA, PROB classmark, wills from 1680–1720, passim.
95   *Ibid.*
96   TNA, C 6/348/11.
97   Appendix: will, l. 46.
98   Kimbell, *An Account of the Legacies, Gifts, Rents, Fees*, p. 134; Chapter 9, pp. 227–8.
99   Appendix: will, l. 338–9.
100 DAC, SCT, Minutes, 1876–1901; Chapter 9, p. 232.
101 ERO, D/DBG 81/1.

Chapter 5

Thomas Plume and his Maldon Trust
Max Earnshaw and Christopher Thornton

Thomas Plume's will, proved in March 1705, reflected the many interests and responsibilities that he accumulated during a long and busy life. The overall nature and value of Plume's bequests have been dealt with in the previous chapter, but can be categorised under three main headings – religion, poor relief and education – although many comprised elements of all three.[1] The principal bequests to Maldon, his likely birthplace, were of considerable local significance. Plume endowed the building of the town workhouse, but as this legacy was not administered in the long term with his other Maldon benefactions it is not discussed here.[2] The remainder of his bequests were focused on the library building erected on the site of the nave and chancel of St Peter's church about 1698 or 1699 and which still bears his name. The room beneath the library was to house Maldon's grammar school, already endowed by the Breeder and Wentworth charities, for which Plume also provided an endowment to support the teaching and clothing of poor boys. Some of the boys were also to be supported as apprentices, and a weekly lecture was to be given in All Saints' church by local clergy. Plume endowed these charitable bequests with property, chiefly Iltney Farm in the neighbouring parish of Mundon, but also two fields in Maldon.

Plume desired his charitable bequests to be managed by trustees and his trust (hereafter described as his 'Maldon Trust') has been in continuous existence for just over three centuries. The trust's minutes do not begin until 1717, the interim being occupied by difficulties in acquiring the assets given in the will for its maintenance, as described in Chapter 4. Thereafter the trustees met twice-yearly and conducted such business as had arisen in the preceding six months. In addition to the minutes, the archive of Thomas Plume's Library contains copious materials for investigating the history of the charity and its activities, including account books, bills, receipts and vouchers, deeds, farm surveys and reports, correspondence, apprenticeship indentures and book borrowing registers, which have recently been catalogued. Each trustees' meeting had different priorities, so the various trust activities appear in the minutes only as necessary, sometimes making a chronological account of its history difficult to trace. Nevertheless, an attempt has been made in this chapter to create a single narrative, structured around four identifiable phases in the trust's history. In each section attention is first paid to the trust's administration and funding and to the form of its charitable scheme. This is followed by an examination of the trust's activities in relation to Plume's bequests, including the lectures, education, apprenticeships and the library itself.

The Maldon Trust's foundation and early years, 1717–81
In his will Thomas Plume nominated a permanent body of trustees to oversee the institution of his trust, as well as ensuring its continuance as an Anglican endeavour (Table 5.1). They were to include two bailiffs from the 'Company' (i.e. the Corporation, the governing body of the borough of Maldon), the recorder (the borough's chief legal officer), the incumbents of the Maldon churches of All Saints and St Mary, and five of the clergy of Dengie and Rochford hundreds, all of whom were to serve until their death or resignation. As an additional precaution he nominated as life members several personal friends, who could be relied upon to establish the trust as he would have wished, including Dr Francis Thompson, John Stevens, Samuel Pond, Mr Brickwood, Thomas Stace and John Straight. Mr Brickwood was probably the lawyer John Brickwood, but he died in April 1706 before the first surviving record of the names of trustees (Table 5.1).[3]

Thompson was overseer to the will and given the power to elect the library keeper as well as instructions to ensure the preservation of Plume's manuscripts.[4] The grammar school's master, William Scarrow, took delivery of at least part of the library in late 1704 and has previously been regarded as the first Plume librarian. However, it is now known from Plume's executor's accounts that Francis Thompson's nephew, also named Francis, had been appointed librarian and schoolmaster by July 1705. It remains uncertain whether he had replaced Scarrow entirely, or whether both men served as schoolmasters, one for the existing grammar school's boys and one for the new Plume charity boys. After Scarrow's death, Thompson certainly served as grammar school master between 1716 and 1720.[5]

The first meeting of the Maldon Trust was held on 12 April 1717, those present being Samuel Pond (bailiff), George Gray, Abraham Bigoss, Alexander Lindsey (vicar of Tolleshunt Major, appointed a trustee after 1706), and Francis Thompson (the schoolmaster and library keeper) (Figure 5.1).[6] A second

Table 5.1 Plume Trustees in November 1706

Thomas Gibson	bailiff of Maldon
Sir Charles Barrington, Bart.	bailiff of Maldon
John Comyns, Esq. Sergeant-at-law	recorder of Maldon
William Bramston, DD	rector of Woodham Walter
Francis Thompson, DD	rector of St Matthew Friday Street and St Peter Cheap (London); president of Sion College
John Marine, clerk	minister of All Saints, Maldon
George Gray	curate of St Mary, Maldon; rector of Heybridge
Francis Thompson	library keeper and schoolmaster
Daniel Horsmanden, clerk	rector of Purleigh
Abraham Bigoss	vicar of Mundon
John Stevens	Maldon, gentleman
Samuel Pond	Maldon, gentleman
Thomas Stace	Maldon, salesman
John Straight	Maldon, linen draper
Nathaniel Plume	Great Yeldham, gentleman

Source: ERO, D/DQs 133/7, p. 30; D/B 3/1/35, 6 November 1706.

meeting a month later was held at 'ye grammar school', but this practice does not seem to have continued. By 1719 some meetings were being held at the King's Head and that inn continued to be used for the purpose during the first half of the century. In the 1760s and 1770s meetings were held at both the King's Head and the Blue Boar.[7] Despite the large number of trustees envisaged by Plume, usually only five or six of them attended the regular half-yearly meetings. Early expenditures included repairs and other expenses at Iltney Farm (1718) and £206 16s 5¾d for finishing the workhouse (1719) (Figure 5.2).[8] The latter payment was made from the funds left by Plume to set up the institution, but thereafter control of the workhouse was handed over to Maldon's parish overseers, who funded its operation through the poor rates.[9]

Although the Maldon Trust possessed a small income derived from two fields in Maldon called Pound Mead and Molehills (later Fairfield and Longfield), purchased by Plume from John Norton in 1702,[10] its chief endowment was the rent from Iltney Farm in Mundon, a parish about four miles east of Maldon in Dengie hundred.[11] The farm lay on the southern bank of the Blackwater estuary and comprised about 200 acres. Its land was mostly a heavy clay, potentially fertile but retentive of moisture and therefore difficult to drain and expensive to cultivate; later commentators such as Arthur Young (1807) were unimpressed

5.1 The opening entry in the Maldon trust's first minute book, recording the meeting held on 12 April 1717. The names of the trustees attending are given, followed by the first item of business, the dispute with Samuel Palmer, the vicar of All Saints (TPL, MA0120).

5.2 A typical entry from the trust's eighteenth-century minute books recording expenditure. Repairs to Iltney Farm by the bricklayer Thomas Gough and the carpenter James Ougham (top and bottom) had been authorised, while the tailor Mr Whitaker had supplied clothing for Dr Plume's charity boys (centre) (TPL, MA0120).

by the heavy land along the shores of the Blackwater.[12] The farm's vulnerability to flooding also meant that it had been protected from the sea's incursions by a sea wall since the Middle Ages.[13]

Iltney Farm had belonged to St John's Abbey, Colchester, in the Middle Ages,[14] but the farm passed into lay hands after the Dissolution. It was later acquired by Ralph Breeder, a wealthy Maldon haberdasher, landowner and alderman, who endowed a grammar school for the town. On his death in 1609 Iltney was not used to support the school, however, but instead passed to his nephew John Wyldes (or Wildes).[15] It is not known how or when Plume acquired the property, but he apparently purchased it having been advised that it was chantry land before the Dissolution and thus deeming it to be an appropriate endowment for his foundation. Although he was mistaken in the detail, as it had been owned by a monastery rather than a chantry, Iltney was certainly former ecclesiastical property.[16]

The tenant of Iltney Farm from 1717 to 1718 was James Bartlett, who had an 11-year lease at £70 per annum but who was allowed a £25 rebate for improving the land with chalk rubbish in April 1718.[17] The rent apparently remained at about this level throughout the eighteenth century, and therefore the trust's income in real terms may have shrunk by more than half by 1800.[18] Combined with the constant drain on resources caused by repairs to Iltney's buildings and sea walls, the trust already struggled to meet its commitments by the 1750s. As a result, salaries paid out of the Iltney estate were frequently reduced or, occasionally, 'sunk' (i.e. unpaid).[19]

How the trust's income was to be spent discharging its charitable responsibilities as set out in Plume's will was clearly open to some interpretation. In 1728 judgement in a legal case between the Plume trustees and the executor of James Plume, who had been Dr Thomas Plume's own executor, concluded that the charities left to the town of Maldon amounted to £62 4s 0d per annum in value (Table 5.2).

In general, the expenditures recorded in the trust's early minutes and accounts correspond to those shown in Table 5.2. The schoolmaster's salary and housing were evidently excluded at this time, as they were organised and paid for separately.[20] Initially, one of the librarian's tasks was to administer the trust's finances, although William Smart, lawyer, town clerk (1741–69), bailiff and alderman (1761–69),[21] gradually emerged as its secretary in the mid-eighteenth century and took over this role. At the early meetings, at least until the early nineteenth century, cash was paid by the tenant of Iltney Farm and simply distributed to creditors until it ran out.

Of Dr Plume's bequests administered by his Maldon Trust the lowest in monetary value was the provision of a weekly lecture for the town. This was to be delivered by a member of the clergy from Dengie or Rochford hundreds in

Table 5.2 Contemporary account of charitable obligations and expenditures of the Plume Trust in 1728

Charitable bequests	Value
To Sion College appointed Visitors of the Library in Maldon	£1 0s 0d
To b[u]y books for such Library	£1 0s 0d
For repairs of the School and Library	Uncertain
For the Lecture from Lady day to Michaelmas	£13 10s 0d
For the dinners of the Lecturers and their friends	£2 14s 0d
For the sexton for tolling the bell	£1 0s 0d
To the poor who attend the lecture	£1 0s 0d
For 6 poor boys schooling	£6 0s 0d
For their clothing	£12 0s 0d
To the Library Keeper for his salary	£17 0s 0d
To him for receiving the rents and distributing charities	£2 0s 0d
To the vicar of All Saints Parish for reading prayers	£4 0s 0d
Total	£62 4s 0d (*recte* **£61 4s 0d**)
Payments made	Value
To taxes and repairs of Iltney Farm	£20 0s 0d
To repairs for the School and Library	£3 0s 0d
To fee farm rent and acquittance	£1 2s 0d
Sub-total	£24 2s 0d
The remaining sum [of] has been duly and proportionately distributed to the several respective charities	£45 18s 0d
Total	£70 0s 0d

Source: TPL, MA0120, 14/03/1728.

'the upper Church' (i.e. All Saints).[22] The lectures began as a weekly event, but by 1717 the cost obliged the Plume trustees to reduce them, for a short time, to fortnightly. This aroused the ire of Samuel Palmer, vicar of All Saints and a choleric character who was already at loggerheads with the other trustees over certain failures in reading the daily prayers, also endowed by Plume, for which he had been paid £4 annually. Palmer conducted a campaign against his fellow trustees from the pulpit and refused to allow the lectures to be delivered in his church.[23] An alternative venue was found at St Mary's church at the lower end of the town near to the Hythe, but the argument became so bitter that recourse was had to a formal complaint to the bishop of London, who supported the trust.[24] Eventually the dispute quietened down and Palmer (d. 1724) resumed his trusteeship and salary.

5.3 A list of the Plume lecturers for 1767 preserved in the first minute book. Underneath is a record of £20 from Iltney Farm's rents being directly paid to Maldon's bailiffs for the poor's coals. The trustees later refused to pay this rent-charge, leading to a case in Chancery (TPL, MA0120).

The weekly lectures continued through the eighteenth and nineteenth centuries, and lists of the lecturers can be compiled from the trust's minutes and other papers preserved in the Plume Library (Figure 5.3).[25] The fees offered amounted to ten shillings, plus a further two shillings on each occasion for a dinner at the Blue Boar Inn adjacent to All Saints' church, a welcome addition to the stipends of the local clergy. The lectures can have been of little hardship to them as by the eighteenth century many of the district's clergy preferred to reside in the prosperous market town and healthy air of Maldon rather than on their marshland cures.[26] Initially, most of the eligible local clergy seem to have contributed: in March 1729 a list of the 'Gentlemen Ministers' of Dengie and Rochford hundreds to lecture at All Saints for the following six months included 17 names, working on a weekly basis by rotation.[27] By 1733 they were receiving 12s each, some £15 12s being expended on 31 lectures for the half-year.[28] By the 1760s the number of clergymen involved had declined, with typically only four or five lecturers dividing up the schedule between them and delivering five or six lectures each.[29] Ten shillings was specified for a quarter-year's salary to the church clerk (sexton) for tolling the bell at the lecture (Figure 5.4),[30] while presence at the lectures was encouraged by payment of another ten shillings to be divided on two Quarter Days between those 'most Godly and indigent poore of Maldon' who had a record of regular attendance.[31]

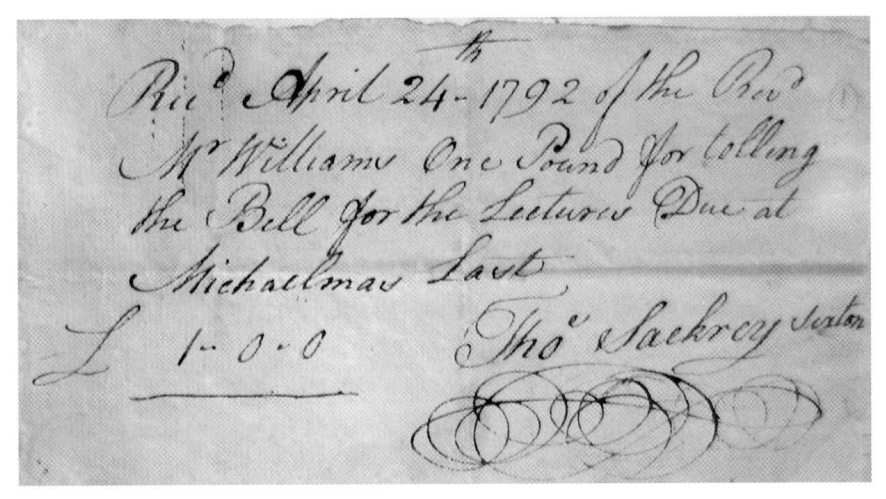

5.4 A receipt from Thomas Sackrey, the sexton of All Saints church, for his half-year's fee of £1 for tolling the bell at Dr Plume's lectures, dated 1792 (TPL, MA0149).

The Maldon Trust also shared responsibility for managing the town's grammar school, which ultimately became known as the Plume School, although Plume was neither the founder nor its main benefactor.[32] A chantry school, apparently founded in the reign of Henry V, had been suppressed in 1548; another school (or possibly more than one) recorded in the late Elizabethan period was probably unendowed and impermanent. In 1609 Ralph Breeder had left £300 to 'maintain a schoolmaster to teach a grammar school in the said town'. His legacy was invested in farm and residential property, held in trust by feoffees who included the bailiffs and aldermen of the borough, and the school was in operation by 1621 under its first master, John Danes, who received a salary of perhaps £30 or more.[33] Later, in 1634, the school's income was augmented under the will of Annastacy Wentworth, who left further property in Maldon to educate three poor boys from Maldon (at £1 a year each) at the school. She had been one of the beneficiaries of Breeder's will, and one of her own executors was Dr Thomas Plume's father.[34]

Ralph Breeder's grammar school was apparently held in the converted St Peter's church,[35] but it had a chequered existence before 1704. After Danes' death in 1639 there had been a gap of 11 years before another schoolmaster was recorded, possibly accounting for Thomas Plume being educated at Chelmsford Grammar School.[36] The school seems to have been resumed in 1650 and it was apparently vigorous enough to survive the reputed collapse of St Peter's church tower on to the nave a few years later. At some unknown point in the late seventeenth century, but probably about 1698 or 1699, Plume erected on the site of the nave and chancel a new two-storey building intended to house the school on the lower floor and his library on the upper floor after his death.[37]

The major part of Dr Plume's expenditure for the support of the school was, then, its rebuilding, which took place at least five years before his death in 1704. His will simply allocated part of his Maldon Trust's Iltney Farm income 'to keep in good repair ye School, & Library room for ever' (see also Table 5.2).[38] Plume did not have to consider the schoolmaster's main salary, which was already provided by Breeder's and Wentworth's benefactions. Instead, he ordered his trustees to maintain at least six poor boys from Maldon or Mundon at the school, and up to ten if funding allowed. Plume's Maldon Trust thereby became responsible for the pupils' fees of £1 a year (the maximum allowed, by a decision of the Maldon Corporation in 1621), and their clothing, which Plume had specified as 'plain gray, or green, coats, breeches, stockings, & shoes … with a Monmouth cap, or hat', for which £2 a year per boy was allocated from Iltney Farm's rents.[39]

Plume's will also specified that two of the foundation's scholars should be supported in becoming apprentices, a significant matter in a town where 'the completion of an apprenticeship entitled the apprentice to become a freeman'.[40] However, no evidence has been found that any Plume apprenticeships were created during the eighteenth century; very possibly the clause was simply overlooked. Nonetheless, Plume's boys were educated and clothed by the trust from 1717 onwards until a major crisis in the school's progress occurred. Under the terms of Breeder's will the schoolmaster was to be appointed by the aldermen and bailiffs of the borough of Maldon, but by 1761 the Whigs, who dominated the Corporation, came into conflict with 'a powerful group of Essex and Maldon Tories' over the election of the town's two members of parliament.[41] The struggle between them was to last eight years, involving disputed borough elections, hotly contested parliamentary elections, legal actions and rising costs, until in 1769 legal judgements left the Corporation with insufficient members to act corporately under its charter of 1555 and it was effectively dissolved.[42] This meant that when the schoolmaster (and Plume librarian), Revd Robert Hay, vicar of Heybridge, died in 1770, no successor could legally be appointed as there were no bailiffs or aldermen to do so.[43]

Dr Plume left all his books, pictures and manuscripts to be preserved in the library room over the school.[44] As the building to house the library and school had already been erected before Plume's death, the immediate task was to transfer those items to Maldon. In late 1704 and early 1705 his executor arranged for several shipments of books in casks from Greenwich and Rochester, apparently via London, and their transfer to the library's upper floor was apparently arranged by the schoolmaster, Revd William Scarrow. One cask packing list survives and begins carefully enough in listing each item as it was removed from the cask, but it soon deteriorates into generalities such as 'four volumes', etc.[45] The original library perhaps comprised *c.*7,400 books and unbound pamphlets, but there have since been many additions. Plume's will allowed only for the relatively small sum of £1 per annum for the purchase of new books out of the Iltney rents, but later the limits were raised.[46]

Relatively little is known about the original fitting-out of the library. By the time that all the legal problems with executing Plume's will had been settled there was a need for safe storage of many papers and documents, and in 1721 a mahogany box of considerable size, with two locks, was purchased for ten shillings.[47] No description of the original bookcases survives, or of the original arrangement of the volumes. Probably then, as now, volumes of similar size were arranged together as they fitted the shelf spaces. Such an arrangement meant that an annotated catalogue was needed so that books could be found by the librarian, and one was produced in 1761 by the newly appointed librarian, Revd Robert Hay.[48]

Thomas Plume specified that his library-keeper should be 'a Scholar, that knows books, M.A. & in holy orders',[49] and these qualifications were held by all the librarians until the death of Revd Isaac Seymour in 1947 (Table 5.3). It was Plume's intention that the librarian's post be supported by a salary of £40 and the provision of a house, for which he allowed £100. The salary was certainly paid, but as the post of schoolmaster and librarian had been combined so the costs were apparently divided between the Plume Trust and the Breeder and Wentworth benefactions, for by 1728 the Plume Trust was contributing only £17 (Table 5.2). Plume had suggested in his will that Mr Brickwood's house be purchased 'if it may bee had, at a reasonable rate'.[50] Mr Brickwood was undoubtedly John Brickwood, member of a Maldon family of lawyers, and the house referred to by Plume was almost certainly his house, the Friars mansion. Brickwood died in April 1706,[51] having bequeathed the Friars mansion 'in my own ... occupation' to his brother Benjamin,[52] and 'Mr Brickwood's house' (again, almost certainly the Friars mansion) was therefore 'not to be had' by the Plume trustees.[53] With Brickwood's house unavailable for purchase, the trustees and Plume's executor instead on 6 November 1706 bought a house near the top of St Peter's Lane (now Market Hill) from Francis Hackett, physician, and his wife Vere, who had moved from Maldon to London. The purchase price was £70. It stood on the west side of the road and was described as 'a Convenient dwelling house near the ... Library'.[54] Later evidence suggests the house was subsequently lost to the trust, perhaps in the disorganisation affecting the trust and grammar school in the later eighteenth century.[55]

As already noted, the librarian also acted as financial officer to the trust, and the first incumbent of this post, Francis Thompson, must have had a strong influence upon the trust's operation, as he remained in post from 1705 until his

Table 5.3 Librarians of Thomas Plume's Library, 1705–2019

1705–43	Francis Thompson, MA (vicar of Steeple, master of the grammar school)
1744–8	Thomas Knipe, MA (vicar of All Saints, Maldon)
1748–60	William Hutchinson, MA (curate of Woodham Walter)
1760–70	Robert Hay, MA (vicar of Heybridge)
1771–3	Laurence Eliot, MA (curate of St Mary, Maldon)
1773–1809	William Williams, MA (vicar of All Saints, Maldon)
1810–44	Charles Matthew, MA (vicar of All Saints, Maldon, and rector of Langford from 1832)
1844–52	Robert Crane, MA (vicar of Tolleshunt Major and Heybridge)
1852–1901	Edward Russell Horwood, MA (vicar of All Saints, Maldon)
1901–7	Alfred Wilson, MA (vicar of All Saints, Maldon)
1907–17	Leonard Hughes, MA, BD (vicar of All Saints, Maldon)
1917–44	Isaac Seymour, MA (vicar of All Saints, Maldon)
1947–66	Sidney Deed, MA (retired headmaster, Maldon Grammar School)
1967–72	Daniel W. Downes, LCP (retired assistant master, Maldon Grammar School)
1972–98	Gwyneth Shacklock, ALA
1972–2001	Olive Earnshaw (assistant librarian)
1998–2001	William John Petchey, MA, PhD (retired assistant master, Ripon Grammar School)
2001–3	Olive Earnshaw
2001–17	Susan Belsham, MA, MCLIP (assistant librarian)
2003–4	John Michael Hayward, MA, MCLIP
2004–19	Erica Wylie, MA
2018–present	Paula Thomson (assistant librarian)
2019–present	Helen Kemp, PhD

Source: http://www.thomasplumeslibrary.co.uk/trustees-staff/ (accessed 22 August 2019). The table has been amended to remove William Scarrow.

death in 1743. Plume had required that the librarian execute a bond in a sum not less than £200 against the embezzlement or removal of books, and this was certainly imposed. After the fourth librarian, Revd William Hutchinson, curate of Woodham Walter, died in 1760, his replacement Revd Robert Hay obtained the key of the library only after placing a bond for 'his faithful execution of the said office of librarian', just as Plume had decreed.[56]

The operation of the Maldon Trust, 1782–1842

Overall, as far as can be ascertained from the surviving material, the trust successfully fulfilled most of Dr Plume's wishes during the first three-quarters of the eighteenth century. It was through no fault of the Plume trustees that the grammar school had fallen into abeyance in 1781. However, there did exist the seeds of a major threat to the trust's finances in a £20 rent charge, payable to the bailiffs of Maldon to pay for coal for the poor, that had been placed upon Iltney Farm by Ralph Breeder when he had bequeathed the farm to John Wyldes.[57] It is not known how diligently this had been applied before Dr Plume's acquisition of the property, and as no mention was made of this obligation in Plume's will it seems possible that he was unaware of it. Initially, his trustees may also have been in ignorance, as it was not directly mentioned in the statement of the Maldon Trust's income and expenditures in 1728, unless represented by the £20 for 'taxes and repairs of Iltney farm' (Table 5.2). Not until 1741 was the matter apparently raised, for in that year the trust allocated to Richard Standish, bailiff and alderman, the sum of £20 'to pay for coals for the poor of the three parishes of Maldon', a sizeable part of the trust's regular income.[58] For the next 40 years £20 was faithfully handed over to a bailiff or, after the Corporation became dormant in 1768, to the churchwardens. For example, in 1779 sums of £8, £6 and £6 were paid to the churchwardens of All Saints, St Peter's, and St Mary's respectively.[59]

In 1782, perhaps prompted by the situation of the grammar school, the Plume trustees examined Plume's will more minutely and, finding no mention of the payment for the poor's coal, determined to cease paying it. The timing might suggest that the trust's financial situation, which had certainly declined in real terms, was coming under pressure. Additionally, the absence of the Maldon bailiffs from the trust owing to the dissolution of the Corporation may have given other trustees greater freedom to act on the issue. The response of Maldon's parish officers, to whom responsibility for supplying the fuel had now fallen, was to bring a Bill in Chancery, which necessitated the trust's books and accounts going to London for some years, thus disrupting its activities.[60] Rather mysteriously, the trust's first minute book, following an entry for 9 April 1783, contains a memorandum stating: 'The following pages of this book containing incorrect entries of the orders and disbursements of Dr Plume's Charities, viz. from page 357 to page 382, the same were ordered to be erased for the purpose of amending the same … '. There is therefore a hiatus in the documentary record of the trust's activities, but in December 1795 the case was finally dismissed with costs on the grounds that (a) the property in question was not sufficiently identified, (b) there was no proof that Plume or his earliest trustees ever recognised the claim and (c) the Chancery case in 1728 between Plume's trustees and his executor had made no mention of the £20 payment.[61] The trust therefore regained control of its books in 1796 and entries in the minute book resumed, although the administrative record remained a little disorganised for a while longer.[62] The mayor of Maldon returned for a second try in 1834, but on that occasion the trustees held firm and the matter was dropped without further legal action.[63]

In January 1813 a memorial or statement was made by the Plume trustees as required under the Act for the registration and securing of Charitable Donations (1812).[64] The trustees were then described as the mayor or chief magistrate of Maldon, the minister of All Saints' church (Revd Charles Matthew), the curate of St Mary's church, the schoolmaster, the library keeper and the ministers of Woodham Walter, Purleigh, Mundon and Heybridge or their curates. Their declaration confirmed that the charity's real estate comprised Iltney Farm in Mundon and 'Norton's land' in Maldon, otherwise the two fields known as Pound Mead and Molehills, which together produced a gross annual income of £212. The charity's objects were described under four headings, which closely followed Dr Plume's original stipulations: (1) to educate and clothe ten charity boys and bind two as apprentices; (2) to maintain a weekly lecture with associated payments; (3) to pay the librarian's salary (£40) and to buy new books (£1); (4) to keep the library and school room in good repair. Any unspent rent from Iltney was to be used to support some poor ministers of Dengie or Rochford hundreds or their families. Nonetheless, by this date the trustees may have interpreted their local responsibilities rather more broadly, perhaps influenced by Revd Matthew, librarian from 1810. In 1813 and 1814 the trustees offered £100 in contributions towards a new burial ground for the combined All Saints' and St Peter's parishes, and in 1831 they made a donation of £20 towards the building of a new gallery in All Saints' church.[65]

As well as successfully repudiating the rent charge of £20 for the poor's coals, by around 1800 the income of the Plume Trust revived, albeit temporarily, owing to the rise in agricultural prices during the Napoleonic Wars. Iltney Farm's rent had increased to £159 10s 0d from Michaelmas 1803, when it was let for 21 years. After Edward Payne bought the lease c.1814–15 he offered an even higher rent of £180 a year for a new one from Michaelmas 1819.[66] It was eventually leased to Payne in 1821 for £215 annually for 20 years, but no sooner had this level been reached than economic conditions worsened. Payne and subsequent tenants complained of an inability to make the farm pay and requested rent abatements. The rent had fallen back to £200 by 1827 before a surveyor's report recommended a reduction to £170 as well as expenditure on the homestead to encourage the tenant to reside on the farm. The decline was significant, as the other components of the trust's income were smaller, comprising the rent of Pound Mead and Molehills, let to Thomas Harvey at £60 p.a., and annuities producing £28 17s 8d.[67]

5.5 Iltney Farm, Mundon, the chief endowment of the Maldon Trust, depicted here on the tithe map of 1841. To the top of the picture (north) lies the river Blackwater with salt marsh along its bank and, to the north-west, drained marsh behind the sea wall. The remainder of the farm was mainly arable, with only a little woodland (TNA, IR 30/12/237).

The problems facing Iltney's tenant farmers during this period are not hard to discern. Mid-nineteenth-century Essex clay-land farms still depended on arable cultivation even though wheat prices had fallen and the crop could be uneconomic. In 1839 Iltney had roughly 149 acres of arable to just 38 acres of pasture, 28 acres of saltings and one acre of woodland (Figure 5.5).[68] The farm's sea wall also needed constant repair and was a heavy drain on profitability, with responsibility for its maintenance being transferred from the tenant to the trustees after 1834.[69] Another limitation was the poor quality of the farm's water supply, with only rainwater available on site until, in 1821, Payne had a well bored (the Maldon Trust contributed £50 towards the expense).[70] Problems increased after 1832 when James Marriage, of the adjacent White House Farm, dug a canal from that farmhouse to a nearby creek, which involved breaching the sea wall; this not only deprived Iltney of its communications on the track along the top of the sea wall, especially to Maldon, but also led to considerable flooding of Iltney's land.[71]

Although a headmaster could not be legally appointed after 1781, attempts were made to keep some sort of school going. Revd Joseph Shinglewood, vicar of Heybridge, served as schoolmaster from 1769 to 1796, although in an unofficial capacity after 1781. He continued to receive the rents of the Breeder foundation, and also taught the Plume charity boys, although the Wentworth charity appears to have been lost or embezzled by this period. Shinglewood was succeeded by his former assistant, William Bugg, who became master of the school and taught the charity boys, again unofficially. Further confusion then arose because the last of the feoffees of the Breeder Trust, Jonas Malden (d. 1795), had neglected the administration of that trust. It was left together with his personal property to his son (of the same name), who seems to have been unaware that he was responsible for the charity and its income, and its tenants refused to pay their rents. Probably as a result of the loss of income to support the master's salary, Bugg ceased teaching the grammar boys and the school closed, but he continued to teach the charity boys, of which there were ten in 1789, on a part-time basis in the lower (former grammar school) room beneath Plume's library.[72] At some point around this time, or a little later, Dr Plume's intention to support apprenticeships for two of the boys may have been rediscovered and brought to the trustees' attention. From 1803 the trust's minute books and other records began to record the names of apprentices, the premiums paid and sometimes the names of their masters.[73]

After the grant of a new borough charter in 1810 the mayor and aldermen appointed a new grammar school master, Revd Francis Waring (1810–32), vicar of Heybridge, but as they found it difficult to reclaim the rents belonging to the school he refused to teach and it remained moribund for many years.[74] The appointment, however, made it clear to local inhabitants that a new grammar school would be just that – a classical curriculum pointing boys to the universities, rather than delivering the more practical education of the old school. The townspeople therefore sought to extend the teaching available for the charity boys to a wider constituency. After a public meeting in 1817 the Plume trustees were persuaded to allow the establishment of a new school in the lower room and to borrow £250 from Revd Matthew to fund an extension to the building. The school was formed under the aegis of the National Society for the Education of the Poor in the Principles of the Established Church (usually abbreviated to forming a 'National School').[75] An additional spur was undoubtedly the establishment of a nearby British School for dissenters' children.[76] To accommodate the changes, a new two-storey extension to the building was constructed. In 1842 some 130 girls were being taught upstairs in the 'library room' using the monitorial system. Presumably the library books were removed, but the pupils would still have been tightly packed, unless 130 was the number of pupils on the roll and not all were present at the same time.[77] The posts of schoolmaster for Thomas Plume's Charity and the National School were then combined in one individual, and the schoolmaster was paid £25 for educating the Plume Boys, the number of whom had been increased to 15 in 1811.[78]

The grammar school was slow in being re-formed, but in 1834 the Breeder charity's rents were regained and under the direction of the Charity Commission the Plume Charity was re-established as part of the school's endowment.[79] A persistent campaign was waged by the grammar school's masters to reclaim the lower room from the National School, particularly by the Revd Salisbury Dunn, who eventually took the matter to the charity commissioners in 1836.[80] During the course of that action it emerged that there had been an underlying confusion over who was entitled to receive the rents of Pound Mead and Molehills (later Fairfield and Longfield).[81] Initially, the £23 rent of the two fields had been paid separately to the Plume librarian, in addition to a charge of £17 on the Iltney estate, in order to augment his salary to £40, as originally decreed by Plume. However, on the death of Francis Thompson the £23 income was swept into the trust's accounts and the librarian's salary paid directly from them instead. As land values changed and increased, the librarian received no extra benefit.[82] From 1807 the excess had been used by the trust 'with the consent of the librarian' to contribute to a capital reserve which stood at £682 10s invested in 3.5 per cent bank annuities producing an annual dividend of £28 17s 8d.[83] In 1836 the Charity Commission determined that the librarian, Revd Matthew, should in future receive the increase in rent as part of his salary, but that the capital sum accrued should be retained for the charity and applied to charitable purposes.[84]

As noted above, to accommodate the National School's female pupils in the upper room the library's books were probably stored elsewhere, perhaps on the upper floor of the new two-bay extension. From the last quarter of the eighteenth century onwards the librarians appointed were more often than not vicars of All Saints (Table 5.3). In 1815 the trustees noted that Dr Plume had allowed £100 for the purchase of a house for the librarian as part of his salary, but they had no evidence that this had occurred (in fact, as already described, the house had been purchased but seems to have later been lost). The trustees therefore decided to apply the additional sum of £5 to his annual salary, representing interest on the £100.[85] Librarians maintained the library collection by making occasional additions, such as, in 1803, Revd Philip Morant's *History and Antiquities of the County of Essex* (1768), which included an account of Plume's legacies to Maldon.[86] In the 1830s Lord Brougham's Commission reported that Revd Hay's library catalogue still existed, that the books and manuscripts were in good condition, that there were approximately 5,530 volumes in the library and that about 20 books had been lost prior to Revd Matthew becoming librarian, with about 10 or 12 books currently on loan.[87]

From the 1843 scheme to the end of the nineteenth century

The legal action of 1836 and its result appears to have drawn the charity commissioners' attention to inconsistencies in the administration of Plume's Maldon Trust. A decree dated 17 July 1839 referred the case to Chancery to enquire further about the ownership of the two fields and who was entitled to receive their rents and profits, to establish the purpose of the charity and to approve a proper scheme for the application of the income from the fields. The result was an entirely new trust deed imposed in 1843, apparently with the intention of restoring Dr Plume's intentions as closely as possible.[88] The scheme had 31 clauses, which may be grouped as follows: Clauses 1 to 7 governed the trustees and meetings of the trust, with ten trustees to be resident in Maldon or within five miles of the town and communicants of the Church of England, two to be members of the Borough Council, another to be the grammar school master and the remainder to be elected with preference for the minister of All Saints, the perpetual curate of St Mary and the ministers of Woodham Walter, Purleigh, Mundon, Heybridge or their curates; Clauses 8 to 14 concerned the minutes, accounts and papers of the charity, and the audit and publication of the accounts in local newspapers; Clauses 15 to 25 set out in some detail the qualifications, responsibilities and salary of the librarian and clerk, and the library's opening hours and borrowing arrangements; Clauses 26 to 29 described the regular charitable payments to be made for the lecture and the education, clothing and apprenticeship of Plume's boys, and what should happen to the money if those charitable objects could not be met; Clause 30 indicated that £200 of the charity's investments should be sold and the money used to restore the library room to its original purpose, with the residue to be used for new books; and Clause 31 concluded by stating that if there was a surplus from the rents and profits of the charity it was to be invested in 3 per cent Consolidated Bank Annuities and the interest spent on the provision of new books and the education and clothing of poor boys from Maldon.

From July 1843 the trustees brought their number up to ten and, following the death (1844) of the incumbent librarian, Revd Matthew, the July 1844 meeting elected Robert P. Crane, vicar of Heybridge, as the new librarian. The trust also moved swiftly to enact certain requirements of the new scheme, arranging the execution of the librarian's bond, the fitting-up of the library room and the expenditure of £10 for books.[89] A published report of the charity's accounts from Midsummer 1845 to Midsummer 1846 reveals its financial situation soon afterwards (Table 5.4). By this date, under the scheme of 1843, the endowment for the schoolmaster's salary was included, but itemised separately within a sub-account.

It seems that financial affairs were not a particular strength of Revd Crane, the new librarian and secretary/financial officer. When Revd Edward Russell

Table 5.4 Summary of accounts of Dr Plume's Charities, Maldon, Essex, 1845–6

Main account – Receipts from Iltney	Value
Carried forward	£66 5s 8½d
Rent of Iltney Farm	£180 0s 0d
Total	£246 5s 8½d
Main account – Payments	
Income tax on Iltney Farm	£5 7s 0d
Clerk's attendance at trustees' meetings	£0 10s 0d
Trustees' dinner	£4 15s 0d
Stationery and advertisement in *Chelmsford County Chronicle*	£3 7s 5d
Lectures	£27 0s 0d
Clerk attending the lectures	£1 0s 0d
Salary of schoolmaster	£20 0s 0d
Boys' clothing	£15 16s 3d
Apprentices' fees and instalments	£57 10s 0d
Insurances	£3 16s 6d
Indentures (for apprentices)	£1 0s 0d
Salary of librarian and secretary	£19 0s 0d
Cleaning library	£0 10s 0d
New books for the library	£12 6s 6d
Poor attending the lectures	£1 0s 0d
Coals and carting	£1 17s 0d
Painter and glazing, carpenters, bricklayer, stonemason	£36 14s 1½d
Cowl for chimney	£2 5s 6d
Incidental expenses	£5 11s 6d
Total payments	£219 6s 9½d
Balance in hand	£26 18s 11d
Total	£246 5s 8½d
Sub-account, Receipts from Librarian's Fields [i.e. Pound Mead and Molehills]	
One year's rent of Librarian's fields	£60 0s 0d
Total	£60 0s 0d
Sub-account, Payments from Librarian's Fields	
Income tax	£1 18s 8d
One year's salary to Librarian	£58 1s 4d
Total	£60 0s 0d

Source: TPL, MA0127, 12/1/23-27, Accounts 1844-49, 1858. Manuscript and printed versions of the accounts disagree by 1s 1d.

Horwood, vicar of All Saints, took office as the trust's chairman in 1850 he was appalled at the condition of its records. Not as to its financial position, for he was apparently quite unable to establish that, but at the complete lack of order in the trust's accounts. No vouchers could be found for much of the income or expenditure and the only course was to draw a line in the books and start again. Crane relinquished office in 1852, but remained a trustee until his death; he was replaced by Revd Horwood as librarian and secretary.[90] A draft balance sheet of Dr Plume's charity for 1854-5 indicates that order had returned by that date. After the charity's regular obligations had been met there was enough of a surplus that year to allocate £50 to poor ministers in Dengie hundred, as had been intended by Plume and directed by the new scheme of 1843; such payments to poor ministers or their families were recorded throughout the remainder of the nineteenth century.[91] In 1897 the ten trustees under the new scheme were the vicars of All Saints (Maldon), St Mary's (Maldon) and Mundon, the rectors of Purleigh, Woodham Walter and Hazeleigh, the grammar school master, the chaplain of Maldon Union Workhouse and two representatives of Maldon Borough Council. At that date the trust's property still included the library contents, Iltney Farm and the two 'Fair Fields' (formerly Pound Mead and Molehills, the librarian's fields).[92]

The financial position of the trust was, however, seriously weakened by the second half of the nineteenth century owing to Iltney Farm's poor performance, as revealed by regular surveys and reports in, for example, 1850, 1861 and 1874.[93] The survey of 1861 shows that it had remained a largely arable farm. Although it was then said to be in a fair state of repair, work was needed on the homestead, its farm buildings and the sea walls, and some of the corn was foul with weeds such as twitch and mayweed.[94] Its farmers evidently struggled and rents were gradually reduced throughout the nineteenth century until in 1896 the farm's poor condition obliged the trust to accept £70 p.a., its rental value nearly two centuries earlier.[95] The immediate context was to be found in collapsing crop prices from the 1870s, which had caused both a national agricultural depression and one felt especially severely on the heavy claylands of south-east Essex. Many farmers were bankrupted, but landlords such as the trust often bore a substantial proportion of the pain.[96]

Despite the depression in the trust's financial circumstances, its work continued. The lectures continued to be supported through the nineteenth century, with the payments for the lecturers having risen to £1 per lecture. In 1848 some 16 poor people attended, 12 receiving 1s 6d each and four only 6d, but usually from eight to ten people shared the payment (Figure 5.6).[97] Payments for lecturers, for the tolling of the bell and for the attendance of poor people were last recorded in the trust's records in 1893.[98] Nonetheless, the educational elements of Plume's bequests continued to be troublesome. In

5.6 A list of 16 poor people attending Dr Plume's lectures in 1848, and the payments made to them. Most attendees by this date were women, many of them widows (TPL, MA0154).

the aftermath of the new scheme, the Plume trustees found themselves unable to accede to the grammar school master's request to return his school to the library's lower room because it was then occupied by the National School. The grammar school's only satisfaction for a period was the rent paid by the National School for the use of 34 feet of the room (its original length).[99] In 1847 the National School relocated to a new building in London Road, Maldon, allowing the grammar school to return to the now empty extension of the Plume Library from 1856, but it moved again after the tower of the former church of St Peter's showed signs of imminent collapse in the 1870s.[100]

The scheme of 1843 had also recognised that the grammar school's master might refuse to educate the Plume boys, and if they were to be rejected in future that the trustees were allowed to arrange alternative education 'in like manner'.[101] As the Plume trustees could not allow the school to return to the lower room, it seems that the charity boys continued to be educated at the National School for a while (the trustees' receiving legal advice that this was permissible). However, in 1848–9 it was agreed that Revd Salisbury Dunn would teach the Plume boys in the grammar school for £10 per annum.[102] After Dunn's death in 1863, however, the new master flatly refused to teach the Plume boys for the fees offered, so they were again attached to the National School with its master to receive annually £20 plus £5 for books.[103] Regular reports as to the progress of the Plume boys were submitted by the National School's master to Plume's trustees, and he was paid occasional sums from Plume funds, as well as the school fees.[104]

The grammar school was now in the final phase of its life as a private school, settling in a house in London Road, Maldon, opposite the new National School building.[105] Although the school began to revive after 1895, under R.L. Ryland, its furniture and equipment were woefully inadequate,[106] especially by the standards required when secondary education became a county function after the passing of the 1902 Education Act. A county education report of 1906 gives some idea of its quality:

> one classroom, also used by the boarders as a dining room, and, across a gravelled yard at the back, a large school-room (formerly a stable, though not so unsuitable as that would seem to imply) in which two classes are always taught together; an old brew house which has been converted into a lavatory and bicycle room, and a shed which makes a sort of covered playground. Another room has been fitted up as a science lecture-room and laboratory, but the equipment is quite inadequate. There is no gymnasium and no art room ... .[107]

As already noted, about 1800 the Maldon Trust appears to have rediscovered its obligation to support two boys as apprentices, and the provision of the

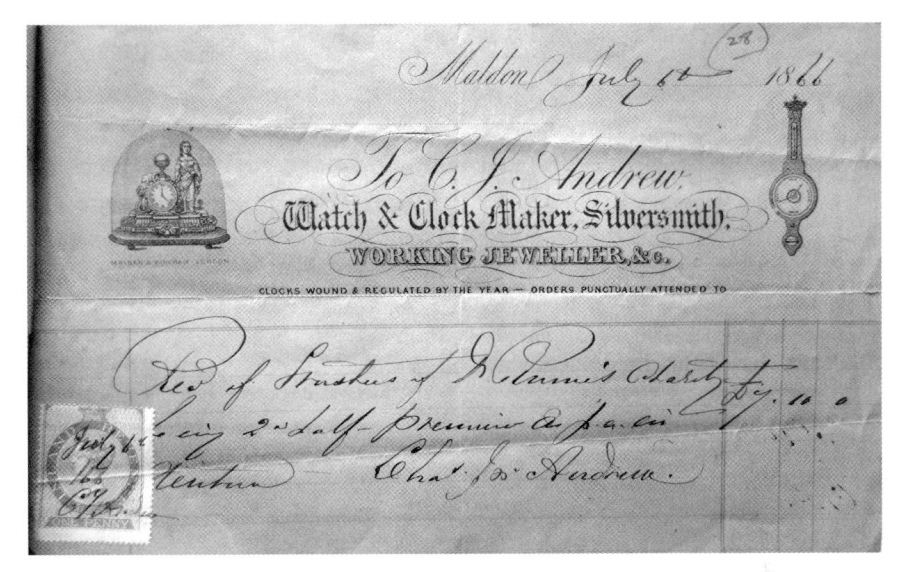

5.7 A receipt from Charles Andrew, a Maldon watch and clockmaker, silversmith and jeweller, dated 6 July 1866, for the second half of the annual premium paid to him for apprenticing a Plume charity boy (TPL, MA0158).

apprenticeships was confirmed by the 1843 scheme. The Plume Library holds a collection of 86 apprenticeship indentures for the period 1803–92, which are best considered as a whole. While they do not form a complete record, they indicate that the apprenticeships typically ran from five to seven years and the premiums paid ranged from £13 to £18, with the most common at £15.[108] Although the majority of placements were within the town of Maldon (St Peter and St Mary parishes), masters were also found in the county town of Chelmsford and the rural parishes of Althorne, Hatfield Peverel, Latchingdon, Rettendon, Rivenhall, Southminster, Steeple, Tillingham, Tollesbury, Tolleshunt D'Arcy, Woodham Ferrers and Woodham Walter (all Essex parishes within a dozen miles of the town). Further afield still were masters in Clerkenwell (London) and in Knottingley (West Yorkshire), an inland port on the river Aire, where the apprentice was a mariner or seaman. Another apprentice was placed with John Finch, master of the ship *Endeavour*. A few boys were apprenticed with their fathers or other close relatives: for example, the boy Simmonds was apprenticed to his uncle Henry Hurrell, a Southminster veterinary surgeon, in 1843.[109]

Many masters were craftsmen in relatively common trades, such as carpenters, wheelwrights, blacksmiths and cordwainers/shoemakers, but Maldon's economy was diverse enough to provide a fairly wide range of future careers for the Plume apprentices (Figure 5.7). Among other masters associated

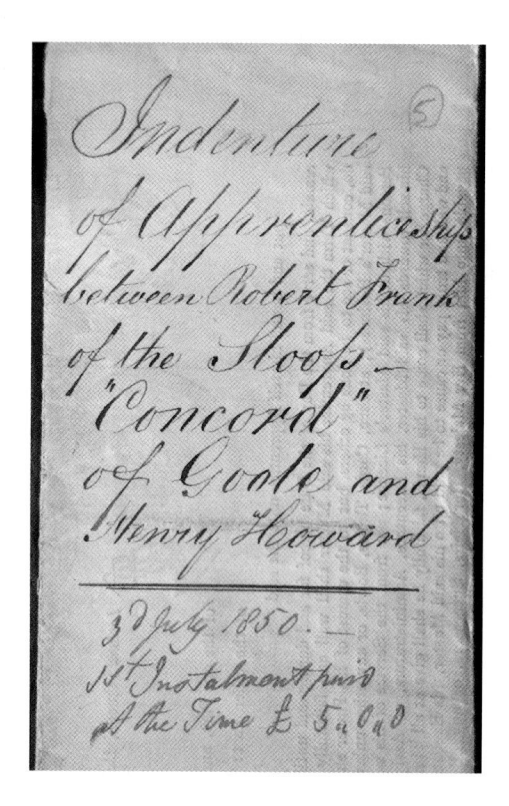

5.8 The cover of an apprenticeship indenture for one of Dr Plume's charity boys, dated 3 July 1850. This was one of the few which involved a maritime apprenticeship (TPL, MA0157).

with the retail trade of the town were cabinet makers (3), watchmaker and jewellers (2), tailors, outfitters and clothiers (2), butchers (2) and bakers (2); one of the bakers was the only female master recorded (Louisa Stow of St Mary's parish, 1844). An apprentice was taken on as a writing and copying clerk to Messrs Crick, attorneys, in 1855, and five others as pupil teachers at the National School in the 1870s. A surprising feature was that no boys were apprenticed to the larger firms in Maldon and Heybridge, such as E.H. Bentall Ltd (agricultural machinery from 1805), John Sadd and Sons Ltd (timber merchants from c.1760) or the Maldon Iron Works Co. (from the 1850s). Unless these firms themselves eschewed the apprenticeships, it seems possible that the trustees preferred to use Dr Plume's charity to support the lesser tradesmen of the town.

More surprising still for a town with such a long-established port was that only two of the apprenticeships were directly related to its maritime activity, with apprentices being placed with masters who were mariners or seamen. A master shipwright was also recorded in the minute book for 1839, while some apprentices, such as carpenters and blacksmiths, may have worked in shipbuilding yards.[110] The policy contrasted with that adopted in some other parts of the county, such as north-east Essex, where the overseers of rural parishes often apprenticed boys to fishermen working in the Harwich fishing fleet.[111] At Maldon it is not known whether the pattern reflects an attitude on the part of the Plume trustees regarding poorer prospects for apprentices in, or higher costs of, maritime employment, or other factors. In general, the apprenticeships seem to have been appreciated by the poor of the town; as one boy said in later life, 'I owe all my advancement in life, under God, to Dr Plume's Charity.'[112] The last apprentice was sponsored in 1894, but the reason for the discontinuation of the Plume apprenticeships thereafter is not clear; possibly the trustees already understood at that stage that a large part of their income from Iltney Farm would disappear.[113]

The charity commissioners had insisted in 1843 that the library be placed in the original location intended by Dr Plume, and this was quickly implemented. The shelving was also replaced when the library was reinstated, some of the regulations concerning the library were renewed or amended,[114] and a new two-volume library catalogue was created by Revd Crane (1848).[115] It was also directed that a lockable box or chest be acquired, with two keys, one for the librarian and one for a trustee; this is probably the large chest in the library, replacing one bought in 1721.[116] A bond was again required of the librarians under the 1843 scheme,[117] and the annual sum allocated for the purchase of new books was increased to £10, with exactly that amount being spent on new books in 1854–5. The new scheme also allowed the trustees to direct any surplus from the charity's rents and profits towards new book purchases.[118]

The Maldon Trust in the twentieth and twenty-first centuries

Changes in national education policy led the charity commissioners to propose a new scheme for the Grammar School charity in 1900, which inevitably impacted upon the existing scheme of 1843 for Plume's Maldon Trust. Initially, there was opposition from the Plume trustees, who felt that the new scheme was contrary to the wishes of the founder (and therefore the scheme approved by the Court of Chancery in 1843), although they countered that they were willing to consider any proposal for the improvement of the library and the extension of its usefulness.[119] However, the changes were subsequently accepted on condition that one-third of the net income of Iltney Farm be used for the maintenance of the non-educational part of the Plume charity and that the trust would appoint two members of the governing body of the school.[120] In 1901 a new scheme therefore amalgamated the Breeder, Wentworth and Plume Trusts, the latter with regard only to its relation to the Grammar School, with the allocation of one-third of Iltney's income to the trust and two-thirds to the school being confirmed in 1905.[121] Thereafter only occasional amounts (e.g. £2 16s 7d in 1909) accrued to the trust, causing it to complain to the school about the absence of income.[122] In 1908, at the request of the Plume trustees, the Charity Commission allowed an amendment to the scheme that enabled the trustees to let land as allotments.[123]

A further Charity Commission scheme under the Endowed Schools Act created the Breeder and Plume Educational Trust in 1910 (by 2019 simply the Plume Educational Trust), which was then endowed with the school's two-thirds share of Iltney's income.[124] The farm was later mortgaged by the Educational Trust, possibly to pay for repairs to its sea wall, but the Plume trustees declined to be a party to the mortgage.[125] The Educational Trust eventually sold the Iltney estate in 1918, yielding a mere £584 17s 10d to Plume's Maldon Trust, which was invested in War Loan Bonds. In 1923 the investment produced £30 0s 2d income.[126] After these changes, support of the Grammar School was permanently removed from the responsibilities of the Maldon Trust. Plume's endowment in this regard was thereafter managed by the Educational Trust, together with its other property at Pleyhill Farm, Hatfield Peverel, and 66 and 68 High Street, Maldon.[127] The Plume trustees did, however, continue to be represented by two places on the Educational Trust.[128]

In October 1917 a meeting of the Maldon Trust considered proposals for the reconstitution of the Charity's scheme, including the possibility of selling the books and pictures and using the proceeds for the erection of a more up-to-date institution (a parish hall or church institute) of more practical value to the town. Although in April the following year it was agreed that no immediate steps should be taken to dispose of them, knowledge of the discussion spread and led to a complaint to the Charity Commission from a former trustee, Revd E.L.B. Kevill-Davies. A public enquiry on 18 March 1919 was adjourned pending a decision as to whether Maldon's war memorial should take the form of a public reading room and library.[129] Subsequently the trustees agreed to a proposal in April 1919 that the Plume Library be rehoused in part of a building to be erected as a war memorial (with modern library and reading room), but the idea was subsequently dropped and the enquiry was closed.[130] In the meantime the Plume Library stayed open, the librarian's salary of £67 was reinstated and the opening hours were set as Wednesday and Saturday afternoons between 2 and 4 p.m. (by application to the librarian).[131]

After these diversions, further attention was paid to the library building and books, both being reinsured for higher sums than before. Investigations were also made concerning the status of the leases of Longfield and Fairfield, then let to Essex County Council (ECC), which had remained in the trust's hands as its landed endowment. In March 1921 the librarian reported that various public bodies and individuals had visited the library, while scholars and antiquarians appreciated the privilege of access to it.[132] Kevill-Davies rejoined as a trustee and became chairman, energetically setting about improving the library with new book purchases, repairs to books, further insuring the books, pictures and oak panelling, obtaining new library furniture, publishing public accounts and considering a proposal to revive the lectures. The trust also gave notice to ECC terminating the lease on Longfield, which was subsequently let to the town council for allotments for seven years at £40 p.a. in 1922.[133] A financial statement from 1923 shows how slender the trust's resources had then become, with combined balances brought forward and annual income comprising £152 7s 9d being set against expenses of £128 5s 1d, leaving just £24 2s 8d in hand.[134]

In 1924 an architect's report recommended urgent and expensive action to save the tower and the library, which both needed repair, and the trustees started a fund for their restoration. The mayor of Maldon, a trustee, agreed to issue an appeal to the town and neighbourhood for the preservation of this 'historical monument and ancient landmark'.[135] The fundraising was slow, however, and in 1929 the trust received further professional advice that the tower was unsafe and ought to be taken down and the library reconstructed. As the trustees of All Saints Parish Council were preparing to build a new parish hall, it was suggested that it could be built on the St Peter's site with the Plume Library incorporated.[136]

In the end the library was saved. Subsequent reports by a SPAB surveyor suggested that the tower was restorable after all, and the combination of local fundraising with a grant from the Pilgrim Trust led to the restoration of the tower in 1930–1.[137] The next problem was the restoration of Dr Plume's library building, which was clearly beyond the means of Plume's Maldon Trust, although work on the foundations at £300 was immediately authorised.[138] A way forward was found in the opening of negotiations with Maldon Borough Council (later the Town Council) to buy the lower room (together with the tower and grounds with the consent of the vicar and churchwardens). In 1931 the mayor extended a loan to the trust of £700 at 5 per cent per annum and this allowed the reconstruction to commence. But by April 1932 the trust had an overdraft of nearly £1,000 and the possibility of selling the building to All Saints' Parish Council was revived if a faculty could be obtained for extending the building. In 1933, after lengthy negotiations during which it emerged that ECC would be willing to lease the lower room as a county library, Maldon Borough Council agreed to buy the whole building for £800. The Plume Trust was awarded the upper floor under a 999-year lease at an annual rent of ten shillings.[139] Thus by 1934 the crisis caused by the condition of the building and the weak state of the trust's finances had largely been overcome, with an adverse balance of only £11 12s 4d. at the end of that year, although money was to remain sparse for the next 20 years.[140]

In 1948 the trust made an application to the Pilgrim Trust for a grant towards the repair of the library contents. A grant of £500 was approved, but subject to the condition that a new scheme should include ECC acting as trustees.

Additionally, the Ministry of Education would agree to a new scheme only if ECC were able to provide assurance that the charity would have adequate funds to function properly. Negotiations between the Plume trustees, ECC and the ministry had started in earnest by 1949–50.[141] In 1952 a new scheme was authorised that changed the charity's title to Thomas Plume's Library and reduced the trustee body to nine: three ex-officio as the rector of St Mary, the vicar of All Saints with St Peter, and the headmaster of Maldon Grammar School, and six representative trustees, comprising three from ECC, two from Maldon Borough Council and one of the incumbents of Heybridge, Mundon, Purleigh and Woodham Walter (acting jointly).[142] The change was apparently regarded as sufficient by the Pilgrim Trust to release their grant, and ECC also committed to paying an annual grant of £250.[143] The Maldon Trust's annual dinner was revived and the reconstituted body met for the first time in September 1952.[144]

The application of the trust's income was simplified by the 1952 scheme, 'in or towards the support of the Library belonging to the Foundation and its contents'. The property of the trust was scheduled as (a) the Library premises held under a 999-year lease from the Borough Council from 29 September 1933, (b) the allotment field (Longfield), formerly Mole Hills, (c) the Grammar School field (Fairfield), formerly Upper Pound Mead and (d) 3.5 per cent War Stock valued at £584 17s 10d and producing £20 9s 4d. The charity's total income was £130 9s 4d, while it had £189 in bank deposit and current accounts.[145] By 2018 the library's assets, beyond the book collection, which was defined as a 'heritage asset' and whose value is effectively unrealisable, included the upper floor of the library building held on a 999-year lease from 1933 at a peppercorn rent from the Town Council (as successor to the Borough Council) and the freehold of Fairfield (6.4 acres), let on a 999-year lease from 1953 at a rent of £75 p.a. to the Plume School.[146] From 1 April 2019 the charity was converted from a simple charitable trust to a 'Charitable Incorporated Organisation', at the same time confirming its official name as Thomas Plume's Library.[147]

Attempts to revive the Plume lectures did not bear fruit until 1975, when a heavily revised form was reinstated by the library trustees at the instigation of Revd Arthur Dunlop as an annual commemoration on the November date nearest the anniversary of Dr Plume's death. Many speakers distinguished in their field have contributed, including well-known political, literary and cultural figures, librarians, museum curators, academic and local historians, and scientists. The latter have included several holders of the Plumian Professorship of Astronomy and Experimental Philosophy at Cambridge University.[148]

Following the reorganisation of the Grammar School's management scheme, a new school was built in Fambridge Road on Fairfield, leased from the

Plume Trust in 1906.[149] As already described above, Plume's Maldon Trust's involvement was now confined to supplying two representatives out of the 12 trustees on the Breeder and Plume Educational Trust, which managed the school.[150] In 2020 Thomas Plume's Library and the Plume School, now a community academy, still enjoy a close relationship. The school's headmaster is an *ex-officio* trustee of the library charity and there are annual visits to the library by the whole of Year 8 (12–13 years old), when *c*.270 pupils view an exhibition of books relevant to their studies prepared by the librarian and her staff. Members of the Friends of Thomas Plume's Library (see below) provide a rota of stewards. The pupils also complete a piece of written work to compete for a history prize which the Friends' trustees award each year.

The first lay librarian was Sidney Deed, retired headmaster of Maldon Grammar School, who was followed by the school's assistant master, D.W. Downes. In 1971 the library appointed a professional librarian, Mrs Gwyneth Shacklock, formerly of Essex county library service. The Maldon historian W.J. Petchey was librarian between 1998 and 2001. An assistant librarian, Olive Earnshaw, appointed in 1972, succeeded him as librarian (2001–3). Erica Wylie (librarian) and Susan Belsham (assistant librarian) were long-serving staff in the early twenty-first century.

Since the late nineteenth century the library has received a number of augmentations. An apparently small number of books were transferred from the Literary and Mechanics' Institute, Maldon, which closed in the 1880s. More were received from the estates of Edward Russell Horwood (d. 1901), former vicar of All Saints and librarian and secretary to the Trust (155 books); Dr J.H. Salter (d. 1932), of Tolleshunt D'Arcy, a general practitioner, sportsman, sporting-dog breeder and horticulturalist (20 books); and R.E. Thomas of Beeleigh Abbey (58 books).[151] Miscellaneous books, none relating to the historic library, were weeded out of the collection by the librarian W.J. Petchey *c*.2000.

While the original purpose of the library had been to facilitate the studies of gentlemen or scholars, who could borrow the books against a deposit of their supposed value,[152] over the years a considerable number of books were lost, either from non-return of such loans or casual removal at times when access was too easy. Not until 1959 was a new catalogue, of Plume's books only, compiled by Sydney Deed and Jane Francis.[153] Even this was incomplete, as the compilers overlooked a number of titles that had been bound with others. Totally ignored were the 2,100 titles (so-called post-Plume volumes) that had accrued over the years. On the initiative of Dr W.J. Petchey, librarian 1998–2001, a start was made to compile a comprehensive catalogue of all the written material in the library. This catalogue, available online, is now complete for both Plume and post-Plume books, and a further catalogue of pamphlets and manuscripts has been added. It is now known that Plume's bequest amounted to 5,800 bound books and 1,600 unbound books and pamphlets.[154]

The modern cataloguing of the library has identified about 700 missing volumes, but from the later twentieth century there have been donations from past users and steps have been taken to find replacements. In February 1987 the trustees of the library agreed to the purchase of Sir John Davies, *The True causes why Ireland was never entirely subdued ...* (London, 1612), a book that had originated from the Plume Library, for the sum of £725.[155] The purchase provided useful publicity and at the same trust meeting Victor Gray, Essex county archivist, suggested the formation of a 'Friends' organisation. In December of the same year The Friends of Thomas Plume's Library was established, later becoming a registered charity; Frank Herrmann was elected its first chairman. The first Friends' lecture was given on 11 April 1988 by Dr W.J. Petchey on the subject of 'Thomas Plume's Maldon'.[156] The Friends have since raised more than £57,000 in support of the library, for conservation, storage and computer cataloguing of books and manuscripts, among other things. Their financial assistance has also enabled the replacement of over 200 of the lost volumes, occasionally even reacquiring one of Plume's original books.[157]

Summary

Over the three centuries of the trust's existence the diligence and success of its trustees can be assessed from the detailed administrative record it has left behind. Like many trusts, it was a self-perpetuating oligarchy and was easily prone to error and many acts of minor (and occasionally not-so-minor) administrative failure. There is, however, no evidence of overt fraud or corruption and with several strong prompts from the Court of Chancery and the charity commissioners it did fulfil most of the duties laid on it by Dr Plume. Among its oversights may be cited a lack of evidence that Sion College was ever paid its £1 annuity for overseeing the library, that support for two of the Plume boys to be apprenticed was not implemented until after 1800, and that support for poor ministers in Dengie hundred was not apparently enacted until the new scheme of 1843.[158] In other regards the trustees discharged Plume's legacies tolerably well, maintaining the lectures (until *c.*1900), supporting the town's grammar school and the education of the charity boys, paying the librarian's salary and keeping the library and school building in reasonable repair. Most importantly of all, at least from an early twenty-first-century perspective, the trust successfully preserved Plume's library and its books, pamphlets, manuscripts and pictures in the room they were placed in so many years ago.

Most of the changes and crises affecting the trust were associated with two underlying fault lines within Plume's legacies to Maldon. The first was that Plume, as a benefactor, was neither the first nor last to miscalculate the balance needed between capital expenditure and investment for future income to maintain the charity's activities. The generally poor return from Iltney, except for a short period during the Napoleonic Wars, and the issues facing its management, such as sea defence, formed a significant backdrop to, and constraint upon, the trust's activities. The second problem faced by the trustees, inextricably linked to that of limited finance, was the multi-faceted nature of Plume's bequests to his home town, which were all rolled into the single charity (with the exception of the workhouse). The structure was perhaps understandable, as Plume would probably have regarded the individual items as indivisible parts of a single scheme. But later uncertainties over the founder's intentions and emphasis, as translated into the proportion of the trust's income that should be devoted to specific bequests, underlay many tensions. The sale of Iltney by the Breeder and Plume Educational Trust in 1918, with hindsight an inopportune moment to realise landed assets, was a major reason for the poverty of the Maldon Trust in the twentieth century. The trust was left with far less room for manoeuvre at a time when its building was in need of serious repair, but fortunately sufficient support emerged, both locally and nationally, for its demolition to be averted. The significant role of local government institutions, especially ECC and Maldon Borough Council, in averting disaster and supporting the trust's reconstitution in the 1952 scheme should be recognised.

The Maldon Trust and its library, now officially Thomas Plume's Library, is today a vibrant part of Maldon's cultural life, with an active body of trustees and a Friends' organisation. It has significantly reinstated and extended its engagement with education in the broader sense since the second half of the twentieth century. Originally, the lectures were a more significant aspect of the charity than is often realised, being allocated around a quarter of Iltney Farm's income in 1728. This element of Plume's conception fell by the wayside around 1900, but in the late twentieth century the trust was able to renew them as a well-attended annual public event. Although the trust is no longer directly associated with schooling, in recent years the renewal of its collaboration with Plume School, built on land left by Plume, has continued to develop. Knowledge of, and access to, the library's important books and manuscripts has been vastly improved through electronic cataloguing and other initiatives, leading to increasing numbers of scholars engaging with the collections.

Notes

1. The authors of this chapter would like to thank R.A. Doe, S. Edward and H. Kemp for their research assistance and J.R. Smith for additional information and his careful and constructive suggestions for improvement. All errors remain our own.
2. For the workhouse see Chapter 4, pp. 109–13; Appendix: Dr Thomas Plume's will, ll. 260–3; J.R. Smith, *The Borough of Maldon 1688–1800: A Golden Age* (Studley, 2013), pp. 362–5.
3. For Brickwood, below, p. 129.
4. Appendix: will, ll. 198–205. For Thompson: Chapter 4, pp. 99–100.
5. TNA C 6/348/11; TPL, MA0113, G.20; W.J. Petchey, *Maldon Grammar School 1608–1958* (Maldon, 1958), 19, 30.
6. TPL, MA0120, 12/04/1717.
7. *Ibid.*, 13/05/1717; 18/02/1719. Examples: 21/03/1729; 13/11/1740; 18/12/1758; 27/07/1774 (King's Head); 20/12/1762, 21/12/1767; 20/12/1775; 08/09/1778 (Blue Boar).
8. *Ibid.*, 12/04/1717; 13/05/1717 (clothing); 22/04/1718 (Iltney); 04/05/1719 (workhouse).
9. Chapter 4, pp. 111–13.
10. Appendix: will, ll. 226–7. For further information on the purchase from John Norton see Chapter 2, p. 33 and Figure 2.4.
11. Appendix: will, ll. 171–3, et seq.; Iltney was an ancient estate first recorded in the late eleventh century (OE 'Elta's island'): P.H. Reaney, *The Place-Names of Essex* (Cambridge, 1935), p. 221.
12. A. Young, *General View of the Agriculture of the County of Essex*, vol. 1 (London, 1813), p. 13; R. Baker, 'On the Farming of Essex', *Journal of the Royal Agricultural Society of England*, 5 (1845) pp. 33–9.
13. The name 'Elteneye in la Walle' suggests it was defended by a sea-wall as early as 1212: Reaney, *Place-Names of Essex*, p. 221.
14. P. Morant, *The History and Antiquities of the County of Essex* (London, 1768), vol. 1, p. 357.
15. Petchey, *Maldon Grammar School 1608–1958*, pp. 9–12; TNA, PROB 11/113/233 (1609).
16. Appendix: will, ll. 171–2; Morant, *History of Essex*, vol. 1, p. 337.
17. TPL, MA0120, 23/09/1717; 22/04/1718.
18. On a simple RPI calculation, an income of £70 in 1718 might equate to one of £135 14s by 1800: https://www.measuringworth.com/calculators/ppoweruk/.
19. Examples: TPL, MA0120, 22/12/1750; 19/12/1751; 05/06/1753; 20/06/1757; 20/12/1762.
20. Below, p. 128.
21. Smith, *The Borough of Maldon*, pp. 65, 124–9, 138–41, 182–3.
22. Appendix: will, ll. 175–80.
23. Payment to vicar: *ibid.*, ll. 246–53; TPL, MA0120, 12/04/1717.
24. The whole dispute is more fully dealt with in Smith, *The Borough of Maldon*, pp. 408–9.
25. TPL, MA0120, MA0121, MA0123, passim; *ibid.*, MA0126, 12/1/2–22, Accounts 1789–1809; *ibid.*, MA0149, Red folder, Lectures, 1792–1893.
26. Smith, *The Borough of Maldon*, p. 12. T. Cox, *Magna Britannia, Antiqua & Nova: or, A new, exact, and comprehensive survey of the ancient and present state of Great-Britain* (London, 1738 edn), vol. 1, p. 691, explained their residence at Maldon 'by reason of the unwholesomeness of the Air where their livings lie'.
27. TPL, MA0120, 31/03/1729.
28. *Ibid.*, 03/11/1733.
29. *Ibid.*, 01/12/1763; 02/12/1766.
30. Payments to sexton: Appendix: will, ll. 186–8; Figure 5.4.
31. Payments to poor: Appendix: will, ll. 189–91; MA0149; MA0154.
32. For a fuller history of the school: Petchey, *Maldon Grammar School 1608–1958*. A modern, more popular synopsis, has been published by S.P. Nunn, 'The Origins, Development and Continuing

Success of the Plume School', in *Maldon The Plume School – Four Centuries of Education (1608–2008)* (Maldon, 2008), pp. 5–28.
33   Petchey, *Maldon Grammar School*, pp. 3–7. Breeder's will is dated 1608 (Old Style), equivalent to 1609 (New Style): TNA, PROB 11/113/233 (1609).
34   *Ibid.*, 17.
35   Chapter 7, p. 178; Smith, *The Borough of Maldon*, 386.
36   Chapter 3, p. 54; Petchey, *Maldon Grammar School*, p. 17.
37   Chapter 7, pp. 178–9; Appendix: will, ll. 134–5.
38   Appendix: will, l. 174.
39   Appendix, will, ll. 192–7. The breeches were replaced with trousers in 1851: TPL, MA0123, 01/07/1851.
40   Smith, *The Borough of Maldon*, p. 82.
41   *Ibid.*, p. 122.
42   *Ibid.*, pp. 122–41.
43   *Ibid.*, 388; Petchey, *Maldon Grammar School*, p. 24. But for the continuation of the school in another form, see pp. 134–5.
44   Appendix: will, ll. 135, 144–5.
45   TPL, MA0113, G.20; TNA, C 6/348/11.
46   Appendix: will, ll. 168–70; Chapter 6, p. 156.
47   TPL, MA0120, 01/03/1721.
48   Chapter 7, p. 181; TPL, MA0159.
49   Appendix: will, ll. 156–7.
50   *Ibid.*, l. 230.
51   ERO, D/P 201/1/2.
52   Will of John Brickwood: ERO, D/ABW 79/74; ERO, D/ABR 15, fo. 305 (probate copy).
53   ERO, D/B 3/1/35.
54   *Ibid.*
55   Below, pp. 131–2, 134.
56   Appendix: will, ll. 146–51; TPL, MA0120, 15/08/1760.
57   The annuity was confirmed and granted by Wyldes in 1609. TPL, MA0155, 06/01/1610; Morant, *History of Essex*, vol. 1, pp. 336–7; Smith, *The Borough of Maldon*, pp. 368–9.
58   TPL, MA0120, 17/06/1741; 07/11/1741. Standish was an apothecary and father-in-law of William Smart: Smith, *The Borough of Maldon*, p. 174.
59   TPL, MA0120, 30/09/1779; ERO, D/DQs 137/3.
60   TPL, MA0120, 14/10/1782; ERO, D/DQs 137/3 (Maldon Corporation papers, statement of Poor Coals case). See also Smith, *The Borough of Maldon*, p. 369, for another account of the case.
61   *The Reports of the Commissioners appointed ... to enquire concerning charities in England and Wales relating to the County of Essex* (London, 1819–37; microfilm in ERO), p. 569; ERO, D/DCf B10/40, pp. 6–7.
62   At the back of the first minute book (TPL, MA0120) are eight pages of notes of trust meetings and financial information for the period April 1796 to June 1801, and a folder containing 15 pages of similar notes also survives for the period April 1796 to July 1800.
63   TPL, MA0121, 07/01/1834; *Reports of the Commissioners*, pp. 573–4.
64   ERO, Q/RSr 3, pp. 1–2; *An Act for the Registering and Securing of Charitable Donations* (The Charitable Donations Registration Act), 52 Geo. III, c. 102 (1812).
65   TPL, MA0120, 04/01/1813; MA0121, 05/07/1831.
66   ERO, D/DOp B45 (various papers and reports regarding Iltney Farm, 1819–20); TPL, MA0120, 11/05/1820 (Edward Payne's new lease).
67   TPL, MA0120, 11/05/1820; ERO, D/DOp B45 (survey report recommending abatement of rent, 16 September 1834); *Reports of the Commissioners*, pp. 573–4. The field was described as Upper Pound Field by this date.

68 ERO, D/CT 247A, B.
69 ERO, D/DOp B45.
70 TPL, MA0120, 03/07/1821.
71 TPL, MA0121, 07/07/1835, and subsequent correspondence with owner of White House Farm re: flooding.
72 Smith, *The Borough of Maldon*, pp. 388–90; Petchey, *Maldon Grammar School*, pp. 24–5, 30.
73 Below, pp. 140–3 and Figures 5.7 and 5.8.
74 Petchey, *Maldon Grammar School*, p. 25.
75 TPL, MA0120, 20/03/1817, 05/01/1818; ERO, D/Cf B10/40, p. 8.
76 M.G.L. Earnshaw, 'The Church on Market Hill' (privately published, 1988).
77 Chapter 7, pp. 180–1; TPL, MA0121, 02/05/1842.
78 *Reports of the Commissioners*, pp. 573–4.
79 Petchey, *Maldon Grammar School*, p. 25.
80 TPL, MA0121, 30/07/1836.
81 The court apparently concluded that the two fields had been purchased by Dr Thomas Plume, from John and Mary Newton, probably in 1702: ERO, D/DCf B10/40, pp. 5–7; above, Chapter 2, p. 33 and Figure 2.4.
82 Compare Tables 5.1 and 5.2, above.
83 *Reports of the Commissioners*, pp. 573–4; ERO, D/DCf B10/40.
84 TPL, MA0121, 05/07/1836; *Reports of the Commissioners*, pp. 573–4. See also ERO, D/DCf B10/40, pp. 7–8.
85 TPL, 03/07/1815; ERO, D/DCf B10/40, p. 6; *Reports of the Commissioners*, pp. 573–4.
86 TPL, MA0120, 26/12/1803.
87 *Reports of the Commissioners*, pp. 573–4.
88 This paragraph based on ERO, D/P 201/25/2 (copy of Plume Library trust deed, 1842/3). See also ERO, D/DCf B10/40; D/DCf Q9.
89 TPL, MA0123, 25/07/1843; 02/07/1844.
90 TPL, MA0123, 29/01/1852; 03/02/1852.
91 ERO, Q/RSr 7/41; D/P 201/25/2 (clause 29). Examples of payments: TPL, MA0123, 02/01/1855; 08/01/1857; 01/01/1862; 05/01/1869; 06/07/1869; 05/07/1870; 09/07/1873.
92 TPL, uncat., Report of the Town Clerk on the Charities of Maldon (January 1897), p. 5; ERO, D/DQs 137/3.
93 TPL, MA0123, 21/08/1850; 02/07/1861; 24/09/1874.
94 TPL, MA0123, 02/07/1861.
95 TPL, MA0123, 29/08/1896; ERO, D/F 63/5/136.
96 P. Wormell, *Essex Farming 1900-2000* (Colchester, 1999), pp. 13–14; E.J.T. Collins, ed., *The Agricultural History of England and Wales, vol. vii, 1850–1914*, Part I (Cambridge, 2000), pp. 374–5; E.H. Hunt and S.J. Pam, 'Responding to Agricultural Depression, 1873–96: Managerial Success, Entrepreneurial Failure?', *Agricultural History Review*, 50/2 (2002), p. 241.
97 TPL, MA0149, Red folder, Lectures, 1792–1893.
98 *Ibid.*
99 TPL, MA0121, 30/07/1836; MA0123, 04/07/1843; 25/07/1843.
100 TPL, MA0123, 05/01/1847, 09/03/1846 (National school). For problems with tower, *ibid.*, 05/07/1875, 06/09/1876, and Chapter 7, p. 185.
101 ERO, D/P 201/25/2, p. 6 (clause 27).
102 TPL, MA0123, 29/08/1843; 04/07/1848; 03/07/1849.
103 *Ibid.*, 03/09/1863.
104 *Ibid.*, passim.
105 Petchey, *Maldon Grammar School*, p. 27.

106 ERO, D/DCf Q15, letter and inventory of school furniture from R.H. Ryland, 05/02/1896.
107 M.E. Sadler, *Report on Secondary and Higher Education in Essex* (Chelmsford, 1906), p. 345.
108 Unless otherwise stated, the following analysis is based upon TPL, MA0157.
109 TPL, MA0123, 04/07/1843; W. White, *History, Gazetteer, and Directory of the County of Essex* (Sheffield, 1848), p. 534.
110 TPL, MA0121, 18/01/1839.
111 For examples: ERO, D/P 8/14/1 (Thorpe-le-Soken); D/P 169/14/1–2, 4 (Kirby-le-Soken).
112 TPL, PP0526, *The Maldonian* (1923); MA0158, item 46, letter from E.R. Horwood, dated 29/10/1881.
113 TPL, MA0123, 13/02/1894.
114 *Ibid.*, 04/07/1843. See also ERO, D/P 201/25/2 (clause 30).
115 TPL, MA0160; MA0161.
116 ERO, D/P 201/25/2 (clause 13). On the basis of examination of the hinge and locks.
117 TPL, MA0120, 15/08/1760; ERO, D/P 201/25/2 (clause 18).
118 ERO, Q/RSr 7/41.
119 TPL, MA0123, 31/03/1900.
120 *Ibid.*, 22/05/1900; 06/08/1900.
121 ERO, D/DCf Q15, Order in Council (15/06/1901) and Order in Council (28/11/1905); TPL, MA0123, 22/05/1900 (agreement to new scheme).
122 TPL, MA0131, 12/2/4 (Maldon Grammar School accounts, 1909); TPL, MA0123, 05/01/1914; 18/01/1916.
123 TPL, uncat., Charity Commission, Scheme, 13 October 1908, pp. 1–3.
124 ERO, D/Cf Q15, Order in Council (19/02/1910); D/B 3/3/696.
125 ERO, D/DQs 137/3 (correspondence dated 1906); D/DCf Q15 (Charity Commission agreements 15/05/1908, 25/06/1912); TPL, MA0123, 10/02/1908.
126 ERO, D/DCf Q15, Charity Commission order for sale of Iltney farm, 21/06/1918; TPL, MA0131, 12/2/7, Letter dated 09/09/1918 from Maldon Grammar School to the clerk of the charity; TPL, MA0123, 08/05/1923.
127 ERO, D/B 3/3/696.
128 For example, in 1922, Revd L.G. Seymour and Mr S.G. Deed: TPL, MA0123, 19/04/1922.
129 TPL, MA0123, 30/10/1917; 16/04/1918; 18/03/1919.
130 *Ibid.*, 08/04/1919; 15/04/1920.
131 *Ibid.*, 08/04/1919.
132 *Ibid.*, 15/03/1921.
133 *Ibid.*, 15/03/1921; 19/07/1921; 29/11/1921; 19/04/1922; 22/08/1922; 08/05/1923.
134 *Ibid.*, 08/05/1923.
135 *Ibid.*, 23/09/1924.
136 *Ibid.*, 23/04/1929; 18/12/1929.
137 *Ibid.*, 28/10/1930; 17/05/1931.
138 *Ibid.*, 17/05/1931.
139 *Ibid.*, 17/05/1931; 17/10/1931; 24/11/1931; 14/04/1932; 04/08/1932; 26/04/1933; TPL, uncat., Minister of Education, Scheme (including Appointment of Trustees), 20 June 1952, p. 4.
140 TPL, MA0123, 22/03/1935.
141 *Ibid.*, 29/04/1948, 10/11/1950; TPL, uncat., papers on 'Plume Library, Maldon', 15/10/1949; 25/04/1950; 30/06/1950, and 'The Plume Library', n.d., after 1952.
142 TPL, uncat., Minister of Education, Scheme (including Appointment of Trustees), 20 June 1952, pp. 1–4; TPL, MA0123, 19/09/1952.
143 TPL, uncat., paper on 'The Plume Library', n.d., after 1952.
144 TPL, MA0123, 29/04/1952; 19/09/1952.

145 TPL, uncat., Minister of Education, Scheme (including Appointment of Trustees), 20 June 1952, pp. 2, 4; TPL, uncat., Charity Commission, Order for vesting in Official Trustee of Charity Lands, 24 February 1953.
146 Inf. from C. Pryke, Hon. Treasurer, Thomas Plume's Library (11/01/2019); http://apps.charitycommission.gov.uk/Accounts/Ends61/0000310661_AC_20180331_E_C.pdf.
147 Inf. from Thomas Plume's Library.
148 http://www.thomasplumeslibrary.co.uk/news-events/the-plume-lecture/
149 TPL, uncat., Plume Box 5, Bundles 5/21 and 5/22 (new Maldon Grammar School leases, 08/05/1906).
150 Petchey, *Maldon Grammar School*, p. 28.
151 TPL, MA0123, 14/07/1902 (Horwood); 14/04/1932; 04/08/1932 (Salter); 22/03/1935 (Thomas). See also online catalogue: www.thomasplumeslibrary.co.uk/catalogue.
152 Appendix: will, ll. 159–67 (opening hours and rules for borrowing); TPL, uncat. note on Library Rules.
153 S.G. Deed and J. Francis, *Catalogue of the Plume Library at Maldon, Essex* (Maldon, 1959).
154 www.thomasplumeslibrary.co.uk/catalogue/the-collections-and-their-catalogues.
155 TPL, uncat., trustees' minutes 09/02/1987 (minute 6); 22/06/1987 (minute 3). The trustees were acting on information obtained through Frank Herrmann and Peter Young (both involved in the book trade), and the book was obtained from Bernard Quaritch Ltd, most of the cost being met by donations.
156 F. Herrmann, 'The Plume Library, Maldon: A New Chapter', in K. Neale (ed.), *Essex 'Full of Profitable Things'* (Oxford, 1996), pp. 245, 247; TPL, uncat., trustees' minutes 09/02/1987 (minute 8); 22/06/1987 (minute 3); 19/10/1987 (minute 3); 22/02/1988 (minute 3).
157 Herrmann, 'The Plume Library', p. 247; http://www.thomasplumeslibrary.co.uk/fotpl/ (accessed 07/01/2019).
158 Lord Brougham's Commission indicated the omission concerning Sion College and the poor ministers: *Reports of the Commissioners*, pp. 573–4.

Chapter 6

Thomas Plume's Library in its seventeenth-century context
David Pearson

Of all the various legacies and benefactions of Thomas Plume, his library is surely the most tangible and visible manifestation that helps to keep his name alive today. Many of his charitable bequests to education, the clergy and the poor made helpful impacts at the time, but their specific identification with Plume has faded over time. His professorship at Cambridge still has his name attached, but few people associate the work of twenty-first-century scientific astronomers with a seventeenth-century clergyman. His library, however, still stands much as he built it, now with a large, bold sign carrying his name. Although he never saw it filled with the books that, during his lifetime, lived on the shelves of his houses in Greenwich and Rochester, those combined collections have been preserved there since 1704, in much the way that he intended, and with relatively little loss. The library was a large one for its time, as one man's holding of books, and is today a valuable survival of the kind of town library of which we used to have more, but which have more usually been absorbed into larger municipal libraries or dispersed. It is a real treasure of bibliographical heritage at both a local and a national level, with books that are interesting individually and collectively. The purpose of this chapter is to outline the shape and content of the library, placing it within the context of other libraries of the time, and to consider Plume's motives and engagement with the books during his lifetime.

Town libraries in the seventeenth and eighteenth centuries
In providing a town library Plume was contributing to a well-established kind of local philanthropy that had gathered momentum during his own generation. Tudor England's libraries were found either within institutions such as

universities or cathedrals or in private houses, and the idea of creating them as resources for the use of a particular settlement evolved during the seventeenth century. They were invariably created through charitable munificence, set going by the gift or bequest of a library of books or money (or both) by an individual with a local connection. Many were attached to, and the responsibility of, a parish church and are commonly known as parochial (or parish) libraries, while others were town libraries, managed by the municipal authority or, as in Plume's case, a body of trustees. Parochial libraries were typically intended specifically for the use of the clergy, while town libraries allowed wider access, but the distinctions are not clear-cut. The earliest such town library in England was established at Norwich in 1608, closely followed by one at Ipswich in 1612; numerous others were created during succeeding decades, including at Bristol (1613), King's Lynn and Colchester (both 1631), and Leicester (1633). In Manchester, the 1653 bequest of Humphrey Chetham (a wealthy local cloth merchant) established a library with a significant endowment, to be managed by a self-electing group of trustees.[1] After the Restoration library-founding continued apace, and Kelly noted that 'more than one-third of the total number of endowed libraries were founded in the years between 1680 and 1720';[2] this included parish libraries as well as town ones, where a number of initiatives contributed to a drive to create libraries to help the clergy in rural areas. In 1685 Barnabas Oley created small libraries in ten parishes in the diocese of Carlisle and in the 1690s Thomas Bray published several works advocating the establishment of parish libraries in both Britain and America.[3] In 1699 Bray founded the Society for the Promotion of Christian Knowledge, which soon became a leading force in the spreading of parish libraries; Plume was one of its founder members.[4] It is clear, therefore, that Plume's ideas for his books were formulated within a well-established framework of recognition of the desirability and benefits of publicly accessible libraries.

The size of the Library

The books that came to Maldon in 1704 constituted Plume's personal library, assembled throughout the course of his working life during the second half of the seventeenth century. The rebuilding of St Peter's church during the late 1690s to house both a school and a library is described in Chapter 7, and it is clear that Plume formed the intention of disposing of his books in this way a decade or more before his death. The latest estimate of size, based on historical information and the recataloguing of the library in the early twenty-first century, is that it originally contained around 5,800 bound volumes and 1,600 unbound pamphlets. For its time, this is a large collection. The private ownership of books was widespread during the seventeenth century, and it is typical to find clergymen, academics and professional men owning libraries of several thousand volumes, but something under 5,000 is much more common than something over. Many sale catalogues survive from the last quarter of the seventeenth century and these, together with other significant collections of the time whose size is known, produce an average figure of 3,000 to 3,500 books for these kinds of library – from people who owned enough books to leave a footprint in the historical record – in the period 1690–1715.[5] John Evelyn (1620–1706), the celebrated diarist and author, had over 5,000 books when he died; Sir William Boothby (1638?–1707), of Ashbourne Hall, Derbyshire, and a noted gentry bibliophile, had around 6,000; Henry Aldrich (1647–1710), dean of Christ Church, Oxford, bequeathed around 3,000 books and a very large collection of music to his college.[6] Plume topped these, but his was not the largest library of his generation; the auction sale of the physician Francis Bernard (1627–98) ran to around 15,000 lots and the celebrated collection of John Moore (1646–1714), which holds the record as the largest of its day, comprised about 30,000 books.[7] Edward Stillingfleet (1635–99), whose library became one of the foundation stones of Marsh's Library in Dublin, owned about 10,000 books.[8] It should be noted, though, that Stillingfleet and Moore were bishops, not mere archdeacons like Plume, and that his library was certainly larger than many other episcopal ones of the time. We do not know the full extent of the library of Thomas Barlow (1608/9–91), bishop of Lincoln, which was divided between Queen's College, Oxford, and the Bodleian, but it seems to have been less than 5,000 books; Henry Compton (1631/2–1713), bishop of London, left a little under 2,000 books to St Paul's Cathedral, as well as some books to Sion College and Colchester Grammar School.[9] Within this overall landscape, we can see that Plume's Library may not have been the biggest but was certainly significantly large and in the upper quartile, statistically, in its day.

The contents
Seventeenth-century libraries of this kind of size typically embraced a wide variety of subjects, covering the spectrum of recorded knowledge. At least half the contents, irrespective of the professional background of the owner, would comprise what today would be classified as theology, including biblical and patristic texts, commentaries and devotional, doctrinal and controversial writings, in a way that would seem a much broader spread to a mind of the time than might be the case now. The rest would cover, in varying degrees, history, literature, classics, geography, travel, science, natural history, medicine, law and other miscellaneous topics. Plume's Library very much fits this mould and it is important, in interpreting its contents, to view it within that contemporary context. Previous writers on the library have seen its breadth of content as a sign that Plume was deliberately developing a resource for posterity rather than for his own use – for W.J. Petchey, 'far from being a "personal working library",

as seen by Sir Frank Francis, this was a deliberately constructed museum of European intellectual history', and Keith Manley thought that 'he must always have intended his library for a wider audience' – but we should treat these assumptions with caution.[10] I believe that Francis (writing in the Foreword to the 1959 printed catalogue)[11] was nearer the mark, supported by the evidence noted below of Plume's use of his books right up to the end of his life, but that is not at odds with the idea that he will have come to realise that the library he had developed was on a scale to be of ongoing use.

Subject classification of early books is a notoriously imprecise game and is prone to the dangers of overlaying modern values or thought-systems on texts produced for people with very different sets of principles. Should Robert Burton's *Anatomy of Melancholy* (1621, Plume owned the third edition of 1628) be classified as medicine, psychology, philosophy, literature or something else? Is Morgan Godwyn's *The Negro's and Indians Advocate, Suing for their Admission to the Church* (1680), of which Plume owned two copies together with the 1681 *Supplement*, a book to classify as theology, politics, social history or something else? Arguing for the Christian conversion and baptism of negro slaves in America against the resistance of plantation owners, it is studied today very much in the context of colonial history and slavery, but Godwyn (and doubtless Plume also) was more concerned with spiritual welfare than political emancipation, which for him would have been an alien concept. The boundaries between theology and ideas that we would today categorise differently can be very blurred in the seventeenth-century context.

We can nevertheless attempt some high-level analysis. Taking what should be a representative sample of the library – the first 900 books listed in the printed catalogue, authors A–B, each allocated one subject subdivision – my assessment is shown in Table 6.1. Although this sample covers only a little over 10 per cent of the total library, it is unlikely that a fuller analysis would significantly change the shape of the graphs that emerge as regards the percentages of books that can be assigned to the various subject categories. A split of 65/35 between theology (in its broadest sense) and all other subjects is not a surprise for a clergyman's library of this period, nor is the breadth of other topics embraced.

A study published in 2010 sought to establish some common patterns of book ownership at the end of the seventeenth century by undertaking a comparative analysis of five auction sale catalogues of the 1680s and 1690s, each devoted to one individual's library, to see which books regularly appeared on people's shelves, irrespective of background.[12] The sample included academics, an Anglican and a nonconformist clergyman, and a baronet. Each of the collections was significantly smaller than Plume's, in the region of 1,000 to 1,500 books. A number of lists emerged – specific books which all five owned, authors whose works appeared in every collection – against which

Table 6.1 Subject analysis of books in the Plume Library (sample)

Subject matter	No.	%
Devotional works, liturgy, works on personal religion	123	13.7
Controversial, doctrinal, political theology; works on contemporary ecclesiastical affairs	334	37.1
Biblical commentaries, expository works, Bibles and Biblical texts	103	11.4
Patristics, early church history	28	3.1
History, including continental, Byzantine and Islamic, ecclesiastical, biography	69	7.7
Current affairs, contemporary history, controversy, politics	69	7.7
Classics, ancient authors, history of the classical world	19	2.1
Philosophy, metaphysics, advice on life	12	1.3
Hebrew and oriental languages, lexicons	11	1.2
Literature	20	2.2
Law	3	0.3
Science, mathematics, natural history, contemporary experimentation	55	6.1
Medicine	17	1.9
Astronomy & related	14	1.6
Other subjects, including education, marriage, geography & travel	23	2.6

Plume's holdings can usefully be compared. The list of writers represented in every library included Church Fathers (Cyril, Gregory Nazianzenus), a range of seventeenth-century theological authors from all parts of the Catholic/Anglican/Nonconformist spectrum (including Lancelot Andrewes, Robert Bellarmine, Henry Hammond, John Owen, Gerhard Voss and Andrew Willet) and orientalists such as Johannes Buxtorf and Thomas Erpenius. It included polymaths and philosophers such as Erasmus, Lipsius, More and Scaliger, legal writers such as Grotius and Zouch, and the antiquary Henry Spelman. Literature was represented by Milton and the sixteenth-century Scots poet George Buchanan, and science by Bacon, Digby, Gassendi and Wilkins. Every one of these authors – and all of those who appear in all five of the sample libraries – is included in Plume's Library. As regards specific books, that earlier study found 30 titles (apart from the Bible) that turned up in every collection, over half of which were classical or patristic texts; other books included Erasmus's *Adagia* (first published in 1500 and much reprinted), Buxtorf's *Hebrew Dictionary* (1607) and doctrinal or expository theological works by William Ames, Daniel Heinsius, Richard Hooker, Joseph Mede and William Pemble. Again, there is a close match between this list and Plume's holdings;

the only titles from the 30 that are not in Plume's Library are the works of the Neoplatonist Roman author Macrobius, Ovid's *Metamorphoses* and *The Causes of the Decay of Christian Piety*, a devotional work first published in 1667 that went through many editions in the seventeenth and eighteenth centuries. This last book was one of the family of devotional works following on from the hugely popular *Whole Duty of Man* (1657), all of which are attributed to Richard Allestree (1621/2–81); we might note that Plume seems not to have had a copy of that either, though he did have two other books 'By the author of the Whole Duty of Man': copies of *The Art of Patience under all Afflictions* (1684) and *The Lively Oracles Given to Us* (1679). He may have felt he did not need devotional books intended for a lay audience, or these books may once have been on his shelves but since lost; either is possible. Overall, the patterns around popular authors and subject coverage that emerged from the five smaller libraries are well mirrored in Plume's larger collection.

In assessing seventeenth-century libraries, we need to recognise the ways in which values have changed between then and now, as regards intellectual or cultural significance. The well-known exhibition of 1967 on printing and the mind of man, which sought to identify the most influential and impactful printed books in western civilisation over five centuries, included 76 books published across Europe (including England) between 1580 and 1700 that were reckoned, 'for the ideas which they brought to the world for the first time, [to be] of prime importance'.[13] Some 23 of those 76 books, in various editions or translations, are to be found on Plume's shelves, and a number of other seminal authors are represented by other works. The absence of Shakespeare is perhaps the most obvious gap to draw modern attention, but it is quite usual to find him absent from seventeenth-century libraries, even large ones. In the literary sphere, Chaucer, Donne, Herbert, Jonson, Marvell and Milton are all represented on Plume's shelves.

Looking at milestones in the development of early modern thinking, we can observe that Plume owned Hobbes's *Leviathan* (a 1670 Latin edition, not the original 1651 English one) and Locke's *Essay Concerning Humane Understanding* (the second edition of 1694), and works by Descartes, Leibniz and Spinoza. Others have commented on the absence of Newton from the library (particularly the 1687 *Principia*),[14] and we might also have expected to find Robert Hooke's *Micrographia* (1665), but Plume's holdings of scientific works are noteworthy in various ways. He owned nearly 30 separate publications by Robert Boyle and, although he had no known connection with the Royal Society, his pamphlets include a number of separate parts of the *Philosophical Transactions* from the 1660s and 1680s. Plume's interest in astronomy, reflected in his bequest to Cambridge, is clearly visible in the number of books in this field that he owned. There are over 100 books that relate directly or partly to astronomy, which may be a small percentage of the collection as a whole but a significant quantity nonetheless for a general library of the time. They include works by well-known major authors such as Brahe, Galilei, Gassendi, Halley, Hevelius and Kepler, alongside more ephemeral pieces such as John Bainbridge's *Astronomicall Description of the Late Comet* (1619). His holdings of medical texts likewise run into three figures, with works by leading medical writers of his own generation such as Charleton, Lower and Willis, and two of the books of William Harvey. He owned the writings of Galen and Hippocrates, and those of significant European medical authors of the sixteenth and seventeenth centuries such as Fernel, Malpighi, van Helmont, Sennert and Tulp. Overall, the library suggests familiarity with, and interest in, much of the culture of scientific experimentation that was flourishing in late seventeenth-century England. The area where the library is noticeably thin is law. Plume did own a number of the standard works on legal theory, such as Grotius on war (*De Jure Belli ac Pacis*; 1650) and Richard Zouch on civil law (*Elementa Jurisprudentiae*; 1652), but a search of the Plume catalogue will show that much of the material classified as law relates to ecclesiastical and parochial law, tithes and matters that we can see being of practical concern to a working clergyman; there is less by way of law reports and suchlike, beyond two volumes of reports of trials held by two well-known early seventeenth-century judges, Sir Henry Hobart (1560–1625) and Sir Edward Coke (1552–1634). Although Plume's Library contains a significant proportion of theological material, as we would expect, it also embraces a broad sweep of the scientific and intellectual enquiry for which we now celebrate the later seventeenth century.

How the Library was developed
We know very little about the ways in which the library was built up by Plume, beyond what can be deduced from evidence in the books. There was a flourishing trade in both new and secondhand books in London and elsewhere throughout Plume's lifetime and he would have had plenty of opportunities to buy books.[15] Petchey thought that Hacket's commissioning of Plume as his book-runner during the Interregnum provided him with a useful apprenticeship – 'in the late 1650s he commenced a life-long acquaintance with the many book-sellers of London'[16] – but he had been buying books for himself before this. There are volumes in the library with inscriptions in Plume's youthful hand whose imprint dates (1640s) and subject matter suggest books he was acquiring in his student days.[17] Imprint dates and inscriptions point to a steady process of ingesting books thereafter, through the rest of his life. Petchey plotted a graph of imprint dates, showing how half the total contents were printed before 1650; he inferred from this that Plume's book-buying declined towards the end of his life, and that he was actively focusing on 'the work of

generations of scholars prior to his own', but there is nothing unusual about seventeenth-century book-owners relying at least as much on the secondhand market as on the new one. He was certainly acquiring books up to the time of his death, as there are books of the late 1690s and early 1700s inscribed by him and a copy of William Assheton's *Vindication of the Immortality of the Soul* (1703) with a note in his hand that it was given him by the author.[18]

Large libraries are sometimes built partly via the gift, purchase or bequest of other large collections *en bloc* – for instance, the buying of Stillingfleet's 10,000 books by Archbishop Marsh in 1705[19] – but this does not apply to Plume as far as we can tell. He did not inherit any sizeable quantities of books from his father or any other relative. Many of Plume's books carry inscriptions, bookplates or other markings from previous owners, but there are no names that occur so frequently as to suggest a bulk purchase. We know that some of his manuscript collections came to him *en bloc*, such as the manuscripts of Robert Boreman (which included within them the papers of Edward Hyde), and Helen Kemp notes that some printed books from Justinian Whitter (d. 1649) are likely to have flowed into Plume's Library via bequest, but there is only a small handful of books carrying Whitter's inscription (see Chapter 8).[20] A 1703 book with an 'ex dono authoris' inscription was noted above and there are a few, but only a few, other books with notes in Plume's hand saying that they were gifts from the author.[21] It seems likely that Plume would have patronised the auction trade in secondhand books that began in London in the 1670s and flourished thereafter, but in the absence of archival or other evidence to substantiate this we can only conjecture.[22] Reflecting on the question of how long Plume sustained his book-buying, we may note a small clutch of books that are likely to have reached the secondhand market not long before his death; John Fitzwilliam (d. 1699), fellow of Magdalen College, Oxford, until deprived as a nonjuror in 1689, bequeathed his books to Magdalen. There are at least two books on the Plume shelves that carry Fitzwilliam's distinctive inscription and which are likely to have come onto the market sometime after 1699 as surplus to Magdalen's requirements, implying the ongoing acquisition of secondhand material into the eighteenth century.[23]

The one piece of documentary evidence that we do have of block purchase by Plume is an undated late seventeenth-century manuscript list written on both sides of two long narrow pieces of paper headed 'Duplicates in folio of my Ld of Ely's'. The second leaf (recto) begins 'In Quarto, et Octavo'. This lists about 350 books, almost entirely theological, with authors, titles, dates (sometimes) and prices; they presumably constitute a group of books that belonged, or had belonged, to a bishop of Ely and were available for purchase as surplus to requirements elsewhere. The books range in date from the late sixteenth to the late seventeenth centuries (the latest imprint date noted is 1681) and prices are

6.1 A typical example of Plume's inscription in a book, from his later years, together with his 'PL' monogram: flyleaf of *The Acts and Negotiations* (1698) (TPL, B01046).

6.2 The more unusual inscription 'Thomas Plume & Amico[ru]m' ('belonging to Thomas Plume and his friends'), on the flyleaf of J. de Mariana, *Tractatus VII* (1609) (TPL, B00152).

typically between four shillings and a pound for folios (more for multi-volume works) and between one and six shillings for quartos and octavos. Around 150 of the books on the list have ink crosses beside them, which spot checks with the library shelves suggest are books selected by Plume. Taking all dates into account, the most likely candidate as the original owner of these books is Peter Gunning (1614–84), bishop of Ely from 1675 until his death, who bequeathed his sizeable library to St John's College, Cambridge, where there would be likely to be duplication of holdings.[24] If this interpretation is correct, this would represent an investment of around £40 in a single transaction to acquire a block of books all at once, and there may have been more like this. Unfortunately, we do not have letters, bills, accounts or other kinds of domestic archive surviving for Plume to enable the picture to be painted more fully.[25]

Plume as an inscriber and annotator

We might be able to construct Plume's acquisition schedule more fully if he had systematically inscribed his books, but his practice in this regard was more occasional than regular. It is, however, not true to say (as Petchey did) that 'he is not to be found among his books'.[26] There are a few more than 50 books in the library in which he wrote his name on the flyleaf or titlepage, typically in the form 'Tho Plume', like the example shown in Figure 6.1. Examples can be found from the beginning, middle and end of his book-buying life, so it was not a habit that was a brief passing phase, but we do not know why he wrote his name like this just sometimes, and not more often. Perhaps the inscribed books were lent out to others? There is one book, a copy of Juan de Mariana's *Tractatus vii de Adventu B. Jacobi Apostoli in Hispaniam* (1609), in which he wrote 'Thomae Plume & Amicorum' ('Belonging to Thomas Plume and his friends'), a book-

6.3 An early example of Plume's inscription, from the flyleaf of *Terence in English* (1641) (TPL, B00206).

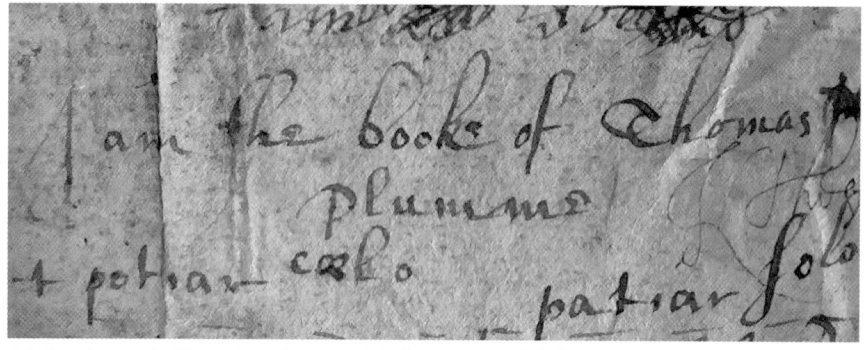

6.4 Another early Plume inscription, with the name spelt 'Plumme', 1643 (TPL, MA0066).

ownership formula that was popular across Europe a century or so earlier, but which is uncommon in the late seventeenth; its existence perhaps supports the theory of loaning (Figure 6.2).[27] The handwriting of the inscriptions in Figures 6.1 and 6.2 is typical of the middle and later part of Plume's life; as a young man, his hand was less angular (the inscription in one of the student books of the 1640s mentioned earlier is shown in Figure 6.3). We might note the bar over the 'm' of Plume here, indicating that at this point in his life he thought of his name as Plumme, the form he used in a small manuscript filled with sermon notes from his younger days (Figure 6.4).

Plume was not a marginal annotator of his books, but he did sometimes add notes to flyleaves, providing contents lists of tract volumes or references to particular passages of text. These are typically abbreviated, in his angular and often difficult-to-read hand, like the examples in Figures 6.5 and 6.6. Many book historians have written about the challenges involved in moving between book ownership and demonstrable use; a book owned is not necessarily one read, and we need to be cautious in assessing the evidence.[28] Many of Plume's books carry no trace of his hand and we should not automatically assume that he read what he bought.

The evidence of his close reading and engagement with many of his books lies not in the books themselves, but in a series of notebooks that survive as part of the library's manuscript collections. There are nine of these – there may

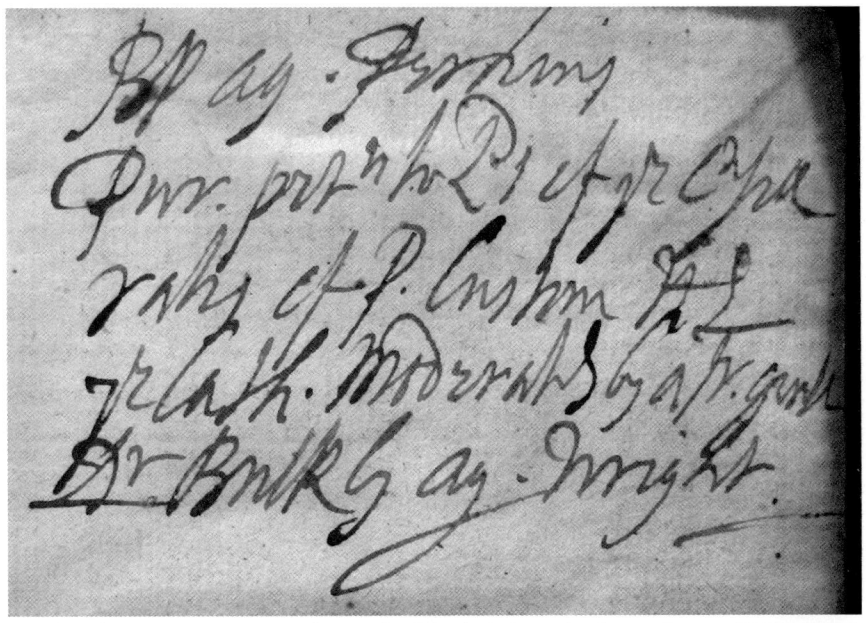

6.5 Plume's manuscript contents list on the flyleaf of a bound volume of tracts: W. Bishop, *A reformation of a Catholike deformed* (1604; and four others, 1590–1623) (TPL, B07423).

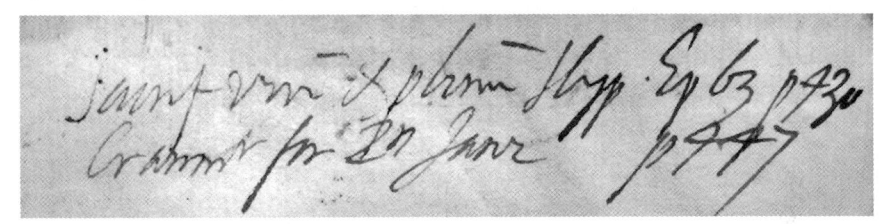

6.6 An example of Plume's flyleaf notes, referring to points in the text with page references (page 430 of this book refers to Cyprian's Epistle 63, page 447 to Cranmer's support for Lady Jane Grey): F. Walshingham, *A Search made into Matters of Religion* (1609) (TPL, B00421).

once have been more – which mostly started life as small blank octavo books simply bound in undecorated sheepskin, then filled by Plume with detailed notes on particular books.[29] They are typically written from both ends, with a contents list of 15 or 20 books for each half and several pages of closely written notes showing how he read through each book page by page, extracting page-referenced points that he considered worth recording (Figure 6.7). Each book-section ends with a note of the date that he finished reading and, although these fall mostly between the late 1650s and the 1680s, the latest one is dated 1703.[30] Helen Kemp describes these more fully in her analysis of the Plume manuscripts, where she points out that the notebooks cover a range of subjects and are not only theological; MA0072 shows Plume's reading of Gassendi's

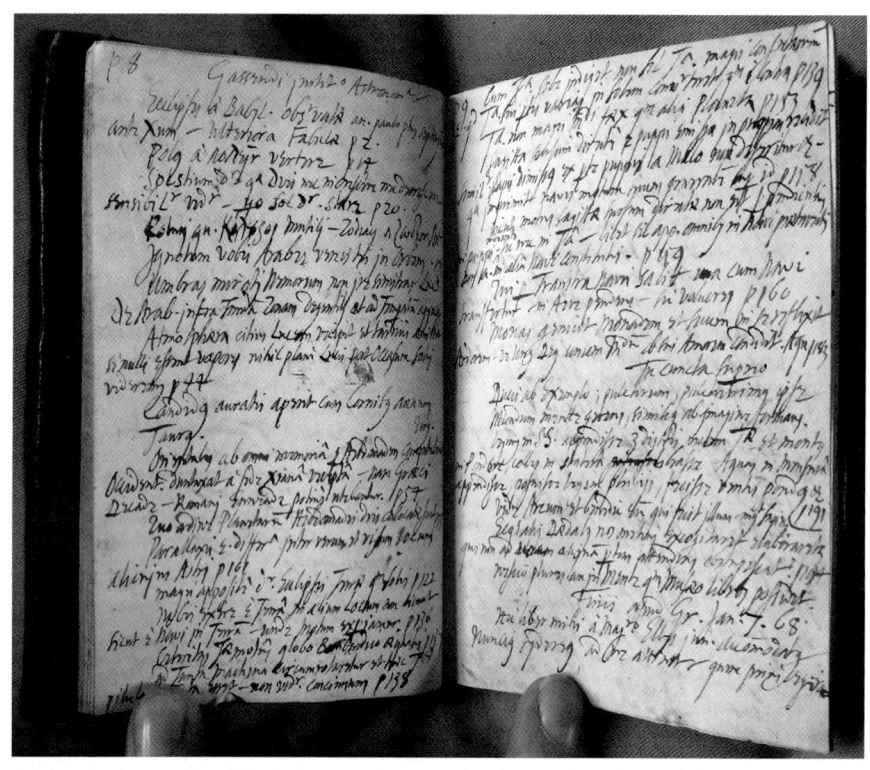

6.7 A typical example of Plume's manuscript notebooks, in which he made his reading notes: TPL, MA0072, showing notes on Gassendi's *Institutio Astronomica* (n.d) (TPL, B06928).

Institutio Astronomica (a book that is no longer in the library and must have gone missing sometime after 1704; Plume perhaps read the first London edition of 1653) and the same author's biography of Tycho Brahe (still there), while MA0054 includes his abstracting of Dugdale's *Monasticon Anglicanum* (1655–73) and Evelyn's *Sylva* (Plume had the second edition, 1670). This kind of noting technique as a way of reading and digesting books was a standard practice that was taught in the seventeenth century, and many other similar notebooks and commonplace books survive (including within the Plume manuscripts). Where the books survive in the library, it is possible to check Plume's page references against the books on the shelves and verify the match; he was certainly using the same editions and there is no reason to doubt that he was reading his own copies. The notebooks demonstrate Plume's use and close reading of his books throughout his professional lifetime.

One kind of inscription that Plume did regularly add to many books, and which remains a mystery, is a monogram that looks like a combination of a P and an L, which is found on the flyleaves of over 500 books; it can be seen in

Figure 6.1. It appears sometimes in books in which he also wrote his name, more often not, and there is at least one instance where it has been written over the name of a previous owner.[31] The distribution pattern suggests the marking of a particular subset of books within the whole – perhaps those at one of his two residences, Longfield or Greenwich? – but no convincing explanation has thus far appeared. It has been suggested that these books may correlate with a batch of books packed in six casks and despatched to Maldon after Plume's death, but examination of this list shows that this cannot be the case.[32]

Plume's bookbindings
Throughout the handpress period, until mechanisation and mass production arrived during the nineteenth century, the binding of books (like their printing) was a handcrafted process and every book, from the simplest pamphlet to the grandest folio, had to be sewn, covered and decorated by hand. This created a spectrum of choice for book-buyers, who could take their books home sewn in paper wrappers or luxuriously bound in richly gilded fine leather; the more they paid, the more sturdily constructed and the more elaborately decorated the end product would be. There were various reasons why people might choose to pay more than was necessary just to have a sturdy book and opt for gilding and decoration: because they liked it aesthetically, because they wished to impress or use their books to demonstrate their social standing, because the book was destined to be a gift, or to seek patronage, or to make a statement about the importance of the book's contents. A mixture of these motives is likely to apply in any individual case, and there are plentiful instances of people who were certainly serious readers of their books but who also spent money on the beautification of their outsides; Plume's contemporaries Samuel Pepys (1633–1703) and John Evelyn (1620–1706) are well-known examples.[33] At the same time, voices were active in the seventeenth century, as in all centuries, to counsel against vain expenditure. Gabriel Naudé's advice on libraries, translated from the French by Evelyn (1661), includes strictures against 'superfluous expences, which many prodigally and to no purpose bestow upon the binding and ornaments of their books … it becoming the ignorant onely to esteem a book for its cover'.[34]

Plume certainly followed the advice of Naudé, rather than the practice of his translator, in the binding of his books. The great majority are in sound, sturdy contemporary bindings, typically leather-covered with very simple decoration, the kind of thing that represented the default option of the time for someone wanting a book that would be thoroughly serviceable and lasting, but without undue prettification for its own sake. Standing in Plume's Library today, the bookshelves do not present us with rows of gilded spines. We know that he was sufficiently wealthy to have been able to afford something more showy should he have desired it – there are plenty of seventeenth-century clergy collections where we can be more sure that rows of plain bindings reflect a modest income level – but, in Plume's case, it is reasonable to assume that he eschewed more flamboyance as a matter of choice. Unlike Pepys and Evelyn, he did not commission personalised armorial binding tools, nor did he succumb to the fashion for bookplates that appealed to so many book owners at the end of the seventeenth century. Of course, many of Plume's books were acquired secondhand and therefore ready bound, and it will generally be found that bindings with less than minimal decoration fall into this category. There are numerous books with late sixteenth- or early seventeenth-century gilded centrepieces, and some with the armorial decoration of previous owners, which were clearly already bound like this when bought by Plume.[35] One or two bindings with more elaborate decoration stand out today, but it seems unlikely that their fanciness, as opposed to their text, was what interested Plume.[36] A late seventeenth-century binding with a more than usually gilded spine turns out to be a presentation copy to Plume, and was doubtless commissioned like that by the donor, not the recipient.[37] One of the books on the list of the bishop of Ely's duplicates, mentioned above, which has a cross beside it and is presumably the copy now in the Plume Library, is described as 'M. Lomini Blackloanae Haeresis Hist. Gandavi 1675, unbound 00–02–08'. This is Peter Talbot's *Blakloanae Haeresis ... Historia et Confutatio*, printed in Ghent (Gandavum) in 1675, and if acquired unbound it seems safe to assume that the plain dark brown calfskin binding that now covers it, decorated only with minimal blind-tooled lines, was what Plume commissioned after he received it.

The fact that Plume's Library is not a showcase of fine binding is no cause for regret; it is, rather, a treasury of sixteenth- and seventeenth-century books in largely unspoiled contemporary condition that provides an authentic window into the experience of books in the early modern period. This is particularly the case with the library's collection of unbound pamphlets, one of its more remarkable, but as yet little explored, strengths. In addition to the bound volumes on the shelves, there are about 1,600 tracts and short books that are not in leather-covered boards but held together with simple stitching, with or without wrappers of paper or manuscript waste. Subject-wise, they fit with the profile of the library more widely; many are theological, others range across the spectrum of knowledge and ideas. Here will be found some perhaps unexpected byways in the thinking of Plume and his contemporaries, such as Edmund Arwaker's *Fons Perennis. A ... Poem on Making Sea-water Fresh* (1686), Richard Boothby's *Breife Discovery ... of Madagascar* (1646) and Cave Beck's *Universal Character* (1657), which was an early proposal for the creation of a universal language, long before Esperanto. There are

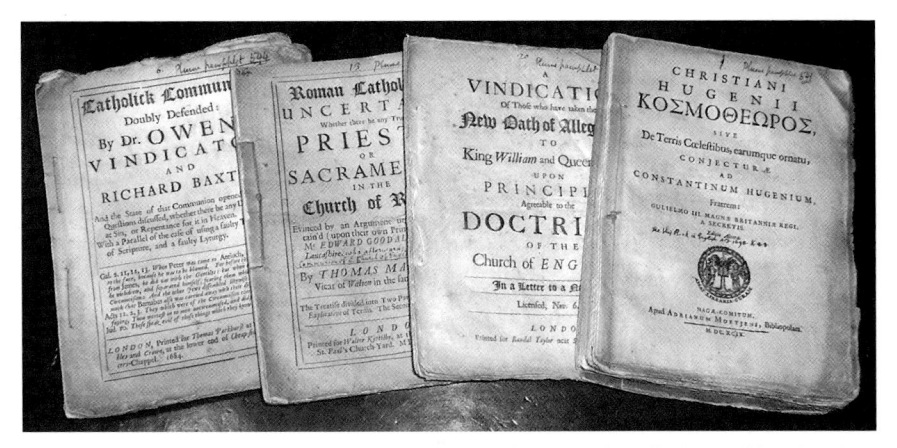

6.8 A representative selection of Plume's collection of unbound stitched pamphlets (TPL).

inevitably rarities here, in the sense of books of which only a few copies now exist, but in toto this is a striking survival of the kind of collection that used to be a typical feature of private libraries of any size. Book-sale catalogues of the late seventeenth and early eighteenth centuries regularly end with lots comprising bundles of stitched pamphlets or unbound tracts and sermons, but finding such quantities all together in the way they were left at the time is now unusual.[38] Historic books have generally come down to us today as a result of being preserved in institutional libraries, and those libraries' practice has commonly been to bind such material up in more permanent formats; otherwise, they have been discarded or destroyed as victims of their ephemeral physical state. Plume's pamphlets manifest a range of construction techniques; some have been covered with modern paper wrappers but many are stab-stitched in original seventeenth-century condition, sometimes with no covers, sometimes with covers of contemporary coloured paper or printed waste, sometimes with wrappers from discarded medieval manuscripts (Figure 6.8). There are a few other libraries of this period whose intact survival includes pamphlet collections, but I am not aware of any English ones on the scale of Plume's.[39] At a time of increasing interest in books as material objects, when we are recognising the importance of considering physical format as an influence upon ways in which books were read and received, the opportunity this collection represents to experience seventeenth-century books in authentic condition should be particularly appreciated.

Plume and manuscripts

Plume's manuscript collections comprised a mixture of his own notebooks and papers and those of several of his clerical contemporaries (they are described in more detail in Chapter 8). In this context it is worth adding that these, too, constitute a rare survival of the kind of assemblages of such material that would once have been commoner than can easily be found today. The wills of seventeenth-century book owners display a range of approaches to personal working papers – sometimes they were to be destroyed, sometimes passed to family members or colleagues. Clergymen and academics naturally recognised the value of the working papers and notes of their fellows and the accumulation of collections such as this was not unusual; what is much less common is their undispersed preservation over several centuries. Thomas Barlow, bishop of Lincoln (1608/9–91), who left most of his printed books to the Bodleian and Queen's College, Oxford, separated out his own manuscript writings to go to his chaplains.[40] John Bowle, bishop of Rochester (d. 1637), directed that his books be sold, but that 'all my written paper books and writings that conteyne my … practise in divinitie' be given to his friend John Moundeford, prebendary of St Paul's.[41] Humphrey Gower, master of St John's College, Cambridge (1638–1711), left most of his books to the college, but 'manuscripts of my own composing' were to go to his friend Edward Brome, fellow.[42]

It is also worth observing that one thing Plume did not acquire was medieval manuscripts, although he would certainly have had both the opportunity and the means to do so. The appreciation of manuscripts as important historical witnesses was well established by Plume's day, through a century and more of antiquarian activity, and we know that he both owned and read Dugdale's *Monasticon*, with its overview of monastic heritage.[43] Many private libraries of his time did embrace manuscript holdings and they featured in numerous auction sales of the late seventeenth century.[44] One of Plume's fellow archdeacons within the diocese of Canterbury, John Batteley, archdeacon of Canterbury (1646–1708, who Plume must have known), had a collection of medieval manuscripts that came to be sought after his death by Robert Harley and others, and other clergymen of Plume's time had similar collections.[45] Plume's Library has a copy of Edward Bernard's catalogue of collections of manuscripts in English private and institutional hands, published in 1697, which was presumably his; it has no markings by him, though a few annotations in a slightly later hand, and is generally in clean condition with few signs of use.[46] The inference is that Plume's interest in the library was as a working tool, a quarry of knowledge and ideas, not as a safeguarder or preserver of heritage; he was a scholar–clergyman, not an antiquary.

Plume's Library, as it seemed to him, and to us
Parish libraries were often designated as belonging to the incumbent and his successors (or some similar formulation), and many town libraries as well as parochial ones were intended primarily for clergy use, although provision was often made to permit access by suitably respectable lay people also. The

poverty of many rural clergymen, and their consequent inability to buy books for themselves, was a key motivator of men such as Barnabas Oley and Thomas Bray, and some of Plume's other charitable bequests show that financial support for poor clergymen was one of his concerns.[47] Local clergymen involved in preaching or giving the weekly lectures for which Plume left provision could be expected to benefit from the storehouse of learning that Plume provided. He clearly intended his library to be more widely accessible, though, with his provision that 'any gentleman, or Scholar, who desires, may goe into it, & make use of any book there or borrow it'.[48] Education, right-thinking and spiritual well-being were surely key purposes in his mind, but Michael Powell has pointed out that civic pride doubtless played a part too in the setting up of town libraries; at a time of growing library foundation, with long-established town libraries at Colchester and Ipswich, it was surely time that Maldon was put on this map?[49] Which it emphatically was, with a library that was not only significantly larger than most but also had its own purpose-designed building, a much less common feature at the time.[50] The most striking thing it lacked, as others have pointed out, was a purchase fund; Plume's will makes provision for an ongoing acquisition budget of only one pound per year, which is clearly no more than a token sum, stipulated by a man who knew what books cost.[51] He presumably thought that his library already contained the necessary sum core of the world's knowledge and thinking, sufficient for generations to come, a narrowness of mental horizons that suggests a dogmatic, conservative or short-sighted mindset – or a combination of all of those?

Fifty years ago, in his Foreword to the printed catalogue of the Plume Library, Sir Frank Francis (then director of the British Museum Library, today's British Library) sought to bring out its key features. He devoted a paragraph to books that are technically rare, in the sense of surviving in only a few copies worldwide, pointing out that 'there are some thirty books apparently new to Pollard and Redgrave', the standard bibliography of English printed books down to 1640 (which was then less comprehensive than its successor is today).[52] While seeing some excitement for experts in this statistic – 'the presence in the catalogue of books new to the two "STCs" adds a touch of piquancy to the catalogue for the bibliographer' – he could not help but express some disappointment over the contents.[53] Although he acknowledged the extensive holdings of scientific, medical and astronomical books, he thought that Plume could have tried harder with literature: 'there is … no Shakespeare, no Marlowe, and plays are, in general, conspicuous by their absence … there is not, alas, an array of striking first editions'.

These kinds of assessment, which are all too common when modern eyes look across historic library shelves, are wide of the mark and fall into the trap of applying today's values about interest and collectability to an age that thought differently. If we wish to understand the past, and not merely judge it by mistaken criteria, we need to appreciate what libraries such as Plume's can tell us about seventeenth-century intellectual priorities. The rarity of particular texts or editions may add bibliographical piquancy but it will not bring streams of people to Maldon to read them, now that the texts of all those STC books are available online in digital facsimile.

Francis was surely closer to recognising the library's great strengths when he focused on its character as 'Plume's own library ... a personal working library of a scholar with wide interests in all fields of learning', which 'has come down to us almost intact'. It contains so much unspoilt evidence at both individual and collective level, of books and of a library in original condition, with much to offer a book-historical generation that has come to appreciate the importance of the book as a whole material object. It is full of books with individual histories manifested in ownership, annotation, evidence of use (or not) and binding, and has great potential to be further explored from these angles. It is not unique for a library of its period to have survived in this way, but its size and scale mark it out as special. It is certainly less celebrated than it ought to be: the literature on the library is noticeably thin, not helped by the self-effacing persona of Plume, on which other writers have commented. It is a significant heritage asset of Maldon, a town that is not short of history. Samuel Pepys's library, less than half the size, is much better known, but so is Pepys the man. Let us hope that this book helps to shine more light on someone who has been more in the shadows of Restoration history, but whose legacies deserve so much more recognition. The library should always be centre stage within that billing.

Notes

1   For good summary overviews of these developments, see T. Kelly, *Early Public Libraries: A History of Public Libraries in Great Britain before 1850* (The Library Association, London, 1966), chapters 4–5 (pp. 68–117), and M. Powell, 'Endowed Libraries for Towns', in G. Mandelbrote and K.A. Manley (eds), *The Cambridge History of Libraries in Britain and Ireland, Volume II 1640–1850* (Cambridge, 2006), chapter 7 (pp. 83–101).
2   Kelly, *Early Public Libraries*, p. 90.
3   M. Perkin (ed.), *A Directory of the Parochial Libraries of the Church of England and the Church in Wales* (London, 2004), p. 34ff.
4   As pointed out by K.A. Manley, 'Thomas Plume', in W. Baker and K. Womack (eds), *Dictionary of Literary Biography: volume 213: Pre-Nineteenth-Century British Book Collectors and Bibliographers* (Farmington Hills, 1999), p. 275; though we may note that Plume appears on a list in the SPCK archives, *c.*1700, of 'members that have neither subscribed (financially) annually nor to the charges of the Charter'. See W.W. Manross, *S.P.G. Papers in the Lambeth Palace Library* (Oxford, 1974), p. 39.
5   D. Pearson, 'The English Private Library in the Seventeenth Century', *The Library*, 7th ser., 13 (2012), p. 382. It is important to stress the footprint word here – this is not the average size of all

6   On Evelyn see G. Mandelbrote, 'John Evelyn and his Books', in F. Harris and M. Hunter (eds), *John Evelyn and his Milieu* (London, 2003), pp. 71–94; on Boothby, P. Beal, 'My Books are the Great Joy of my Life', *The Book Collector*, 46 (1997), pp. 350–78; on Aldrich, W. Hiscock, *A Christ Church Miscellany* (Oxford, 1946), chapter 2 (pp. 17–30), Henry Aldrich, book-collector, musician, architect.

7   BL, ESTC r34405, *A Catalogue of the Library of ... Francis Bernard* (London, 1698), and see J. Burnaby, 'Bernard, Francis (bap. 1628, d.1698)', *ODNB* (Oxford, 2004); J. Ringrose, 'John Moore and his Books', in P. Fox (ed.), *Cambridge University Library: The Great Collections* (Cambridge, 1986), pp. 78–89.

8   M. McCarthy, *All Graduates and Gentlemen* (Dublin, 1980), p. 38ff.

9   W. Poole, 'William Barlow's Books at Queen's', *Insight* (Michaelmas 2013), pp. 3–7 (https://www.queens.ox.ac.uk/publications/insight-michaelmas-term-2013); N. Ramsay, 'The Library and Archives to 1897', in D. Keene, A. Burns and A. Saint (eds), *St. Paul's. The Cathedral Church of London 604-2004* (New Haven, CT, 2004), pp. 413–29.

10 W.J. Petchey, *The Intentions of Thomas Plume* (Maldon, tercentenary edition, 2004), pp. 19–20; Manley, 'Thomas Plume', p. 277.

11 F.C. Francis, 'Foreword', in S.G. Deed and J. Francis, *Catalogue of the Plume Library at Maldon, Essex* (Maldon, 1959), pp. vii–ix.

12 D. Pearson, 'Patterns of Book Ownership in Late Seventeenth-Century England', *The Library*, 7th ser., 11 (2010), pp. 139–67.

13 J. Carter and P. Muir, *Printing and the Mind of Man: A Descriptive Catalogue Illustrating the Impact of Print* (London, 1967).

14 Petchey, *Intentions*, p. 3.

15 J. Raven, *The Business of Books* (New Haven, CT, and London, 2007), chapter 4 'The Late Stuart Trade'.

16 Petchey, *Intentions*, p. 8.

17 E.g. E. Lubinus, *Clavis Graecae Linguae* (1640); *Terence in English*, (1641); see Fig.6.3. We also know from his undergraduate account book (TPL, MA0118) of 1646–50 that he was buying books then.

18 Other examples from the last decade of his life, inscribed by him, include J. Locke, *A Letter to the ... Bishop of Worcester* (1697); *The Acts and Negotiations ... at Ryswick* (1698).

19 See above, note 4.

20 Chapter 8, p. 215. Examples of books with Whitter's inscription are M. Pflacher, *Analysis Typica* (1587); J.H. Alsted, *Thesaurus Chronologiae* (1624); R. Dallington, *Aphorismes* (1629).

21 Another example is G. Bright, *A Treatise of Prayer* (1678).

22 On book auctions, see Raven, *Business*, pp. 106–12. There are some books in the Plume Library which demonstrably passed through the auction trade of the late seventeenth century – e.g. a copy of J. Mayer, *Many Commentaries in One* (London, 1647), which has the inscription of Ambrose Atfield (d. 1684). Atfield's library was sold by auction in London in 1685 and this book was lot 106 in the sale catalogue (*Catalogus Variorum Librorum ... Amb. Atfield*, 1685).

23 J. Cappel, *Historia Sacra* (1613); W. Ames, *Bellarminus Enervatus* (1629).

24 The only other bishop of Ely who would fit the available dates, before Plume's death, would be Francis Turner (1637–1700), who was deprived as a nonjuror in 1690. We might wonder whether the books came from the bequest of books that John Patrick (1632–95) left his brother Symon, who succeeded Turner as bishop of Ely and who died in 1707, but if so they would almost certainly carry John's ownership inscription, which is not the case. I am grateful to Kathryn McKee, of St John's College Library, for her help and advice on Gunning's books there today.

25 There is one stitched pamphlet of household accounts – partly recycled from someone else's paper manuscript of some kind – that details various kinds of domestic expenditure c.1700–2, but it is confined to things such as food and candles and does not refer to books (TPL, MA0111, Bundle E.49).

26 Petchey, *Intentions*, p. 11.
27 On the phraseology, see G.D. Hobson, 'Et Amicorum', *The Library*, 5th ser., 4 (1949), pp. 87–99; the tag is most immediately associated with the French statesman and bibliophile Jean Grolier (1489/90–1565), who had it tooled onto bindings, but many other people also adopted it for book inscriptions.
28 E.g. S. Colclough, 'Readers: Books and Biography', in S. Eliot and J. Rose (eds), *A Companion to the History of the Book* (Oxford, 2007), pp. 50–62.
29 Chapter 8, pp. 210–11.
30 TPL, MA0072, in which he noted finishing Edward Hyde's *History of the ... Civil Wars* (1702) on 29 April 1703.
31 R. Bolton, *Last and Learned Works* (1632), on whose flyleaf the monogram has been written across an earlier seventeenth-century inscription ('Wm Scrafton his booke').
32 TPL, MA0113, G.20.
33 H.M. Nixon, *Catalogue of the Pepys Library at Magdalene College ... Vol. VI, Bindings* (Woodbridge, 1984); M. Foot, 'John Evelyn's Bookbindings', in F. Harris and M. Hunter (eds), *John Evelyn and his Milieu* (London, 2003), pp. 61–70; on this subject more generally, see D. Pearson, *English Bookbinding Styles 1450–1800* (New Castle, DE, 2014), pp. 10–12.
34 G. Naudé, tr. J. Evelyn, *Instructions Concerning Erecting of a Library* (London, 1661), p. 61.
35 E.g. P. de Mornay, *Fowre Books* (1600); R. Greenham, *The Workes* (1605); L. Molina, *Liberi Arbitrii cum Gratiae Donis ... Concordia* (1595) (all gilt centrepieces); Thomas Aquinas, *Summa Totius Theologiae* (Paris, 1615), has the gilt armorial stamp of Sir Robert Naunton (1563–1635).
36 A number of these are noted in Petchey, *Intentions*, pp. 22–3.
37 Bright, *A Treatise of Prayer*, with Plume's inscription on the flyleaf 'Tho Plume Ex dono Autoris doctissimi amicissimiq.'; its contemporary binding with a gold decorated spine in arc and arrowhead style stands out on the shelves as noticeably more gilded than most of the books around it.
38 Atfield's sale, for example (note 18 above), concluded with 12 lots of 'Bundles of pamphlets in folio' and 53 lots of 'Bundles of pamphlets in quarto'. The number of pamphlets in a bundle was sometimes listed, between 12 and 20, but was usually unspecified.
39 The library of John Forbes (1628/9–1712), nonconformist minister in Gloucestershire, which is now preserved more or less intact in the Thomas Fisher Library at the University of Toronto, includes around 300 unbound pamphlets alongside *c.*1300 bound volumes; his library is overall, therefore, on a smaller scale than Plume's.
40 Barlow's will: TNA, PROB 11/407/226.
41 D. Pearson, 'The Libraries of English Bishops, 1600–40', *The Library*, 6th ser., 14 (1992), p. 237.
42 Gower's will: TNA, PROB 11/520/273.
43 TPL, MA0054, as noted above.
44 R. Beadle, 'Medieval English Manuscripts at Auction', *The Book Collector*, 53 (2004), pp. 46–63.
45 On Batteley, see C.S. Knighton, 'Batterley, John (bap. 1646, d.1708)', *ODNB* (Oxford, 2004), and C.E. and R.C. Wright (eds), *The Diary of Humfrey Wanley, 1715–1726* (London, 1966), vol. 1, p. 15 and the further references identified there; George Davenport (d. 1677) gave *c.*70 medieval manuscripts to Cosin's Library, Durham in 1670; Thomas Man (1655?–90), fellow of Jesus College, Cambridge, gave *c.*80 medieval manuscripts to the College.
46 E. Bernard, *Catalogi librorum manuscriptorum Angliae et Hiberniae in unum collecti; cum indice alphabetico* (Oxford, 1697); B04508.
47 Perkin, *Directory*, 35–6; Chapter 1, pp. 16–17; Chapter 4, pp. 106–7.
48 Appendix: Dr Plume's will, ll. 161–3.
49 Powell, 'Endowed Libraries', pp. 88–9.
50 It has been pointed out that only Thomas Tenison's library at St Martin in the Fields, London (1684), and Marsh's Library in Dublin (1701) share this distinction (Powell, 'Endowed libraries',

p. 96); to this list we should add Cosin's Library in Durham, built by him in the late 1660s and opened in 1669. See A.I. Doyle, 'John Cosin (1595–1672) as a library maker', *The Book Collector*, 40 (1991), pp. 335–57.

51 Appendix: Dr Thomas Plume's will, ll. 168–70; Powell, 'Endowed Libraries', p. 96; noted also by Petchey, *Intentions*, p. 14, and Manley, 'Thomas Plume', p. 278.
52 Francis, 'Foreword', p. viii.
53 By 'STCs' Francis meant the two bibliographies that at the time of writing were the authoritative listings of all English books printed before 1701.

Chapter 7

The Plume Building
James Bettley

I have erected over ye School at Maldon, a Library-Room to which I give all my books, & pictures.[1]

Thomas Plume erected the building that was to house his library on the site of the medieval church of St Peter, retaining only the west tower. St Peter's was a large parish, entirely surrounding that of All Saints, and included within it the important medieval institutions of Beeleigh Abbey and St Giles' Hospital. Indeed, the earliest record of St Peter's is a document of 1189 confirming the grant of St Peter's and All Saints, together with other churches and land, to the Premonstratensian canons of Beeleigh; Roger Mantell had made the grant in 1180, enabling the canons to move from Great Parndon (near Harlow) to Maldon.[2] As early as 1244 the parishes of St Peter's and All Saints were combined 'by reason of their leanness and poverty', and from 1379 St Peter's seems to have been used principally by the Fraternity or Guild of the Assumption of Our Lady.[3]

Little is known about the medieval building, apart from the tower. It is thought that Plume's building occupies the site of the medieval nave (Figure 7.1), and that the chancel projected further east; in 1929 F.W. Chancellor discovered that 'the brick walls of the library had been built upon the ancient foundations of the original nave of the Church'.[4] The tower was built in the fifteenth century and may well have replaced an older one.[5] It is constructed mainly of flint rubble, with limestone dressings, and has angle buttresses and battlements. The original entrance was through a west door, now blocked at the base and used as a window. Above the west doorway is a window with two cinquefoiled lights and Perpendicular tracery, while, above that again, lighting what was originally the second stage of the tower, are square-headed windows

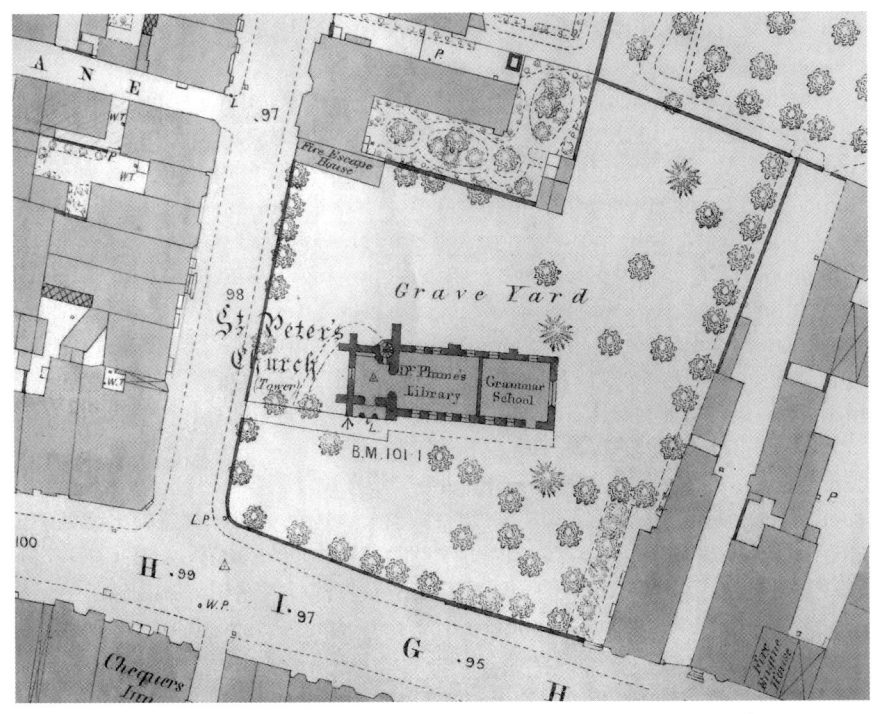

7.1 The location of St Peter's church and Dr Plume's Library in 1873, showing the subdivided ground floor and the portico (OS map 1:2500).

in the north, south and west walls. The former bell-chamber has a single cinquefoiled light in a square head on all four sides. In the north-east corner is a stair-turret that was originally higher than the battlements.

Excavation beneath the floor of the tower in 1999 revealed some medieval tiles, at least one of which was of a type that was made in Danbury (about four and a half miles from Maldon on the main road to Chelmsford) between 1278 and 1350. Rather than being evidence of an earlier tower, it is thought that the tiles may have been salvaged from Maldon's Carmelite friary following its dissolution in about 1538.[6]

After the suppression of the Guild of the Assumption of Our Lady in 1539, St Peter's continued to be used for baptisms, marriages and burials; Alderman John Morris, in his will of 1609, asked to be buried inside the church, a marriage was recorded in 1691 and baptisms in 1694.[7] For regular services, however, parishioners of St Peter's were required to attend All Saints. In 1577 the archdeacon of Essex formally instructed the churchwardens of All Saints and St Peter's to combine their functions and arrange for parishioners of St Peter's 'to be placed according to his degree' in All Saints, and in 1612 it was said that 'parishioners of St Peter do usuallie resort and come' to All Saints.[8] In

1837 it was reported that 'divine worship ceased to be performed in St Peter's church' in 1662.[9]

A document associated with the suppression of the Guild refers to the church being used also as a school, and this continued; it may well have been used for that purpose by William Lowth, who was teaching in Maldon in 1581.[10] In 1609 Ralph Breeder left money for the foundation of a grammar school in the town, and when this was put into effect in 1621 the school was housed in St Peter's.[11] When, in 1628, letters patent were issued allowing St Mary's, Maldon's third church, to appeal for funds to repair its collapsed tower, reference was made to 'Saint Peter having the ruynes thereof (by the consent of the Bishop) converted to a publique Schoole'.[12] The antiquary Richard Symonds, who visited Maldon in 1639, noted of St Peter's that 'this church is turned into a Grammar Schoole'.[13]

The rebuilding of St Peter's may be said with some certainty to have been completed by 1699.[14] In that year a new bell was cast by James Bartlet of Greenwich, with the inscription 'THIS BELL WAS NEW CAST AT THE CHARGE OF THOMAS PEVME [sic] D D AD^N OF ROCH^R AND MN^R OF GREENWICH 1699 IACOBUS BARTLET ME FECIT'.[15] The existing frame, which appears to have been made in the sixteenth century to take four bells, was adapted for a single bell.[16] What cannot be said with any certainty is the state of the medieval building at this time. The archdeacon's court heard in 1572 that the building was in decay, in 1580 that the chancel was out of repair and in 1591 that the church was 'far out of reparacon'.[17] The word 'ruynes' was used in 1628, yet the building remained in use; the building's poor condition may have been exaggerated in order to make a better case for funding the repair of St Mary's. The tower was in sufficiently good repair for money to be spent on the bells, including new bell ropes, in 1647, 1653 and 1664.[18] The supposition is that shortly after this there was some disaster, such as the upper part of the tower collapsing on to the nave. The account closest to the event, Morant's *History and Antiquities of Essex* (1768), refers to 'the body of [the church] being down'.[19] Subsequent accounts say that the church 'fell into ruins', 'fell down about 1665', and so on.[20] W.J. Petchey wrote in 1958 that 'about 1664 the crumbling upper stages of the fifteenth century tower cracked and slid down, destroying the ancient church beneath', supporting this version of events by reference to the fallen towers of St Andrew, Heybridge, and St Mary, Maldon.[21] Petchey wrote later that Plume 'chose to reconstruct the tower ... despite the considerable expense involved and although it was irrelevant to his principal project of housing his books', and saw a symbolic contrast between the medieval ecclesiastical tower and the modern secular library building: it represented the relationship, so important to Plume, between Church and state.[22]

There have been so many repairs to the tower over the centuries, particularly between 1870 and 1981 (as described below), that it is almost impossible to say what repairs belong to what period. Close examination of the fabric does not support Petchey's proposition that much of it was rebuilt in medieval style in the late seventeenth century, which would indeed have been a highly unusual course of action. Some of the brickwork, on the other hand, appears to date from Plume's time.[23] Petchey himself, although he continued to maintain that the tower was 'almost entirely a late-seventeenth century replacement', conceded that there was no proof that the tower really had fallen in about 1665.[24] Plume may simply have decided that in order to achieve his aim of housing both a library and a school a two-storey building was needed and it was therefore better to demolish what was there already and start again, rather than trying to adapt the nave and chancel. The tower was adapted to provide an entrance to the first-floor library. This may have been a symbolic gesture on his part, or simply a practical expedient; he clearly saw some need for a tower rather than simply providing a staircase, for he went to the trouble of having a new bell cast. It was probably at this time that the outside door was inserted at the base of the stair-turret. The stairs led up to a new floor that was inserted in the lower stage of the tower, at the level of the upper floor in the new building. This cuts across the tower arch, which was retained and thus frames the entrance to the library. The tower was repaired using red brick, most visibly in the battlements and stair-turret.[25]

The new building, in contrast to the tower, is essentially domestic in character, being built of red brick with quoins, platband and keystones of stone that were probably reused from the church. It was originally only five bays long. The windows are of timber, with mullions and transoms forming a cross, and leaded lights. Sir Nikolaus Pevsner commented, 'That an archdeacon of Rochester should have felt a library to be of more use to his native town than the rebuilding of a parish church is a noteworthy sign of the period about 1700',[26] and the form of the building suits its secular purpose. The only visible evidence of medieval work is a fragment of carved stone fixed to the north wall of the ground-floor interior. It appears to be a capital of a column, but it is clearly not *in situ* and is supported by a post-medieval bracket. Two pieces of Tudor stained glass from the church, with the arms of Henry VIII impaling Jane Seymour and fragments of the royal arms of Henry VIII, are now in the west window of All Saints.[27]

The only record of significant work to the building in the eighteenth century occurs in 1752, when the trustees ordered 'that the tyling at the Library be ripped & the Rafters repaired where wanted and that such other Repairs be forthwith done there as are wanting'.[28] There was a suggestion, in 1790, that the church might be demolished in order to lay out a bowling green in the churchyard for the diversion of patrons of Edward Bright's salt-water bath on the Blackwater, but this idea seems to have died, with Bright, later that year.[29] In 1805 the sundial

7.2 The Plume Building, c.1840–50, engraved by Harris Bros, London and published by P.H. Youngman, Maldon. Note the portico at the entrance to the tower (ERO, A13366).

was painted and gilded by Thomas Limner, presumably the same sundial that is now at the east end of the south wall, and which is probably contemporary with Plume's building.[30] The face is of lead sheet folded over a wooden frame, with gnomon and brackets of wrought iron. It carries a motto, 'Non sine lumine' (not without light). In 1814 William Barker took down and rebuilt part of the east end of the building, and the following year payment was authorised to Francis Barker, bricklayer, and John Cook, carpenter, for work done at the school and library, and it was ordered that new gravel be laid on the path outside.[31]

In 1817, however, came a major change. The grammar school's master was appointed by the Corporation, the town's governing body, but this did not function between 1769 and 1810, when a new Corporation was set up by royal charter. The grammar school languished as a result, and ceased to occupy the Plume Building.[32] In 1817 the Plume trustees decided to use their funds to establish a school for 'the Education of the Children of the Poor in the principles of the Established Church', and the National Society for Promoting Religious Education made a grant of £50 for the purpose of enlarging the building.[33] It was extended eastwards by two bays, in closely matching style, with an outside door in the second bay from the east (Figure 7.2); the National School opened the following year. John Cook was the main contractor for the work, the contract sum being £89 13s, although his total bill came to £123 0s 3½d.[34] The Revd Charles Matthew, vicar of All Saints, loaned the Trust £125 to cover the costs of 'the late alterations and improvements in the School Room and Library'.[35] In 1819 Francis Barker was employed to make a new doorway in the tower.[36] This no doubt refers to the present south door, for in 1820 John Cook erected a portico to shelter it.[37] This timber structure fitted between the buttresses on the south side of the tower and consisted of four columns and carved brackets supporting an entablature and pediment.[38] In 1830 the trustees ordered the tiles to be taken off the whole building ('being greatly out of repair') and replaced with slates.[39]

Further major changes came in 1843, when the High Court of Chancery confirmed a new scheme for the administration of Thomas Plume's Charity. The National School moved out; it had quickly outgrown the building, which was reported to have accommodated 'about 270 poor children of both sexes' (the boys' schoolroom was on the ground floor, the girls' on the first).[40] Among other things, the new scheme allowed for £200 to be spent 'in restoring the Library room to its original purpose & fitting up the room & furnishing it with Book Cases, & such other things as may be requisite & necessary'.[41] A total of £74 1s was paid to James Beale, including £33 for making and fixing six bookcases, and in 1844 he supplied 32 yards of green worsted tammy 'for drapery to bookcases'.[42] It is not known how the books had been organised before that, but the shelving system recorded in early catalogues suggests that it must have been similar. George Brown (blacksmith) supplied two large iron columns for supporting the library floor to take the weight of the books.[43] A further indication of the new era that had opened for the library was the commissioning in 1844 of the framed rules of the library, painted by Robert Nightingale and including a miniature portrait of Plume and his coat of arms (Figure 7.3). The painting cost £4 10s, plus 3s 6d for the board and 5s 6d for the frame, made by Beale, who also hung the library's pictures on brass-headed nails. At the same time Nightingale cleaned and repaired the painting of Archbishop Laud.[44]

It is doubtful how much of the interior of the library room survives from the seventeenth century. A lot of the panelling (especially that in the 1817 extension) was imported from elsewhere and had to be adapted to fit its new location; James Beale's invoice in 1843 also included considerable work to the 'wainscot'.[45] The following year Francis H. Hearn was paid for cleaning, staining and varnishing all the old wainscotting in both the library and the end room on the 'school side'.[46] The early seventeenth-century overmantel with enriched arches and baluster pilasters is notable, but it is not known when it was

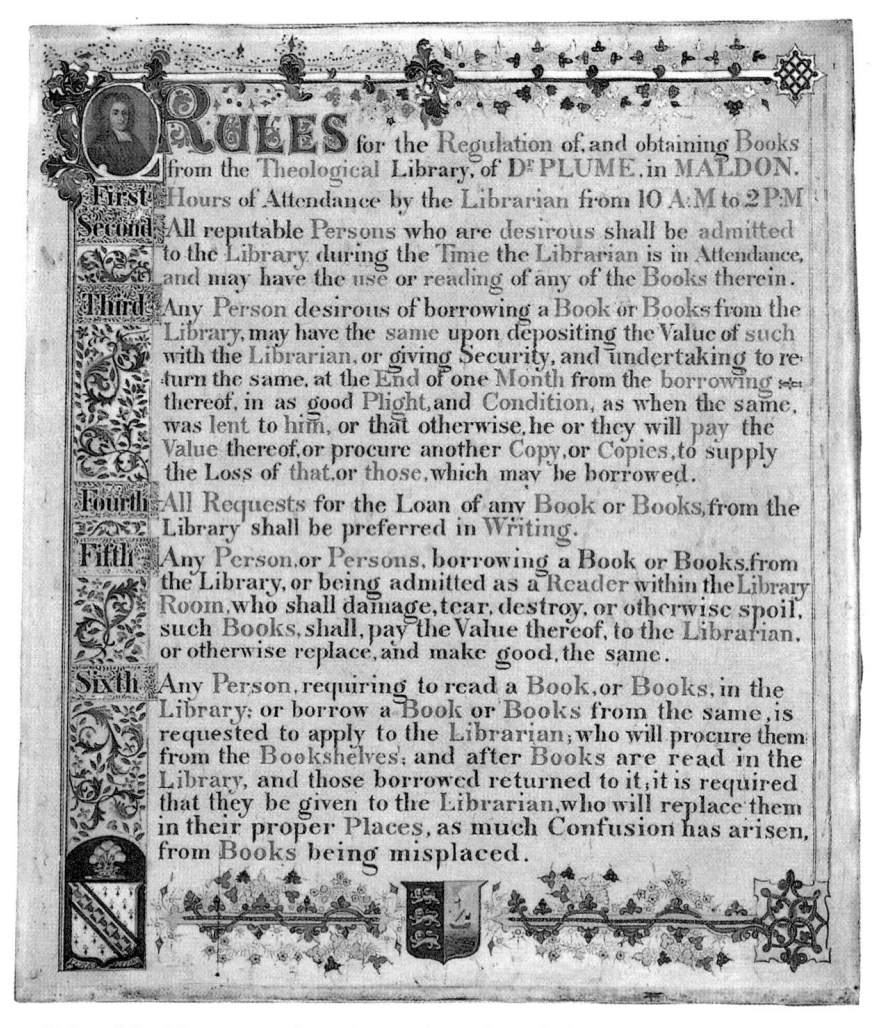

RULES for the Regulation of, and obtaining Books from the Theological Library, of D[r] PLUME, in MALDON.

First Hours of Attendance by the Librarian from 10 A:M to 2 P:M

Second All reputable Persons who are desirous shall be admitted to the Library during the Time the Librarian is in Attendance, and may have the use or reading of any of the Books therein.

Third Any Person desirous of borrowing a Book or Books from the Library, may have the same upon depositing the Value of such with the Librarian, or giving Security, and undertaking to return the same, at the End of one Month from the borrowing thereof, in as good Plight, and Condition, as when the same, was lent to him, or that otherwise, he or they will pay the Value thereof, or procure another Copy, or Copies, to supply the Loss of that, or those, which may be borrowed.

Fourth All Requests for the Loan of any Book or Books, from the Library shall be preferred in Writing.

Fifth Any Person, or Persons, borrowing a Book or Books, from the Library, or being admitted as a Reader within the Library Room, who shall damage, tear, destroy, or otherwise spoil, such Books, shall, pay the Value thereof, to the Librarian, or otherwise replace, and make good, the same.

Sixth Any Person, requiring to read a Book, or Books, in the Library; or borrow a Book or Books from the same, is requested to apply to the Librarian; who will procure them from the Bookshelves; and after Books are read in the Library, and those borrowed returned to it, it is required that they be given to the Librarian, who will replace them in their proper Places, as much Confusion has arisen, from Books being misplaced.

7.3 Rules of the Library, 1844, by Robert Nightingale, including miniature portrait of Thomas Plume (TPL).

introduced into the building.[47] The actual fire surround, however, was made in 1927, by G.H. Tunmer & Son of Maldon; older photographs show a plain white surround, probably the marble chimneypiece supplied by A. Malcholm of Fullbridge in 1843 (Figure 7.4).[48] There is another fireplace in the 1817 extension (now blocked), and two fireplaces in corresponding positions on the ground floor. The latter have surrounds with bolection moulding.[49] The plan drawn in 1920 by the inspectors from the Royal Commission on Historical Monuments shows a fireplace in the south wall, between the fourth and fifth bays from the east (where there is now a buttress), but no other evidence has

7.4 Interior of the Library, 1920. Note the old fire surround, replaced in 1927, and the gas fittings on the bookshelves, removed in 1925 (Historic England, BB056869).

been found for a fireplace in this position. The two chimneystacks on the north wall have been reduced to below the level of the eaves. They are clearly additions to the original fabric, and remains of brickwork beside them appear to be of blocked windows. It is therefore likely that the library and the 1817 extension were originally without fireplaces; it would certainly have been the norm for a library in the seventeenth or early eighteenth century not to be heated.[50] The school room, however, had a fire by the mid-eighteenth century, because it was recorded in 1837 that 'about 70 years ago ... Latin scholars possessed the exclusive privilege of being taught near the fire'.[51]

Some form of heating was in place in the library room by 1801, when William Draper supplied a set of fire irons and a fender, and a coal and wood bin was purchased.[52] Work in 1820 may well have included a new chimney, as C. Comyns Parker supplied 3,000 bricks, Francis Barker was paid for work to a chimney and John Cook made a coal box.[53] There is another reference to a new chimney (and stove) in 1843, when William Hearn supplied lead for the gutters on the new chimney, John Terling supplied a stove, fender and irons, and Edward Knight a coal scuttle and scoop.[54] Gas lighting had been installed by 1896, but had been superseded by electricity by 1925, when the fittings were removed from the bookcases.[55]

Plume specified that the library room was for his pictures as well as books. The small collection consists of 12 portraits, as well as 'Salvator Mundi' by a

7.5 Interior of ground floor in use as a Masonic Hall, 1864–99. The iron columns were inserted in 1844 to support the library floor (by kind permission of the Brethren of the Lodge of St Peter, number 1024 in the Province of Essex).

follower of Hans Memling. All are seventeenth-century journeyman copies of well-known paintings, and the subjects of the portraits reflect Plume's own loyalties to the monarchy and to the Church of England as established by law: Richard III, Edward VI, Mary I, James I, Charles I and Charles II; John Whitgift and William Laud, archbishops of Canterbury, Ralph Brownrig (or Brownrigg), bishop of Exeter, and Brian Duppa, dean of Christ Church, Oxford. Brownrig's portrait has only recently been correctly identified, having previously been thought to be of Dr James Ussher, archbishop of Armagh. Plume's own portrait hangs in the Moot Hall; by the terms of his will, he forbade his portrait ever to be brought into the library. Later additions to the collection include a portrait of the Revd Robert P. Crane, Plume Librarian 1844–52, very possibly the work of Robert Nightingale.[56] The library also contains a celestial globe, made by William Carey. It was purchased in 1829, and the paper is watermarked 1824. It was one of a pair (costing £17 1s, plus 12s 6d carriage), and they replaced an old pair that had worn out. It is not known what became of the terrestrial globe.[57]

With the National School established in London Road, a new use was needed for the rest of the building. The grammar school, which occupied various buildings before a permanent home was built for it in 1906–7, used the room at the east end of the library (the upper floor of the 1817 extension) for a time, as recorded by W.J. Samms, a pupil in 1859–64. He described the room as 'a fine old room for an Old School with its dark oak panelled walls and door opening into the Ancient Library, but the school fittings were just dreadful, and the forms real back-achers. As to lavatory or convenience there were none, it was a school room and nothing more.'[58] Work to the schoolroom ('Mr Dunn's room') undertaken by various contractors in 1858, including making new desks and seats, suggests that its new use began in that year; it continued until at least 1876, when Ewan Christian, architect to the Ecclesiastical Commissioners, warned of the danger of fragments of the tower falling on to children coming to school.[59]

From 1864 to 1899 the base of the tower and part of the rest of the ground floor were used by St Peter's Lodge of Freemasons and, later, the Plume Chapter of Royal Arch Freemasons (created in 1891) for their meetings (Figure 7.5). The Revd E.R. Horwood, vicar of All Saints from 1850 to 1901 and Plume Librarian from 1852, was a freemason and chaplain of St Peter's Lodge.[60] Various maps and plans show that the ground floor was subdivided at this time, with a partition between the third and fourth bays from the east.[61] The ground floor, or part of it, was later used by boy scouts as a meeting hall.[62]

From 1870 the condition of the building, and in particular the tower, began to be a cause for concern; major repairs were carried out, intermittently, over more than a century. Ebenezer Saunders inserted iron tie rods in 1870,[63] and in 1875 the trustees asked for a report on the tower from Ewan Christian on the basis of which repairs were started. In a second report in 1876, once scaffolding had been erected and he was able to inspect the building more closely, he found that 'the whole of the upper part of the turret has separated from the tower and only waits a very moderate impulse to send it to the ground'. He even suggested taking down the top of the tower and replacing it with a lighter timber structure to cover the bell floor.[64] Repairs were carried out by Saunders in 1875–6, which included the fitting of an iron band round the outside of the tower at the level of the bell-chamber (Figures 1.5, 7.6); his bill came to £83 18s 6d, which included repairs to the roof of the library.[65] When the Royal Archaeological Institute visited Maldon in 1876 the tower was under scaffolding and 'soon to be demolished'. The mayor 'positively declined to give his consent to an internal inspection', but the temptation of what lay within was so great that his warnings were ignored; those who ventured inside 'were well rewarded for their trouble and courage'.[66] A portion of the tower actually fell between trustees' meetings, so their and Christian's concerns were justified. The only casualty, however, was an indirect victim of the work. After the scaffolding had been taken down a timber carriage laden with the poles ran out of control down Market Hill and collided with a wagonette, killing the vicar of Great Totham, the Revd M.G. Dennis; no blame was attached to Saunders or his employees.[67] In 1879 Saunders was asked to re-erect the weather vane on the tower.[68]

7.6 St Peter's Tower in 1928, showing the iron bands added to the belfry in 1875–6 (TNA, WORK 14/1239).

The repairs proved ineffective, and concerns were raised again in 1907. This time a report was prepared by P.M. Beaumont, a Maldon architect and one-time borough surveyor. He had examined the tower five or six years previously and found it to be in much the same condition as it had been then, apart from small cracks that had been filled and the carrying out of other minor repairs. He recommended injecting cement grout under pressure into the cracks and pointing the joints of the rubble with cement. He also noticed that the arch between the tower and library appeared to be spreading, and advised replacing a broken tie rod.[69] Repairs to the tower were again an issue in 1916, when the trustees agreed to spend three guineas.[70]

In 1920 the building was inspected by the Royal Commission on Historical Monuments (England) in preparation of the second volume of the *Inventory of the Historical Monuments in Essex* (1921). The inspectors described the condition of the tower as 'bad', having been 'badly shaken by air raids, so that the face of the wall is in places falling away'. Their conclusion was that 'the building is more interesting as a library, and architecturally is comparatively of little value'.[71] Although the building was included in the inspectors' list of monuments 'especially worthy of preservation', it was not scheduled under the Ancient Monuments Acts, although it was often assumed to be; it was finally listed Grade I in 1951.[72]

A further report was commissioned by the trustees in 1924, this time from Duncan Clark, a Colchester architect. He found the tower to be 'badly cracked & in a serious condition', and recommended repairs costing £800. He also advised rebuilding the south-east corner of the main building and part of the east wall, for a further estimated £100.[73] There was talk of a public appeal, but no action seems to have been taken until 1927, when Clark's practice (Duncan Clark & Beckett) prepared detailed drawings of the tower.[74] The Plume trustees agreed to contribute £100 to the appeal that had been launched by the mayor and the vicar of All Saints.[75]

Matters came to a head in 1929. The year before Duncan Clark had been replaced as architect by F. Wykeham Chancellor of Chelmsford, who inspected the building with Arthur Heasman, architect in charge of historic buildings at HM Office of Works.[76] Chancellor's conclusion was that the tower was unsafe and should be taken down; the library building was in a dilapidated condition ('the present condition of the brick walling … is largely due to the defective state of the original foundations') and, in Chancellor's opinion, should be rebuilt.[77] Estimates for demolishing the tower were obtained. All Saints were in the process of selling their church hall; it was suggested that a new one might be built on the site of the library, incorporating its panelling and pictures.[78] This was the revival of a proposal first made in 1918, when building a modern library and reading room was suggested as a war memorial.[79] News of the proposed demolition reached the Society for the Protection of Ancient Buildings, and its secretary, A.R. Powys (himself an architect), wrote to the trustees offering his services: 'It would be a real pity to destroy it!'[80] In December 1929 he reported that it would be feasible to repair the tower: 'There is not a doubt as to whether the tower is worth preserving. It is of considerable interest and buildings of its age are none too common'. His suggestions included stitching the cracks together with roofing tiles laid horizontally, a favourite method of the SPAB at that time. He estimated that the work could be done 'at a cost of £400 to £800 and nearer £400 than £800', as opposed to the £2,200 estimated by Chancellor and Heasman. In view of the state of the tower the trustees decided that the more valuable books should be removed to Barclays Bank for safe keeping.[81]

7.7 St Peter's Tower under scaffolding during restoration work in 1930 (SPAB).

7.8 The Plume Building, 1932, after the completion of repairs (SPAB).

Powys and Chancellor worked together on the repairs, having agreed a compromise that the work could be done for £1,070; Powys admitted that the tower was in a worse state than he had thought, because much of the deterioration had been concealed by ivy. The restoration included removing the iron bands added in 1875–6 and replacing them with a continuous bonding belt of reinforced concrete below the belfry floor (Figure 7.7). The work, which was carried out by Sherling & Son of Maldon, was completed by May 1931, leaving the trustees with a debt of £270.[82] Meanwhile, there was the question of the library building. The trustees no longer wished to work with Chancellor, whom they considered too expensive. While work on the tower was in progress Powys had sent down a young architect named David E. Nye, who had been awarded the first SPAB scholarship in 1930, so that he would learn from the complicated restoration, as well as send reports back to Powys. He clearly impressed the trustees, who appointed him to restore the library building. He estimated the cost of repair at £820, to make the walls and foundations safe by underpinning; a slate damp course was also inserted. The total bill, including new electric light and heating installation and repairs to all the windows, came to £999.[83]

While work was in progress the trustees were discussing with the Borough Corporation the possibility of selling all or part of the library building (not including the tower, which remained church property). Their offer of the ground floor was declined 'owing to the present financial situation & the need for economy'. There were also discussions about converting the ground floor to a parish hall; Nye prepared a scheme, but it was thought unlikely that the diocese would allow the building to be extended and the idea was dropped.[84] When the trustees inspected the completed work in April 1932 (Figure 7.8) they 'expressed their entire satisfaction with the work on the fabric and the interior', but were left with a deficit of £452 16s 4d on the accounts for 1931 and an overdraft at the bank of nearly £1,000.[85]

An approach from the county library provided part of the solution. Maldon's public library had outgrown its present accommodation at The Friary, and it was thought that the ground floor of the Plume Building would provide sufficient space not only for the circulating library but also for a reference library and magazine room. The mayor, A.L. Clarke, indicated that the Corporation would be prepared to purchase the Plume Building for a town library, an offer which the trustees accepted.[86] The trustees agreed the legal document of agreement on 26 April 1933; it was sealed on 19 May.[87] Under the agreement, the Corporation purchased 'the Plume Building adjoining St Peter's Church Tower' from the trustees for £800 and granted the trustees a 999-year lease of the upper floor for 10s per annum. Conditions of the lease included right of access from the ground floor as well as externally, and an undertaking by the Corporation 'to carry out during the term all structural and other external repairs, including the roof'.[88] The public library occupied the ground floor until the new branch of the county library in White Horse Lane opened in 1993. Since 1998 the ground floor has been occupied by the Maeldune Heritage Centre.

The library was reroofed in 1965 and the north wall was underpinned in 1976; the metal fire-escape on the north side of the building was erected in the same year. But it was the tower that continued to be the principal cause of concern. David E. Nye prepared a report on the unstable condition of the parapet in 1950.[89] Following a report by John H. Gibbs in 1977 and another by Purcell Miller Tritton & Partners in 1979, further work was carried out in 1980–1, including the complete removal of the upper part of the stair-turret: the architect, John Burton, had discovered that the structure of the turret was standing free of the tower from the belfry level up, just as Christian had done a hundred years earlier. Repairs to the south wall of the library, including resin injection, enabled a buttress at the south-east corner of the building to be removed. No major structural work has been carried out since then.[90]

St Peter's churchyard remained in use until the cemetery in London Road was opened in 1855; it was formally closed for burials on 1 July 1856.[91] In 1766 a faculty was granted permitting part of the churchyard to be taken for widening Market Hill, to make the road 'more safe and commodious for His Majesty's subjects'; the work was promoted by John Coe, a leading merchant of the town.[92] In 1827 the trustees contributed £22 12s towards the cost of building a wall round the churchyard.[93] The road was again widened under a faculty granted in 1926; this involved moving seven graves. The parochial council opposed the scheme, partly because they considered it unnecessary, but also because they took expert advice (from Duncan Clark) and were told 'that if the works of road-widening … are carried out, the result will undoubtedly be that the Tower will collapse within a very short time'.[94]

Although the churchyard was closed, it remained church property. In 1920 the vicar of All Saints, the Revd I.L. Seymour, had made a provisional agreement to sell the churchyard to the Borough Corporation for 1s, and in 1923 the Corporation applied for a faculty to use the churchyard as a public open space. A further application followed to erect a public convenience north-west of the tower, facing Market Hill. Both applications were withdrawn when it became apparent that the vicar had no right to dispose of the churchyard, as the freehold belonged to four lay impropriators, whose identity could not easily be established; in the face of such complications, the Corporation dropped the scheme.[95] In 1947 the next vicar, the Revd John R. Lewis, inquired whether the Ministry of Works would accept guardianship of the tower, but the Ministry felt that as the tower formed the entrance to the library it was an integral part of it and should not be treated separately.[96]

In 1974 the Borough Corporation and Maldon Rural District Council were abolished and replaced by Maldon Town Council and Maldon District Council, with different levels of responsibility. The churchyard and tower were conveyed by the Church Commissioners for England to Maldon Town Council in 1996, and at the same time the library building was transferred from Maldon District Council (successors to the Borough Corporation, who had purchased it in 1933) to the Town Council.[97] The entire building and churchyard thus became the property of the Town Council, although the library's lease of the upper floor was not affected. A number of restrictive covenants applied, principally that the property was to be used only for 'civic cultural and community purposes'.[98]

The Plume Building is essentially utilitarian, and was apparently erected by Plume with the minimum expenditure. Some stones from the old church were recycled, the medieval tower was reused and the new materials (bricks, tiles, timber) would have been readily available locally. There is no unnecessary ornamentation, and the only seeming extravagance was the casting of a new bell. The interest of the building lies not in its architectural qualities but, as Pevsner observed, in the sheer fact that Plume thought a library more useful than a rebuilt church. Its lasting significance is as a purpose-built library that still performs its original function, at least as far as the upper storey is concerned (and allowing for the changes to the structure and the interior that this chapter has documented). Such buildings are usually found in the precincts of cathedrals and colleges, not in small market towns. When built it was a rare thing, and its survival has made it even more so, and while the contents of the Library, in terms of the individual books, are less remarkable, their continuing presence in the room built to house them adds to the exceptional rarity of Thomas Plume's Library.

Notes

1. TNA, PROB 10/1387; Appendix: Dr Thomas Plume's will, ll. 134–5. I am grateful to the late Max Earnshaw for references to Plume Trustees' minutes (TPL, MA0120, MA0121, MA0123), and to John Smith for references to records of the Archdeaconry of Essex (ERO).
2. W. Page and J.H. Round (eds), *VCH Essex*, vol. ii (London, 1907), p. 172.
3. L. Hughes, *A Guide to the Church of All Saints, Maldon* (Maldon and London, 1909, reprinted 2006), pp. iii and 14; W.J. Petchey, 'The History of the Church before c.1650: the Vanished Church of St Peter, Maldon', in S.P. Nunn (ed.), *St Peter's, Maldon's Redundant 'Middle Church'* (revised edn, Maldon, 1984), p. 3. P. Morant, *The History and Antiquities of the County of Essex*, vol. i (London, 1768), p. 333 and Page and Round, *VCH Essex*, p. 172 have 1306 rather than 1244, but Hughes explains why they were in error. Page and Round, *VCH Essex*, p. 516 have 1388 rather than 1379, but this appears to be based on the Guild Certificate made in Chancery, 12 Richard II, in which it is stated that the fraternity was ordained in July 1379 (TNA, C 47/39/55).
4. TPL, uncat. report by Chancellor, 12 February 1929; Petchey, 'The History of the Church before c.1650', p. 4; Nunn, *St. Peter's*, pp. 18–19.
5. Royal Commission on Historical Monuments (England), *An Inventory of the Historical Monuments in Essex*, vol. ii (London, 1921), p. 178 says late fifteenth century; the National Heritage List for England list entry number 1256632 says late fourteenth.
6. W.J.R. Clark, 'Maldon, St Peter. Excavation within the Tower, 1999', *Essex Archaeology and History*, 3rd series, 31 (2000), pp. 263–4; W.J.R. Clark, 'Excavations in St Peter's Tower, Maldon', *Essex Journal*, 36/1 (2001), pp. 7–11.
7. ERO, D/P 201/1/3-4 (St Peter, parish registers, 1556–1695, 1695–1750); Petchey, 'The History of the Church before c.1650', p. 4. The churchyard continued to be used for burials until 1855.
8. ERO, D/AEA 10; D/AEA 26; Petchey, 'The History of the Church before c.1650', p. 4.
9. *The Reports of the Commissioners appointed ... to enquire concerning charities in England and Wales relating to the County of Essex* (London, 1819–37), p. 576.
10. W.J. Petchey, *Maldon Grammar School 1608–1958* (Maldon, 1958), pp. 5, 7.
11. *Ibid.*, pp. 11–12. For more information on the history of the school and its relationship with the Plume Trust see Chapter 5, pp. 127–8, 134–5, 144, 147.
12. ERO, D/B 3/3/661.
13. Quoted by Petchey, 'The History of the Church before c.1650', p. 4.
14. There is no trace of a faculty, which would normally have been required for the demolition of the old building. The fact that it had already fallen out of regular ecclesiastical use, and that the bishop had already given permission for the church to be used as a school, may have meant that one was not necessary.

15 C. Deedes and H.B. Walters, *The Church Bells of Essex* (n.p., 1909), p. 77. The bell was scrapped in 1922 and the metal used to recast and augment the bells at All Saints (David Sloman, pers. comm., 2015). For the date of completion of the building, cf. W.J. Petchey, *The Intentions of Thomas Plume* (Maldon, 1985), pp. 11–12.
16 D. Sloman and E. Watkin, *English Heritage Bell Frame Survey for Essex* (n.p., 1993).
17 ERO, D/AEA/7, 11, 15.
18 ERO, D/B 3/3/310; Petchey, *Maldon Grammar School*, p. 19. It is not known what became of the old bells; if the tower did indeed collapse they might have fallen with it, although the bell frame appears to have survived.
19 Morant, *History of Essex*, vol. i, p. 333.
20 W. White, *History, Gazetteer, and Directory of the County of Essex* (Sheffield, 1848), p. 512; F.R. Kelly (ed.), *The Post Office Directory of Essex* (London, 1874), p. 149.
21 Petchey, *Maldon Grammar School*, p. 19.
22 Petchey, *Intentions*, p. 12.
23 *Ibid.*; H. Wyatt, 'Preserving the Plume: towards an Analytical Evaluation of the Building Fabric with Particular Focus on Site Context, Available Documentary Evidence, Morphology and Repair Strategies', unpub. submission for the Frank and Patricia Herrmann Award (2015), pp. 27–35.
24 Petchey, 'The History of the Church before c.1650', pp. 2–3.
25 Wyatt, 'Preserving the Plume', p. 27.
26 N. Pevsner, *Essex* (Harmondsworth, 1954), p. 265.
27 Nunn, *St Peter's*, p. 10.
28 TPL, MA0120, 18 June 1752.
29 Letter, John White of Maldon to John Strutt of Terling Place, 4 February 1790 (by kind permission of Lord Rayleigh); J.R. Smith, *The Borough of Maldon 1688–1800: A Golden Age* (Studley, 2013), pp. 442–3.
30 TPL, MA0147, box 3/3/2. Similar work is recorded in 1846 by George Hearn (MA0147, box 3/17/12). Thomas Limner is mentioned as a plumber and glazier in Smith, *Borough of Maldon*, p. 260.
31 TPL, MA0147, box 3/5/3; *ibid.*, MA0120, 2 January 1815.
32 Chapter 5, p. 32.
33 TPL, MA0120, 7 July 1817; *Reports of the Commissioners*, pp. 574–5.
34 TPL, MA0147, box 3/6/1–21.
35 TPL, MA0120, 5 January 1818.
36 TPL, MA0147, box 3/9/3.
37 *Ibid.*, box 3/10/6.
38 A print of about 1840–50 (Figure 7.2; ERO, A13366) shows a simpler structure than this, but it is known from early photographs. It was there when the RCHM inspectors visited in 1920 (they considered it to be early eighteenth century); it is not shown on a plan of 1927 (ERO, D/F 8/406). Clark, 'Maldon, St Peter', pp. 263–4, and 'Excavations in St Peter's Tower, Maldon', pp. 7–11, concluded that the base of the tower had been refurbished and the south doorway made in 1864, but this cannot be so.
39 TPL, MA0121, 5 January 1830.
40 J.R. McCulloch, *A Dictionary, Geographical, Statistical and Historical of the Various Countries, Places, and Principal Natural Objects in the World* (London, 1842), vol. ii, p. 260; Hughes, *Guide*, p. xxxiii. Purpose-built replacement premises in London Road were not erected until 1847.
41 TPL, MA0140, 'Fitting up Dr Plume's Library' (account book); cf. White, *Directory*, p. 513.
42 TPL, MA0140; MA0147, box 3/16/8, 3/18/6. Additional shelving was provided in 1848 and 1952–3 (MA0147, box 3/19/6, 3/30/1–6).
43 TPL, MA0147, box 3/16/10.
44 *Ibid.*, box 3/17/4, 3/18/9; H. Scantlebury, *Robert Nightingale: The Life and Times of an Essex Artist* (n.p., 2007), pp. 9–10.

45 TPL, MA0147, box 3/16/8.
46 *Ibid.*, box 3/18/3.
47 Royal Commission on Historical Monuments (England), *Essex*, vol. ii, p. 178.
48 TPL, MA0147, box 3/16/13, 3/29/21; accounts for 1927-29 in ERO, D/B 3/3/769; Royal Commission on Historical Monuments (England), *Essex*, vol. ii, opp. p. 176.
49 Wyatt, 'Preserving the Plume', p. 49.
50 SPAB file, Plume Library Building, report by D.E. Nye, 11 September 1930; cf. Wyatt, 'Preserving the Plume', p. 39.
51 *Reports of the Commissioners*, p. 576.
52 TPL, MA0147, box 3/2/1. For William Draper, clockmaker, see Smith, *Borough of Maldon*, pp. 289-90.
53 TPL, MA0147, box 3/10/4, 6-7.
54 *Ibid.*, box 3/16/1, 9, 15.
55 *Ibid.*, box 3/27/22 (cleaning out gas burners and pipes, 1896), box 3/29/18 (staining bookcases and taking off gas fittings, 1925).
56 Petchey, *Intentions*, p. 12; The Public Catalogue Foundation, *Oil Paintings in Public Ownership in Essex* (London, 2006), pp. 214-17; R.A. Doe, 'Exit Ussher, enter Brownrig: The Tale of a Portrait in the Plume Library, Maldon', *Essex Journal*, 45/1 (2010), pp. 5-7.
57 TPL, MA0123, 6 January 1879; MA0135, 18 May and 15 June 1829.
58 Petchey, *Maldon Grammar School*, p. 27; S.P. Nunn, 'The Origins, Development and Continuing Success of the Plume School', in *Maldon: The Plume School – Four Centuries of Education (1608-2008)* (Maldon, 2008), pp. 13-14.
59 TPL, MA0147, box 3/22/14; *ibid.*, Christian's report, 20 June 1876.
60 E.A. Fitch, *Maldon and the River Blackwater* (Maldon, n.d.), p. 20; Clark, 'Excavations in St Peter's Tower, Maldon', p. 10, citing S.P. Nunn, *Maldon and the Handshake of History* (*Maldon and Burnham Standard*, 17 March 1988); S.P. Nunn, pers. comm., 2015; painting of interior in Maldon Masonic Hall, Cromwell Hill.
61 OS Map 1:500, sheet LIV 6.2 (1873 edn). The parts are labelled 'Dr Plume's Library' and 'Grammar School', but the plan is clearly of the ground floor, not the upper floor, and the partition on the upper floor is between the second and third bays from the east: that is, between the library and the 1817 extension. The same division of the ground floor is shown in the plan drawn by the Royal Commission in 1920 (Inspectors' notes in Historic England archive, Swindon), although in 1910 the trustees had agreed to make the two ground-floor rooms into one (TPL, MA0123, 14 February 1910).
62 *Chelmsford Chronicle*, 2 July 1926, p. 3; ERO, D/B 3/3/769, application by Plume Trustees to Carnegie United Kingdom Trust, 1931.
63 TPL, MA0147, box 3/24/7.
64 TPL, MA0123, 20 April, 6 July, 17 August, 31 August 1875, 6 September 1876; *ibid.*, uncat., Christian's report, 20 June 1876; *Chelmsford Chronicle*, 11 August 1876, p. 4; 18 August 1876, p. 5.
65 TPL, uncat., Saunders' letter, 17 August 1875, and account, November 1876.
66 *Building News*, 31 (1876), p. 138; Royal Archaeological Institute of Great Britain & Ireland, *Colchester Meeting, August 1 to 8, 1876: Full Report of the Proceedings* (Colchester, 1876), p. 58.
67 *Chelmsford Chronicle*, 16 November 1876, p. 8.
68 TPL, uncat., Saunders' letter to trustees, 6 May 1879; TPL, MA0123, 7 July 1879. David E. Nye personally regilded the vane in 1930 (SPAB file, St Peter's Tower).
69 TPL, MA0123, 21 January 1907, 28 August 1907; *ibid.*, uncat., Beaumont's account, 17 December 1908.
70 TPL, MA0123, 18 January 1916.
71 Inspectors' notes in Historic England archive, Swindon; RCHM(E), *Essex*, vol. ii, p. 178 (photographs of interior of library opp. p. 176). Damage by Zeppelin raids is also mentioned in an appeal for funds by the mayor 'to our American friends' (ERO, D/B 3/3/769).

72 Royal Commission on Historical Monuments (England), *Essex*, vol. ii, pp. xxiii, xxv; TNA, HLG 51/667; National Heritage List for England list entry number 1256632.
73 TPL, MA0123, 23 September 1924.
74 ERO, D/F 8/406. These show a partition dividing the base of the tower, but there is no indication of its purpose.
75 TPL, MA0123, 25 January 1927.
76 TNA, WORK 14/1239.
77 TPL, uncat., Chancellor's report, 16 February 1929.
78 TPL, MA0123, 23 April 1929.
79 *Ibid.*, 16 April 1918, 8 April 1919, 15 April 1920.
80 ERO, D/B 3/3/769.
81 TPL, MA0123, 23 April, 18 December 1929; ERO, D/B 3/3/769.
82 TPL, MA0123, 17 May 1931; SPAB file, St Peter's Tower.
83 SPAB file, Plume Library; TPL, MA0123, 17 May 1931; *ibid.*, uncat., Nye's report of work completed, 20 June 1932. Nye (1906–86) went on to design the Embassy Cinema, Maldon, 1936, and although he maintained his association with the SPAB throughout his career he is now better known as a cinema architect.
84 TPL, MA0123, 17 October, 24 November 1931. Under the Disused Burial Grounds Act 1884, 'It shall not be lawful to erect any buildings upon any disused burial grounds, except for the purposes of enlarging a church, chapel, meeting-houses, or other places of worship'.
85 *Ibid.*, 14 April 1932.
86 *Ibid.*, 4 August 1932.
87 *Ibid.*, 26 April 1933; ERO, D/B 3/3/769.
88 ERO, D/B 3/3/769; TNA, HLG 51/667.
89 TNA, WORK 14/1239.
90 TPL, uncat., 'Plume Building' file, 1875–1995, report and other notes; Wyatt, 'Preserving the Plume', pp. 53–4.
91 ERO, D/B 3/3/726.
92 ERO, D/DHt O16.
93 *Reports of the Commissioners*, p. 576.
94 ERO, D/B 3/3/726; D/CF 65/34; *Chelmsford Chronicle*, 2 July 1926, p. 3. A stone set in the boundary wall records the widening and notes that the land taken remains the property of the church and consecrated ground.
95 ERO, D/CF 62/26. The Town Clerk was only able to establish the names of the lay impropriators in 1840: Benjamin Baker in right of his wife Frances, Joseph Pattisson, William Hutley and Robert Eden.
96 TNA, WORK 14/1239.
97 Local Government Act 1972.
98 TPL, uncat., conveyance and extract from H.M. Land Registry (title number EXC554518) with Maldon Town Council.

Chapter 8

'All my Manuscript-papers of my own hand': Plume's collection of handwritten texts
Helen Kemp

In his will of 1704 Dr Thomas Plume directed his friend and trustee Dr Francis Thompson 'to convey all my Manuscript-papers of my own hand, to bee carefully preserved in ye Study of the aforesaid Library'.[1] At a first glance this seems to refer to documents written by Plume himself, but a closer inspection of the papers in the Plume Library reveals that around three-quarters of them were originally written by individuals *other* than Plume. Unpacking the precise wording in the will could suggest that Plume referred to his 'Manuscript-papers' as the unbound items in the collection and considered the handwritten notebooks part of the 'books'. In this chapter, however, I will refer to the bound and unbound handwritten items together as the 'manuscripts'. The instruction to Dr Thompson is curious, as Plume indicated neither his rationale for carefully preserving the notebooks and papers nor their expected future function. In contrast to the books, which could be borrowed upon application to the librarian and secured by a deposit, there is no mention of whether the manuscripts should be consulted in the future.[2] This chapter will present an analysis of the manuscript collection and what it can show about Plume's life and this part of his legacy. Following a brief discussion of the relevant historiography, the authors and genres of the manuscripts will be examined, together with the ways in which Plume acquired them.

Study of the manuscripts
The manner in which Dr Thompson transported the manuscript papers from Plume's residence(s) to the Library building in Maldon is not evident, nor is the way in which they were ordered upon arrival in the Library 'Study'. During this period the term 'study' could refer to either a reading space or room, or

alternatively a cupboard or archive location, though the reference to them being 'carefully preserved' suggests the latter meaning.[3] Regardless of the material form of the 'Study' envisaged by Plume, however, it does seem that the manuscripts were intended to be on hand for consultation, even if only for a limited clerical audience who might wish to refer to them. An example of such use can be seen in one particular manuscript that contains an index started in 1707, providing evidence that someone – perhaps the librarian – used the manuscript three years after Plume's death.[4] It is unlikely, however, that users of the library would generally have been inclined to annotate the manuscripts, since those documents had at that point become institutional property.

Previous studies of the manuscripts
Plume's manuscripts have interested historians since the early twentieth century, although the texts have been approached with different purposes in mind. Andrew Clark (1856–1922), an Oxford scholar and rector of Great Leighs (from 1894), had been inspired, following the exciting rediscovery of 'several bundles of papers' in the Library's mahogany chest, to make an inventory of the contents, and his appraisal of the collection resulted in the first iteration of the Plume manuscript catalogue.[5] In contrast to the printed books, a cataloguing exercise had not taken place for the manuscripts until then.[6] Clark's disappointment in the content of the manuscripts is palpable in his 1904 article for the *Essex Review*, where he reported that his 'awakened hopes … have been dispelled by an examination of the papers'.[7] Reading between the lines of Clark's article, it can be surmised that the manuscript papers he referred to as being found in the chest were exclusively what now constitute the bundles of papers classified as A to I.[8] The manuscripts in these bundles are unbound, which is in contrast to the remaining 109 handwritten notebooks and papers, most of which are enclosed within pasteboards or limp vellum covers. It seems likely that at the time of Clark's research the bound notebooks were kept in a separate place within the library and were therefore differentiated from the unbound papers. During the seventeenth century the separation of printed and manuscript books on library shelves was becoming increasingly common, but it appears that by the time of the arrangement of Thomas Plume's Library *four* distinctions were made between material forms of texts: printed books, unbound pamphlets, handwritten books and unbound papers.[9]

Clark had hoped to find appropriate material in the rediscovered papers to furnish a biography of Plume where he could identify the context for Plume's endowments of the school, library and Cambridge professorship. Although he later went on to write one article devoted to analysing the contents of a 'pocket book' belonging to Plume, and another article about one of Plume's notebooks, Clark concluded that the appropriate evidence did not exist in the manuscript papers.[10] He did find some consolation on realising that Dr Edward Hyde had used the reverse sides of a pair of letters to finish a sermon, since the letters exposed evidence for the availability of commodities such as wine and coinage during the Civil Wars.[11] This, Clark observed, would not normally be revealed by sermon notes.[12] Clark also mentioned in his article that he had found a theological treatise, but he thought this item would be of interest only if it had been written by a prominent religious leader.[13] These glimpses into Clark's Edwardian construction of history show that his interest was concentrated around elite political and socio-economic activities, a more narrowly defined concept of history than the wider cultural appreciation that can be taken today.

W.J. Petchey, writing in the 1980s for his published Plume Lecture *The Intentions of Thomas Plume*, again did not discuss the manuscript collection in its entirety, but instead focused on two of Plume's notebooks.[14] His examination led him to concur with Clark that the notebooks did not reveal anything of significance about Plume's intentions concerning his legacy, although he commented that they 'can provoke a useful search of the books'.[15] Petchey did not expand on the meaning of this latter statement, although Plume's notebooks do reveal some evidence of his own reading. More recently, R.A. Doe has addressed Plume's reading activities, focusing on Plume's churchmanship and mentorship by bishop John Hacket.[16]

The previous studies of Plume's manuscripts have therefore focused specifically on his own writings and the information that can be gained from them concerning his life and motivations. My own interpretation of the collection takes a different perspective because it addresses the collection as a whole, using manuscripts written by different authors. This approach enables a broader understanding of why Plume had accumulated these documents and shows the ways in which the mid-level clergy generally used and valued their handwritten work. The new perspective will also allow a different insight into Plume's motivations for wishing to 'carefully preserve' the notebooks and papers in the Library. With this in mind, each of the 484 manuscript items have been individually examined so that an appraisal can be made of the content, language, authorship and material form of each document.

Recent studies involving other manuscript collections have been concerned with specific aspects of manuscript culture: texts collected for their historical value and rarity; evidence for a particular person's reading and the mechanics of facilitated reading (where a scholar was employed to interpret text for their patron); or 'scribal culture', where manuscripts are copied out by hand for circulation and publication.[17] Recent scholars have also been particularly interested in the political aspects and applications of reading.[18] Plume's collection is different from the objects of these studies in both its composition and the context in which it can be approached, mainly because Plume's manuscripts are mostly made up of what can be called 'working papers': not only notes from reading made by a range of different people but also drafts of sermons and treatises, correspondence and accounts. This shows Plume as a different type of collector: one who saw value in the ordinary and everyday production of work and self-education.

The perspective taken here helps to show the significance of the handwritten alongside printed texts, how the seventeenth-century clergy used them for their professional role, and how they were saved for posterity from destruction. In order to give an illustration of the collection overall, the following sections will address the types of document found there, the issues of why and how their original creators made and used them and the various ways in which Plume acquired them. First, however, it would be helpful to introduce the main authors and the characteristics of their texts.

The known authors and their texts
There are varying degrees of certainty with which authorship of a manuscript can be determined. For example, the presence of a signature does not necessarily indicate original authorship, but could instead denote subsequent ownership. Certain manuscripts, however, make references to people or places that can provide evidence for an author's identity. For example, one writer, Lady Barbara Hyde, can be identified by connecting three pieces of evidence from her notebook: the presence of her initials 'BH' in three places; the presence of her son's handwriting in the early part of the book; and her reference in the text to various relatives including her sons, her brother and her sisters-in-law.[19] Many of the manuscript books and papers in Plume's collection do not contain enough clues to establish the author's identity. However, once identity *has* been firmly established in one manuscript, careful comparison of the hand and cross-referencing with contextual information can help to ascribe authorship in others.

Thomas Plume
Using this method of identification, just over a quarter of the manuscripts in the collection can be attributed to Thomas Plume. The earliest examples of Plume's work are three notebooks that Plume filled with records of sermons he heard in Maldon and Chelmsford between the ages of 12 and 15.[20] One of these notebooks is inscribed at the front: 'Thomas Plume His Booke Anno Domini 1643', and another: 'Plume his sermon booke'.[21] The vicar of the united Maldon parishes of All Saints and St Peter in Maldon between 1620 and 1649 was Mr Israel Hewitt, sometimes referred to by Plume in his notebooks as 'Mr Huits'.[22] As has been shown in Chapter 3, Plume attended Chelmsford Grammar School, where the curriculum would have included instruction on how to take

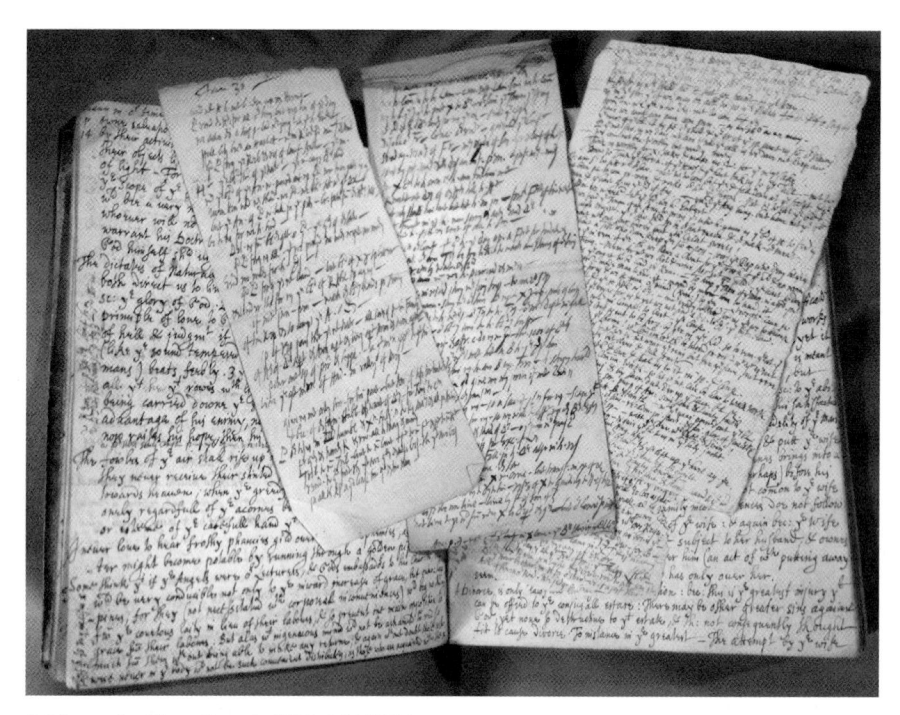

8.1 Loose leaf insertions in TPL, MA0017.

notes on sermons.[23] These note-taking skills would also be useful after Plume had left formal education, when recording his reading from books.

Most of Plume's own writings were made in English, although he used Latin and Greek in approximately 10 per cent of his work. Generally, if the note-takers in Plume's collection had read a book in Latin or Greek, their preference was to take the resulting notes in those languages as well. A good example of this is Plume's reading of Philipp Andreas Oldenburger's *Notitia rerum illustrium imperii* (1668) where his notes are in Latin to match the text in the book.[24] Another example is the notes taken by the preacher at Eythorne (Kent), who read works in Greek and made his notes using the same language.[25] Most of Plume's manuscripts are comprised of sermon notes: from sermons he heard or preached, or notes he made for future sermons.

The remainder of his own manuscripts are made up of reading notes, correspondence, verses and accounts. Plume reread and reused many of his notes, and there is also evidence that he read at least 32 of the other texts, which contain annotations made by him. For example, Plume created an index in Justinian Whitter's miscellany and wrote a title on two of Robert Boreman's texts.[26] Evidence for this rereading and recycling of manuscripts appears in more than 50 of the handwritten items. As well as complete notebooks or folios of text, Plume also made use of individual scraps of paper for his notes. Some of the scraps can be found within the bound notebooks, serving as either page markers or extractions of useful information from within, as illustrated by Figure 8.1.

Reference to the catalogue of printed books shows that Plume owned many of the books that he read, and in many cases his reading notes can be matched to the specific printed books he owned and left to the Library. One notebook written by Plume that can be dated to the 1650s (after he left Cambridge and before he was presented to his living at Greenwich) comprises notes about various books that he had read while living at Nonsuch Palace.[27] R.A. Doe has argued that Plume was resident in that part of Surrey owing to his connections with bishop John Hacket, who was sequestered at his rectory in Cheam, less than a mile away.[28] This idea is supported in Plume's biography of John Hacket, where he commented that he would often go into London to buy books for Hacket, and also by the fact that apartments at Nonsuch Palace were available to be leased during the 1650s. Living at Nonsuch gave Plume ready access to his mentor and was also convenient for visiting London.[29]

During the period encompassing the 1660s to the 1680s, however, Plume used eight notebooks dedicated to his reading notes on topics ranging from philology and philosophy, theology and jurisprudence; the catechism and divine character; history, geography, war and politics.[30] The latest entries in the books were made during the 1680s, when Plume's handwriting had deteriorated so much as to be virtually illegible; as Clark commented, it is a wonder that he could read it himself.[31] It is possible that Plume had a particular health condition that affected the legibility of his handwriting. An indication of this can be found in a letter from Joseph Carte (1636–1707), vicar of Leigh in Kent from 1662, who wrote to Plume finishing on the following note: 'I was glad to see your hand writing the certain indication of your health that it may continue for many years is the prayer of, sir, your humble servant.'[32] This may point to Plume having an unknown health condition, which in its early stages affected his handwriting intermittently but got progressively worse over time. However, the recent discovery by Sue Edward of Plume's original will shows that Plume was still able to write neatly right up until the time of his death,[33] as seen in the several sentences he personally added. Since Plume did not as a rule annotate his printed books, this makes his manuscript notebooks even more valuable as a source for his concerns and interests.

The changing legibility of his hand leads to the question of how useful Plume may have thought his writings would be to subsequent readers. His legible writings, and those of many of the other authors, could indeed have been read and understood, and perhaps were meant to be of practical help to future readers, in the same way they had been used before their arrival at the library.

However, in keeping all the papers by every author, regardless of their legibility or practical use, it is possible that Plume saw them more as a historic cache of information relating to the time in which they were written that formed a memorial to their authors. Plume relayed, in his biography of John Hacket, the story of how the bishop lost many manuscripts as well as books during his sequestration from Holborn, and perhaps Hacket's experience motivated Plume to preserve scholarship that was vulnerable to destruction.[34]

Dr Robert Boreman (d. 1675)

Robert Boreman's manuscripts form the second largest body of documents by one author. Boreman attended Westminster School and Trinity College, Cambridge, receiving his Batchelor of Arts degree in 1632.[35] He was elected a fellow of Trinity in 1632 and went on to receive his Master of Arts in 1635, after which he became tutor and lecturer in Hebrew.[36] He was ordained in 1638 in Peterborough.[37] At the Restoration he was awarded the title of doctor of divinity and presented to the rectory of Blisworth in Northamptonshire.[38] Three years later he became rector of St Giles-in-the-Fields and a prebendary of Westminster Abbey in 1667.[39] Boreman's manuscripts were not referred to in his will, but they were acquired by Thomas Plume around the time of his death, along with those that had belonged to Boreman's close friend and associate Dr Edward Hyde. Boreman published eight of his own texts in addition to the sermons and treatise he posthumously published on Hyde's behalf.[40]

Boreman's papers begin in the 1640s, when he was a fellow at Trinity, and continue until the year of his death in 1675. The account book that shows his income until a month before his death is particularly interesting because it details donations and patronage received from prominent figures, including Lady Alice Dudley (1579–1669), whose funeral sermon Boreman later published.[41] Although this notebook contained information relating to parish business, Boreman chose to pass it to Plume with his other papers. This was a book that Boreman wrote in personally, rather than one kept by a clerk or curate, and it is likely that he considered it to be his own property, especially considering that it referred to income generated from his living. Boreman died at Greenwich, where his family lived, and was buried in St Alfege's church, where Plume was vicar.[42] It is possible that they had met some years before through their mutual association with John Hacket during the 1650s, as Petchey places Boreman at Cheam from anecdotes in Plume's notebook.[43] In any event, Boreman described Plume in his will as one of his 'very loving friends' and left him five pounds to buy a mourning gown.[44] Although there is no mention of Boreman's manuscript papers in his will, Plume's possession of them indicates that they must have been given to him shortly before or after Boreman's death, as discussed later in this chapter.

8.2 Side view of TPL, MA0106 showing construction.

The majority of Boreman's writings were in English, although he authored a slightly higher proportion of Greek and Latin manuscripts than Plume and occasionally used Hebrew script interspersed with the other languages in certain of his texts. Robert Boreman's handwriting also changed over time but, in contrast to Plume's, remained neat and legible. Boreman's general practice was to use individual sheets of paper, sewn together to form his own notebooks, which were constructed in preparation for writing (Figure 8.2). To illustrate this further, one notebook attributable to Boreman has had a page cut out, leaving a 20mm stub but resulting in no loss of text.[45] The manner in which the page was cut out suggests that the notebook was at least compiled, and perhaps sewn together, before the writing took place. This may mean that the volume of notes was made to fit a previously prepared notebook. Richard Holdsworth's 1651 treatise to students suggested that they should buy paper books in a portable octavo format, demonstrating that this type of book could be purchased already made up.[46]

The 12 bound notebooks attributable to Robert Boreman, on the other hand, seem to have performed a more formal function than his sewn-paper books. Some were acquired by him on special occasions, perhaps as gifts: one example of this is a book with decorated pasteboards, which he used as a grammar.[47] The remainder of Boreman's bound notebooks represent a more permanent and formal record of his writing than those that remain unbound, as can be seen in the pre-publication version of his text 'Antidote Against Swearing' and the related sermon 'Sweare Not', which formed earlier versions of a text that appeared in print in 1662.[48] The bound form of these manuscripts present a sense of being more complete and polished compared with the more draft nature of the unbound texts.

Dr Edward Hyde (1607–59)
Dr Hyde's father was Sir Laurence Hyde (*c.*1562–1642), a lawyer who became attorney to Queen Anne in 1614.[49] His brother Alexander (*c.*1596–1667) was the bishop of Salisbury, and their cousin was the more well-known Edward Hyde, earl of Clarendon (1609–74).[50] Dr Hyde was at Westminster and Trinity at the same time as Robert Boreman, and was also ordained in 1638, in Salisbury, receiving his doctor of divinity and first living just before the Civil Wars.[51]

In contrast to the note-taking methods of both Thomas Plume and Robert Boreman, most of Edward Hyde's writings are contained within bound notebooks. There are only three unbound sermons, together with a dis-bound Exposition on Psalm 25, which was split up at a later date into individual sermons.[52] Dr Hyde's practice was to utilise all available space on the page using very small handwriting; however, there are numerous blank pages in his notebooks, suggesting that he was not short of paper but instead filled the pages in an economical manner. The prevalence of bound notebooks in his materials may be an indication of Hyde's slightly higher social status and ready access to funds, compared with the other two writers. Edward Hyde authored 31 of the manuscripts preserved in the Library, comprising reading notes, sermons, papers of mixed content and the Exposition on Psalm 25. In contrast to Plume's own manuscripts, only five of these documents were written wholly in English; six were in Latin and the remainder in a mixture of Latin, English, Greek and Hebrew. The time-span of the documents ranges from 1629 to 1657, two years before his death in 1659. Hyde's handwriting was consistently clear, although always tightly packed onto the page, and did not significantly change over time.

Other authors not conclusively identified
MA0114, also known as 'Bundle H', comprises 68 loose-leaf sermons ascribed to a clergyman named Robert Browne. This attribution is derived from an address label from his father, Anthony Browne, forming part of the paper used for one of the sermons (Figure 8.3), 'To my very loveinge sonn / Mr Robert Browne in Kent / give these I praye you'. Andrew Clark suggests that a certain Robert Browne who received the MA degree from Magdalen College, Oxford, would fit the dates of the sermons (although *Alumni Oxoniensis* does not place this Robert Browne in Kent).[53] However, in terms of clergymen named Robert Browne known to have been operating in Kent, there are two further possibilities as candidates for authorship: one who was vicar of Selling or 'Sellynge' in the 1540s, and another (rather long-lived) Robert Browne (1577–1675) who was rector of Stapleford.[54]

Although Plume emerged as a royalist supporter following his time at university, he also owned notebooks clearly written by a non-conformist preacher and supporter of parliament during the Civil Wars, who preached in

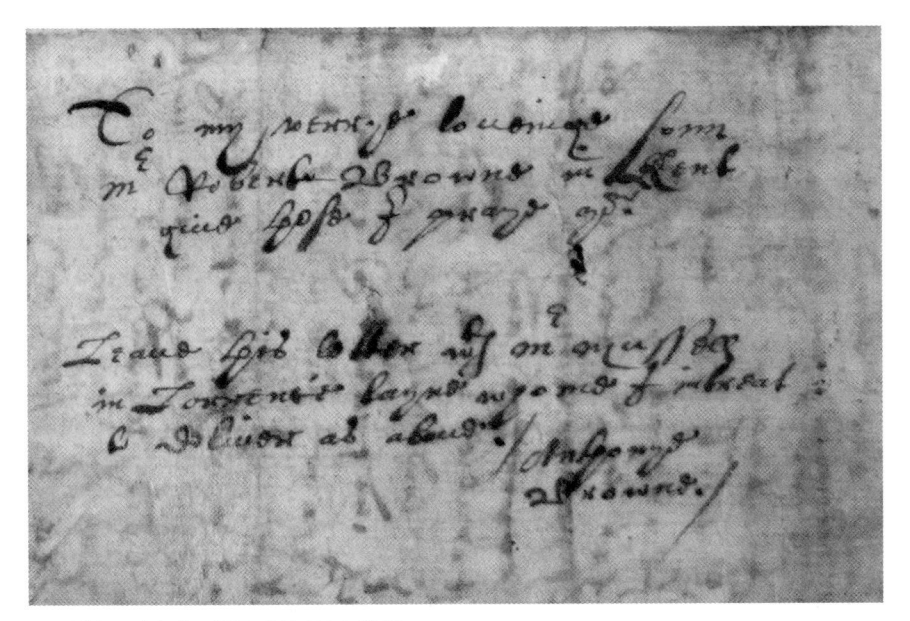

8.3 Address label in TPL, MA0114, H.25.

the parishes of Eythorne and Tilmanstone. The three notebooks in the Plume Library belonging to this clergyman were entitled 'The Third Booke', 'The Sixt Booke' and 'The Seventh Booke'; presumably the others in the series were not acquired by Plume.[55] The notebooks are similar in size, measuring in the region of 200mm × 150mm × 40mm, and are bound in seventeenth-century calf with blindlines (plain/uncoloured lines stamped onto the leather) over pasteboards. They each contain several sermons on different topics, written over a period of time and collected together in one place. These notebooks contrast with the single sermon written on unbound paper by the same author, showing that clergymen did not always adhere to a single method in their writing practices.[56]

It is difficult to ascertain the identity of the preacher at Eythorne (Kent) during this period. John Monyns (1609–1707) had been instituted as the rector there in 1642 and it is likely that he was sequestered shortly afterwards in the same year and succeeded by another preacher.[57] A plausible candidate for author of these sermon notebooks is Nicholas Billingsley, MA. Billingsley was a former Master of Faversham Grammar school, and recorded as rector of Tilmanstone (he also held the living of Bettleshanger) between 1644 and 1651 (this coincides with the dates set out for preaching sermons in Eythorne and Tilmanstone in the notebooks' indexes).[58] Billingsley had taken over from the sequestered royalist rector Moses Capell, whose appointment had ended in 1642. Another possibility could be Edward Hudson, who, on 26 May 1643, made a petition to the House of Lords because the archdeacon of Canterbury had refused to induct him as rector of Eythorne.[59] The Lords found the archdeacon and his two associates guilty of 'Oppression' and they were ordered to appear before them so that appropriate recompense for Hudson could be decided.[60] This indicates that Edward Hudson had been conducting the duties of rector in Eythorne but was unpaid for the living. However, in the absence of conclusive evidence that he was in post at the time the notebooks were written, their author will be referred to as 'the Eythorne preacher'.

In each of the three notebooks the Eythorne preacher inserted his own indexes on the penultimate page and back pastedown to show when, and where, he had delivered each sermon, and it can be seen from these indexes that he also preached in the nearby parishes of Tilmanstone and Northbourne, Kent.[61] Plume also created an index in 'The Third Booke' and made some annotations on another page, which shows that he also found the contents of that particular book to be useful.[62] Plume's index refers to the biblical texts used by the Eythorne preacher in the composition of his sermons.[63] Perhaps this suggests that Plume's interest was in the scriptural references rather than the political content of the sermons. However, although Plume owned 21 printed thanksgiving sermons in support of, or issued by, the monarchy, three further printed sermons he owned were issued by parliament, giving thanks for parliamentarian victories.[64] Plume owned printed books representing all sides of religious debates, and this practice was not at all unusual during the period. However, the ownership of these printed parliamentarian sermons seems harder to reconcile with Plume's royalist stance because they stood directly against the king rather than against a theoretical position on Church practice or scriptural meaning to be debated and analysed by scholars.

Material form of the manuscripts

In terms of their material form, the manuscripts appear in a range of sizes. The largest is 547mm × 212mm × 5mm and comprises the list of the book values or prices of books belonging to the bishop of Ely dating from the late seventeenth century, discussed in Chapter 6.[65] One of the smallest notebooks in the collection, at 131mm × 79mm × 23mm, 'signed T Pindarus' on the pastedown, is bound in calf over pasteboards with a gold border and contains reading notes on the subjects of the Vision of Cyrus, the Scythians, the Amazonians and Plutarch's *Life of Theseus*.[66] There was a Thomas Pindar, rector of Weston in Suffolk in 1543, who could have been the original owner or scribe.[67] The majority of the notebooks and papers, however, are around 140–160mm tall and 98–120mm wide, making them pocket-sized and transportable. During the early seventeenth century, once writing paper had been folded in two, pages were approximately 300mm × 200mm, indicating that many of the manuscripts in the Plume collection are on the small side.[68] At that time most of the paper in use in England came from

France, Germany, Italy and Switzerland, although there had been a paper mill in Dartford from 1585.[69] The material form of manuscripts can indicate how they were used by the original and subsequent owners and finding evidence for authorship can help to show how the manuscripts came into Plume's possession. However, there is a third aspect that helps to demonstrate how and why Plume valued the documents, and that is the type of content they contained.

Genre

There are five main categories of content found in the manuscripts: sermons, treatises, reading notes, miscellanies and common-placing, and, finally, household items (including correspondence). The categorisation of items can be problematic when they were started for one reason and then reused for another. In most cases the original use – if that can be established – has been employed here. Occasionally an exception has been made, as, for example, in the case of the piece of paper addressed to Robert Browne, where the original use was 'correspondence' but the subsequent use was for drafting a sermon. In this case the category of 'sermons' has been used, because this was its *main* use. In addition, it forms part of a set of sermons by Browne, so to label this manuscript as 'correspondence' would be misleading.

Sermons
Two-thirds of the whole collection can be considered under an umbrella category of 'Sermons', which comprises three distinct types of document. The first is a record of the sermons that a note-taker heard being preached and these examples range from simply a few words on the theme or structure of the sermon to a more extensive transcription. The second comprises drafts of future sermons, and either includes details taken from scripture on which to base the theme of the sermon or represents what Clark referred to as 'pulpit notes, such as divines placed on their pulpit-cushion to aid memory'.[70] The third type in this category is completed sermons: polished texts to be read verbatim or intended for publication.

Discerning the difference between sermons *preached* by the writer and sermons *heard* by the writer can be problematic. An obvious indication that the sermons were heard rather than composed is the presence of a preacher's name at the beginning of the notes. A good example is the notebook containing notes from sermons attended by Edward Hyde in Cambridge, where he records the speaker and their college affiliation: for example, 'Mr Nailer of Sidney' and 'Mr Duncan of Pembroke'.[71] Another (though less reliable) indicator is the appearance of the handwriting: an extensive transcription made at the time of the sermon could result in poor legibility owing to the speed with which the notes were taken. The messy handwriting of an unknown scribe prompted a later reader to write in the front that he thought the content 'seems to be notes taken fro[m] Dr Baylye, as they were preaching'.[72] In contrast, sermons delivered by the author rather than heard can often be identified by a date and place being inserted *after* the text. A good example in Plume's collection of sermons preached by the author are those by the Eythorne preacher, who noted the specific locations where and dates when he had delivered his sermons.[73]

Completed sermons intended for publication represent another form of this genre. As discussed in Chapter 3, John Hacket (1592–1670), bishop of Lichfield and Coventry, left Plume his manuscript sermons, which Plume later published as *A Century of Sermons* (although the manuscripts themselves are not present in the collection).[74] There are, however, two small sermon notebooks in Plume's collection written in Hacket's hand, although unsigned by him.[75] In contrast, Robert Boreman kept manuscript pre-printer versions of his publications. He drafted one such treatise in 1648 'intended first for ye pulpitt and now cast into a continued treatise', and published it in print as *An Antidote against Sweareing* in 1662.[76] The original sermon he developed the treatise from is also present in the collection, as are his notes on Matthew 5.34, which formed the basis for the sermon.[77] Although the sermon category is the largest, the remaining genres of manuscript, discussed below, can be particularly revealing in terms of their writers' interests.

Treatises
Religious writing was often addressed to specific religious communities and aimed at strengthening an existing communal identity.[78] Lay readers were keen to read expositions written by professional clergy that interpreted doctrine and provided references to further readings to enhance their understanding.[79] Several manuscripts in the collection comprise drafts of tracts, treatises, expositions and commentaries, some of which later appeared in printed form. For example, Robert Boreman published a treatise in favour of tithes, *The Country-man's Catechisme*, in 1651, an earlier manuscript version of which appears in the collection.[80] This manuscript includes many erasures, and it is likely that it would have needed to have been written out again in fair copy in order to be passed by the licenser and for the use of the compositor.[81]

Another manuscript exposition existing in two parts in the collection is entitled 'The brief meaning or sum[m]arie exposition of the Apocalypse', written by an unknown author.[82] The illustration in Figure 8.4 representing the Four Evangelists is taken from a drawing in the margin of this manuscript.[83] The theme of apocalypse is also present in Robert Boreman's Latin verses on Nebuchadnezzar's vision.[84] Warren Johnston argues that, although apocalyptic ideas had been used by radical factions during the Civil Wars to justify their opposition of the monarchy, during the Restoration Anglicans also used these

8.4 Four Evangelists image in TPL, MA0113, G.12.

ideas politically in favour of monarchy and episcopacy.[85] This is significant for the collection in that it embodies one of the ideological concerns reflected in the whole collection of manuscripts. Henry More (1614–87) wrote extensively on the apocalypse post-Restoration and Thomas Plume had a number of his books on this and other subjects. More was a fellow at Christ's at the time Plume was a student there, but extensive searches have failed to establish any links between them.[86]

Another draft treatise in the collection, later published by Lancelot Andrewes (1555–1626) as *A summarie view of the government both of the old and new testament*, is present in Plume's manuscripts in another person's hand.[87] The signature of 'John Simpson' and the date '1640' appear at the end of the document, while the first page states that the document is 'the copie of Bp And. work as he left it'.[88] The inclusion of this note indicates that the text was scribally copied from one of Bishop Lancelot Andrewes' own manuscripts prior to it going to print in 1641. The handwriting in both the signature and the accounts corresponds precisely with the style of lettering in the main body of text, suggesting that John Simpson was the scribe who copied the work. The curate for St Mary's Church in Maldon c.1619–42 was named John Simpson, but there were other clergymen of the same name operating in London who could have equally been the author.[89]

Reading notes
The breadth of subjects of interest to seventeenth-century Anglican clergymen is indicated by the notebooks containing reading notes. The genres of reading include history, from Greek historians Xenophon and Plutarch – read by the Eythorne preacher and an unknown scribe, possibly Thomas Pindar, whose signature appears in the manuscript – via Renaissance historians Francesco Guicciardini and Paulo Sarpi – read by Boreman and Plume – to more recent histories from authors such as William Dugdale, William Camden and the earl of Clarendon – also read by Plume.[90] Another sixteenth-century Italian Protestant author, Girolamo Zanchi (1516–90), was also popular. Records of three readings of his work exist, by Boreman, Hyde and an unknown scribe, and Plume also owned a printed book by Zanchi.[91] Plume read political philosophy in Hobbes' *Leviathan* (1651) and Descartes' *Opera Philosophica* (1664), and he read natural philosophy in, for example, Robert Boyle's *Natural Philosophy* (1663/1671).[92] Edward Hyde read *De Emendatione Temporum* (1583) by Joseph Justus Scaliger (1540–1609) and *Chronicle of Eusebius* (1606) and Plume read the notes that Justinian Whitter had made on a work by Julius Caesar Scaliger (1484–1558) regarding 'De Intelligentiis' (from the *Exotericarum exercitationum libri*).[93]

Also present are notes on reading from books on astrology and astronomy by Tomasso Campanella and Pierre Gassendi; these authors were read by Hyde, Boreman and Plume.[94] Aristotle was read by many of the note-takers, including Boreman, Hyde, Justinian Whitter and two unknown scribes. They were interested in Aristotle's *Rhetoric*, noting down his vocabulary, metaphysical terms, 'categories' and writings on behaviour, politics, the soul, cosmology, birth and death, and the history of animals.[95] Cicero's speeches were read by Hyde and two unknown scribes (signatures of R. Groome and Thomas Beconus are present), in particular *Pro Quinctio* and *Pro Roscio Amerino*.[96] These classical authors were read side by side with Doctors of the Church, such as Thomas Aquinas, who was read by Hyde and Whitter, and early Church Fathers such as Theodoret and Chrysostom, read by both Hyde and Boreman.[97]

There are two references to the reading of contemporary drama: Plume read Ben Jonson's *Everyman in his Humour* (1601/1616) and copied out a few verses, and Hyde read 'Mr Randolphs Comaedie called the Jealous Lovers Aug 6. 1632'.[98] There is a connection between these readings, as Thomas Randolph was a contemporary of Edward Hyde at Westminster School and Trinity, and became part of Ben Jonson's circle of followers.[99] Plume owned another comedy by Randolph and a copy of the works of Ben Jonson.[100] John Hacket also had a connection to Ben Jonson through their collaboration in the translation of Francis Bacon's work *Advancement of Learning* (1605) into Latin.[101] These reading subjects illustrate the broad spectrum of learning available to scholars during the university years and beyond. The reading of contemporary texts – in some cases shortly after they were published – shows the continued scholarly engagement of these manuscript writers in the political, religious and cultural developments of the time.

Miscellanies and common-placing
Notebook miscellanies were common during the early modern period.[102] They could be created by one author to record more than one type of content; alternatively, the notebook could become a miscellany when a subsequent owner added information of a different genre. One of Plume's own notebooks contains a 'Recipe for Infection or Sickness' and parish accounts paid and unpaid next to notes from the Psalms, Paul's Epistles and Church synods, and a reference to genealogy.[103] A further example is Thomas Plume's notebook used to record sermons he had heard, together with Greek vocabulary.[104] Edward Hyde started a notebook to record or draft letters to his brothers Thomas and Henry but, following a section of blank pages, inserted a series of entries headed 'Carmina' (poems) and later on inscribed notes of the play by Randolph discussed earlier.[105] Common-placing, on the other hand, involved placing extracts from texts under pre-written alphabetically ordered headings.[106]

It could be argued that useful information such as those items contained in the examples above was not meant to be segregated into different places, but formed a complementary body of knowledge for the author to draw on in one place. This is particularly likely in the case of Thomas Plume's notebook, which he completed while at grammar school, where Greek vocabulary found a common ground with sermons in the language of the New Testament. Plume used the university workbooks long after he had completed formal education: for example, there are annotations in Plume's hand in the book previously owned by Edward Hyde, which Plume did not receive until the 1670s.[107]

Household and accounts
In other cases, however, household information such as correspondence, recipes and accounts could have been incorporated into a notebook or document merely in lieu of other writing space being available. This seems to be the case where the manuscript was started by one person and then the available space on the page was reused by another person. For example, Thomas Plume drafted a letter on the back of one of Robert Boreman's verses and

Robert Browne reused a piece of paper addressed to him by his father to write a sermon, as shown in Figure 8.3.[108] In some cases, therefore, the appearance of different genres of writing within one manuscript was merely arbitrary and at other times deliberate, but in most cases it is apparent from the material form of the text. The content with which Thomas Plume was more concerned – the clergy scholarship in the manuscripts – was sometimes joined by more random information, which he would not necessarily otherwise have kept.

In terms of single items and fragments, however, one example of a household item Plume kept was a recipe, catalogued as being for brewing but – judging by the ingredients – perhaps a form of purging medicine instead: '4 oz senna, 2 oz Rhubarb, 2 oz Polipody, 4 oz of Seeds, 1 oz Epithenam. Putt them into foure gallons new Ale; before it hath done working [in a droastring] bag'.[109] There are also several items of correspondence, one example being a letter from George Gifford (d. 1686), 'Gresham professor of divinity in 1661 and president of Sion College in 1677' and grandson of George Gifford (1547/8–1600), curate of the united parishes of All Saints and St Peter, Maldon in 1578.[110] Gifford wrote to Plume:

> I met Mr Kent yesterday who tould me your journey was put of & that you Intended to come this way today. I have sent that if you could, I might hasten your coming; because my father is in London & hath a great desire to speake with you, but by reason of his shortnes of time in towne, cant possibly come so far. You would doe him & mee a great favour if you could possibly meet him at my house at dinner a little after 12 a clock. Pray send word If you can come. Your Assured friend G. Gifford.[111]

George Gifford was rector of St Dunstan's in the East, and this letter indicates that Plume was planning to travel into the area near London Bridge on business. Why did Plume keep this particular letter for so many years after it had served its purpose, among all the other correspondence he must have received? Was it in memory of George or his father? The household items generally do not necessarily have a practical value for the clergyman's role in the same way as sermons and reading notes might. To try to understand why Plume might have kept these papers, therefore, it would be useful to know how he acquired the manuscripts.

How Plume acquired the notebooks and papers

Thomas Plume acquired the manuscripts in two main ways – friendship gift and family inheritance – although it was also possible that he could have bought some of them in secondhand sales and auctions. There is also evidence that other individuals whose work appears in the collection acquired manuscripts in the same manner, and a system of pro-active collection, as opposed to mere accumulation, emerges from these transactions. Similarly, there is a sense of a

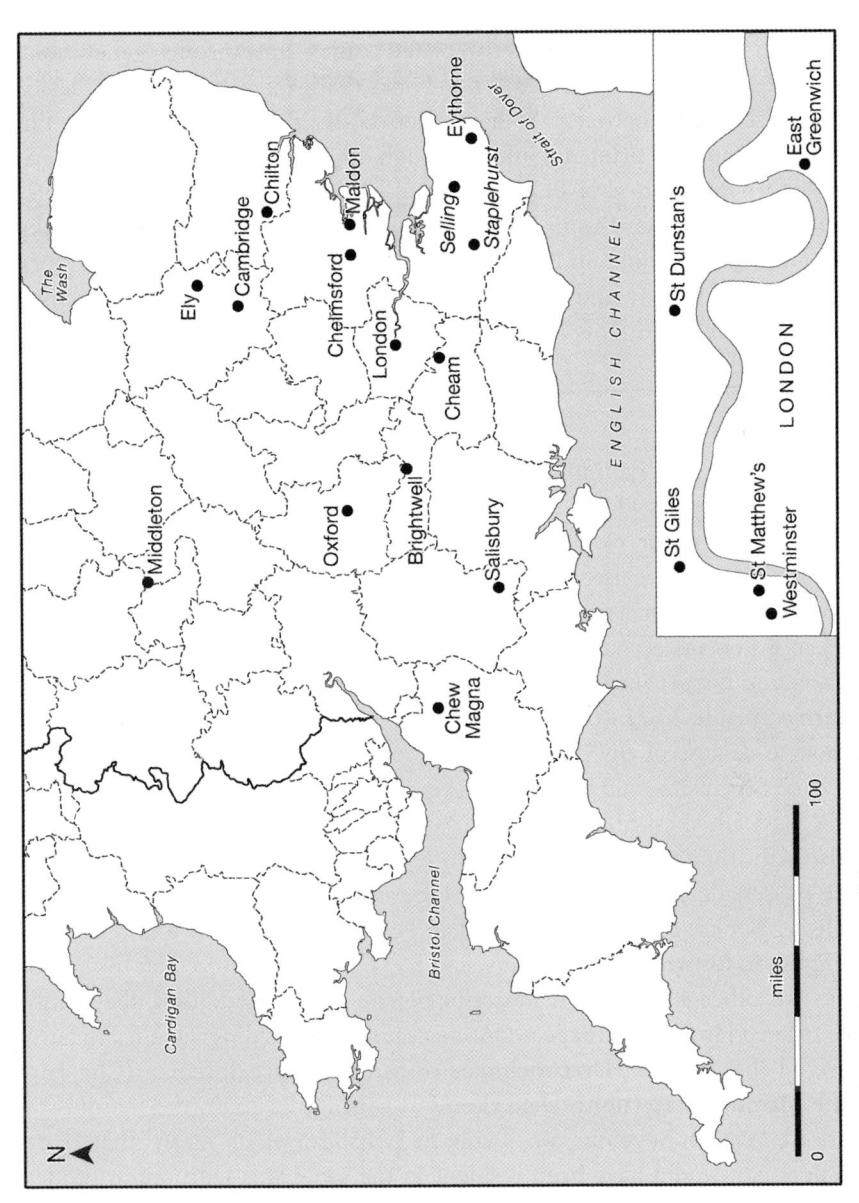

8.5 Map showing the origins of the manuscripts.

baton being passed from one user to the next, with the former's death – or the recognition of its approach – as the catalyst. This type of transmission contrasts with the usual picture of a republic of letters, or the circulation of texts between readers and writers who worked together to produce texts during their lifetimes. The way in which families passed completed manuscripts through generations is mirrored in the gifting of blank notebooks, with many of the examples of such gifts seemingly between brothers. There is also a relationship between the manuscripts and the printed books: although it has not been possible to prove that Robert Boreman gave Plume his books in addition to his manuscripts, there is a precedent for this in Plume's acquisition of Justinian Whitter's books and notebooks. The map in Figure 8.5 shows the locations where the authors originally created the manuscripts and the sphere of geographical space within which they circulated. This is significant as it demonstrates the wide-ranging scope of Plume's network across the south and east of England.

Friendship gift
Evidence for the precise timing of Robert Boreman's gift of his own manuscript collection to Thomas Plume can be found in Boreman's account book relating to his time as rector of St-Giles-in-the-Fields in London (1663–75).[112] This particular document is useful because it shows the date when Boreman last used it, thus providing a small timeframe for Thomas Plume's acquisition of it. The final entry in Boreman's account book is 5–12 October 1675.[113] Boreman's will does not mention his personal library of printed books or manuscripts, but instead confirmed that he had instructed his brother, Sir William Boreman (c.1612–86), on how to dispose of any possessions not mentioned specifically in the will.[114] Therefore Boreman would have either given Plume his manuscripts in the month before his death or asked his brother to pass them on to Plume afterwards.

Also at the time of his death Robert Boreman had Edward Hyde's manuscripts in his possession, having kept them for the past 16 years. Hyde had bequeathed his 'lesser bookes that is to say lesse than Folio' to his nephews and his books in English to his wife and daughters, and had entrusted to Boreman his 'paper books': in other words, his manuscript notebooks.[115] In addition, the family were to keep Hyde's loose papers for one year before deciding whether to burn them, on the advice of Dr Hinchman 'or as Mr Robert Boreman (Chaplain to the Marquis of Hertford) shall desire'.[116] During the 1650s the marquis of Hertford, William Seymour, was living in Wiltshire, which means that Hyde and Boreman would have been resident in the same area with opportunities for meeting in person.[117] Slips of paper in Boreman's hand inserted into two of Hyde's notebooks show that Boreman read not only Hyde's sermons but his other 'paper books' as well (Figure 8.6).[118] Three years after Hyde's death, Robert Boreman published *The True Catholick's Tenure* in Hyde's name, which

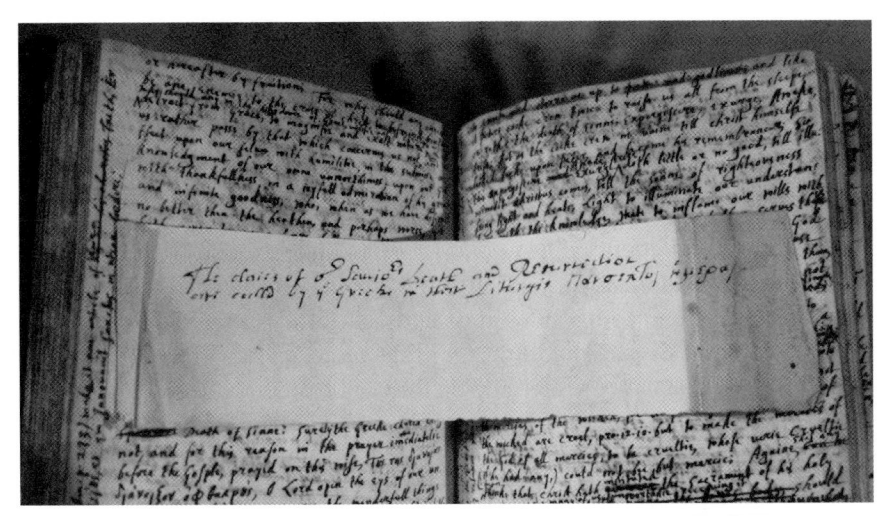

8.6 Robert Boreman's slip of paper in Edward Hyde's notebook TPL, MA0044.

contained a second title, *Allegiance and Conscience not Fled out of England*, comprising sermons Hyde had preached in 1649.[119]

Another case where eight manuscripts – and also at least three books – were acquired through friendship gift was that of Justinian Whitter (d. 1649). Whitter's will stated that Thomas Plume of Yeldham (possibly Dr Thomas Plume's father) was to be one of the executors in the event of his wife Mary either remarrying or dying before the full execution of his will had taken place.[120] Whitter did not specifically mention his books and manuscripts, but they would have been included under 'the rest of any monie and goods' that he left to Mary Whitter. It is possible, therefore, that they passed to Dr Plume through Thomas Plume senior having involvement with Whitter's will.[121] It would have been usual for a clergyman's books to be left to a son or nephew, although Whitter's son John was a child at the time of Whitter's death and he does not appear in the alumni records of Oxford or Cambridge, suggesting either that he did not survive or that he did not go into the Church.

Family inheritance
One of Plume's own notebooks contains the name John Plume and the date 1636 on the cover.[122] As has been seen from Chapter 2, the most likely owner of this book was Dr Plume's half-brother. John Plume's work involved arithmetic and calculations, and this may reflect his training as a merchant. The table at the start of John's notes is described as serving 'to reckon anie number', and he produced further pages on the addition of money and weights.[123] Thomas Plume would have been six years old at the time of John's death, meaning that the book would have been kept for him until he was old enough to make use of it. Plume

started making use of John's notebook two years into his time at university, as his initial inscription reads June 27/1648.[124] He continued using the notebook for arithmetic and calculations: for example, he noted calculations for amounts of rye, wheat, barley and oats[125] through posing questions to be answered, such as: 'So yt now say if 120 bushels cost 280 shillings, what will one bushel cost?'[126]

At a later date Plume again wrote in this notebook, recording his reading of Descartes' *Meditations on first philosophy*.[127] Plume owned the 1654 edition of Descartes' *Meditations*, printed in Amsterdam, and the connection can be made between the reading notes and the book from which Plume compiled them.[128] There is an inscription on the front pastedown of the book reading 'Thomas Knight 8 October 1659' and on the back pastedown '15 October 1660' (presumably when Thomas Knight finished reading it himself). One candidate for the original owner of this book is a Thomas Knight who was a scholar at Sidney Sussex College, Cambridge, and a vicar in Hertfordshire at the end of his life; he died in 1660.[129] The inscription gives the purchase price as 6s 2d, amended from a previous figure, perhaps to show the price that Plume paid.[130] Thomas Plume did not always ascribe a date to his reading, but the last date found in John Plume's notebook is 1688, showing that Thomas had used the notebook intermittently for 40 years, and on his death it had been in the family for at least 68 years. His reading shows his ideological persuasion as well as his interest in contemporary intellectual thought. The secondhand purchase of the Descartes' *Meditations* reflects the final way in which Plume may have acquired some of the manuscript notebooks in the collection.

There are other instances where the notebooks were passed from brother to brother. One notebook containing a variety of different content is inscribed on the front pastedown 'Sam: Plume', indicating that it may have belonged to Dr Plume's elder brother Samuel before Thomas Plume used it.[131] This same handwriting appears in the front part of the notebook noting various lessons in Latin.[132] The other main authors were also given notebooks by their brothers. John Boreman was one of Robert Boreman's elder brothers and is referred to in the will of Sir William Boreman.[133] In a notebook entitled 'Greek Manuscript', which contains Robert Boreman's notes on Conrad Gessner's *Historia Animalium*, there is a signature of John Boreman on the front flyleaf, suggesting that it had previously been owned by him.[134] Such notebooks could also be given as gifts rather than just 'hand-me-downs'. One of Edward Hyde's notebooks was given to him by his brother Thomas as a gift, as indicated in the inscription on the front flyleaf: 'Ed Hyde from THH'.[135]

Secondhand purchase

The final example of how Thomas Plume acquired his manuscript books is by secondhand purchase. In the same way that Plume purchased pre-owned

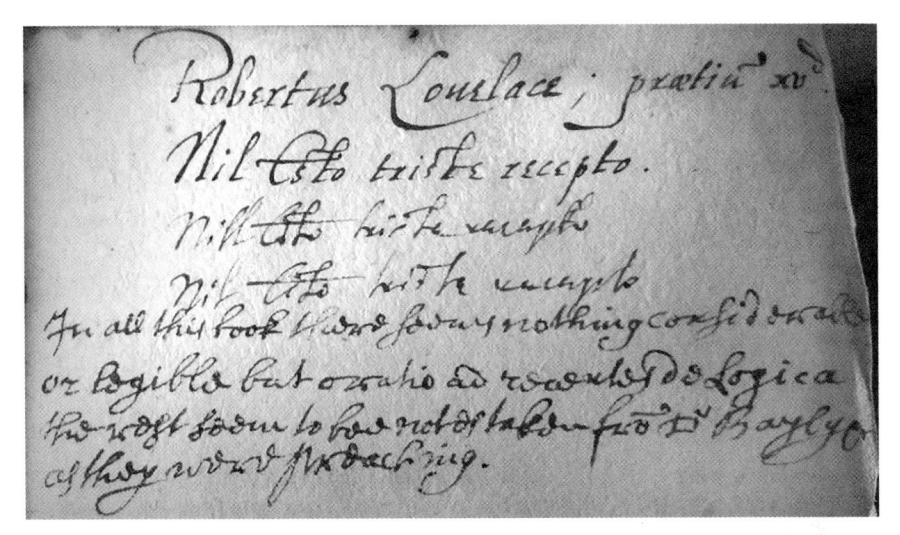

8.7 Inscription in front leaf of TPL, MA0053.

printed books secondhand, as in the example of Descartes's *Meditations*, it is likely that he also bought manuscript books in this way. However, this cannot be definitely proven as there is only one manuscript showing a purchase price (Figure 8.7). The notebook, which shows a purchase price of 15d, is bound in calf with gold ornaments and it is also possible that the blank notebook was bought for this price, rather than one which had already been used. The inscription on the title page reads:

> Robertus Lovelace; praetiu[m] xvd
> *Nil esto triste recepto*
> *Nil esto triste recepto*
> *Nil esto triste recepto* [let nothing be received sadly]
> In all this book there seems nothing considerable
> or legible but *oratio ad recentes de logica* [a lecture to young men about thought]
> the rest seem to bee notes taken fro[m] Dr Baylye
> as they were preaching.[136]

It is likely that Robert Lovelace, whose name appears on the first line, also wrote the three lines *Nil esto triste recepto*. Two further manuscripts contain this phrase in the same handwriting.[137] However, it is possible that a different writer, who subsequently acquired the book, wrote the second part of the inscription. Although both parts are in black ink, the reason for suggesting that there were two different scribes is the different styles of the letter 'e' in the two sections. There is no apparent connection between Robert Lovelace and Thomas Plume, apart from Lovelace's family hailing from Kent and Plume becoming archdeacon of Rochester in 1679.[138] Lovelace was a vicar in Hertfordshire and died in 1673 (no will has been traced), and it is possible that Plume bought the notebook in a sale after his death.[139] It could be argued that Plume was interested in this content, as he owned other examples of sermon notes taken by auditors. Three individuals from the same family with the title Dr Bayly could have been the preacher referred to in the notebook: Lewis Bayly (1575–1631) and his sons John Bayly (1595–1633) and Thomas Bayly (d. 1657). Plume owned a printed book of sermons by John and another book by Thomas regarding the Royal Charter; Lewis Bayly was particularly renowned for his preaching.[140]

Therefore, it was through a combination of inheritance, living gift, family connections and perhaps purchase that the collection came together. This suggests that Plume was known and trusted as an active collector of manuscript working papers and that he may have sought them out in sales in a similar way to the printed books. This endeavour may have an origin in Plume's dismay that Hacket had lost important books and manuscripts during his sequestration from Holborn.

Conclusion
The manuscript collection taken as a whole provides an insight into Thomas Plume's development as a clergyman, from his studies as a schoolboy, through his education at Chelmsford and Christ's, to his continued educational development and professional work. In addition, from what remains of his written work and the work of the other authors of the manuscripts, reading and writing trends emerge that emphasise the variety of genres in which these clergymen were interested. The authors of the manuscripts read widely in the history and geography of nations, as well as the history of the Church, and were particularly interested in the Italian writers of the sixteenth century. To aid their own professional development they made notes from sermons preached by others as a preparation for writing their own, and sometimes wrote their sermons out in full for publication. Many of the manuscripts contain readings from different genres within one document, and a few perform multi-purpose functions. They read each other's work, and the notebooks belonging to other individuals continued to be read long after the original author had inscribed them and they had arrived in Plume's possession.

Thomas Plume collected manuscripts both from his contemporaries and also from those of a generation earlier, and it is apparent that he knew some of these individuals personally. However, he was also in possession of work created by people with whom no obvious connection can be established. It is likely that he was given these manuscripts by friends and intermediaries or bought them in secondhand sales. As he specified that the notebooks and papers were to be 'carefully preserved', it is likely that he acquired them with a thought toward their future value and relevance, for both himself and the scholarly clergymen he wanted to provide for after his death. Specifically, Plume collected other people's *scholarship*. The household papers that are present in most cases had been repurposed for use with the notebooks. This shows that Plume, and the clergymen who gave him their work, were selective in what they saved and passed on. Plume was not merely a 'hoarder' of manuscripts: there was a valid reason for accumulating them.

However, Plume did not keep these items only for their practical value. Plume's manuscript collection contains evidence of the day-to-day working lives of the clergy during the seventeenth century – clergy from both sides of the political divide during the Civil Wars – and it is unusual in that so many items have survived. The careful preservation of these manuscripts by their original creators, intermediaries and Plume himself through the tumultuous times of the seventeenth century speaks of a desire to memorialise the people who created them through saving their life's work from deliberate destruction or neglect.

Notes

1 TNA, PROB 10/1387; Appendix: Dr Thomas Plume's will, ll. 144–5. This chapter has been adapted from H. Kemp, 'Collecting, communicating, and commemorating: the significance of Thomas Plume's manuscript collection, left to his Library in Maldon, est. 1704', PhD thesis (University of Essex, 2017), Chapter 4.
2 *Ibid.*, ll. 161–3.
3 See 'study, n.' OED Online. *Oxford University Press*, 8 September 2016, entries 7a and 8a.
4 TPL, MA0015, fo. 37r.
5 TPL, PP1960. On 2 March 1721 the Plume Trustees' minutes recorded that: 'It is ordered that Mr Thompson be paid ten shillings for the Mahogenie Box for the use of the Trust to put ye Books and Writings and Deeds of the several Estates to them belonging': TPL, MA0120.
6 The printed books arrived at the Library with a packing list, which served as an initial catalogue, and further catalogues were made by the serving Librarians in 1761 and 1848 and the Trustees in 1959 and 2004. See further: http://www.thomasplumeslibrary.co.uk/catalogue/the-collections-and-their-catalogues/.
7 A. Clark, 'Plume MS papers', *ER*, xiii (1904), p. 30.
8 Comprising TPL, MA0107 to MA0115.
9 D. McKitterick, *Print, Manuscript and the Search for Order, 1450–1830* (Cambridge, 2003), pp. 12–13.
10 Clark, 'Plume MS papers', p. 30; A. Clark, 'Dr Plume's Notebook', *ER*, xiv (1905), pp. 152–63, 213–20 and xv (1906), pp. 8–24; *idem.*, 'Dr Plume's Pocketbook', *ER*, xiv (1905), pp. 9–20, 65–72.
11 Clark, 'Plume MS papers', p. 31.
12 *Ibid.*
13 *Ibid.*
14 W.J. Petchey, *The Intentions of Thomas Plume* (Maldon, 2004); TPL, MA0029 (formerly MS 7) and MA0017.
15 Petchey, *Intentions*, p. 9.

16　Chapter 3, pp. 63–5; TPL, MA0029.
17　C.J. Wright (ed.), *Sir Robert Cotton as Collector. Essays on an Early Stuart Courtier and his Legacy* (London, 1997); P. Beal, *In Praise of Scribes: Manuscripts and their Makers in Seventeenth-Century England* (Lyell Lectures in Bibliography, Oxford, 1998); H. Woudhuysen, *Sir Phillip Sydney and the Circulation of Manuscripts 1558–1640: The Procreative Pen* (Oxford, 1996); H. Love, *The Culture and Commerce of Texts: Scribal Publication in Seventeenth-Century England* (Amherst, MA, 1998).
18　K. Sharpe, *Reading Revolutions: The Politics of Reading in Early Modern England* (New Haven, CT, 2000); P.E.J. Hammer, 'The Use of Scholarship: The Secretariat of Robert Devereux, Second Earl of Essex, c.1585–1601', *The English Historical Review*, 109 (1994), pp. 26–51.
19　TPL, MA0092.
20　TPL, MA0066; MA0076; MA0096.
21　TPL, MA0066; MA0076.
22　J. and J.A. Venn (eds), *Alumni Cantbrigiensis*, Part 1 to 1751, vol. II, Dabbs-Juxton (Cambridge, 1922). For more on Israel Hewitt, see Chapter 2, pp. 40–1.
23　D. Cressy, *Literacy and the Social Order: Reading and Writing in Tudor and Stuart England* (Cambridge, 1980), p. 6; K. Narveson, *Bible Readers and Lay Writers in Early Modern England: Gender and Self-Definition* (Abingdon, 2012), p. 31.
24　TPL, MA0111, E.41. The printed book is in TPL, B06356.
25　TPL, MA0048.
26　TPL, MA0056; MA0107, A.45 and MA0107, A.47.
27　TPL, MA0029.
28　J. Hacket, *A Century of Sermons upon several remarkable subjects preached by the Right Reverend Father in God, John Hacket, late Lord Bishop of Lichfield and Coventry; published by Thomas Plume* (London, 1675), p. x (TPL, B01512).
29　Hacket, *Century of Sermons*, p. liii; D. Lysons, 'Cheam', in *The Environs of London: volume 1: County of Surrey* (online edition) (London, 1792), pp. 137–58.
30　TPL, MA0005; MA0029; MA0047; MA0050; MA0054; MA0065; MA0072; MA0074; MA0099.
31　Clark, 'Plume MS papers', p. 31.
32　TPL, MA0111, E.5.
33　Chapter 4, p. 97.
34　Hacket, *Century of Sermons*.
35　Venn and Venn, *Alumni Cantbrigiensis*, Part 1 to 1751, vol. I Abbas-Cutts.
36　J.J. Smith, 'Boreman, Robert (d. 1675)', *ODNB* (Oxford, 2004); (http://www.oxforddnb.com/view/article/2903, accessed 19 September 2016).
37　Venn and Venn, *Alumni Cantbrigiensis*, Part 1 to 1751, vol. I Abbas-Cutts.
38　Smith, 'Boreman, Robert (d. 1675)'.
39　*Ibid.*
40　These included treatises on tithes, swearing, the value of a university education, two funeral sermons and an account of a fratricide.
41　TPL, MA0002; R. Boreman, *A Mirrour of Christianity, and a Miracle of Charity; or, A true and exact narrative of the life and death of the most virtuous Lady Alice Dutchess Duddeley. Published after the sermon in the church of St. Giles in the Fields by R.B. D.D. rector of the said church on Sunday the 14th of March, MDCLXIX* (London, 1669) (no copy is present in TPL).
42　D. Lysons, 'Greenwich', in *The Environs of London: volume 4, Counties of Herts, Essex and Kent* (London, 1796), pp. 426–93. British History Online http://www.british-history.ac.uk/london-environs/vol4/pp426-93 (accessed 1 August 2016).
43　Petchey, *Intentions*, p. 7.
44　TNA, PROB 20/260, will of Robert Boreman, line 30.
45　TPL, MA0111, E.20.

46 C. Burlinson, 'The Use and Re-Use of Early Seventeenth-Century Student Notebooks: Inside and Outside the University', in J. Daybell and P. Hinds (eds), *Material Readings of Early Modern Culture, 1580–1730: Texts and Social Practices* (Basingstoke, 2010), p. 231. Holdsworth is believed to have devised Plume's curriculum at Cambridge: R.A. Doe, 'The Churchmanship of Thomas Plume (1630–1704): A Study of a Career in the Restoration Church of England', MA dissertation (University of Essex, 2005), p. 21.

47 TPL, MA0091.

48 TPL, MA0024; MA0030. R. Boreman, *An Antidote against Swearing: To which is annexed an appendix concerning an assertory and promissory oath in reference to the statutes of the two now flourishing sister universities. Also a short catalogue of some remarkable judgments from God upon blasphemers, &c. By R Boreman, D.D. and Fellow of Trinity Colledge in Cambridge* (London, 1662) (TPL, B03364).

49 'Horrobin-Hyte', in J. Foster (ed.), *Alumni Oxonienses 1500–1714* (Oxford, 1891), pp. 748–84.

50 Ibid.

51 Ibid.

52 TPL, MA0111, E.34; MA0111, E.35; MA0111, E.36; MA0112. MA0112 (Bundle F) has been counted as one item for the purposes of this analysis.

53 Clark, 'MS papers', p. 32.

54 See Venn and Venn, *Alumni Cantabrigienses*, and Clergy of the Church of England Database, Person ID: 39422, http://db.theclergydatabase.org.uk/.

55 TPL, MA0026; MA0036; MA0039. There is no record of the other books in the series in the British Library or The National Archives.

56 TPL, MA0111, E.23.

57 Cambridge Alumni Database; 34% of parishes were affected by sequestration in 1642. See G.L. Ignajatijevie, 'The Parish Clergy in the Diocese of Canterbury and the Archdeaconry of Bedford in the Reign of Charles I and under the Commonwealth', PhD thesis (University of Sheffield, 1986), p. 107.

58 T.S. Frampton, 'List if Forty-Five Vicars of Tilmanstone. Compiled with Notes', *Archaeologica Cantiana*, 20 (1893), p. 112. My thanks to Catharina Clement for this reference.

59 'House of Lords Journal Volume 6: 25 May 1643', in *Journal of the House of Lords: Volume 6, 1643* (London, 1767–1830), pp. 61–3. The archdeacon of Canterbury at the time was William Kingsley (1584–1648).

60 'House of Lords Journal Volume 6: 25 May 1643', pp. 61–3.

61 TPL, MA0026; MA0036; MA0039.

62 TPL, MA0039, fo. 1v and penultimate folio.

63 'John 8:56, P[salm] 136:5 give thanks to ye L[or]d, Heb. 4:1–2, Heb 11:17 Abr[aham] off[e]red up Is[aac], M[atthew] 5:8 Bl[essed] pure in H[ear]t, L[uke] 36:25 [...] in your life torment, J[ohn] 4:23 K[ee]p ye H[ear]t [...], Exodus 5:1 K[ee]p ye, P[salm] 1–5–1 O give thanks to ye L[or]d & call up[on] h[is] n[ame].'

64 R. Vines, *Magnalia Dei ab Aquilone; set forth in a sermon preached before the right honourable the Lords and Commons, at St Margaret's Westminster, upon Thursday Iuly 18, 14644, being the day of publike thanksgiving for the great victory obtained against Prince Rupert and the Earle of Newcastles forces neere Yorke* (London, 1644) (TPL, B04419); C. Herle, *Davids song of three parts: delivered in a sermon preached before the right Honorable the House of Lords, at the Abby-Church in Westminster, upon the 15. day of June, 1643. Being the day appointed for publike thanksgiving for Gods great deliverance of the Parliament, citie and kingdome, from the late most mischievous conspiracy against all three* (London, 1643) (TPL, B02961); S. Marshall, *The song of Moses the servant of God, and the song of the Lambe: opened in a sermon preached to the Honorable House of Commons, at their late solemne day of thanksgiving, Iune 15. 1643. for the discovery of a dangerous, desperate, and bloudy designe, tending to the utter subversion of the Parliament, and of the famous city of London* (London, 1643) (TPL, B02869).

65 TPL, MA0006.
66 TPL, MA0090.
67 A. Suckling, 'Weston', *The History and Antiquities of the County of Suffolk*, vol. 1 (Ipswich, 1846), pp. 97–101.
68 W.A. Churchill, *Watermarks in Paper in Holland, France, England etc. in the XVII and XVIII centuries and their interconnection* (Amsterdam, 1935), p. 42.
69 Churchill, *Watermarks in Paper*, p. 40.
70 Clark, 'Plume MS papers', p. 30.
71 TPL, MA0093.
72 TPL, MA0053. This notebook will be discussed further later in the chapter.
73 TPL, MA0036; MA0039; MA0048.
74 There is no record of these manuscript sermons being extant, and the consensus view is that they went to the printer and were not returned. Hacket, *Century of Sermons*.
75 TPL, MA0045 and MA0059. With thanks to Dr Noah Millstone for providing two images of Hacket's handwriting, from which I was able to make this identification.
76 TPL, MA0024; Boreman, *An antidote against swearing*.
77 TPL, MA0030.
78 R.D. Sell and A.W. Johnson, *Writing and Religion in England 1558–1689: Studies in Community-Making and Cultural Memory* (Abingdon, 2009), p. 1.
79 Narveson, *Bible Readers and Lay Writers*, pp. 22–3.
80 TPL, MA0113, G.19; R. Boreman, *The Country-mans Catechisme: or, The Churches plea for tithes. Wherein is plainely discovered, the duty and dignity of Christs ministers, and the peoples duty to them. By R.B. B.D. Fellow of Trin. Col. Camb.* (London, 1652 [i.e. 1651]) (not present in TPL).
81 R.B. McKerrow, 'The Relationship of English Printed Books to Authors' Manuscripts during the Sixteenth and Seventeenth Centuries: The 1928 Sandars Lectures', in C.M. Bajetta (ed.), *Studies in Bibliography* (2000), p. 26.
82 TPL, MA0111, E.26 and MA0113, G.12.
83 TPL, MA0113, G.12, fo. 2v.
84 TPL, MA0113, G.4.
85 W. Johnston, 'The Anglican Apocalypse in Restoration England', *The Journal of Ecclesiastical History*, 55/3 (2004), p. 469.
86 See Venn and Venn, *Alumni Cantabrigienses*.
87 L. Andrewes, *A summarie view of the government both of the old and new testament whereby the episcopall government of Christs church is vindicated out of the rude draughts of Lancelot Andrewes, late Bishop of Winchester: whereunto is prefixed (as a preamble to the whole) a discovery of the causes of the continuance of these contentions touching church-government out of the fragments of Richard Hooker* (Oxford, 1641) (not present in TPL).
88 TPL, MA0113, G.1, fo. 1r.
89 W.J. Petchey, *A Prospect of Maldon 1500–1689* (Chelmsford, 1991), p. 233.
90 TPL, MA0090; MA0048; MA0106; MA0111, E.20; MA0029; MA0050; MA0054; MA0072.
91 TPL, MA0041; MA0042; MA0111, E.22; Girolamo Zanchi, *Clariss. viri D. Hier. Zanchii Omnium operum theologicorum tomi octo [...]* (Geneva, 1619) (TPL, B05690).
92 TPL, MA0029; MA0050; MA0007; MA0054.
93 TPL, MA0055; MA0071; J.J. Scaliger, *Thesaurus temporum, Eusebii Chronicorum Canonum omnimodae historae libri duo, interprete Hieronymo* (Leiden, 1606); G.C. Scaligero, *Iulii Caesaris Scaligeri Exotericarum exercitationum liber XV. De subtilitate, ad Hieronymum Cardanum : In fine duo sunt indices: prior breuiusculus, continens sententias nobiliores: alter opulentissimus, pene omnia complectens* (Hanover, 1620).
94 TPL, MA0055; MA0113, G.10; MA0072.

95 TPL, MA0027; MA0009; MA0097; MA0057; MA0087; MA0068; MA0077; MA0105.
96 TPL, MA0031; MA0009.
97 TPL, MA0041; MA0089; MA0068; MA0011; MA0040; MA0018; MA0111, E.16.
98 TPL, MA0095; MA0016.
99 W.H. Kelliher, 'Randolph, Thomas (bap. 1605, d. 1635)', *ODNB* (Oxford, 2004).
100 T. Randolph, *Cornelianum dolium; Comœdia lepidissima, optimorum judiciis approbata, & theatrali coryphœo, nec immeritò, donata, palma chorali apprimè digna. Auctore, T.R. ingeniosissimo hujus ævi heliconio* (London, 1638) (TPL, B00694); B. Jonson, *The Workes of Benjamin Jonson* (London, 1640) (TPL, B06128). The other volume of the *Workes* in the TPL catalogue with standard no. B60127 was a post-Plume addition.
101 F. Bacon, *Baconiana, or, Certain genuine remains of Sr. Francis Bacon, Baron of Verulam, and Viscount of St. Albans in arguments civil and moral, natural, medical, theological, and bibliographical* (London, 1679), p. 60 (TPL, B03614).
102 See J. Eckhardt and D.S. Smith (eds), *Manuscript Miscellanies in Early Modern England* (Abingdon, 2014).
103 TPL, MA0070.
104 TPL, MA0096.
105 TPL, MA0016.
106 For example, see TPL MA0001, which is a common-place book containing theologically themed extracts.
107 TPL, MA0009.
108 TPL, MA0113, G.3; MA0114, H.25.
109 TPL, MA0109, C.41. Culpepper's *Complete Herbal* says that Polypody 'by itself it is a very mild and useful purge; but being very slow, it is generally mixed by infusion or decoction with other purging ingredients'; http://www.complete-herbal.com/culpepper/polypody.htm (accessed 1 June 2020). Epithemum was also a purge for 'black or burnt choler, … purging the veins of the choleric and phlegmatic humours'; http://www.complete-herbal.com/culpepper/dodder.htm (accessed 1 June 2020).
110 B. Usher, 'Gifford, George (1547/8–1600)', *ODNB* (Oxford, 2004); http://www.oxforddnb.com/view/article/10658 (accessed 14 September 2016).
111 TPL, MA0110, D.38.
112 TPL, MA0002.
113 *Ibid.*, fo. 18v.
114 TNA, PROB 20/260, will of Robert Boreman, lines 54–6.
115 TNA, PROB 11/298/753, will of Edward Hyde, lines 26–8.
116 *Ibid.*, lines 29–32.
117 D.L. Smith, 'Seymour, William, first Marquis of Hertford and second duke of Somerset (1587–1660)', *ODNB* (Oxford, 2004); (http://www.oxforddnb.com/view/article/25182, accessed 14 November 2014).
118 TPL, MA0008, 'Practical observations out of the Old Testament', and MA0044, 'Sermons'.
119 E. Hyde, *The True Catholicks Tenure, or A good Christians certainty which he ought to have of his religion, and may have of his salvation. By Edvvard Hyde D.D. sometimes fellow of Trinity Colledge in Cambridge, and late rector resident of Brightwell in Berks.* (Cambridge, 1662) (TPL, B06545).
120 Suffolk Record Office, Bury Archive, IC500/1/106/21, will of Justinian Whitter 1648, line 32.
121 *Ibid.*, line 19.
122 TPL, MA0007.
123 *Ibid.*, fo. 2r.
124 *Ibid.*, fo. 1v.

125 *Ibid.*, fo. 18v.
126 *Ibid.*, fo. 18v.
127 *Ibid.*, fo. 49v.
128 Renati Descartes, *Meditationes de prima philosophia: in quibus dei existentia, & animae humanae à corpore distinctio, demonstrantur. His adjunctae sunt variae objectiones doctorum virorum in istas de Deo & anima demonstrationes; cum responsionibus authoris* (Editio ultima prioribus auctior & emendatior. ed.) (Amsterdam, 1654) (TPL, B04832).
129 Venn and Venn, *Alumni Cantbrigiensis*, vol. IV Kaile-Ryves.
130 A simple Purchasing Power Calculator would say the relative value is £41.70. This answer is obtained by multiplying £0.31 by the percentage increase in the RPI from 1660 to 2015. http://www.measuringworth.com/ukcompare/relativevalue.php. The salary of a journeyman mason or bricklayer was between 2s and 3s per day.
131 TPL, MA0095, front paste-down.
132 *Ibid.*, fo. 1r.
133 TNA, PROB 11/384/89, will of Sir William Boreman of East Greenwich, Kent, 1686.
134 TPL, MA0027.
135 TPL, MA0013.
136 TPL, MA0053, fo. 1r. With thanks to Mr Peter Foden for help with the translation.
137 TPL, MA0022; TPL, MA0083.
138 Venn and Venn, *Alumni Cantbrigiensis*, vol. I Abbas-Cutts.
139 *Ibid.* There is an alternative view that Lovelace bought the notebook new for 15d, that the notes from Dr Bayly's sermons were his own and that a later reader or owner inserted the second part of the inscription. This is less likely in my view, as Lovelace's livings were in Hertfordshire and his family came from Kent, whereas all three Dr Baylys preached mainly in Wales, Worcestershire and the West Country. Lewis Bayly also spent a short period of treasurer of St Paul's Cathedral. J. Gwynfor Jones and V. Larminie, 'Bayly, Lewis (c.1575–1631)', *ODNB* (Oxford, 2004); (http://www.oxforddnb.com/view/article/1766, accessed 19 December 2016).
140 J. Bayly, *Two sermons; The angell guardian. The light enlightening. Preached by Iohn Bayly ...* (Oxford, 1630) (TPL, B03004); T. Bayly, *The Royal Charter granted unto kings* (London, 1649) (TPL, B00319). Gwynfor Jones and Larminie, 'Bayly, Lewis (c.1575–1631)'.

Chapter 9

'His works do follow him': Dr Thomas Plume and his Kent legacies

Catharina Clement

Dr Thomas Plume left 76 legacies in his will and of these about one-third were poor relief, educational or religious bequests covering the county of Kent. For the purposes of this chapter Kent incorporates the Rochester Diocesan area in the time of Thomas Plume, including Deptford and Greenwich. The main part of his Kentish legacy was the Stone Castle Charity (later Trust), which also administered a number of the smaller donations made under his will. This charity was also known as the Plume Trust, but is referred to throughout by its original name to distinguish it from its namesake in Essex. While some of these bequests were one-off payments, others were long-term charities for which he laid out the guidelines and trustees in his will. These legacies will be dealt with in two specific categories: relief of the poor, and educational and religious funding. A final section will deal with his main donation: the foundation and development of the Stone Castle Charity. However, this chapter will first discuss the parameters set by Plume's will and the ensuing problems these created for his executor.

Thomas Plume owned Stone Castle Farm, near Dartford, in Kent, which he had purchased earlier in his clerical career. Whether he ever resided there or merely acquired the estate as a financial asset is unclear. However, towards the end of his lifetime Plume started to consider the best way to dispose of this property and conceived a complex plan to benefit the poor clergy of the diocese of Rochester. His will left detailed instructions for the implementation of the Stone Castle Charity, which was to be set up to administer this and other legacies. Plume also leased land on the Isle of Grain from the dean and chapter of Rochester, which he placed at the disposal of the trustees for the same purpose. The complexity of his will, and in particular the above trust, created considerable difficulties for his executor, James Plume. Many of the bequests had timescales attached to them, which James Plume found hard to fulfil. While his executor appeared on occasions to be very tardy in carrying out Plume's wishes, much of this was inevitable owing to the sheer volume of legacies he had to handle. Other issues focused on the lack of clarity in some of Dr Plume's bequests or the manifold instructions contained in his will, leading to confusion on the part of both James Plume and some of the beneficiaries. This resulted in two chancery cases between 1706 and 1710: one brought by James Plume against the rector and others of Greenwich and a second one by all of Dr Plume's beneficiaries against the executor of the will. Some of Thomas Plume's gifts were never enacted, because of a lack of either clarity or oversight. James Plume died before all the Kentish legacies had been successfully resolved and this may also explain why some never came to fruition.

Relief of the poor

Plume wrote at the end of his long will and testament:

> but all the rest I give to Charity, that is my whole Estate, not otherwise disposed of by this my Will. If any of my kindred or any else, upon any pretence, oppose this my last will Hee shall forfeit his legacy, or any benefit by it. Though I give all my goods to feed the poor, and have not charity, it will profit mee nothing.[1]

In this passage Plume provided a clue to the main purpose of his will. Although his stated intention was to give most of his worldly goods for the poor, it must be done with the right attitude – love – or there would be no heavenly reward awaiting him. Charitable giving was expected of the clergy and wealthier citizens, but it had to be done out of a sense of care, not just of duty. Tony Doe suggests that Plume's own notion of salvation may have been formed as a young man, combining aspects of both Calvinist and Arminian concepts of salvation.[2]

Maximillian Buck, vicar of Kemsing and Seal in Kent, dedicated his *Anniversary Sermon on the Martyrdom of King Charles I* to Dr Plume. This sermon was delivered towards the end of Plume's life and acknowledged Plume's 'charity towards the poor'. In return for this dedication, Plume ensured that Buck received a small legacy in his will as a 'poor divine'.[3] It is, therefore, no surprise that the relief of the poor accounts for nine of Plume's Kentish bequests.

Bromley College was a charity founded by Bishop John Warner of Rochester under his will of 1666 (Figure 9.1). Warner intended that it should provide 'for the residence and maintenance of twenty clergymen's widows, of small incomes, to be elected out of any diocese; but a preference was always to be given to the widows belonging to the diocese of Rochester'.[4] Plume gave £100 to the Trustees of Bromley College 'for the better maintenance of the Widdows

9.1 Bromley College, Kent, founded in 1666 by the bishop of Rochester as an almshouse for the widows of clergymen, was one of the Kent charities to receive an endowment from Dr Plume (engraving by A.C. Breden, published in *The Builder*, 19 April 1890).

there for ever'.[5] Widows were paid £20 per annum by the charity. In Bromley College's chapel, on Tablet two, Thomas Plume is listed as a benefactor of the charity. The inscription would probably not have met with Plume's approval, as he did not wish his name to be attached to any of his legacies. It took James Plume 18 months to settle this legacy to Thomas Elliott, who was possibly the master or treasurer of Bromley College.[6]

That Plume also left a bequest to the poor of East Greenwich is perhaps the least surprising of all his gifts, as he was vicar of the parish of St Alfege's for his entire clerical career. Although the amount of £10 seems small in comparison with some of his other bequests and given his longstanding connection with the local community, it was nevertheless a standard sum to leave for parish poor relief at the time. John Loton, curate of Chatham and overseer to several of Plume's legacies, also left £10 in his will for poor widows of his parish. In contrast to his tardiness in paying out some of the gifts, James Plume distributed this particular payment within ten days of Plume's death.[7]

Dr Plume was equally concerned that the poor of Greenwich and Deptford should be provided with shelter in their time of need. Almshouses were generally set aside for the elderly, infirm or widows. Plume owned 'four brick

Houses in Debtford in Dog-kennel-Row', which he bequeathed to the poor of East Greenwich to occupy free of charge and to be named the Archdeacon's Almshouses. William Dawes, one of the witnesses to Plume's will and Plume's tenant at the vicarage, owned the middle house in Dog Kennel Row. His property was required to create the almshouses and so Plume ordered that, if possible, Dawe's house be purchased for that purpose for a sum of between 10 and 12 pounds. The intent was to save the parish of Deptford the cost of poor relief, with the buildings to be maintained by the churchwardens of East Greenwich.[8] However, this was a far from straightforward gift. James Plume brought a chancery case against the rector and churchwardens of East Greenwich in 1707 because various legacies and charities at Greenwich were still under dispute and had not been implemented within the timescales laid down in Plume's will.[9]

While the four houses in Dog Kennel Row were not part of the overall dispute, nevertheless there is no indication that Dawes had accepted the executor's offer to buy his house there. In 1707 James Plume made it clear that the almshouses had yet to be established.[10] Indeed, these properties were never used for their intended purpose, probably being overlooked among all the legal wrangling. Later, in 1811, the land that these houses had stood upon was acquired by the Greenwich churchwardens. St Alfege vestry minutes for 11 August 1811 note:

> The Churchwardens informed the Vestry that understanding the Ground alluded to had never been in the Possession of the Parish for the Purpose intended by the Will of the Donor but in that of other Persons who from the great length of Time they had held it could not be dispossessed but by an expensive Process at Law.[11]

However, a bit of bargaining led to an agreement to reimburse the owners with the £45 they had laid out for the land, which was in turn leased out for rental income. The profits were to be 'applied to the Relief of Poor Widows of this parish who shall from time to time be elected to inhabit the Jubilee Almshouses'.[12] John Kimbell, churchwarden of Greenwich, summed it up well: 'That which was once lost through Negligence & Inattention has been regained by perseverance and is now in possession of its lawful Owner, the Poor of the Parish of Greenwich.'[13] Although the legacy was never used for its original purpose, the parish had managed to fulfil the spirit of Plume's will a century later.

The largest of Plume's properties was Stone Castle. He, therefore, gave 'to the Minister and church wardens of Stone for their poor five pounds to bee paid by the Tenant within three months after my decease, and five shillings every Christmasse day for ever, out of the rent of Stone Castle'.[14] There is no indication James Plume paid out the £5, but this was the responsibility of the tenant of Stone Castle. Plume's annuity of 5s to the poor was administered by the Stone Castle Charity, with the first reference to its payment being recorded in 1739, when Stone vestry records open with a reference to £6 16s having been received from the Trustees of Stone Castle for 'the use of the poor of the parish of Stone and distributed among them the Sunday following'.[15] This payment was for the arrears due at Christmas 1732, which would indicate that the charity was paying the annuity for the first time, dating back to Plume's death. Stone Castle Charity maintained this payment of 5s per annum well into the nineteenth century, even if payments were sometimes late and rolled up into several years at a time. However, in 1908 the charity commissioners agreed to a new scheme that consolidated this gift with three others for Stone parish into one charity.[16]

Another bequest for the poor was £5 per annum to the parish of Longfield, the centre of Plume's archdeaconry and his official place of abode. Payments were to be administered by the Stone Castle Charity and doled out twice a year to the Longfield churchwardens. In addition to poor relief these sums were to cover the cost of maintaining Plume's grave in Longfield churchyard. The year 1755 saw a payment of £4 10s made to the poor of Longfield, with presumably the remaining 10s going towards the upkeep of his gravestone. During 1787 some £4 8s 9d was paid out, the difference being the deduction of Land Tax, which was not revoked until 1809. These payments were made until 1889, when an alternative plan was proposed by the Trustees to commute this annual gift to the poor into a £100 lump sum payment to restore Longfield church. The proposal was rejected by the charity commissioners as not being in the spirit of Plume's will. Another suggestion was to use some of the £100 towards the 'erection of a suitable memorial to Archdeacon Plume in the shape of an East Window or a tablet to his memory in the Church'.[17] This was something Plume would have considered ostentatious and not in keeping with his request for a simple gravestone and inscription. The vicar, although unsuccessful in this attempt, turned to Cambridge University for a lasting memorial. A stained glass window was donated by them to Longfield church with a fitting inscription that ended: 'His works do follow him'.[18]

Plume's jurisdiction and interests, as archdeacon of Rochester, also included the Medway towns of Rochester, Strood and Chatham. He, therefore, left a bequest of £20 to be distributed among the poor of those three places. The overseers of this bequest were the mayor of Rochester as well as four local ministers. Dr Plume ordered that this legacy should be paid within one month of his death; however, the executor's accounts show that it was not disbursed until September 1705.[19]

John Wright, the mayor of Rochester, was also paid £50 by James Plume for the relief of poor tradesmen in Rochester. Dr Plume had granted this sum to the city of Rochester 'to bee lent out upon good security by the Mayor, &

Aldermen, to five poor tradesmen for ever, gratis'. No mayoral accounts survive for this period to discover how this was eventually allocated. However, this type of legacy was in keeping with other similar gifts made for that purpose to Rochester Corporation. For example, in 1724 the dean and chapter of Rochester had donated £50 to be lent to young freemen and tradesmen of the city. The idea was to set up young men in business and so to avoid them becoming a burden on parish poor relief.[20]

A further bequest to the poor under Plume's will benefited the Sir John Hawkins Knight Hospital for poor seamen. Plume considered that there was in excess of £100 of his money in the hands of its paymaster Madox in the Chatham Chest (Figure 9.2), a fund to pay pensions to Royal Navy disabled seamen, but his executor's accounts show that only £93 4s 5d was actually available. John Loton, Mr Stubbs, the rector of Woolwich and chaplain at Greenwich hospital, and the governors of the hospital were to be responsible

9.2 The Chatham Chest, where funds were kept from 1588 to pay pensions to disabled Royal Navy seamen, and in which Plume had deposited money. It is possible that he had assisted with the recurring crises in the fund's liquidity in the later seventeenth century, and he bequeathed his money kept there to poor seamen (National Maritime Museum, Greenwich, L4474).

for the administration and selection of seamen to benefit from the donation.[21] The £100 was distributed to six poor seamen: John Peterson, John Cole, Robert Knap, Walter Martin, Robert Arnold and John Sinclear, who all received £15 10s 9d each. The payment had finally been agreed in December 1707, and James Plume's delay in this case might have been in the hope of benefiting more than six seamen, as the attorney Thomas Power wrote in a letter to his counterpart at Strood on 4 October 1707: 'the executor who thinks more poor men might have beene partakers'.[22] The six recipients had to sign a draft instrument agreeing to the terms of the payment scheme drawn up by the attorneys and governors. The deputy governor of the hospital was to pay each man one shilling weekly and if one died before the fund was exhausted the balance would be redistributed among the remaining recipients. On the death of all six seamen any remainder could be allocated to other new almsmen of the hospital.[23]

Although Dr Plume remained a bachelor, he made it clear in his will that he was in principle not averse to the idea of marriage: 'And because I would show that I have no ill opinion of marriage, I bequeath one hundred pounds to the placing of ten Maids in marriage, being above twenty four years old, of civill life & who have lived in one service above seven years.'[24] A maid in Plume's understanding was both an unmarried woman and a loyal servant. He split the bequest equally between the parish of East Greenwich and the Medway towns, stipulating that his oldest maid should be one beneficiary and Mrs Woods' old maid another of the recipients. For Greenwich the executor paid out £40 in June 1705 towards four maids placed in marriage, which included Elizabeth Rutter, who was Plume's eldest maid. According to the February 1707 chancery case, James Plume stated that he had distributed £50 to the churchwardens of East Greenwich on that account. His expenditure on the testator's behalf is recorded until October 1707, but there is no mention of the balance of £10 being paid out.[25]

The remaining £50 was dispersed to John Loton, a Stone Castle trustee and vicar of Chatham, in May 1705 for five maids from the various Medway parishes, named by James Plume as Mary Lake, Mary Caster, Mary Baynard, Francis Dadson and Mary Burford. Marriages took place for Mary Lake and Mary Baynard in the cathedral and Strood parish church respectively. No trace has been found of the marriage for Mary Caster within the Medway parishes. However, the bequests paid out in favour of Francis Dadson and Mary Burford were not quite in accordance with Dr Plume's bequest, as Francis was a male threadsman who married Mary, a maid, at St Nicholas, Rochester in October 1705, for which they received £20 jointly.[26] This anomaly was probably a decision by John Loton rather than the executor, as he would have supplied the names of the maids. There is no mention of Mrs Woods' old maid at St Margaret's being one of the five recipients, but perhaps she was Mary Caster.

Educational and religious bequests

Thomas Plume, raised in a Puritan household, appreciated the need for a good education. Thus, four of his Kent bequests targeted the schooling of the poorer sort. His second codicil revoked the legacy of two further houses in Dog Kennel Row, Deptford, left to his executor, and instead assigned them for the benefit of 'the Grey-coat School in E. Greenwich to clothe, & teach two boys in the said school, for ever'. Plume had been involved in the founding of the school in 1677.[27] Although the bequest was eventually carried out, it was the subject of the chancery case James Plume brought in 1707. Several leases in the eighteenth century indicate that this bequest was administered by the Trustees of Grey Coat School and provided rental income, so that two local poor boys could be suitably clothed and educated. The education consisted of 'reading, writing and cyphering (mathematics)'.[28] By 1810 this land realised £15 per annum in income.[29]

A second gift for the education of poor children was made by Plume for 'five pounds p[er] Annu[m] to ye Curate of Grain, or any sober man, that shall teach their children at school there, if hee may bee had at that rate'. This legacy was to have been administered by the Stone Castle Charity.[30] Grain parish register shows the curate to have been Thomas Dycker in 1705, but neither he nor anyone else ever received any annual fee for educating the Grain children. An explanation may be suggested by Archbishop Thomas Secker's *Speculum*, which indicates that the parish was in a bad state of neglect in the early and mid-eighteenth century. Richard Hancorn, vicar of the nearby parish of Stoke, advised in a letter of 8 December 1759 to Secker: 'Dr Plume left £5 a Year tow[ar]ds a School. None for many Years. One will be set up to teach the Ch[ildre]n the Cat[echism] at least, if not to read[,] also it is hoped the Arrears will be p[ai]d to it.'[31] There is no mention in the Trust's earliest surviving accounts of any payment, yet the charity commissioners' annual report of 1843 still listed the gift as part of the Plume charity for Kent. The only other indication comes from the minutes when the trustees received correspondence from the vicar of Grain in 1895-6: 'Notice from the Vicar of Grayne, Kent claiming on behalf of that Parish arrears of a rent charge of £5 per annum devised by the Will of Dr Plume in 1705 and which the latter stated had never been paid'.[32] The receiver also noted that a similar request had been referred to the charity commissioners in 1866. Despite these two letters, the minutes state that no action was taken about the legacy or arrears. Plume's will had stated that if no suitable person could be found the legacy would revert back to the charity for other purposes, but it appears that no attempt was ever made to implement it.[33]

Another educational bequest was the funding of a series of lectures at Dartford and Gravesend, to be administered and paid for out of the Stone Castle Charity. A suitable preacher was to deliver these lectures on a Wednesday or Saturday, alternating between the two venues. Both the preacher and sexton were to be rewarded for their efforts, but the emphasis was on the religious education of the poor: 'I give also ten shillings a quarter to bee divided amongst the most indigent, & Godly Poor, that most frequently resort to this lecture.'[34] In 1755 the total cost of the lectures, clerks, sextons and poor of both parishes was £20 4s, an amount still being paid out in 1787 and throughout the nineteenth century.[35]

In 1899 the vicar of Dartford challenged these unchanged payments, suggesting that they should have been reviewed periodically by the trustees of Stone Castle Charity when the augmentations were reassessed:

> If that had been done the value of each Lectureship would have been increased from £17 12s p.a. to £88 p.a. The Sexton in each church from £1 p.a. to £5 p.a. and the Poor in each place from £1 p.a. to £5 p.a. As you are aware all of these bequests have been decreased of late years.[36]

It was agreed in 1900 that the convoluted payments described above should cease and instead each town would receive £60 per annum for the lectures. This sum was to go to the second assistant curate, presumably for providing the lectures in each town. Payment of £60, however, appears to have been interpreted as for both towns, as the following few years saw £30 dispersed to each town annually and this amount was incorporated into the new Plume Charity in 1909. During 1948 a proposal was put forward to increase the sums to £100 each in future.[37]

In the spirit of Plume's legacy Revd Roger Knight preached the 2008 Advent Sunday sermon at Holy Trinity, Dartford, in his capacity as one of the trustees of the current charity. His sermon was on the emphasis of the wide-ranging legacies left by Thomas Plume and his ability to tolerate all religious viewpoints. Dartford parish continues to receive £1,850 from the charity annually to carry on Plume's wish to support the teaching ministry.[38]

Dr Plume also recognised that the cathedral laity were often in poor circumstances and so ordered that his executor was to pay 'Twenty pounds to the poor Officers of Rochester Church Organist & Lay Clerks & any poor schollars, sons of poor men to be distributed among them [...] & in remembrance of mee Mrs Eyers 2 Children'.[39] Many of the choristers were scholars at the King's School attached to the cathedral and the lay clerks were often training for the ministry. Mrs Elizabeth Ayerst was the widow of the Revd Thomas Ayerst, vicar of Shorne, who died in 1688. Three of their sons were King's scholars at the cathedral, with William Ayerst and John Gunsley Ayerst being the intended recipients of Plume's legacy. Here Plume invested in the education of both children and impoverished young men. James Plume paid out this gift on 8 May 1706.[40]

The greater part of Plume's estate in Kent went towards religious causes. By far the largest individual religious bequest was the establishment of the Stone Castle Charity, which was to augment the livings of poor ministers within the diocese of Rochester. This legacy is discussed in a separate section at the end of the chapter.

Dr Plume had already spent £200 of his own money on improving the condition of the vicarage at East Greenwich. His will contained a further £10, which could be used for any necessary repairs by his successor. A property owned by Plume in Church Street, Greenwich, was left to his successors in perpetuity for their benefit, provided that John Turner (Plume's successor at St Alfege, Greenwich) did not sue for dilapidations to the vicarage house. However, Turner was involved in two separate court cases about the dilapidations, so by default the property went to James Plume to cover his costs. James Plume's accounts show that he received three years' rent from William Dawes for this property in October 1707.[41]

Thomas Plume also bequeathed £50 to the dean and chapter of Rochester towards the maintenance of the cathedral, which was settled quite promptly. This was the first gift listed in his will, but is rather strangely worded. He was archdeacon of Rochester and a canon of the cathedral; however, he seems to distance himself from the building by calling it 'their Cathedrall'.[42] Perhaps this was the voice of Dr Plume, stating that he preferred his parish at Greenwich and rectory at Longfield to the grandeur and pomp of the cathedral. He, likewise, opted for a simple burial at Longfield rather than an interment within the cathedral grounds, which would have befitted his status as an archdeacon. His predecessor, John Lee Warner, was buried inside the cathedral with a prominent monumental inscription.

The second codicil redistributed the £100 originally intended for a hundred poor Kent parishes. Among the new recipients were 'poor Divines' or 'other good Christians' in the deanery of Tonbridge and Malling. Plume allocated £20 to this group and named 'Mr Wintely, Mr Beak and Mr Buck' as being worthy beneficiaries.[43] James Plume was relatively quick in paying out this legacy to the above three ministers plus the 'poor divine' Mr Francis Dudson. However, the executor seems otherwise to have ignored Plume's requirements in this respect; the overseers of this bequest were bypassed and James Plume paid out £24 to these four ministers rather than the £20 specified in the will.[44]

An annual payment of £5 was also to be settled 'upon the Rector of Longfield […] for ever'. In order for this to happen Dr Plume indicated that £120 was to be made available to purchase 'some estate of inheritance' that was to be administered by a trust.[45] His executor made no effort to implement this part of the will and stated in the 1706 chancery case that he did not consider the land earmarked in Longfield as suitable. Indeed, James Plume felt he was entitled to use the interest on the £120 for his own benefit. It was only in 1734 that a suitable piece of estate, at Ridley, was acquired by the Stone Castle Charity to implement this legacy. Even they were lax in making payments, as the rector of Longfield had to remind them in 1831 that the income had not been received for a number of years.[46]

Thomas Plume added £25 to a bequest of £5 left under the will of Mark Cottle towards the erection of a charnel house at St Alfege's churchyard. These mortuaries were unusual by the late seventeenth century, but Plume may have been influenced by the recent addition of one to the nearby St Nicholas church at Deptford. The executor paid out the funds for the building of the charnel house to the churchwardens of East Greenwich in June 1706. A stipulation of Plume's will was that the money was released on condition that the building would be completed within a year of his death.[47] This was an issue, as the funds were not released until 18 months after his death and the project had obviously not been completed by February 1707, when James Plume brought his chancery case against (among others) the churchwardens of East Greenwich. He challenged them to indicate 'when and w[h]ere and within what time the said Charnell house was built if any such there were and what summe and summes of money were deposited and actually paid for the materialls and workmanship thereof'.[48] There is no surviving record of the charnel house being erected, but the building may have been destroyed in the collapse of St Alfege's church in 1710. It is also possible that no attempt was ever made to construct the charnel house, just as the almshouse was never implemented.

Stone Castle Charity
Thomas Plume's main charitable focus for Kent was the augmentation of the livings of poor ministers within the diocese of Rochester:

> I would have the Trustees distribute in augmentation of poor Parsonages, & Vicarages, in the Diocesse of Rochester, not worth £60 p[er] Annum, to the severall Incumbents, who lead sober lives, & conform to the Church of England, and hold but one Living, yet not allowing to any one place, or Minister more than ten pounds p[er] An[num].[49]

Plume's only stipulations were that 'Town-Malling' should be a permanent recipient and that as many deserving cases should be included as the estate could maintain.[50]

The endowment of this charity was to be Plume's house at Stone Castle and the surrounding estate, which had an annual rentable income of £74 at the time of his death. Dr Plume was also quite clear in his will how this and several other bequests should be administered. He ordered that a trust should be set up to be known as the Stone Castle Charity with Dr Francis Thompson (a

London clergyman who was Plume's close friend and colleague) and 20 other ministers from named parishes within Rochester diocese to act as trustees. The Stone Castle bequest and several others were the subject of a protracted chancery case started in 1706, which was not resolved until 1710.[51] According to the eighteenth-century Kent historian Edward Hasted, the charitable trust was not operational until long after Plume's demise:

> This charitable devise of Dr Plume did not take place till some years after his death, owing to a suit in chancery, carried on by the trustees with his executor and heir at law, which was heard in 1710, when this charity, by the decree then given, was put under proper regulations, and the trustees as appointed in the doctor's will (twenty clergymen of the diocese of Rochester) were made perpetual feoffees. The first feoffment was dated in 1722, by which the trust of this charity was vested in the twenty trustees by name, and the several uses of it declared, but many difficulties still arising, nothing further was done in it till 1734.[52]

Most of this information tallies with the abstract of feoffment of 1798, which is the only surviving record of the charity's early history.

While many things have changed during the 300 years or so of the charity's life, the structure has remained largely unchanged. The 20 named parishes were to provide successive trustees to carry on the charity on the decease or removal of the existing ministers. Initially 13 ministers were named in the will to act as trustees; all were known to Plume and alive when he made his will just a few months before his decease. Despite Hasted's assertion that little was done before 1734, there is some evidence to the contrary. In 1706 nine of the minsters named by Dr Plume were involved in the suit against the executor, James Plume, and two new 'trustees'.[53] Although they may not have set up the charity yet, the named trustees were actively seeking to get Plume's legacy established:

> And the said Trustees appointed by the said Will for the Charitable uses in the said County of Kent are very willing and desirous that the said estates may be employed an[d] setled according to the purport and true meaning of the said Will in all things wherein they humbly pray [for the] Direccion of this honourable Court.[54]

On 8 May 1710 the case was finally heard in Chancery, with the Lord Chancellor ruling that Samuel Keck, Master of the Rolls, was to draw up a deed of feoffment (Trust Deed) to outline the structure of and regulations for implementing and running the charitable trust.

There is no indication as to why the trust was not officially formed, as ordered in Plume's will and instructed by the Court of Chancery in 1710, until 1722 under a deed of feoffment. However, the 1798 recital does seem to indicate that Plume's will was taken as the original basis of the charity and that this first feoffment was conveying the grants and possessions nominated under Plume's will from the originally named trustees to their successors. This deed apparently decreed that upon the number of trustees named falling to seven they were to set up a new agreement, electing the new trustees to form a full complement of 20. Only four were required to form a quorum and upon the death or removal of a minister their successor could serve the charity in the interim, but was not a trustee until duly elected and named in the revised feoffment. By 1722 only four of the original trustees were still alive, which created an issue with the running of the trust. It would appear that this resulted in the remaining trustees finally setting the charity up along the lines instructed by the court.[55]

Our next insight into the trustees derives from the 1734 indenture of land in Ridley, purchased to augment the living of Longfield. Of the trustees included in the 1722 deed of feoffment, ten were still alive and active over a decade later. According to the 1798 abstract several further agreements were processed over the eighteenth century when the trustees reached the minimum number required to operate the charity. However, evidence of the identities of actual trustees between 1734 and 1787, from the date the first minute book survives, is non-existent. At the front of the earliest minute book 20 'trustees' are listed for 1787, but many of these were succeeding ministers, not trustees listed in the last agreement.[56] Over the next century various new agreements were entered into, but the number of trustees and qualifying parishes remained exactly the same. This did not change until the latter decades of the twentieth century, when parishes either united or ceased to exist. In the twenty-first century four of these parishes are no longer represented by trustees, two are presently vacant and three new ones have been added. The total number of trustees is now 19, with Gravesend having two parishes represented.[57]

The agreement of 1722 specified that the trustees were to meet twice yearly within 14 days of Lady Day and Michaelmas 'to audit adjust and settle the account and application of the Profits and for management of the Trusts' at Stone Castle Farm. In order to fulfil this requirement a receiver was to be appointed from among the trustees or else someone suitably qualified and 'such person giving the Security directed by the Decree'.[58] Provision was also made under the feoffment allowing the trustees to lease out or rent property or land owned by the Stone Castle Charity for 21 years under an indenture.[59] By this means the trustees could raise income to run the charity and carry out the intentions expressed in Plume's will.

Thomas Plume bequeathed three legacies to maintain the charitable trust that he desired to be set up to augment poor ministers and fund a series of weekly lectures, as well as administer several other smaller gifts. The main

9.3 Stone Castle, near Gravesend, Kent, an estate bought by Dr Plume in the late seventeenth century. After his death it became the main endowment of his Stone Castle Charity (engraving published in 1829 by George Virtue, 26 Ivy Lane, London).

income was from Stone Castle Farm (Figure 9.3), which was rented out to the Talbot family for most of the eighteenth century. By 1786 the value had risen and John Talbot was paying £119 per annum for the lease of the castle and surrounding farmland, which covered about 240 acres. Dr Plume also held a lease for marsh and upland on the Isle of Grain from the dean and chapter of Rochester. He settled this upon the trust with the proviso that they could sell the lease and purchase a piece of freehold land for the same purpose. His third gift to the trust was '£340 odd pounds due to mee from the City of London, for w[hi]ch I have their receit and is paid at Guild-hall every halfe yeare after four pounds p[er] cent interest'.[60] This being, according to the chancery decree issued in 1710, Orphan Stock.[61]

Although the charity was not fully operational until 1734 the trustees did undertake certain tasks before that date. It would appear that they were collecting the above rental income and interest from the Orphan Stock as per a conveyance of lease & release dated November 1734, but this money was being accrued and banked by the Accountant General of the Court of Chancery until such time as the Stone Castle Charity was able to implement the decree of the court in full. Whether the Stone Castle Charity used some of this initial income to augment any livings prior to 1734 is unclear.[62] As described earlier, the trustees were also active immediately after Plume's demise in identifying a piece of suitable freehold land in the parish of Longfield that would yield £5 per annum for the maintenance of the rector of Longfield. Plume had stipulated that the gift should be set up in 'such manner in Trust or otherwise for that purpose as by Councill learned in the Laws, shall in that behalfe bee advised'. While Plume did not specify a particular trust to carry out this part of his will, the attorney general insisted 'that the Trustees for [the Stone] Castle Charity and their Successors for the time being are very proper persons to be made Trustees for the augmentacion of this Rectory at Longfeild'. Delays in settling this bequest were initially down to James Plume and the lengthy chancery case, but it took the trust another 24 years to finally acquire a piece of land for that purpose.[63]

Included in the decree issued in 1710 was an instruction that both the lease for the marsh and 'Upland' on the Isle of Grain plus the Orphan Stock should be sold 'and the Money vested in purchasing Lands of Inheritance'.[64] No date of sale is given for these assets, but the sale and funds in the bank had realised £1,275 2s in 1734, giving enough capital to purchase Tudeley Farm, Tudeley, near Tonbridge in Kent. This covered about 60 acres and was secured in November 1734 for £1,150 5s from William Davis, vicar of nearby Shipbourne. The land tax paid on Tudeley Farm in 1755 suggests that its value was about half that of Stone Castle Farm at that time. By 1786 it achieved a rental income of £32 per annum and was leased to a David Harries.[65]

Tudeley Farm produced a reliable source of income for the charity for nearly 150 years, but was deemed to be insufficient for the needs of the charity by the 1870s. Stone Castle Charity's expenditure tended to outstrip income by this period. This was partly due to the downturn in agriculture towards the latter half of the nineteenth century and also to the increased cost of maintaining the farms and estates. Therefore, a decision was made in 1882 to sell Tudeley Farm, with the agreement of the charity commissioners, 'for the purpose of obtaining more extended powers of investment of the money to be produced by the sale than in the purchase of 3 per cent Consols with a view to the production of a larger amount of income to the Trustees'.[66] The sale realised £4,670 11s 2d, which was made available to purchase freehold ground rents in London. These investments yielded a much larger return per annum than the rents from the farm.

By 1812 Stone Castle Charity had a large surplus and profits sitting in its bank account that were not being utilised and for which no provision had been made in Plume's will or the Decree of Chancery in 1710. The trustees sought legal advice upon 'the propriety of applying the Surplus of Money in the hands of the Treasurer so as to produce an annual profit', but were advised they could not proceed without the approval of the Court of Chancery. In 1814 the Master of the Rolls directed the trustees to approve a scheme whereby the charitable intentions of Dr Plume's will would be fully implemented, allowing the trust's surplus funds to be invested in government or other securities in the name of the archdeacon of Rochester and the treasurer of the trustees, with the dividends to be paid to their half-yearly accounts.[67]

The Stone Castle trustees decided to invest in 3 per cent Consols or consolidated bonds to the value of £1,515 3s in 1814, for which they laid out £1,000. The receiver purchased further Consols periodically over the next ten years to a total value of £3,500 by 1824. In that year the whole lot had to be sold, as noted in the minutes of the Stone Castle Charity: 'Ordered that the sum of £3,500 3 per cent Consols standing in the Trustees Names, be sold as soon as may be, and the produce invested in Exchequer Bills, towards defraying the Expenses of the Buildings, in order that the Trust may not lose their Benefit of the present price of the Funds'.[68] However, this arrangement appears to have been to the detriment of the trust, as the Consols were sold off at only 93 per cent of their true value and the newly acquired Exchequer Bills returned less than 2.5 per cent interest per annum. Exchequer Bills, unlike Consols, could be redeemed at short notice.

Stone Castle Farm proved a more long-term drain on the resources of the charity than Tudeley Farm. The above-mentioned Exchequer Bills were specifically purchased in order to rebuild Stone Castle, which by 1824 was in a dilapidated condition. These could be redeemed piecemeal as instalments became due to the builders. In total £3,600 was spent on the rebuilding work, leaving a balance in hand of just £13 5s 8½d on completion of the work in March 1829 to meet all other costs in running the charity. More was actually spent on the new building than its value for insurance purposes: £3,000 in 1826. Although there is a gap of 50 years or so in both the accounts and minutes for Stone Castle Charity, it can be surmised that around 1839 more money was expended on the restoration of the Old Tower at Stone Castle.[69]

Despite the trust's need for additional funding to rebuild the old castle, there was no attempt made to sell off any of the surrounding woodland at the time. In 1755 the immediate castle and farm estate covered 198 acres, with the woodland encompassing another 42 acres from which income was derived by tendering out contracts to fell the underwood. From the 1841 tithe apportionments it is apparent that little had altered in terms of acreage, apart from the sale of Mount Wood.[70] During 1894 another application was made to the charity commissioners to sell stock for the repair of Stone Castle. On this occasion the cost of repairs amounted to £511 3s 7d and left a balance in hand of a mere £70 11s 8d in 1896, with cheques being retained until sufficient funds were available to meet augmentations as well as a resulting overdraft at the bank. The charity commissioners proposed a scheme whereby the investment cashed in could be restored, but the receiver estimated that the reserves would not be back to their current level under this scheme until 1910. Eventually a decision was reached in 1898 to sell off the estate to raise capital and prevent further dwindling of the charity's assets on repairs. Several bids were received and Stone Castle Farm was finally sold for £25,825 to the cement manufacturers Messrs Johnson & Co. Out of these proceeds £10,225 15s was used to purchase property in various parts of London and £14,646 16s 4d invested in 2.75 per cent Consols.[71] The main endowment left by Plume in Kent, Stone Castle Farm, had therefore proved to be a millstone around the neck of the charity, as it drained the resources of the trustees in the long term, restricting their ability to meet their charitable obligations during the nineteenth century.

While it is possible that augmentations were paid out from 1710 onwards, there is no record of any transaction before 1755. In that year £50 was paid out to an unknown number of ministers. By 1787 the sum had been reduced to £40 per annum and covered just four ministers.[72] Concerns were growing among the trustees that the original instructions in Plume's will were no longer adequate to meet the changing circumstances in the late eighteenth century. In 1792 the charity sought legal opinion 'to ascertain what latitude the Trustees may take in estimating the value of Livings for augmentation and also whether they may be permitted & in which degree to augment the peculiar within the diocese of Rochester'.[73] One of the issues raised was whether perpetual curacies were covered under Plume's intentions. Revd John Powell, curate of Plaxtol, had applied for assistance in 1792 and by 1793 learned counsel had judged that it was in order for the trust to grant him an augmentation, which they did for £10 per annum. Eight additional augmentations of £10 each were awarded between 1792 and 1796, suggesting that the maximum payment had not been changed and that the charity was in a good financial position to meet all of these costs.[74]

Prior to 1798 payments to the poor ministers had been administered in an ad hoc manner rather than centrally organised. The new trustees ordered that in future a voucher system was to be put in place and each minister or his representative had to come to Stone Castle at the time of the trust's meetings and sign the voucher in return for their augmentation. By 1812 the £10 limitation per minister was seen as somewhat restrictive and trustees ordered their lawyers to apply to the Court of Chancery for a review of the conditions under which they could operate. The charity wanted to extend the scope of its awards to include curates as well as ministers, and to be able to exercise discretion in awarding augmentations as well as increasing the maximum amount of an augmentation they could settle on an individual incumbent.[75]

In 1814 the Master of the Rolls directed that, as the cost of living had increased since the time that Plume made his will, the trustees could use any surplus funds and profits to augment poor livings valued at less than £250 per annum within the diocese of Rochester. The stipulation was that the incumbent should hold only one living and that the trustees could award a maximum augmentation of £30 per year to an individual minister.[76] This ruling greatly increased the scope of the trust's ability to augment poor livings and at a rate that was more in keeping with the costs of the nineteenth century. Four of the existing benefactors had their payments increased from £10 to £25 per annum.

Over the next 50 years there were many disputes about qualifying livings and earnings, as well as some odd requests. Revd George Harker of Rochester St Nicholas wanted £60 to clear a debt incurred in repairing his vicarage, but the trustees rejected the application as 'the object of it not being within the Trusts declared by Dr Plume's Will'.[77] It became clear to the receiver that many incumbents were failing to declare their total income and so in 1834 a new order was made that, in future,

> every application for augmentation being made the Clerk obtain from each applicant a statement in writing particularizing the gross & net annual value of the preferment held by such applicants & it is requested that such statement shall contain the particulars of the Land Tax, Poor Rate, & other Rates & annual necessary charges on the Living to the Governors of Queen Anne's Bounty or to other persons.[78]

Later that decade each minister had to declare whether his living had a vicarage attached and if he resided there as well any part of the Easter offering he received.[79]

This was to cause great friction between ministers and the trustees in the latter part of the nineteenth century, when under straitened circumstances the Stone Castle Charity insisted that the congregation of each minister match the trust's grant usually by means of an Easter offering. By 1876 the charity was paying out 11 augmentations at an average rate of £15 per annum, somewhat less than had been awarded 40 years earlier. In 1880 the Revd A. Jackson of All Saints, Northfleet, was advised that 'the Trustees regretted being unable to continue the grant which had hitherto been made to him in consequence of the funds at present at their disposal being sufficient only to meet applications which appeared to the Trustees to be more pressing than his'.[80] He had received the princely sum of £15 per annum, which the charity could no longer afford. Due to the downturn in agriculture in the third quarter of the nineteenth century, estates faced declining rental income and rising costs. This impacted on the Stone Castle Charity's ability to augment the livings of many poor ministers, despite having applied to the charity commissioners in 1876 to change the maximum qualifying earnings from £250 to £300 p.a. and the level of augmentation from a maximum of £30 to £50 p.a.[81]

Although the charity wished to increase the overall awards to the poorest ministers, they increasingly made further demands on the parishioners to match their grant. Revd J. Christie of Southfleet wrote in 1884:

both he and the Churchwardens considered that the Parish should by degrees do something towards augmenting the Vicars stipend but that as the Population consisted of mostly the labouring Class it was not possible [...] and as the Patrons of the Living had already made up a considerable deficit in the current expenses he hoped that the Trustees would not make it a condition for the continuance of a grant from Dr Plume's Charity that an equal amount should be subscribed by the Parishioners.[82]

Because Revd N. Willis of Ifield stated in 1884 that he could not get any additional subscriptions as 'the population of the district consist[ed] with one or two exceptions of struggling farmers and poor labouring men', his grant was reduced from £25 to £15 per annum.[83] The following year he was advised it would be removed completely unless he proved he had grovelled to the parish and sought outside donations. This he did and was awarded £20 for his trouble, only to have it removed again three years later when his benefice united with another small one at Nurstead and took his annual income above the £300 threshold.[84]

Revd Willis' story was a typical one of increasing harassment employed by the charity in the late nineteenth century to get poor ministers to drop their claims, which may leave a question mark over the activities of the charity 180 years after its institution. It certainly was no longer operating under the intentions and spirit of Plume's will. Much income was being spent by this period on small ad hoc gifts to churches, schools and other institutions that had little bearing on supporting poor ministers, while the awards to ministers were being drastically cut or no longer guaranteed. Somewhere along the line the charity had lost sight of its role and purpose.

The sale of Stone Castle in 1898 finally refocused the trustees and resulted in an increase in the annual grant to £60 per annum from 1900. That year a record number of 21 augmentations were paid out to assist poor incumbents, a figure that had risen to 24 by 1910. During the early twentieth century grants continued to be made, but alterations in the situations of the clergy within the diocese necessitated changes in the structure of the awards. In 1929 the charity commissioners gave more discretion to the trustees in terms of grants and recognised the charity as the Plume Trust. By 1947 the archbishop of Canterbury had put in an appeal to raise all benefices to a minimum of £500 per annum, leaving fewer dependent on the charity. Just a year later the trust increased its grant to a maximum of £100 per annum and made it possible for a beneficiary to hold two livings, as well as including new parishes within the diocese in the scheme. Today the trust welcomes applications from "necessitous" beneficed and licensed clergy in most parishes of the present Diocese of Rochester and the Archdeaconry of Southwark and can make grants of up to £3,000. In 2019 the Dr Plumes Trust had an income of approximately £21,469 and expended about £15,010 in various grants and other costs.[85]

Conclusion

Dr Thomas Plume acquired property with the intent of leaving a lasting legacy for the poor clergy of the diocese of Rochester. In total, 19 bequests in Plume's will related to Kent and 16 of them were intended to benefit the poor. Charitable giving towards poor relief was expected of Dr Plume as a prominent clergyman, but it is worth noting that most of his educational and religious bequests were also targeted at the less well-off. Access to education would encourage boys and young men to pursue a clerical career, while Plume's scheme to augment poor livings would attract more learned ministers to Kent parish churches.

It is rather difficult to place Dr Thomas Plume's charitable giving in the context of that of other philanthropists in the late seventeenth or early eighteenth century. His smaller donations in Kent were generally in keeping with those of other clergy and the middling sort in society. In comparison with other clergymen of his status, he appeared to be very wealthy and had no immediate family to whom he could leave his estate. Plume's will covered many pages, as opposed to the mere side and a half of that by John Lee Warner, his predecessor at Rochester, who came from a wealthy Norfolk family. However, the most significant differences lay in the sheer number of legacies and total value of his charitable giving. Warner had closer family ties, but the amount he bequeathed to charity was negligible given that he was the nephew of Bishop Warner of Rochester, who had left sizeable donations to both the clergy and fabric of the church. Bishop Warner's will was the only comparable one found in Kent in terms of the sums involved and the proportion of charitable giving, so Plume's Kentish legacies do not seem typical of a middle-ranking clergyman of the period.[86]

Although at times the progress of the Stone Castle Charity (now Trust) was rocky, it survived to continue in its present format. While Dr Plume wanted to leave an enduring gift, he had no desire for his name to be associated with it. Similarly, he requested that the almshouses in Deptford should be named after his office, not him. He had little truck with ostentatiousness, leaving only a small bequest towards the fabric of the cathedral church and nothing for his own parish church. His funeral was to be low key, with a burial in Longfield churchyard accompanied by a simple and humble monumental inscription. There was to be no memorial in the church itself and he rejected the cathedral as his final resting place, although it had been the preference of his predecessor. However, some of his long-term beneficiaries decided that his name should be remembered by attaching it to the largest Kent legacy, the Stone Castle Charity. While the name was not legally changed until 1929, the charity was referred to by Kent historians as Dr Plume's Trust or Gift from about 1770 and by the charity digest in 1843. The desire by Victorians to publicise philanthropy and good works also prompted the vicar of Longfield to add a more fitting memorial to Dr Plume inside the church. This was achieved in the 1890s, despite attempts by the charity commissioners, who wished to follow the instructions and spirit of Thomas Plume's will, to thwart the plan.

It is true that several aspects of Plume's minor Kentish bequests were ignored or forgotten. This was partly due to the general complexity of Dr Plume's will, the legal challenges involved and the widespread geographic nature of the gifts.[87] However, the impression is also gained that internal squabbling at East Greenwich parish church ensured that two of his smaller gifts were never implemented, while the time delay in setting up the Stone Castle Charity meant that others were passed over or not established until long after his death. His executor, James Plume, was not perhaps as incompetent or self-centred as he might first appear. The legal challenges were to clarify the complex nature of the many bequests in Plume's will and, although his handling of the gifts sometimes appeared tardy, this had more to do with the large number of legacies and widespread nature of Plume's largesse.

Clearly, much effort was expended in the centuries following Plume's death to carry out his intentions. This was evident in the nineteenth century, when an unfulfilled Greenwich legacy was finally brought to fruition, even if not as directed in Plume's will. Plume had set out the conditions under which the Stone Castle Charity should operate, but he had failed to foresee that the endowments would generate considerable profits or that livings would change in scope and value. The trustees' hands were tied, as they did not have the power to utilise these profits for the benefit of more clergymen. In order to fully realise Plume's real intentions, the Stone Castle trustees had to resort to law in the nineteenth century to ensure that the full value of the trust's assets could be used for the benefit of poor livings.

At other times the trustees lost sight of the purpose of the trust. In the early nineteenth century much time and money was expended on Stone Castle, often to the detriment of the poor clergy. Later in the century some income was spent on other causes not directly connected with poor livings, which led to fewer and diminishing augmentations and clergymen having to justify their claims. By the late nineteenth century neither Tudeley Farm nor the Stone Castle estate were still viable assets and so were sold off. More appropriate rental property was acquired, allowing the charity to refocus its position. In the twentieth century most of its income was deployed in the maintenance of poor livings, which was more in the spirit of Plume's will. From that time onwards the charity has adapted to changing circumstances and in the early twenty-first century is still an active charity working to benefit poorer clergymen within the diocese of Rochester.

Notes

1 TNA, PROB 10/1387; Appendix: Dr Thomas Plume's will, ll, 453–8.
2 Chapter 3, pp. 63–6, 85–6.
3 M. Buck, *An Anniversary Sermon on the Martyrdom of King Charles the First* (London, 1702). For Buck's legacy see this chapter, p. 254.
4 S.R. Shepherd, *The Bromley Magazine* (Bromley, 1845), Issues 1–9, pp. 210–11.
5 Appendix: will, ll. 543–4.
6 C. Freeman, *The History, Antiquities, Improvements ... of the Parish of Bromley, Kent* (Greenwich, 1832), p. 85; http://www.londongardensonline.org.uk/gardens-online-record.asp?ID=BRO011; TNA, C 6/348/11, Attorney General v Bernard, 1706.
7 Appendix: will, l. 40; TNA, C 6/348/11; PROB 11/583/4, Will of John Loton, 1722.
8 Appendix: will, ll. 46–53.
9 TNA, C 6/550/309, Plume v unknown, 1706.
10 *Ibid.*
11 GHC, G 3:2, St Alfege, Greenwich, vestry minutes 1796–1813.
12 *Ibid.*
13 GHC, John Kimbell, manuscript of the Charities of Greenwich, fo. 105. The Jubilee Almshouses were founded in 1809 on George III's jubilee.
14 Appendix: will, ll. 545–7.
15 DAC, SCT, Details of Stone Castle Charity, 1755; MAC, P352/8/1, Stone parish, vestry minutes, 1739–1825.
16 DAC, SCT, Accounts, 1787–1829; MAC, P352/25/2, correspondence, 1896–1927.
17 Appendix: will, ll. 314–19; DAC, SCT, Details, 1755; Accounts, 1787–1829; Minutes, 1787–1839; Minutes, 1876–1901.
18 Sue Rogers, secretary at Longfield Church, dates the window to *c*.1890; http://www.kentarchaeology.org.uk/Research/Libr/MIs/MIsLongfield/MIsLongfield.htm (accessed 3 June 2020).
19 Appendix: will, ll. 33–6; TNA, C 6/348/11, fo. 7.
20 Appendix: will, ll. 37–9; TNA, C 6/348/11, fo. 7; MAC, RCA/L6/2, Rochester City Council Charity records, Deed of Gift, 16/01/1724.
21 Appendix: will, ll. 505–07, 523–7; TNA, C 6/348/11, fo. 7.
22 MAC, CH108/191/1, Sir John Hawkins Knight Hospital records, Plume bequest 16/09/1705; CH108/92, Letter Thomas Power to John Walsall, 4 October 1707.
23 MAC, CH108/194, Draft of instrument, 1707.
24 Appendix: will, ll. 67–81.
25 TNA, C 6/348/11, fo. 7; C 6/550/309. The four Greenwich maids were Anne Ramsey, Ann Burr, Anne Brewer and Elizabeth Rutter.
26 TNA, C 6/348/11, fo. 7; MAC, DRc/S02, Rochester Cathedral register, 1694–1754; *ibid.*, P306/1/12, Rochester St Nicholas marriage register, 1673–1727; P150B/1/3, Strood St Nicholas register, 1695–1715.
27 Appendix: will, ll. 518–22; J. Kimbell, *An Account of the Legacies, Gifts, Rents, Fees & appertaining to the Church and Poor of the Parish of St Alphege Greenwich, in the County of Kent* (Greenwich, 1816), p. 77.
28 Kimbell, *An Account*, pp. 76, 86, 94; TNA, C 6/550/309; LMA, LMA/4442/01/01/01/13–16, John Roan School Records, Leases & Deeds in Greenwich, Deptford & Lewisham, 1723–1766.
29 Kimbell, *An Account*, p. 76.
30 Appendix: will, ll. 337–9.
31 MAC, P314/1/1, Grain parish register, 1653–1768; J. Gregory (ed.), *The Speculum of Archbishop Thomas Secker* (Woodbridge, 1995), pp. 280–1.
32 Charity Commissioners, *Digest of the Reports made by the Commissioners of Inquiry into Charities ...* (London, 1843), pp. 61–2; DAC, SCT, Minutes 1876–1901.

33 DAC, SCT, Minutes 1876–1901; Appendix: will, ll. 339–40.
34 Appendix: will, ll. 271–83.
35 DAC, SCT, Details, 1755; Accounts, 1787–1829.
36 DAC, SCT, Minutes, 1876–1901.
37 DAC, SCT, Minutes, 1901–1952; Account Book, 1876–1911.
38 Revd R. Knight, 'The Word Made Flesh' (Holy Trinity Dartford, Advent 2008): http://www.cuxtonandhalling.org.uk/teaching.htm (accessed 3 June 2020).
39 Appendix: will, ll. 461–8.
40 TNA, C 6/348/11, fo. 7; MAC, DRc/Ac/04, Rochester Cathedral minute book, 1695–1706, (Book 10) fos 7, 25a, 42, 66a, (Book 11) fos 3, 13, 36, 55, 66, (Book 12) fos 2, 12, 24, 30a, 41a, 50a, 62a, 69a; *ibid.*, P336/1/02, Shorne parish register, 1644–1812. It is uncertain whether either child benefited from this legacy, as both had left the cathedral school by 1705.
41 Appendix: will, ll. 320–33; TNA, C 6/348/11, fo. 7; C 6/550/309.
42 Appendix: will, ll. 31–2; TNA, C 6/348/11, fo. 7.
43 Appendix: will, ll. 528–33.
44 TNA, C 6/348/11, fo. 7. The four poor divines were; John Winteley of Groombridge, Maximilian Buck of Kemsing, Thomas Beake and Francis Dudson.
45 Appendix: will, ll. 487–95.
46 DAC, SCT, Indenture, the Revd Mr Lamb to the Trustees of Stone Charity, 7 May 1734; *ibid.*, Minutes, 1787–1839; TNA, C 6/348/11, fo. 3.
47 Appendix: will, ll. 41–5; TNA, C 6/348/11, fo. 7.
48 TNA, C 6/550/309, fo. 2; E. Hasted, *The History and Topographical Survey of the County of Kent*, vol. 1 (Canterbury, 1797), p. 416.
49 Appendix: will, ll. 285–90.
50 *Ibid.*, ll. 290–94.
51 *Ibid.*, ll. 264–306; TNA, C 6/348/11.
52 Hasted, *The History and Topographical Survey*, vol. 2, pp. 391–2.
53 Appendix: will, ll. 295–306. John Hope, a trustee named in the chancery case, was buried on 18 January 1706, so the suit must have been prepared prior to that date.
54 DAC, SCT, Abstract of Deed of Feoffment, 1798.
55 Appendix: will, ll. 295–313; TNA, C 6/348/11, fo. 3; DAC, SCT, Deed of Feoffment, 1798.
56 DAC, SCT, Indenture, the Revd Mr Lamb, 7 May 1734; *ibid.*, Deed of Feoffment, 1798; *ibid.*, Minutes, 1787–1839 (front page). The new agreement in 1798 listed the existing trustees and new ones, who were elected. Many of those listed in the 1787 minutes were not elected trustees, but successive ministers permitted under the original agreement to serve on the charity until a new agreement was required to be drawn up; i.e. when the actual named trustees dropped to seven.
57 Excel spreadsheet of 2015 trustees supplied by Kevin Ross at Dartford Almshouse Charity.
58 DAC, SCT, Deed of Feoffment, 1798.
59 *Ibid.*
60 *Ibid.*; Accounts, 1787–1829; Details, 1755; Appendix: will, ll. 264–6, 334–6, 340–2, 343–7; TNA, C 6/348/11 fo. 3.
61 Orphan Stock was a form of commodity or bond on the Stock Exchange, whereby the estates of wealthy orphans could be open to speculation by relatives and others.
62 DAC, SCT, Deed of Feoffment, 1798; Indenture, the Revd Lamb, 1734.
63 Appendix: will, ll. 492–4; TNA, C 6/348/11 fo. 3.
64 TNA, C6/348/11, fo. 3.
65 DAC, SCT, Deed of Feoffment, 1798; Details, 1755; Accounts, 1787–1829.
66 DAC, SCT, Minutes, 1876–1901; P.J. Perry, *British Agriculture, 1875–1914* (Abingdon, 2006), pp. 1–55, for the state of English farming in the late eighteenth century.

67 DAC, SCT, Minutes, 1787–1839.
68 DAC, SCT, Accounts, 1787–1829; Minutes, 1787–1839.
69 *Ibid.*
70 DAC, SCT, Details 1755; Accounts, 1787–1829; Stone, Kent, tithe award schedule, 1838, http://www.kentarchaeology.org.uk/Research/Maps/STO/02.htm (accessed 3 June 2020).
71 DAC, SCT, Minutes, 1876–1901.
72 DAC, SCT, Details, 1755; Accounts, 1787–1829.
73 DAC, SCT, Minutes, 1787–1839.
74 *Ibid.*
75 *Ibid.*
76 *Ibid.*
77 DAC, SCT, Minutes, 1787–1839.
78 *Ibid.*
79 *Ibid.*
80 DAC, SCT, Minutes, 1876–1901.
81 *Ibid.*
82 DAC, SCT, Minutes, 1876–1901.
83 *Ibid.*
84 *Ibid.*
85 *Ibid.*; Accounts, 1876–1911; Minutes, 1901–1952; Diocese of Rochester, Plume's Trust details, http://www.rochester.anglican.org/content/pages/documents/1480072875.pdf (accessed 27 June 2020); Charity Commission Reports, Dr Plumes Trust, reg. char. 254048, http://apps.charitycommission.gov.uk/Showcharity/RegisterOfCharities/CharityWithoutPartB.aspx?RegisteredCharityNumber=254048&SubsidiaryNumber=0 (accessed 27 June 2020).
86 For further discussion of this general issue, Chapter 4, pp. 114–15.
87 For a summary, Chapter 4, pp. 103–5.

Chapter 10

'A studious, and learned Professor of Astronomy and experimentall philosophy': the Plumian professors at Cambridge from 1707 to the present day

Mark Hurn

The inescapable backdrop to Thomas Plume's bequest to astronomy and the creation of the Plumian Professorship is the foundation of the Royal Observatory in Greenwich.[1] The Observatory was completed on the site of a small fort on a hill in Greenwich Park by 1676. This observatory was founded not just for the abstract study of astronomy: like other European powers (the Paris Observatory was founded just a few years earlier, in 1671), the British were well aware of the vital importance of astronomical navigation to a maritime nation. The king appointed the Revd John Flamsteed as the Astronomical Observator to supervise the Observatory's work.[2] These two great foundation stones may well have been in Plume's mind when he made out his will, for Plume had been the vicar of Greenwich since 1658, would have seen the Observatory constructed and would have got to know Flamsteed and his family during this time. Plume was not a scientist or a member of the Royal Society himself, but he acquired the history of the Royal Society for his library along with some other scientific texts. At Greenwich he witnessed the dramatic effects of royal patronage on astronomy in Britain at first hand and this may well have stimulated the idea of doing something similar himself.

In a letter written shortly after Plume's death Flamsteed recalls him as a 'Friend and neighbour' and mentions that they had discussed together candidates for the professorship.[3] Indeed, it is very likely that, through Flamsteed, Plume would have heard news of the great names in astronomy at the time, such as Isaac Newton and Edmond Halley. It also may be that Flamsteed lent, or recommended, books to Plume. In 1764 the then Plumian professor, Robert Smith, wrote in his copy of *Kosmotheoros* (1698) by Christiaan Huygens that reading that book had inspired Plume to leave the money for a chair of astronomy in his will.[4] Huygen's book speculated about life on other planets and how alien life might fit into Christian theology.

Plume's will set out his plan for the study of astronomy in Cambridge and the investments to be allocated for its funding, which totalled £1,902 12s 2d, in some detail.[5] It is clear that his intention was to build an observatory, equip it, and maintain a professor of astronomy. The professor was required to educate 'scholars and gentlemen' not just in astronomy but also in globes, navigation, natural philosophy, dialing and practical mathematics. In addition, the professor was required to read at least two lectures a year in Latin and deposit copies in the University Library; furthermore, there is some detail as to how the lectures were to be promoted.[6] Plume also gave details of the people he wanted to run the professorship: these were Dr Francis Thompson,[7] Dr Covell (master of Christ's College) and Dr Bentley (master of Trinity College), with advice from Newton, John Ellys (master of Caius College) and Flamsteed.

There was a long tradition of wealthy church dignitaries, like Plume, making benefactions to the University of Cambridge, such as Archbishop Parker in the sixteenth century. But perhaps closer in time (and sentiment) would be the royalist Tobias Rustat (1608–94). In 1667 Rustat, a benefactor of Jesus College who also had a strong interest in books, gave Cambridge University library an endowment to buy 'the choicest and most useful books'.[8]

In order to support Plume's professorship, the immediate action of the university was to purchase a country estate in the Cambridgeshire village of Balsham to provide a regular income. The estate, now known as Plumian Farm, was purchased in 1706 for £1,845 and consumed most of Plume's endowment.[9] There was, therefore, nowhere near enough remaining money to build and equip an observatory on the model of Greenwich. At Greenwich the building works alone had cost £520, and individual instruments such as a mural arc (a scale designed to measure star positions accurately) cost £120, while Flamsteed's salary was £100 and that of an assistant £26.[10] It must have been obvious that Cambridge could have very quickly spent the remaining capital setting up an observatory, and been left with little to maintain the professor over time. Instead, a small observatory was built over the Great Gate of Trinity College in 1706 and remained in use until it was demolished in 1797, having been unused for half a century.[11] John Flamsteed had not been in favour of this site, arguing that the observatory should be independent of the colleges.[12]

Table 10.1 The Plumian Professors, 1707–2017

Name	Lived	Period as Professor
Roger Cotes	1682–1716	1707–16
Robert Smith	1689–1768	1716–60
Anthony Shepherd	1721–1796	1760–96
Samuel Vince	1749–1821	1796–1821
Robert Woodhouse	1773–1827	1822–27
George Airy	1801–1892	1828–36
James Challis	1803–1882	1836–82
George Darwin	1845–1912	1883–1912
Arthur Eddington	1882–1944	1913–44
Harold Jeffreys	1891–1989	1946–58
Fred Hoyle	1915–2001	1958–72
Martin Rees	1942–	1973–91
Richard Ellis	1950–	1993–99
Jeremiah Ostriker	1937–	2001–04
Robert C. Kennicutt, Jnr.	1951–	2005–17
Christopher S. Reynolds	1971–	2017–

Since Plume's bequest there have been 15 Plumian professors (Table 10.1). Each one is deserving of a book to themselves, but by dividing them into three groups I hope to give a flavour of the astronomical work they have carried out for over three centuries, during which astronomy has seen great changes and discoveries.

The mathematical astronomers (1707–1821)
These Plumian professors worked in the mathematical tradition of Newton. Plume had a candidate in mind for the first professorship, as Flamsteed wrote to William Whiston – who later succeeded Isaac Newton as Lucasian Professor of Mathematics at Cambridge – explaining that 'Dr Plume … [had] fixed upon an ingenious Young Man that about 3 years ago was my servant for his professor'. However, Flamsteed advised that Plume's choice did not have the required language skills and that Plume had then decided to leave the decision to the trustees. Subsequently, the masters of the three colleges proposed Roger Cotes, a young man of Trinity, for the appointment, but a great deal of tension between the trustees over both the location of the observatory and the identity of the Professor is apparent from Flamsteed's correspondence at this time.[13]

Flamsteed wanted Whiston to persuade the masters to consider John Witty, who had been educated at St John's, as 'he has attain'd that knowledge which the Dr. respected as absolutely necessary in his professor'. Flamsteed was insistent that Plume's wishes, rather than the trustees' personal preferences, should be adhered to. Whiston replied that in his view it was a fait accompli and 'past remidy'.[14] Flamsteed then wrote to Newton saying that the master of Trinity's decision to appoint a candidate without consulting the other trustees was 'I fear directly contrary to the Archdeacon's designe wherewith I am apt to thinke none of the Trustees in Cambridge were so well acquainted as I am'. He was worried that this decision would set a 'very ill' precedent for future elections.[15]

Indeed, **Roger Cotes** was successfully elected as the first Plumian professor on 16 October 1707 and worked very closely with Newton himself. He helped Newton revise his famous book the *Principia* (first published in 1687, revised edition 1713). In particular, he took up the study of the tides, lunar motions and the orbits of comets. He also began the construction of an observatory at Trinity College. Sadly, Cotes died at the young age of 32 and was never able to fulfil the great promise he had shown. Newton is recorded as saying 'if he had lived we might have known something'.[16] Flamsteed seems to have been kept informed about the developments made at the Cambridge observatory by Cotes' assistant Stephen Gray, who wrote to him to divulge 'anything there worth your knowledge'. In September 1708 Gray reported that a proposal for a new catalogue of fixed stars was in production to rival Flamsteed's own, which Gray thought was not to be bettered.[17]

The second professor, **Robert Smith**, was the cousin of Roger Cotes and published two books by Cotes posthumously. He was mainly based at Trinity College, where he was the master from 1742 to 1768, but he was also vice chancellor of the university from 1742 to 1743. He bequeathed some of his own money to add to the Plume bequest and improve the observatory above the gate at the college. Another bequest led to the Smith's Prize for mathematics. His academic reputation was based on his book *Complete System of Opticks* (1738), which went through many editions and promoted Newton's theory of light. He was also interested in the mathematics of music, writing *Harmonics, or the Philosophy of Musical Sounds* (1749).[18]

The next professor, **Anthony Shepherd**, was a member of the Board of Longitude and a friend of the navigator Captain James Cook (1728-79). Cook is said to have named the Shepherd Islands in Vanuatu after his friend. At that time navigation at sea was very much dependent on accurate astronomical tables, the production of which the Board of Longitude supervised. Shepherd himself was neither a great observer nor calculator; indeed, he had a reputation for laziness and absenteeism.[19] His *Tables for Correcting the*

10.1 Samuel Vince (1749–1821), Plumian Professor of Astronomy, University of Cambridge (1796–1821), c.1821 (engraved by R. Cooper, drawn by T. Wageman and published by T. Clay, London, 1821) (by kind permission of the Univ. of Cambridge, Institute of Astronomy).

Apparent Distance of the Moon and a Star from the Effects of Refraction and Parallax (1772) was over 900 pages long, but he is said to have written only the four-page Preface himself.[20]

Samuel Vince (Figure 10.1) took over as Plumian professor after the death of Shepherd in 1796, but he was not to have access to an observatory at Cambridge, as the one at Trinity College was demolished in the following year. The son of a bricklayer, he had risen from a lowly social position having been spotted as a talented boy at 12 years old by a local clergyman who provided him with an education. He graduated from Gonville and Caius in 1775 as senior wrangler and won Smith's Prize and the Copley Medal of the Royal Society in 1780. His major work in astronomy was *A Complete System of Astronomy* (published in three volumes 1797–1808).[21]

The observatory directors (1822–82)

These Plumian professors had responsibility for the new Cambridge Observatory and its observational work, although sometimes for limited periods.

10.2 Early nineteenth-century print of Cambridge Observatory (possibly by J. & H.S. Storer of Cambridge, c.1829) (by kind permission of the Univ. of Cambridge, Institute of Astronomy).

In 1822 **Robert Woodhouse** was elected to the Plumian Professorship. He had graduated from Gonville & Caius College as senior wrangler and won the Smith's prize for 1795. He came to astronomy through mathematics, where he had helped reform mathematical methods, breaking with the fluxions of Newton and adopting the continental notation for calculus. He was associated with a group of 'university reformers' who were influential in setting up the new university observatory. The new observatory (completed in 1823) was slightly outside the town, to the west of Cambridge on the Madingley road, and was not associated with any particular college (Figure 10.2). As Plumian professor he was also director of the observatory and took up residence in the east wing of the observatory. In 1823 he married Harriet Wilkins and in 1825 they had a son, Robert. However, what might have become a happy home rapidly became a place of sadness as first Harriet died on 31 March 1826 and then Woodhouse himself on 23 December 1827.[22] There is a suggestion that the water supply at the observatory was contaminated.

The next Plumian professor was another young Cambridge student, **George Biddell Airy**. As a young man, Airy had suffered from astigmatism and had worked out the correct optical prescription for spectacles that would cure this problem of the eyes.[23] Airy had a gift for organisation. The observatory

10.3 Sir George Biddell Airy (1801–1892), Astronomer Royal (1835–81) and Plumian Professor (1828–36), caricatured in *Punch* magazine, May 1883. The reference is to the famous time ball on Flamsteed House, Greenwich (Royal Observatory Greenwich) (Sciencephotolibrary, C045/4372).

had been equipped only with rather small telescopes to start with, but Airy was responsible for designing and obtaining a world-class telescope for Cambridge: the Northumberland Refractor. This was a telescope with an 11.5-inch object glass, which became the principal instrument of the observatory for many years and which still remains there. Although Airy was not director of the observatory for long he was responsible for many improvements, and remained interested in it even after he had taken up the post of Astronomer Royal in Greenwich in 1836. He became one of the leading scientific authorities in Victorian Britain, advising the government on technical matters and holding the post of Astronomer Royal for 46 years.[24] Among his many achievements was the promotion of the Greenwich Observatory regarding navigation, for which he was caricatured in *Punch* as the Greenwich time ball (see Figure 10.3), which had been installed in 1833 for the benefit of shipping in the Thames. Some 50 years later Airy's astronomical and geodetic work contributed to the international recognition of Greenwich as the prime meridian.[25]

Airy recommended as his successor the Revd **James Challis** (Figure 10.4). In 1846 Challis had an opportunity to discover the planet Neptune using the Northumberland telescope, Airy having suggested that a search for an eighth

10.4 Revd James Challis, Plumian Professor (1836–82), in 1874 (Photograph portrait by Maull & Polybank, London) (by kind permission of the Univ. of Cambridge, Institute of Astronomy).

planet should be made based upon irregularities observed in the orbit of Uranus. However, his lack of conviction and laborious methods led to failure, with the honours for discovery going to the Berlin Observatory.[26] Challis became overburdened by the practical side of managing the observatory, particularly the publication of his observations, and in 1861 passed the directorship to John Couch Adams (1819–92) while retaining the Plumian Professorship until his death in 1882.

The theoreticians (1883–present)

For these professors, the running of the Cambridge Observatory was not their principal concern, and their work would use images and data from far more powerful telescopes in more favourable locations (including in space). This period has seen Newtonian physics superseded by the Relativity of Einstein and the development of quantum physics.

When Challis died the professorship passed to a son of the famous Charles Darwin, **George Howard Darwin**. He was very much a theoretician, rather

10.5 Einstein and Sir Arthur Eddington, Plumian Professor (1913–44), in the garden of the Cambridge Observatory, 1930 (Sciencephotolibrary, C001/0943).

than an observer, and his main interest was in the study of the tides.[27] A delightful picture of Cambridge at the time of G.H. Darwin can be obtained by reading *Period Piece* (1952), by his daughter Gwen Raverat.[28]

In 1913 the opportunity arose to reunite the professorship with the directorship of the observatory. The electors made the bold decision to appoint a young man, who had already shown himself to be an able mathematician and astronomer and who was to become perhaps the most famous Plumian professor: **Arthur Stanley Eddington** (Figure 10.5).

Eddington's importance is due to his association with Einstein's General Theory of Relativity. Eddington prepared a report on General Relativity in 1918 and was a natural choice to lead an experiment to test the new (and very controversial) theory.[29] The experiment involved travelling to the island of Principe (off the west coast of Africa) to observe the total eclipse of the sun in 1919. Photographs taken during the totality of the eclipse showed that the light of distant stars is deflected by the gravity of the sun exactly to the amount predicted by Einstein's theory. The triumph of providing the first experimental evidence for General Relativity was followed up by a book that explained the new theory in English.[30] The work was important after the First World War, when many scientists were prejudiced against Einstein's theories (which had been published by Einstein in German). Eddington was a Quaker and a conscientious objector during the war, and it has been suggested that his advocacy of Relativity was motivated by a desire to establish peace with Germany.[31]

Eddington's other great contribution to astronomy was his work on the physics of stars, including his establishment of the mass–luminosity relation, an equation that states how the luminosity (brightness) of a star is related to its mass. This work and other contributions on stellar physics are discussed in his famous book *The Internal Constitution of the Stars* (1926).[32]

Eddington's reputation is somewhat clouded by his refusal to accept the idea of black holes and his humiliation at a scientific meeting of Subrahmanyan Chandrasekhar, who proposed some of the first theories for them.[33] Eddington's fascination with the mathematical relations between physical constants, particularly the fine-structure constant (which defines the strength of electromagnetic interaction between particles), was and is today considered as an unproductive eccentricity by most physicists.

Eddington was a great populariser of astronomy, writing books aimed at the general public. He also dealt with the religious and philosophical questions that scientific advances had raised.[34] It may seem surprising that no comprehensive, modern critical biography of Eddington has been written, but this is partly a reflection of his very wide and profound contributions to the subject; indeed, he still attracts much attention from scholars in many fields.

After Eddington's unexpectedly early death in 1944, the next Plumian professor **Harold Jeffreys** was more a mathematician and geophysicist than an astronomer. His books *The Earth* (1923) and *Theory of Probability* (1939) went through several editions. He is also credited with some pioneering studies of the central core of the earth, but he never accepted the theory of continental drift.[35]

Jeffreys' appointment marked a separation of the Plumian Professorship from the directorship of the observatory. The limitations of Cambridge as an observing site (the low altitude and the cloudy weather) had increasingly led astronomers to use mountaintop observatories instead, such as Palomar in California, which have the advantage of being above low-level cloud, giving both clearer views of the stars and many more nights of observing.

The next Plumian professor was certainly one of the most famous and possibly the most colourful. **Fred Hoyle**, like Eddington before him, was quite a public figure and, also like Eddington, his celebrity was based on solid scientific achievements. In a classic paper known as B2FH, after the surname initials of the authors, Hoyle and his co-authors laid down the basic principles of how the chemical elements are formed in stars, a process known as nucleosynthesis.[36]

Hoyle was prominent in developing the subject of cosmology – the scientific study of the origin and development of the universe. Hoyle proposed the 'steady state' theory, with the 'continuous creation of matter' in very small quantities. He posited an eternal and, on the largest scale, essentially unchanging universe, explaining the phenomenon astronomers now call 'dark energy'.[37] Hoyle opposed the rival cosmological theory, in which the universe develops over time from a precise moment in time, calling it a 'big bang'.[38] However, evidence from radio astronomers backed Hoyle's opponents, and now the Big Bang theory is the generally accepted theory in cosmology.

In 1967 Hoyle founded the Institute of Theoretical Astronomy (IOTA), based in its own building in the grounds of the Cambridge Observatory. The two institutions were united to form the Institute of Astronomy in 1972. Academic politics over the appointment of an additional professor of astrophysics at the new Institute led Hoyle to resign as Plumian professor in 1972,[39] but he continued to work in astronomy, among other fields, for the rest of his life.

Alongside his scientific work, Hoyle had become quite a successful writer of science fiction. Perhaps his best novel was *The Black Cloud* (1957). He also co-authored, with John Elliot, *A for Andromeda* (1962), based on the TV series they had written together.

Following on from Fred Hoyle was **Martin Rees**, a director of the Institute of Astronomy for many years, who in 1995 became, and remains at the time of writing, the Astronomer Royal. His astronomical work concerns the black holes thought to power the activity of quasars. He has also studied the mysterious gamma ray bursts, powerful bursts of radiation that occur at times from distant galaxies. Lord Rees, now very much a public figure, has written a number of books explaining his scientific work and speculating on the future of the human race.[40]

Richard Salisbury Ellis was also a director of the Institute of Astronomy for most of his tenure as Plumian professor, his astronomical work including the study of the large-scale structure of the universe. He was part of the Supernova Cosmology Project, which showed that the expansion of the universe is still rapidly accelerating.[41]

Jeremiah Ostriker, born in New York, was the first Plumian professor to be born outside of Britain. His astronomical work particularly involves the concept of dark matter, the idea that the universe largely consists of matter that cannot be seen, but which reveals itself only by subtle effects. The exact nature of dark matter is still very much a problem for astronomers.[42]

10.6 Robert C. Kennicutt, Jr, Plumian Professor (2005–17), in 2008 (by kind permission of the Univ. of Cambridge, Institute of Astronomy).

The next Plumian professor was **Robert C. Kennicutt Jr** He is known for the Kennicutt–Schmidt law, which relates the gas density in galaxies to the formation rate of stars. He is the principal investigator for a survey of nearby galaxies using the Spitzer Space Telescope.[43]

In October 2017 **Christopher S. Reynolds** took over as the latest Plumian professor. He completed his PhD at the Institute of Astronomy in Cambridge in 1996 and, before moving to Cambridge, had been Professor of Astronomy in the Department of Astronomy at the University of Maryland since 2009. His research interests involve high-energy astrophysics, such as the accretion of material onto the black holes in the centres of galaxies.[44]

The period of the Plumian Professorship has seen enormous changes in the practice and theory of astronomy. The professorship has always been regarded as one of the highest status roles in astronomy, not just in Cambridge, but in Britain and the world. The early professors worked in the mathematical tradition of Newton, the later ones in the relativistic astrophysics inspired by Einstein. Some had responsibility for observatories at Cambridge and elsewhere, while others worked purely as theorists. Technology and advances in science have made the practice of astronomy rather different now from what it was in Plume's day, but the holders of the Plumian Chair have always been at the very forefront of astronomical research. Many important scientific developments have therefore been assisted by the intention of Thomas Plume all those years ago.

Notes

1. The description of the Plumian Professorship in the title to this chapter is a quotation from Plume's will; see Appendix: Dr Thomas Plume's will, ll. 363–5.
2. The title 'Astronomer Royal' emerged over time. In his will, Plume describes Flamsteed as 'Royall Mathematician at East Greenwich': TNA, PROB 10/1387; Appendix: will, ll. 407–08. For Flamsteed's biography see *ODNB*.
3. RGO, 1/33, fo. 130, Flamsteed to Whiston 13 February 1705/6, quoted in E.G. Forbes, L. Murdin and F. Willmoth, *The Correspondence of John Flamsteed, the First Astronomer Royal*, vol. 3, 1703–1719 (Bristol, 2002).
4. This book is held in the Library of Trinity College, Cambridge (T.49.21).
5. Appendix: will, ll. 353–420.
6. There is little evidence that even the early Plumian professors complied with the details of these stipulations. For example, if they deposited copies of their lectures in the library there is no surviving record.
7. A Doctor of Divinity (1639?–1715?): ACAD (A Cambridge Alumni Database); http://venn.lib.cam.ac.uk/ (accessed 3 September 2014). He is mentioned several times in Plume's will: see Chapter 4, pp. 99–100.
8. J.W. Clark, *Endowments of the University of Cambridge* (Cambridge, 1904).
9. CUL, University Archives D.XII. 14.
10. D. Howse, *Greenwich Time and the Discovery of the Longitude* (Oxford, 1980).
11. R. Willis, *The Architectural History of the University of Cambridge, and of the Colleges of Cambridge and Eton*, ed. J.W. Clark (Cambridge, 1886), p. 191.
12. Forbes *et al.*, *The Correspondence of John Flamsteed*, vol. 3, p. 484, n. 3.
13. *Ibid.*, p. 291.
14. *Ibid.*, pp. 291, 293.
15. *Ibid.*, p. 295.
16. R. Gowing, *Roger Cotes – Natural Philosopher* (Cambridge, 1983), p. 141.
17. Forbes *et al.*, *The Correspondence of John Flamsteed*, vol. 3, p. 483.
18. G. Cantor, 'Smith, Robert (bap. 1689, d. 1768)', *ODNB* (Oxford, 2004); http://www.oxforddnb.com/view/article/25891 (accessed 9 February 2017).
19. L. Taub, 'Shepherd, Anthony (1721?–1796)', *ODNB* (Oxford, 2004); http://www.oxforddnb.com/view/article/25330 (accessed 9 February 2017).
20. A. Shepherd, *Tables for Correcting the Apparent Distance of the Moon and a Star from the Effects of Refraction and Parallax* (Cambridge, 1772).
21. A. McConnell, 'Vince, Samuel (1749–1821)', *ODNB* (Oxford, 2004); http://www.oxforddnb.com/view/article/28306 (accessed 9 February 2017).
22. H.W. Becher, 'Woodhouse, Robert (1773–1827)', *ODNB* (Oxford, 2004); http://www.oxforddnb.com/view/article/29926 (accessed 9 February 2017).
23. J.R. Levene, 'Sir George Biddell Airy F.R.S. (1801–1892) and the Discovery and Correction of Astigmatism', *Notes and Records of the Royal Society of London*, 21/2 (1966), pp. 180–99.
24. A. Chapman, 'Private Research and Public Duty – Airy, George and the Search for Neptune', *Journal for the History of Astronomy*, 29 (1988), p. 121.
25. Chapman, 'Airy, Sir George Biddell (1801–1892)'; A. Chapman, 'Airy, Sir George Biddell (1801–1892)', *ODNB* (Oxford, 2004).
26. T. Standage, *The Neptune File: Planet Detectives and the Discovery of Worlds Unseen* (London, 2000).
27. G.H. Darwin, *The Tides: and Kindred Phenomena in the Solar System* (London, 1898).
28. G. Raverat, *Period Piece* (London, 1952).
29. A.S. Eddington, *Report on the Relativity Theory of Gravitation* (London, 1918).
30. A.S. Eddington, *The Mathematical Theory of Relativity* (Cambridge, 1923).

31 M. Stanley, 'An Expedition to Heal the Wounds of War. The 1919 Eclipse and Eddington as Quaker Adventurer', *Isis. Journal of the History of Science Society*, 94 (2003), pp. 57–89.
32 A.S. Eddington, *The Internal Constitution of the Stars* (Cambridge, 1926).
33 A.I. Miller, *Empire of the Stars: Friendship, Obsession & Betrayal in the Quest for Black Holes* (London, 2005).
34 K. Price, *Loving Faster than Light: Romance and Readers in Einstein's Universe* (Chicago, IL, 2012).
35 B.A. Bolt, Obituary of Harold Jeffreys, *Quarterly Journal of the Royal Astronomical Society*, 31 (1990), pp. 267–71; L. Runcorn, 'Sir Harold Jeffreys (1891–1989)', *Nature*, 339/6220 (1989), p. 102.
36 M. Burbidge, G. Burbidge, W. Fowler and F. Hoyle, 'Synthesis of the Elements in Stars', *Reviews of Modern Physics*, 29 (1957), pp. 547–650.
37 F. Hoyle, 'A New Model for the Expanding Universe', *Monthly Notices of the Royal Astronomical Society*, 108 (1948), p. 372.
38 S. Mitton, *Fred Hoyle: A Life in Science* (London, 2005).
39 *Ibid.*, p. 287.
40 M. Rees, *Our Final Century: A Scientist's Warning: How Terror, Error, and Environmental Disaster threaten Humankind's Future in this Century – on Earth and Beyond* (London, 2003).
41 Personal homepage: http://www.eso.org/~rellis/ (accessed 30 January 2017).
42 Personal homepage: http://www.astro.princeton.edu/people/webpages/jpo/ (accessed 30 January 2017).
43 Personal homepage: https://www.as.arizona.edu/people/faculty/rob-kennicutt (accessed 22 June 2020).
44 Personal homepage: https://www.astro.umd.edu/~chris/Site/Welcome.html (accessed 13 October 2017).

Appendix:

Dr Thomas Plume's will

A transcript of the original version of Dr Thomas Plume's will preserved in TNA, PROB 10/1387.

General observations
1. Punctuation and spelling are set out as in the original.
2. Pages and lines are transcribed as in the original, but numbered for ease of reference.
3. Plume signed every page 'Tho. Plume', which we have not added to the transcription.
4. Catchwords, duplicating the first word on the following page, have not been transcribed.

Abbreviations in the manuscript
Words with clear abbreviation marks have been extended using square brackets. A few other words have been similarly extended for clarity. Plume also used the following standard abbreviations.
ye = the
yt = that
ym = them

Manuscript hands
Hand A. The first part of the will, labelled below as Part I, is largely written in one hand, apparently by a clerk taking instruction from Dr Plume.
Hand B. The second part of the will, labelled below as Part II, is largely written in different hand, apparently by another clerk taking instruction from Dr Plume.

Hand C. Small sections of the text in both Parts I and II are in Dr Thomas Plume's own hand, reproduced below in *italics*.
Three other hands have also been identified, and are indicated below, as follows:
Hand D
Hand E
Hand F

Note also that deletions in the text of the original will are shown with ~~scored~~ text.

[Part I]

Covering page
My last will 8br4 1704[1]

p. 1

1   Da Domine, ut quae ex immensâ bonitate tuâ mihi elargiri
2   dignatus es, in quorum cunqβ manus devenerint, in tuam cedant Gloriam.[2]

3   God direct me in ye making my last will, as may most
4   make for his Glory, ye benefit of his Church, & my own soul's Good
5   in the day of his great account.

6   In Nomine Domini Amen.[3]

7   I Thomas Plume of E. Greenwich D.D. Minister tho' most undeserving
8   being in reasonable good temper of body, &, God be praised, of a sound
9   & disposing mind, & memory, doe make this my last Will, & Testament,
10   in manner, & form following.

11   First, I humbly resign my spirit into thy hands, O blessed Jesu, who
12   didst give up thy spirit into ye hands of thy Father, from thy body
13   crucified for my sins, by which passion, I strongly hope, & trust, to have
14   my many sins, (which I heartily repent of) forgiven, & that my soul,
15   & body, shall escape ye due punishment thereof in ye world to come. Amen, Lord Jesu.

16   2. For ye interment of my body, I will that my Cousin
17   James Plume of Lambeth, & Dr Thompson, & Mr Rawson
18   in an herse carry it to Longfield Church-yard, & there bury it in
19   a brick't grave, giving rings of eight shillings value, to ye Dean,
20   Prebendaries, & Petty-Canons of Rochester, & neighbour-Ministers, that
21   shall bee at my funeral there, (viz.) Mr Peirson, Mr Loton, Mr Thornton,
22   Mr Swinden, & all ye other Trustees named in my Will following. <u>as alsoe to Dr Cade,</u>
23   <u>Mr Thomas Powers, and Mr Watson of Greenwich & Mr Crump of</u>
24   <u>Rochester.</u> I desire but small attendance, & an ordinary black Coffin; but a fair
25   black stone, to bee laid upon me with this inscription.

---

1   I.e. 4 October 1704. October was the eighth month in the ecclesiastical calendar commonly in use from the twelfth century until 1752: C.R. Cheney (ed.), *Handbook of Dates for Students of English History* (1978 edn), p. 5.

2   Grant, Lord, that the effects which out of your great goodness you have deemed fit to lavish on me may turn, no matter whose hands they come down to, to your glory.

3   In the name of the Lord Amen.

26 Hic subtus jacet Archidiaconus Roffensis:
27 Peccatorum maximus, utinam et Poenitentium.
28 Nomen quaere in libro Vitae;
29 Veniet, iterum, qui me in lucem reponet dies.[4]

30 Concerning the trifles of my worldly Goods,
31 First, I order my Executor to pay to ye Dean, & Chapter of Rochester,
32 towards ye repair of their Cathedrall, fifty pounds.

33 2dly I order my Executor to pay to ye Mayor of Rochester, within
34 one moneth after my decease, twenty pounds, to bee distributed amongst
35 the Poor of Rochester, St. Margarets, Stroud & Chattham, as the
36 Mayor, Mr Loton, Mr Ax & Mr Wren, *and Mr Beresford* shall think meet.

p. 2

37 3dly I give to ye City of Rochester, fifty pounds, to bee paid within
38 a moneth after my death; to bee lent out upon good security, by the
39 Mayor, & Aldermen, to five poor tradesmen for ever, gratis.

40 I also give ten pounds to ye Church-Wardens of E. Greenwich, to ye poor of E. Greenwich.

41 Old Mark Cottle, left in my hands five pounds towards
42 building a Charnel-House, in E. Greenwich-parish-Church-yard, which
43 I order my Executor to pay to ye Church-Wardens, & also to pay them
44 five & twenty pounds more, of my own mony, for that use. <u>if they build
45 it within one year after my decease.</u>

46 I have four brick Houses in Debtford, in Dog-kennel-row,
47 where, my tenant Dawes, hath ye middle one, which I order my
48 Executor to buy of him, if hee will sell it, for ten or twelve
49 pounds, & to give them all for ever, for Almes-Houses for, ye poor
50 of E. Greenwich, to inhabit gratis, & to bee called, The Archdea-
51 cons Poor Almes-Houses; ye Church Wardens of E. Greenwich keeping
52 them in repair, and saving ye parish of Debtford from any charge, by such as they
53 thither send.

54 I give to Mr Rob[er]t Plume of Withersfield for his two sons

---

4 Beneath here lies the Archdeacon of Rochester:
The greatest of sinners and, I pray, of penitents.
Look for his name in the book of life;
The day which will lead me back into the light will come again.

55 that shall bee living at my death, ten pounds a peice, to bee paid to
56 him for them, by Dr Thompson, to whom I order my Executor to pay
57 the said summs, accordingly.

58 Item, I give my Curate then being, five pounds, & a ring of ye named value.

59 And I give five pounds to Francis, Nephew of Dr Thompson.
60 I forgive Mr Wheelock, & his son Abraham, ye one hundred pounds
61 they owe mee, & order their bonds to bee given them, on condition
62 that he pay his Sisters Anne & [ ][5] Wheelock fifty pounds
63 between them *& Mr Watts minister of Orpington ten pounds.*

64 I give my eldest maid, living with mee at my death, ten pounds
65 & my youngest five pounds.
66 ~~And I give two pounds to Elizabeth Royston, my old Maid.~~

67 And because I would show that I have no ill opinion of
68 marriage, I bequeath one hundred pounds to the placing of ten

p. 3

69 Maids in marriage, being above twenty four years old, of civill life &
70 who have lived in one service above seven years; five whereof I
71 would have to bee in E. Greenwich; & therefore leave ye Minister and
72 Church Wardens thereof, fifty pounds to bee disposed of by ym, for yt purpose,
73 in equall portions, willing my own eldest Maid, living with mee at my
74 death, should bee one of ye number, ~~& Talbot's wive's sister~~
75 ~~another, if then living, & not married~~. The other five maids to bee chosen
76 out of Rochester, St Margaret's Stroud or Chattham, whereof Mrs Wood's
77 old maid of St Margarets, to bee one, if living.

78 And I order my Executor to pay ye remaining fifty pounds
79 to Mr Loton, Minister of Chattham, for ye other four maids, as hee,
80 & ye Church Wardens of Rochester, & Chattham, shall think best to choose,
81 & distribute, by equall portions to ye said five.

82 All my Household Goods (excepting my ready mony, plate,
83 & books) viz: Apparel, black cloth, & bedding &c. whether at E. Greenwich,
84 or Rochester, I order Dr Thompson, & Mr Rawson & Mr Berisford, to
85 choose any one thing first for themselves, & afterwards sell, or divide

---

5 There is a space here for a missing forename. Plume either did not know, or more probably could not recall, the name of the second sister as he was dictating the will.

86   the rest, amongst any ten poor Ministers of Rochester Diocess, such
87   as they shall see, need most, & as deserve best.

88   But I leave my bed & furniture of my chamber at Stone-Castle
89   to my Tenant there, for ye time being, to accommodate any of
90   my Trustees, when they please to lodge there, from time to time. *for ever.*

91   My own House in Maldon, wherein Mr Carr did live,
92   I give to my cousin Nathaniel Plume of Yeldham, & his Heirs
93   for ever. Likewise ye shop wherein Folgier now kills, & uses his trade,
94   of five pounds, p[er] Annu[m] rent. Also my lands called Smithfield,
95   which John Brown uses, & pays fourteen pounds p[er] An[num]. All these I
96   give to him, & his Heirs for ever: & also ~~an hundred pounds in~~
97   ~~mony, as a token of my love to him~~ *all my morgage*
98   *mony lent to M[r] Gyon,* in hopes hee will recover the
99   family wasted by others.

100 And I give Mr William Plume of Laerbretto[n][6] near Colchester, ~~ten~~ *twenty* pounds.
101 And I give Mr Hoell of London, in Shire lane, ten pounds.

p. 4

102 And I give Mr Dorrell of Holbourn Millainer, ten pounds.

103 And also I give to my man, Thomas Allen, living with mee at
104 my death, five pounds

105 And I also order my Executor to pay Mr Allix about ye Charter-
106 house one hundred pounds, to give to poor French, Protestant-Ministers
107 especially, or other French Laymen, at his discretion, & thank him for
108 his translation of Nectarius.

109 And I give one hundred pounds more, to bee dispersed among
110 an hundred parishes in ye Diocess of Rochester, giving every parish twenty
111 shillings, unless those to whom I have made greater bequeathments,
112 in my will, before. This shall be paid to ye Trustees of Stone-Castle,
113 to distribute to ye *ministers &* and Church Wardens of ye severall parishes for the Poor.

114 And I give one hundred pounds to ye Corporation for propagating
115 the Gospel beyond sea, to bee disposed of by them accordingly.

---

6   Layer Breton.

116 And I give two hundred pounds, & all ye residue of my personall
117 Estate, not disposed of in this my last will, for ye purchasing, & providing
118 Tenements, & a stock, for setting ye poor of Maldon to work according
119 to Mr Commins's direction, & his draught, sent mee by Dr Thompson,
120 & I doe appoint those named for the School, Trustees for this Charity
121 also, & desire of them to employ some poor of Munden in it. *& Country about.*
122 <u>I give the mortgage of Mrs Melsops</u>
123 <u>house for this Charity. Dec. 28, 1703.</u>

124 I give one hundred pounds to Mr Edward Brooke
125 *Mnr of Hadlow in Kent & Curat of Woodham Water*
126 *in Essex.*

127 *I also give one hundred pound to Mr John Pully m[i]n[iste]r*
128 *of Fordham in Essex for himself & children.*

129 *Whereas Charles Huggett may claim equity of redempt[ion]*
130 *of Mrs Melsops House in Fulbridg Street I do bequeath*
131 *Him to be payd by my Executor ten pounds for his release*
132 *of the same, though the House is not worth so much*
133 *as it owes mee*

p. 5
134 I have erected over ye School at Maldon, a Library-room
135 to which I give all my books, & pictures, (but forbid my picture now in
136 Mr Pond's house to bee ever brought into my Library.) together with
137 my large map of ye World, to bee sent from Roch[este]r & E. Greenwich, & set
138 up at Maldon, as Dr Thompson and ye Trustees think best. for which,
139 I appoint my Executor, to pay him all charges, & likewise leave ye
140 Doctor an hundred pounds, to bee paid to him within half a year,
141 after my decease, by my Executor, for his care, & pains in my affairs,
142 & make him overseer of my Will, & a Trustee, for electing a Library-
143 keeper, & all other Charities given out of my Estate, & desire him
144 to convey all my Manuscript-papers of my own hand, to bee carefully
145 preserved in ye study of the aforesaid Library.

146 The Library-keeper shall give two hundred pounds bond
147 at least, not to embezell my books; nor to lend them out, without
148 sufficient pawn, to buy ye same again, to my Trustees at Maldon, ye
149 Ministers, & Gentlemen named below, who shall require bond of him also,
150 upon forfeiture of his trust, to goe out peaceably, upon a Quarter's

151 warning, that they may put in another as they shall think fit, with ye
152 approbation of ye Governours of Sion Coll[ege] London, for ye time being,
153 whom I desire to take account thereof, for which I leave yt College
154 twenty shillings, p[er] An[num], out of Iltny Estate for ever, & for ye visiting,
155 & determining any matters about it.

156 The Keeper of this Library, shall be a Scholar, yt knows books, *M.A.*
157 & in holy orders, & may bee some Minister yt has a neighbouring living,
158 & can *or shall* reside in Maldon, or ye school master himself, or any other of
159 good learning, & life, yt will be engaged to attend every morning &
160 afternoon (except Sundays) two hours in ye Library room, or in his house
161 near to it, in all, four hours p[er] diem, yt any Gentleman, or Schollar
162 who desires, may goe into it, & make use of any book there or borrow
163 it, in case he leaves a vadimonium,[7] with ye keeper, for ye restoring thereof,
164 fair & uncorrupted, within a short time, or else, therewith to buy another
165 of ye same kind, & goodness. *He shall suffer no stranger to bee*
166 *there alone w'out a voucher, for his Honesty & his own promise*
167 *not to carry away or deface any Book.*

p. 6

168 And because new books are daily printing, I will yt twenty
169 shillings p[er] annum be paid out of my Iltny Estate yearly for ever, to
170 buy any yt shall bee most desired by ye Library keeper.

171 The Farm of Iltny in Munden having been (as I have credibly heard)
172 a Chantry land given to Maldon but alienated by King Henry ye eighth;
173 I now restore, & give for ever to ye Town of Maldon for ye uses following.

174 First to keep in good repair ye School, & Library room for ever.
175 2dly to maintain a weekly lecture, from Lady day to Michaelmass for ever,
176 allowing ye several neighbouring Ministers of Dengy, or Rochford-
177 Hundred, yt shall bee chosen to preach it weekly, ten shillings for their
178 sermon, & two shillings for his own, and his friends dinner, at ye blew boar
179 Inn or elsewhere, if ye Trustees order it, upon Wednesday or Saturday,
180 as they shall agree, in ye upper Church at Maldon.
181 But upon ye first Wednesday, or Saturday in August for ever, I allow
182 twenty shillings out of Iltny lands, towards ye dinner of them yt shall there
183 meet, & shall then take ye accounts of ye Tenants, let, & set ye Farm,
184 consider ye repairs of ye houses, ditches, Marsh-Walls, take care to pay ye

---

7   i.e. a legally binding bond or pledge.

185 quit-rent, survey ye Library, & doe any thing else requisite for ye farm
186 & my donations, allowing the Sexton, ten shillings for each of ye two
187 quarters, for tolling ye bell for ye Lecture, to bee paid ten shillings upon
188 Midsumer day, & ten shillings at Michaelmass.

189 And likewise ten shillings at each of ye said two quarter days, to bee
190 divided among ye most Godly indigent Poor of Maldon, that repair to
191 this lecture, prayers, & sermon most constantly.

192 And farther out of ye profitts of Iltny lands, I order ye Trustees
193 to keep six poor boys, out of Maldon, or Munden, & doe allow ye Master
194 twenty shillings p[er] an[num] for each boy's schooling, & each of those boys
195 forty shillings p[er] an[num] towards his clothing, in plain gray, or green coats,
196 breeches, stockings, & shoes, as far as it can bee made to goe, with a
197 Monmouth cap, or hat.

198 The Trustees of this matter, I nominate, ye two annual Bayliffs of Maldon,
199 (if they communicate with ye Church of England) & ye Ministers of
200 All Saints parish Maldon, ye Curate of St Maries there, ye schoolmaster,
201 the Library keeper, & also ye Ministers of Woodham-Water, Purlegh,

p. 7

202 Munden, Heybridge or Curates, for ever, or any five of them, upon trust,
203 to dispose all things, as they see good, for ye fulfilling of this will. I also
204 appoint Mr Brickwood, Mr John Stevens, Mr Samuel Pond, Mr John Pond,
205 Trustees for their lives <u>and Mr Stacy and Mr Strait Dec. 28 1703</u>

206 I give to ye upper Church in Maldon in Essex, twenty pounds, to buy
207 them plate for ye Comunion-table in All Saints Church; in thankfullness
208 for my baptism there, August ye 7th 1630 out of my own plate.

209 Item I bequeath to Chelmsford school twenty pounds to bee laid out
210 in books, for ye use thereof, in a standing Library, in thankfulness for
211 my education there out of my own plate.

212 Whatsoever rent is due at my death, out of any estate of mine in Essex,
213 I give to those Trustees, to bee expended in some of ye Charities abovementioned,
214 as also what is due upon Skelton of Iltny his bond.

215 I would have ye Library keeper if fit rebus agundis,[8] to bee entrusted
216 to receive ye rents of ye Farm, & pay ye Ministers yt shall be chosen
217 by ye Trustees, for their pains presently after ye lecture, & also the
218 Sexton, or Clark, & poor, their severall ten shillings at Midsumer, &
219 Michaelmas, & also ye expence of twenty shillings, ye first week
220 in August, for which I bequeath him yearly, forty shillings more out
221 of Iltny Estate.

222 After ye charge of repairs, taxes, Wall-charges (which if extra-
223 ordinary, abatements must be made, by all persons proportionably) &
224 after ye preacher's salary, ye children's schooling, & clothes, ye Sexton, &
225 ye poor, are discharged, together with ye Library keeper's salary of
226 seventeen pounds p[er] annum, added to his twenty three pounds p[er] an[num] out of
227 ye lands in Maldon lately purchased of Mr Norton, making his salary
228 full forty pounds p[er] an[num] & a dwelling house, near ye Library, to bee
229 purchased for him, & his Successors, with an hundred pounds, I bequeath
230 for yt purpose (Mr Brickwood's if it may bee had, at a reasonable rate)
231 & over & above ye aforesaid two pounds p[er] an[num] for his receiving &
232 paying ye rent as aforesaid, besides what he may get for his
233 preaching, or procuring sermons, when any of ye appointed Ministers

p. 8

234 fail their turns, after ye discharge of all these things, ye remaining rent
235 of Iltny farm, shall augment ye number of ye children to ten, or put
236 some of ym out apprentices, & ye rest ye Trustees shall dispense in charity
237 to some poor Ministers in Dengy Hundred, or to their Widdows or Children
238 as they shall think best.

239 <u>I give one hundred pounds to Mrs An Beale of Westminster.</u>[9]

240 And I give one hundred pounds to Christ College
241 in Cambridge on condition they allow an annual Exhibition of
242 six pounds towards ye maintenance of one scholar educated at Maldon
243 but if there bee none from thence to bee given to one educated at
244 Chelmsford, & in default of both, to any yt is educated in any part of
245 the County of Essex. *or at Brentwood*

---

8   Fit 'for carrying matters out', i.e. 'fit for purpose'.
9   This passage is clearly an interpolation in a different hand. It led to Dr Plume's executor bringing a court case against Mrs Beale accusing her of forgery. The forename of Mrs Beale was clearly written 'An' which would normally be extended as An[ne], but her name was Audrey. See Chapter 4, p. 104.

246 The Minister of All Sts parish or whosoever reads
247 the prayers before the Lecture & at other times
248 shall be allowed 20 shillings every quarter
249 of the an. out of Iltny Estate for ever
250 for constant reading morning pr dayly.
251 About eleven a clock & five att night or sooner
252 in Winter for wh[ich] he shall have twenty shillings
253 every quarter.

254 I likewise give out of my personall Estate one thousand
255 pound for buying in of Tyths to small livings in any
256 great Towns or Villages where the living is not
257 worth an hundred pounds to be augmented as Dr Thompson
258 & Mr Stubs & the governours of ye Corporation of ministers
259 children shall think fitt.
260 I also give w[ha]t remains of my personall Estate in
261 the Excheq[ue]r towards erecting a Work House for ye poor
262 of Maldon & neighb[ourin]g villages as Mr Cumins & the Trustees
263 for ye school shall think best to order.

[Part II]

p. 9

264 I bought of Mr. Etkins the Mannor of Stone-Castle
265 for about £1500 lying in Stone parish, or Swanscome in
266 Kent, which lets for £74 p[er] Annu[m], lands, woods, & houses.
267 All this estate, and whatsoever appertains to it, I settle
268 upon the following trustees, neighbour ministers, &
269 their successors in their Livings, or Benefices for ever
270 for the uses following.

271 1st to maintain a weekly lecture at Dartford, or Gravesend,
272 every Wednesday, or Saturday morning, from the 25th of March
273 till Michaelmasse alternatin[g], or one year at Dartford, &
274 the next at Gravesend. for w[hi]ch the severall Preachers
275 shall have ten shillings for their sermon, and two shillings
276 for their dinner, & their friends paid them. And the
277 Sexton ten shillings a quarter, during the time of ye said lecture
278 for tolling the bell. I give also ten shillings a quarter to bee
279 divided amongst the most indigent, & Godly Poor, that most
280 frequently resort to this lecture, also twenty shillings, each

281 of the two quarters, wherein ye Lecture is preached, to
282 the Minister of the Parish, for his reading prayers before
283 the said Lecture in the morning, & for ye use of his Pulpit.

284 2dly Out of this mannor, & the estates given, whatsoever shall
285 arise besides, I would have the Trustees distribute in augmentation
286 of poor Parsonages, & Vicarages, in the Diocesse of Rochester,
287 not worth £60 p[er] Annum, to the severall Incumbents, who
288 lead sober lives, & conform to the Church of England, and
289 hold but one Living, yet not allowing to any one place,

p. 10

290 or Minister more than ten pounds p[er] An[num]. Of these augmentations,
291 I would have Town-Malling ever partake, the rest I
292 leave to be named by the Trustees, & their Ecclesiasticall
293 Successors for ever, as they shall see best deserve, and most
294 need, & to as many as the Estates given will maintain.

295 The Trustees of this Charity I name, are, Dr Thompson,
296 Mr Loton, curate of Chatham, Mr Berisford Vicar of Halling
297 ~~Shall have ten pounds p[er] An[num] augmentation out of [Grain]~~[10]
298 Also Mr Pierson Vicar of Higham, Mr Thornton Rector of Stone,
299 Mr Price Vicar of Dartford, Mr Harris Vicar of Northfleet,
300 the Rector of Milton, the Rector of Gravesend, Mr Raty
301 Vicar of Rydly, the vicars of East-Greenwich, & of Plumsted
302 and of Eltham. The Rector of Crayford, Mr Hope Rector
303 of Swanscome, Mr James Wallis vicar of Falkham, Mr Will[iam]
304 Hopkins vicar of Horton-Kirby, Mr Thornton Minister of Ludsdown,
305 Mr Swinden vicar of Shorne, Mr Gibson Vicar of Friendsbury.
306 And the vicar of Cobham, & their Successors in their Benefices for ever.

307 Which Trustees I order to meet twice a year at Stone Castle
308 where the Tenant shall bee allowed, out of his rent, twenty shillings
309 to provide them a dinner each time, within one fortnight before
310 or after Lady day, or Michaelmasse, as the major part
311 of them shall appoint, & then take order for ye rent, & all needful
312 repayrs, and payments of ye severall Augmentations, as ye
313 Majority of the Trustees there present shall agree upon.

---

10   This deleted line is difficult to read clearly.

p. 11

314 3ly I appoint that the Ministers w[h]o are Commissioners for Stone-Castle
315 Charity, & other bequests at Dartford, & Grain, do, out of
316 the rents of those estates, pay five pounds p[er] An[num] for ever,
317 by halfe yearly payments, to the Church wardens of Longfield,
318 for ye poor of Longfield, and keeping my grave, & gravestone
319 in good repair for ever.

320 4ly I bequeath to the same Trustees my house in Greenwich
321 which I bought of the Robinsons, & now built, wherein Daws lives,
322 for the benefit of the succeeding vicars of E. Greenwich for ever.
323 Provided that my successor there sue not my Executor
324 for any Dilapidations of the vicarage house, which I have made
325 better then ever. Having laid out above two hundred pounds
326 of my own proper estate to make it habitable, & keep it in
327 sufficient repair as it is in this year 1704. Notwithstanding
328 this, if ye vicar w[h]o succeeds mee shall molest, or sue my Executor,
329 James Plume, for further dilapidations, I give to my Executor
330 yt house of Daws, w[hi]ch I built, to defend himselfe in Law, till
331 the vicar give him a discharge from all dilapidations, upon his
332 receit of ten pounds, w[hi]ch I leave him to repayr, what shall
333 bee thought necessary.

334 5tly I bequeath to ye same Trustees my lease of Marsh & Upland in
335 the Isle of Grain, w[hi]ch I hold of the Church of Roch[este]r now in the
336 occupation of Sam[uel] London, for augmenting poor parsonages, or
337 vicarages in ye Diocese of Rochester, and five pounds p[er] Annu[m]
338 to ye Curate of Grain, or any sober man, that shall teach their
339 children at school there, if hee may bee had at that rate, otherwise
340 the said £5 p[er] An[num] is to bee disposed of, as the rest is. This last named
341 lease, I allow them to sell, if they think good, & purchase freehold land
342 with ye mony, for ye same purpose, to save ye trouble of renewalls.

p. 12

343 6tly I give them also to the same purpose of augmenting
344 poor vicarages the £340 odd pounds due to mee
345 from the City of London, for w[hi]ch I have their receit
346 and is paid at Guild-hall every halfe yeare after
347 four pounds p[er] cent interest.

348 *7ly I will that the A[rch]D[eaco]n of roch[este]r for ye time*
349 *being, shall every an[num] at his visitation take the*
350 *Trustees Account of the disposall of this Charity*
351 *& determin any matters of difference about it*
352 *at any convenient time.*

353 I have in the bank of England one thousand
354 pounds and in the Chamber of London
355 Orphan-stock seven hundred pounds
356 Principall mony purchased September
357 14th 1702. of John Mabb assignee, for
358 Sir Nathaniell Hern, and also two hundred
359 and two pounds twelve shillings and two
360 pence purchased of John King Mercer or
361 Merchant of London the same day. All these
362 summes I give and bequeath to erect an
363 Observatory and to maintein a studious, and
364 Learned Professor of Astronomy and
365 experimentall Philosophy, and to buy him

p. 13

366 and his successors, utensills, & instruments,
367 quadrants, telescopes etc & to buy, or rent,
368 or build an house, with or near the said
369 observatory; which Observatory, is to preserve
370 the said instruments in, fro[m] time to time,
371 for the use of the said Professor for the
372 time being, and the house to reside in; or
373 if hee bee resident in a Colledge, to lett, and
374 to reserve the rent for himselfe; but so,
375 as any ingenous Scholers or Gentlemen, may
376 resort to him, at all proper seasons, to bee instructed,
377 and improved by him, in the knowledge of Astronomy,
378 the Globes, Navigation, Naturall Philosophy,
379 Dialling, and other practicall parts of the Mathematicks,
380 in, or near Cambridge; And that hee bee obliged
381 to read in the Latin tongue, and Lecture every
382 term, or at least two, in every year, making,
383 or procuring, a suitable oration in latin,
384 before each lecture, to recommend the said
385 Sciences to the study of his Auditory, and to

p. 14

386 Print or to leave a fair manuscript in quarto,
387 one copy every year, in the University Library,
388 of such Lecture, to bee preserved there, among
389 their Archives, and to bee bound up together,
390 when they shall come to a fit volume,
391 by himselfe, or his next Successor, as
392 they were delivered, in the Physick-school
393 or elsewhere, according to the appointment
394 of the vice chancellour. Of the reading
395 of which Lecture I desire the Beadle to
396 give notice, in every Colledge, viva voce,
397 as they do for Consiosum ad Clerum;[11] for
398 which the Professor shall content them
399 or else shall cause only the School-bell
400 to bee rung, or both, as the Vice Chancellour
401 shall order. And I will that Doctor
402 Francis Thompson, Dr Covell, Master of
403 Christ's Colledge, and his successors there
404 the Mathematick Professor for the time being,
405 *Dr Bently M[aste]r of Trin[ity] Coll[ege]*
406 *with ye advice of Mr. Newtin in London,*

p. 15

407 Mr John Ellys Custos of Caius College, and Mr Flamsted
408 the Royall Mathematician at East Greenwich,
409 or their Survivors, shall constitute, make
410 or alter, such statutes and orders for the Election,
411 residence, qualifications and performances, as shall bee
412 most requisit[e] for the perpetuation & benefit of
413 the said Professor, and the improvement of Astronomy
414 and Naturall Philosophy, enjoyning him to keep a
415 boy or two to assist him in his observations, &
416 teach them Physicks, Mathematics, Navigation, &
417 Astronomy, if I settle not these statutes myselfe.
418 I will that the Principall mony bee not removed
419 from the Bank, till they have a very good purchase
420 to make with it. [ ][12] This is my last will & testament,

---

11   Translation uncertain; perhaps 'council to the clergy'.
12   A small space exists here, presumably intended to signify the start of a new section of the will dealing with James Plume and his executorship.

421 of which I declare Mr James Plume of Lambeth, scarlet-
422 dyer, my sole Executor, and do renounce all other pretended
423 wills, or Deeds of Gift, or bonds, or judgements, which I
424 hear the Shipsides falsely and impudently pretend.
425 Professing before God, in verbo sacerdotis, & morientis hominis[13]
426 I never made them any such, though I have forgiven
427 him an hundred pound bond, or two, made to mee.
428 To my sole Executor James Plume, for his pains, and
429 fidelity in discharge of my charities, I do bequeath all
430 my stock in the East India company, and all bonds due to
431 mee from them, at, or before Midsummer one thousand
432 seven hundred and four.

p. 16

433 But the thousand pounds paid to the United East India company
434 by mee. July. 21. 1704. as also another thousand pounds paid
435 them upon my account, by my Cousin James Plume July. 28.
436 1704. I will that the said two thousand pounds should
437 bee employed for makeing good my charities as to the
438 Workhouse for the poor of Maldon, Munden, & neighbo[u]r
439 Parishes, and other charities specified in my will,
440 and not be claimed by my Executor to whom I
441 have above willed all my East India stock, and
442 bonds only, w[hi]ch were due before these, or before
443 Midsummer 1704. Moreover I give to my
444 said Executor, and to his heirs for ever, the house, or
445 houses in Debtford, where Bat the Gardiner, and the
446 Widdow Stansby, & Watts, now live, the Mortgages &
447 Purchases whereof, are in Mr Powers' hands or keeping.
448 I also give him the thirteen pounds per An[num] due to
449 mee from the Treasury, for the debt of Sir Rob[ert] Viner,
450 which I hope the justice of the nation will one day make good.
451 I also give him three hundred pounds due from Lindsey ye Goldsmith.
452 Those Legacies I give him to requite his pains as Executor,
453 but all the rest I give to Charity, yt is my whole Estate, not
454 otherwise disposed of by this Will. If any of my kindred
455 or any else, upon any pretence, oppose this my last will
456 Hee shall forfeit his legacy, or any benefit by it.
457 Though I give all my goods to feed the poor, and

---

13 'upon my word as a priest, and a dying man'.

458 have not charity, it will profit mee nothing.
459 Blessed are the dead that dye in the Lord.
460 Come, Lord Jesu, come quickly.

p. 17

461 *Item I give Twenty pounds to the poor Officers of*
462 *rochester Church Organist & Lay Clerks &*
463 *any poor schollars, sons of poor men to be*
464 *distributed among them all, as Mr Bairstow, Mr*
465 *Peirson m[i]n[iste]r of Higham, Mr Thomas Huggins &*
466 *Mr Lavender shall think fitt to distribute*
467 *willing each of them twenty shillings for their pains*
468 *& in remembrance of mee Mrs Eyers 2 children.*
469 *And I hereby declare that this & the four sheets*
470 *of paper hereunto annexed containing in number seventeen*
471 *sides of paper to every of w[hi]ch sides I have sett my*
472 *hand to be my Last Will and Testam[en]t & in*
473 *Testimony thereof have hereunto sett my Hand & Seal*
474 *this 2ᵈ day of 7ber An[n]o Do[min]i 1704*
475 *Tho. Plume*
476 Signed sealed published &
477 declared by the said Testator
478 Thomas Plume as & for his
479 last Will & Testament in the
480 presence of us who have sett
481 our hands as witnesses hereunto
482 at the request & in the presence
483 of the said Testator
484 Wm Dawes
485 Francis Gillett
486 Tho: Power[14]

---

14 Two annotations on this page:
(1) This Will was shewed to Dr Francis Thompson at the tyme of his ex[am]i[n]a[t]ion taken in Chancery on the parte & behalfe of James Plume Executor of the last will & testam[en]t of Thomas Plume de[cea]sed, compl[ainan]t ag[ain]st Anne Beale defend[dan]t. A Trevor
(2) This Will was shewn to William Dawes Francis Gillett & Thomas Power att the times of their exa[m]i[na]c[i]ons taken in Chancery on the p[ar]t of the Attorney Gen[er]al att the Relation of S[ir] John Ellis Knt and others comp[lainan]ts against William Barnard and others Def[endan]ts. A Trevor

p. 19 [*recte* p. 18][15]

487 October. 20th 1704. I bequeath one hundred and
488 twenty pounds to be disposed of in some estate of inheritance
489 for setling of five pounds p[er] An[num] for ever, upon the Rector of
490 Longfield, and his successors for the time being
491 for ever, in augmentation of that Rectory
492 and to bee setled in such manner in Trust or
493 otherwise for that purpose as by Councill learned
494 in the Laws, shall in that behalfe bee advised,
495 and thought meet.
496 Tho Plume
497 Signed, sealed, published, and
498 declared, by the said Testator
499 Thomas Plume, as, & for a
500 codicill of his last will & testament
501 in the presence of us
502 Edward Waite
503 Francis Gillet
504 Randall Danson.[16]

505 November. 4. 1704. What mony of mine is in Chatham chest left there by
506 Paymaster Madox, I give to poor seamen, to bee distributed among them
507 soon after my death, as the Governours, & Mr Loton & Mr Stubs shall think fit.
508 and I will that the number of the children at Maldon, before
509 mention'd shall bee ten, two whereof shall bee yearly
510 put out apprentices either by sea, or land. *& also*
511 *I will, that Mr Nathaniel Plume of Yeldham bee a Trustee for*
512 *to inspect the severall charities left to Maldon ministers,*
513 *or poor people & have power besides to name another in whom*
514 *he can repose Trust & let the recorder be of ye quorum*
515 *either in person, or by his hand writing*
516 *& if any difference happens the last decision shall bee in ye B[isho]p*
517 *of ye Diocess.*

---

15 This page is numbered 19, but it is evident that the original is misnumbered and this is actually p. 18. There is no sign that a page has been removed or that content is missing.

16 This section annotated as follows:
This paper writing or Codicill was shown to Edward Waite Francis Gillett and Randall Danson att the times of their exa[mina]cion taken in Chancery on the part of the Attorney Generall at the Relation of Sr John Ellis Knt and others compl[ainan]ts against William Barnard and others def[endan]ts. A Trevor

p. 20 [*recte* p. 19]

518 I revoke out of my Will the gift of my two houses in Deptford from
519 my Executor Mr James Plume, & bequeath them to the
520 Minister, & Church wardens and Trustees of the
521 Grey-coat School in E. Greenwich to clothe, &
522 teach two boys in the said school, for ever.

523 I revoke also the hundred pounds to the one hundred
524 parrishes in Kent, since I now give more than that
525 summe, deposited long since by Pay Master Maddox
526 in Chattham Chest, to the poor seamen of S[i]r John
527 Hawkins' hospitall there as above said.

528 I leave twenty pounds to bee distributed by Mr Higgins,
529 and Mr Cart & Mr Burliston to poor Divines especially, or
530 other good Christians within the Deanery of Tunbridge or
531 Malling as they shall think fit, and particularly to
532 Mr Wintely, Mr Beak, and Mr Buck, within three
533 months after my decease.

534 I revoke the thousand pounds given in my will for buying in of Impropri-
535 ate Tithes to augment small Livings as Dr Thompson, Mr Stubs, &
536 the Governours of the Corporation of Ministers sons should think
537 fit, but do give four hundred pounds to Augment the vicarage of
538 All Saints in Maldon by buying impropriate tithes, or so much
539 glebe as may bee had for the same, for which the Incumbent
540 shall bee Resident and take care for dayly prayers.

541 Also I give to the corporation of ministers sons, for ye reliefe of
542 clergymen's Widdows and Orphans one hundred pounds.

543 I also bequeath one hundred pounds to the Trustees of Brumly College
544 for the better maintenance of the Widdows there for ever.

545 I give to the Minister and church wardens of Stone for their poor five pounds
546 to bee paid by the Tenant within three months after my decease, and five
547 shillings every Christmasse day for ever, out of the rent of Stone Castle
548 upon condic[i]on that the church wardens do give a discharge in full from
549 any other claim upon that part of Mr Took's estate which I bought of Mr
550 Etkins.

551 Tho: Plume
552 signed & sealed in the p[re]sence of
553 Edward Waite
554 Wm Dawes Randall Danson

p. 21 [*recte* p. 20]

[The grant of probate]

p. 22 [*recte* p. 21]

This last Codicil was shewed to Edward Waite,
William Dawes and Randall Danson att the time
of their exa[m]i[na]t[i]ons taken in Chancery of the p[ar]t of
the Attorney General att the relation of S[i]r John Ellis knt &
others compl[ainan]ts ag[ain]st William Barnard and others def[endan]ts
(and this certificate is here written for want of room on
the said last Codicill)
A. Trevor

Bibliography

Manuscript sources

Archives in private ownership
Letter, John White of Maldon to John Strutt of Terling Place, 4 February 1790 (by kind permission of Lord Rayleigh)

The British Library (BL)
ESTC r34405, *A catalogue of the library of ... Francis Bernard* (London, 1698)

Cambridge University Library (CUL)
UNIVERSITY ARCHIVES
D.XII. 14, purchase of estate in Balsham, Cambs., 1706

Dartford Almshouse Charity (DAC)
STONE CASTLE TRUST RECORDS (SCT)
Abstract of Deed of Feoffment, 1798
Accounts, 1787–1829; 1876–1911
Details of Stone Castle Charity, 1755
Indenture, the Revd Mr Lamb to the Trustees of Stone Charity, 7 May 1734
Minutes, 1787–1839; 1876–1901; 1901–52

Essex Record Office (ERO)
A13366, album of cuttings, prints, photographs and drawings relating to Essex churches, 1783–1885
D/ABR 8, fo. 248, will of Daniell Peake, 1668
D/ABR 15, fo. 305, will of John Brickwood, 1707 (probate copy)
D/ABW 19/74, will of William Hale, 1582
D/ABW 49/83, will of John Turnidge, 1628
D/ABW 53/184, will of John Soan, 1636
D/ABW 56/143, will of John Danes, 1638
D/ABW 59/47, will of Robert Brooke, 1647
D/ABW 77/136, will and codicil of William Carr, 1702

D/ABW 79/74, will of John Brickwood, 1707

D/AEA/7, 10, 11, 15, 26, 42, Archdeaconry of Essex, act books, 1572–3, 1576–9, 1579–80, 1590–2, 1611–13, and 1638–40

D/B 3/1/3, Maldon Borough, custumal, 1155–1760

D/B 3/1/19, Maldon Borough, court book, 1606–31

D/B 3/1/20, Maldon Borough, court book, 1631–64

D/B 3/1/34, Maldon Borough, record book, 1573–1661

D/B 3/1/35, Maldon Borough, enrolment book, 1661–1741

D/B 3/1/36, Maldon Borough, enrolment book, 1741–1869

D/B 3/3/80, Maldon Borough, chamberlains' account for 1635

D/B 3/3/81, Maldon Borough, chamberlains' account for 1648

D/B 3/3/98, Maldon Borough, chamberlains' account for 1673

D/B 3/3/108, Maldon Borough, chamberlains' account for 1624

D/B 3/3/159, Maldon Borough, misc. records, 1619–1812 (minute of assembly 4 November 1619)

D/B 3/3/183, Maldon Borough, rental, 1687

D/B 3/3/289, Maldon Borough, chamberlains' account for 1620

D/B 3/3/293–308, 310, 311, 319, 493, 502, Maldon Borough chamberlains' accounts for 1623–44, 1647, 1662, 1697, 1649, 1715

D/B 3/3/393/3, Maldon Borough, poll for new vicar, early 1620

D/B 3/3/393/25, Maldon Borough, Corporation resolution 14 March 1621

D/B 3/3/410, Maldon Borough, lease of house called Schoolmasters, 1650

D/B 3/3/501, Maldon Borough, chamberlains' account for 1702

D/B 3/3/578/24, Maldon Borough, proceedings and decree in Court of Record, 1632 (copy, c.1840)

D/B 3/3/622, Legal papers concerning Maldon Grammar School and trust estate of Ralph Breeder of Maldon, haberdasher, 1773–1898

D/B 3/3/661, Charitable Brief (Letters Patent) for the repair of the parish church of St Mary, Maldon (notes St Peter having been converted into a 'publique schoole'), 18 July 1628

D/B 3/3/664/1, Maldon Borough, court papers, depositions and bill (copies, 1819)

D/B 3/3/696, Maldon Borough, documents relating to the Breeder and Plume Educational Trust, 1901, 1930

D/B 3/3/726, Maldon Borough, papers concerning schemes to convert St Peter's churchyard to public open space, and widen roadway at junction of Market Hill and High Street, 1921–6

D/B 3/3/769, Maldon Borough, file of correspondence, including accounts for 1927–9; application by Plume Trustees to Carnegie United Kingdom Trust, 1931; appeal for funds by the mayor 'to our American friends'

D/B 3/11/13, Maldon Borough, conveyance of property in Heybridge, 25 August 1696

D/B 3/12/2, Maldon Borough, petition to the king, c.1660

BIBLIOGRAPHY

D/CF 62/26, Faculty St Peter, Maldon, 1923

D/CF 65/34, Faculty, St Peter, Maldon, 1926

D/CT 247A, B, Mundon tithe apportionment and map, c.1841

D/CT 306A, B, Salcott tithe apportionment and map, 1839

D/CT 365A, B, Tolleshunt Knights tithe apportionment and map, 1839

D/DB T610, Deeds to cottage and land in St Peter, Maldon, 1681–1819

D/DBG 81/1, Letter to James F. Hough, Headmaster, from Bursar of Christ's College, Cambridge, explaining that the Exhibition founded by Dr Plume of Maldon was abolished in 1860, with extract of the relevant statute, 1925

D/DCf B10/40, Brief for the Defendants and Report in Chancery Court suit Attorney General v. Revd Charles Matthew and others (trustees) relating to administration of Dr Plume's Charity, 1843

D/DCf Q9, Papers and documents relating to the administration of Dr Plume's Charity, c.1835–95

D/DCf Q15, Papers and documents relating to Breeder and Plume Educational Trust (Maldon), 1856–1973

D/DCm Q1, Printed Articles of Visitation and Enquiry ... within the Archdeaconry of London, c.1780

D/DHt O16, Faculty to widen road by taking part of churchyard of St Peter's, Maldon, 1766

D/DHt T174/11, deed of piece of land near Maldon hythe, 1687

D/DOp B45, Valuation of property of Plume's Charity: Iltney Farm, Mundon, 1834

D/DQs 137/3, Letters, legal opinions and expenses relating to the recovery of properties belonging to Ralph Breeder's Charity and particularly to Iltney Farm in Mundon, 1786–1840

D/DWd 8–13, 16, 17, deeds of Plume family's house in High Street, Maldon, 1633–1711

D/F 8/406, St Peter, Maldon, tower, plans 1927–31

D/F 63/5/136, Valuer's notebook, incl. Iltney Farm, Mundon, 1896–7

D/P 8/14/1, Apprenticeship indentures, Thorpe-le-Soken

D/P 123/1/1, Hazeleigh parish register, 1589–1812

D/P 132/1/1, St Mary, Maldon, parish register, 1558–1662

D/P 132/1/2, St Mary, Maldon, parish register, 1653–1722

D/P 169/14/1–2, 4, Apprenticeship indentures, Kirby-le-Soken

D/P 201/1/1, All Saints, Maldon, parish register, 1559–1669

D/P 201/1/2, All Saints, Maldon, parish register, 1595–1750

D/P 201/1/3, St Peter, Maldon, parish register, 1556–1695

D/P 201/1/4, St Peter, Maldon, parish register, 1695–1750

D/P 201/5/4, All Saints and St Peter parish, Maldon, accounts, 1716–53

D/P 201/12/1, All Saints parish, Maldon, accounts, 1731–1800

D/P 201/12/4, All Saints parish, Maldon, accounts, 1792–1803

D/P 201/25/2, copy of provisions of Plume Library trust deed, 1842–3

D/P 275/1/1, Great Yeldham, parish register, 1560–1812

Q/RSr 3, Register of charity memorials, 1813–53
Q/RSr 7/41, Accounts of Plume Charity, Borough of Maldon, 1855
T/B 288/14, letter about demolition of a house in Silver Street, Maldon, 1757

Greenwich Heritage Centre (GHC)
G. 1A/1.1, Greenwich parish overseers accounts, 1690–1703
G. 1A/2.1, Greenwich parish churchwardens accounts, 1616–63
G 3:2, St Alfege, Greenwich, vestry minutes 1796–1813
John Kimbell, manuscript of the Charities of Greenwich

Historic England/National Monuments Record (Swindon)
National Heritage List for England list, entry numbers 1256632 and 1338030
Royal Commission Inspector's notes and plan of library building, 1920

Hoare's Bank
Customer ledgers 2, 3, 5
Daily cash book (7 July 1684)

Kent Local History Centre (KLHC)
DRa/VpM1, citation for a visitation of the Deanery of Malling
DRa/VpRl, citation for a visitation of the Deanery of Rochester

London Metropolitan Archives (LMA)
LMA/4442/01/01/01/13–16, John Roan School Records, leases and deeds in Greenwich, Deptford and Lewisham, 1723–1766
LMA/4442/02/01/01/001, Orders of Mr Roanes Schoole
P78/ALF/001–2, St Alfege, Church Street, Greenwich, parish registers (on microfilm X094/109)

Medway Archives Centre (MAC)
PARISH RECORDS
P150B/1/3, Strood St Nicholas parish register, 1695–1715
P306/1/12, Rochester St Nicholas parish marriage register, 1673–1727
P314/1/1, Grain parish register, 1653–1768
P336/1/02, Shorne parish register, 1644–1812
P352/8/1, Stone parish, vestry minutes, 1739–1825
P352/25/2, Stone parish, correspondence, 1896–1927

ROCHESTER DEAN & CHAPTER RECORDS
DRc/Ac/04, Rochester Cathedral minute book, 1695–1706, books 10–12
DRc/Ac/2/2, Chapter book 1

DRc/Arb/2, The Red book
DRc/S02, Rochester Cathedral register, 1694–1754

ROCHESTER CITY COUNCIL RECORDS
RCA/L6/2, Deed of Gift, 16/1/1724
RCA/O2/1, Register of Freemen 1663–1711, microfilm 375

SIR JOHN HAWKINS KNIGHT HOSPITAL RECORDS
CH108/92, Letter Thomas Power to John Walsall, 4th October 1707
CH108/191/1, Plume bequest, 16/9/1705
CH108/194, Draft of instrument, 1707

The National Archives (TNA)
C 6/348/11, Attorney General v Bernard, 1706 (concerning charitable bequest under will Thomas Plume archdeacon of Rochester, of Cambridgeshire, Essex and Kent)
C 6/362/46, Plume v Beale, 1710
C 6/550/309, Plume v [unknown], 1706
C 11/1486/32, Plume v Fleetwood, 1730
C 11/2637/18, Fage v Bishop of Lincoln, 1717
C 47/39/55, Guild certificate, Fraternity of the Assumption in the church of St Peter, Maldon
C 108/15, Deeds relating to Maldon, Heybridge, Layford, Tollesbury, Earls Colne, East Hanningfield, Bradwell etc., Essex, 1377–1686
E 134/9JasI/Mich38, depositions in case Maldon Corporation v Robert Sprignell, 1611
E 134/6and7ChasI/Hil10, papers dealing with case Maldon Corporation *v.* Thomas Plume, 1631, 1632
HLG 51/667, Ministry of Health records, Purchase of Plume building adjoining St Peter's Church tower, 1932–33
IR 30/12/237, tithe map, Mundon, 1841
PROB 3/27/188, Plume, James, Vauxhall, parish of Lambeth, county Surrey, esq. Anne Plume relict and adtrix (17 October 1728)
PROB 6/45, probate act book, 1670
PROB 10/1387, will of Dr Thomas Plume, 1704 (original)
PROB 11/113/233, will of Ralph Breeder, 1609
PROB 11/123/64, will of Benjamin King, 1613
PROB 11/123/117, will of Henry Wentworth, 1613
PROB 11/125/553, will of Thomas Plume, 1615
PROB 11/140/281, will of Edward Hastler, 1622
PROB 11/159/401, will of Paul Dewes, 1630
PROB 11/165/637, will of Annastacy Wentworth, 1631
PROB 11/260/616, will of John Soan of Maldon, 1656
PROB 11/298/753, will of Edward Hyde, 1660

PROB 11/319/164, will of John Greene, 1666
PROB 11/354/546, will of John Stevens of Maldon, 1677
PROB 11/384/89, will of Sir William Boreman of East Greenwich, Kent, 1686
PROB 11/407/226, will of Thomas Barlow, Bishop of Lincoln (d. 1691)
PROB 11/481/24, will of Dr Thomas Plume, 1704 (probate copy)
PROB 11/520/273, will of Humphrey Gower, Master of St John's College, Cambridge (d. 1711)
PROB 11/583/4, will of John Loton, 1722
PROB 11/762/41, will of Anna Plume, 1748
PROB 20/260, will of Robert Boreman, 1675
SP 22, orders and papers of the Committee for Plundered Ministers, 1642–53
SP 28/355/3, accounts of the revenues of Rochester Cathedral, 1644–6
WORK 14/1239, Office of Works file, St Peter's Church tower

The National Portrait Gallery
NPG, D9375, Engraving of Sir John Comyns, by George Vertue after an unknown artist, 1744

Royal Greenwich Observatory (RGO)
RGO 1/33, fo. 130, Flamsteed to Whiston 13 February 1705/6

The Society for the Protection of Ancient Buildings (SPAB)
File, Plume Library Building, incl. report by D.E. Nye, 11 September 1930
File, St Peter's Tower

Suffolk Record Office (SRO)
Bury Archive Office, IC500/1/106/21, will of Justinian Whitter 1648

Thomas Plume Library, Maldon (TPL)
For online catalogues of books, 1761, 1848, 1959 and 2004 see: http://www.thomasplumeslibrary.co.uk/catalogue/the-collections-and-their-catalogues/
Note that books in the Plume Library have a standard number, in the form B00000.
MANUSCRIPTS
MA0001, 'Notebook on theological commonplaces'
MA0002, 'Notebook of parish accounts for St Giles-in-the-Fields 1663–75'
MA0005, 'Notebook on theological commonplaces'
MA0006, 'List of books with prices from the bishop of Ely's collection'
MA0007, 'Notebook containing calculations and reading notes'
MA0008, 'Notebook of theological commonplaces'
MA0009, 'Reading notes on classical texts'
MA0011, 'Reading notes on theology and church history'

BIBLIOGRAPHY

MA0013, 'Reading notes on rhetoric, proverbs and figures'
MA0015, 'Treatise on England's economic status'
MA0016, 'Draft correspondence, poetry and drama'
MA0017, 'Miscellany of reading notes, commonplaces and sermons heard'
MA0018, 'Reading notes on Chrysostom's oration on Genesis, and sermon notes'
MA0022, 'Notes for Sermons on 2 Timothy 3 and 4'
MA0024, 'Draft treatise entitled An Antidote Against Swearing'
MA0026, 'Eight sermons preached in Kent 1645–1650'
MA0027, 'Notes from reading Aristotle'
MA0029 (formerly MS 7), 'Notes from reading on theological topics between 1650/1 and 1656'
MA0030, 'Sermon entitled "Sweare Not"'
MA0031, 'Miscellany of correspondence, commonplaces and reading notes'
MA0036, 'Thirteen sermons preached in Kent 1645–1650'
MA0039, 'Ten sermons preached in Kent 1645–1650'
MA0040, 'Reading notes from Byzantine and Germanic authors'
MA0041, 'Theological commonplaces and notes from reading'
MA0042, 'Notes from reading two books by Giralamo Zanchii'
MA0044, 'Sermons preached in various locations during 1638–1646'
MA0045, 'Sermons on Galatians and Psalm 15'
MA0047, 'Reading notes made between 1661–1668'
MA0048, 'Four sermons followed by reading notes from Roman and Greek authors'
MA0050, 'Reading notes made between 1667–1684'
MA0053, 'Sermons heard in Hertfordshire'
MA0054, 'Notes from reading history, natural philosophy and theology between 1663–1692'
MA0055, 'Notes from reading natural philosophy, geometry, astrology, physiology and mathematics'
MA0056, 'Miscellany of sermon notes, reading notes, Hebrew grammar and accounts'
MA0057, 'Commonplace book for natural philosophy and physics'
MA0059, 'Sermons on Psalm 101, Matthew 21 and Galatians 5'
MA0065, 'Notes from reading between 1660–1687'
MA0066, 'Notes on the Psalms and sermons heard in Maldon in 1640s'
MA0068, 'Study of physics and philosophy, including calculations'
MA0070, 'Miscellany notebook of sermons, reading notes, accounts, genealogy and a recipe'
MA0071, 'Miscellany notebook of astrological diagrams, reading notes, sermon notes and accounts'
MA0072, 'Reading notes made between 1667–1692'
MA0074, 'Reading notes made between 1659–1668'
MA0076, 'Sermons heard in 1640s'
MA0077, 'Reading notes and draft theological treatise'
MA0083, 'Sermons heard in Hertfordshire'

MA0087, 'Reading notes on logic'
MA0089, 'Reading notes on theological topics'
MA0090, 'Reading notes on the visions of Cyrus, Scythians, Amazons, Hercules and Plutarch's thesis'
MA0091, 'Notebook of Latin commonplaces'
MA0092, 'Exposition on Septuagint and notes from sermons heard in Salisbury 1636–1640'
MA0093, 'Notes from five sermons preached in Cambridge and notes on prayer'
MA0095, 'Notes from reading (oratory, cosmology and drama) and letters'
MA0096, 'Miscellany of Greek vocabulary, reading notes, sermons heard in Chelmsford in the 1640s'
MA0097, 'Notes from reading, sermons and scripture notes 1640s'
MA0099, 'Reading notes made between 1657–1687'
MA0105, 'Notes from reading'
MA0106, 'Notes taken from Geoffrey Fenton's 1599 translation of Francesco Guicciardini's *History of Italie*'
MA0107, Bundle of loose-leaf papers (Bundle A)
MA0107, A.21, 'St Jo. 20:29'
MA0107, A.23–39, sermon notes by Thomas Plume
MA0107, A.45, 'St. Jo. 19:30'
MA0107, A.47, 'St. Luke 24:36'
MA0108, Bundle of loose-leaf papers (Bundle B)
MA0108, B.1–29, 39, 48, sermon notes by Thomas Plume
MA0109, Bundle of loose-leaf papers (Bundle C)
MA0109, C.27–32, 34, sermon notes by Thomas Plume
MA0109, C.39, 'Fragment dated Grenwich[sic] Jan. 97', Thomas Plume
MA0109, C.41, 'A recipe for brewing'
MA0109, C.48, 'at foot of hill, funeral', Thomas Plume
MA0110, Bundle of loose-leaf papers (Bundle D)
MA0110, D.1, 42. Items by Thomas Plume
MA0110, D.38, 'A letter asking a friend to meet his Father [London]'
MA0111, Bundle of loose-leaf papers (Bundle E)
MA0111, E.5, 'Letter relating to money due'
MA0111, E.8, 'Notes in an abbreviated form on the back of an address label, addressed to Plume at the house of Lady Mary Armine (1594–1676)'
MA0111, E.11, 'Letter dated 11th December 1701 proposing joint hire of a coach from London to Dartford'
MA0111, E.16, 'Collections from Chrysostom on Genesis 1648'
MA0111, E.20, 'Notes from Paulo Sarpi's *History of the Council of Trent*'
MA0111, E.22, 'Note from tract: "de malis angelis" by H. Zanchius'
MA0111, E.23, 'The fruit who it is'
MA0111, E.26, 'Latin exposition on the apocalypse', see also MA0113, G.12

BIBLIOGRAPHY

MA0111, E.34, 'What is determined in God's'
MA0111, E.35, 'Sermon on St. John 14:23'
MA0111, E.36, 'Sermon on Gen. 6:5, 7'
MA0111, E.41, 'Reading notes from a book Notitia Imperii'
MA0111, E.49, 'Old commonplace book'
MA0112, Exposition of Psalm 25 divided into individual sermons, using the Book of Common Prayer numbering of verses (Bundle F)
MA0113, Bundle of loose-leaf papers (Bundle G)
MA0113, G.1 'Scribal copy of Lancelot Andrewes treatise on "The forme of church government"'
MA0113, G.3, 'Latin verses on Psalm 49:20'
MA0113, G.4, 'Latin verses on Daniel 2: Nebuchadnezzer's 1st vision'
MA0113, G.12, 'Treatise "The brief meaning of the Apocalypse"'
MA0113, G.19, 'Draft treatise on tithes dated 1648'
MA0113, G.20, 'Inventory for Plume's books shipped from Greenwich to the Library in six casks dated 29 November 1704'
MA0114, Bundle of loose-leaf papers (Bundle H)
MA0114, H.25, 'The second use of'
MA0115, Bundle of loose-leaf papers (Bundle I)
MA0117 (formerly MS 30), 'Latin phrase book with notes from sermons and anecdotes'
MA0118 (formerly MS 31), 'Notebook for verses continued as a record of expenditure at university 1646–1650'
MA0119 (formerly MS 25), 'Notebook of anecdotes and reading notes 1650s'
MA0120, Minute Book (of Dr Plume's Trustees), 1717–1826
MA0121, Minute Book (of Dr Plume's Trustees), 1827–43
MA0123, Minute Book of Dr Plume's Trustees, Maldon, 1845 (1843–1968)
MA0126, 12/1/2–22, Accounts 1789–1809
MA0127, 12/1/23–27, Accounts 1844–49, 1858
MA0131, 12/2/4, Maldon Grammar School accounts, 1909
MA0131, 12/2/7, Letter dated 09/09/1918 from Maldon Grammar School to the clerk of the charity
MA0135, Dr Plume's Trust's Expenditure 1822–1837
MA0140, 'Fitting up Dr Plume's Library'
MA0147, Bills and receipts for library and school buildings and furniture and fittings, 1789–1999
MA0149, Red folder, Lectures, 1792–1893
MA0154, Lectures – attendance by poor, payments & correspondence, 1848–90
MA0155, 6/1/1, rent charge document, Iltney farm, 1610 (copy)
MA0157, Apprenticeship indentures, 1803–88, incl. typescript list by Gwyneth Shacklock (n.d.)
MA0158, item 46, letter from E.R. Horwood, dated 29/10/1881
MA0158, Red folder, Apprentices *c.*1842–1894, receipts, letters and indentures

MA0159, A Catalogue of the Books found in the Plume Library: viz January 1st 1761 by R. Hay, MA, Librarian

MA0160 and MA0161, Revd Robert Crane's catalogue. A duplicate manuscript catalogue of the books now found in Archdeacon Plume's library in Maldon, commenced 24th July 1848 (2 copies)

PP0526, *The Maldonian*, an incomplete collection of the Maldon school magazine

PP1960, 'Clark, A., Essex Library Notes' (from Bodl. MSS Eng. Misc., C, 42–3)

Uncat., Beaumont's account, 17 December 1908

Uncat., catalogue of pictures

Uncat., Chancellor's report, 12 February 1929

Uncat., Chancellor's report, 16 February 1929

Uncat., Charity Commission, Order for vesting in Official Trustee of Charity Lands, 24th February 1953

Uncat., Charity Commission, Scheme, 13th October 1908

Uncat., Christian's report, 20 June 1876

Uncat., conveyance and extract from H.M. Land Registry with Maldon Town Council (title number EXC554518)

Uncat., letter to the Plume Library dated 7 March 1975, from T.E. Mathew, Rouge Dragon Pursuivant of Arms, The College of Arms, London, E.C.4

Uncat., Minister of Education, Scheme (including Appointment of Trustees), 20th June 1952

Uncat., note on Library Rules

Uncat., Nye's report of work completed, 20 June 1932

Uncat., paper on 'The Plume Library', n.d., after 1952

Uncat., papers on 'Plume Library, Maldon', 15/10/1949; 25/04/1950; 30/06/1950

Uncat., Plume Box 5, Bundles 5/21 and 5/22 (new Maldon Grammar School leases, 08/05/1906)

Uncat., 'Plume Building' file, 1875–1995

Uncat., report of the Town Clerk on the Charities of Maldon (January, 1897)

Uncat., Saunders' letter, 17 August 1875, and account, November 1876

Uncat., Saunders' letter to trustees, 6 May 1879

Uncat., Trustees' minutes, 1987–8

Trinity College Cambridge, Library

T.49.21, copy of C. Huygens, *Kosmotheoros* (1698)

The Wisbech & Fenland Museum

Wisbech Town Library, A6.17, Michael Antonius Frances de Urrutigoyti, *De Ecclesiis Cathedralibus Erumque Privilegiis et Praerogativus Tractus* ... (Lyons, 1665)

Printed primary sources, including acts of parliament

An Act for the Registering and Securing of Charitable Donations (The Charitable Donations Registration Act), 52 Geo. III, c. 102 (1812).

Building News, 31 (1876).

Calendar of State Papers Domestic, Charles I, Charles II, William III (HMSO, 1858–1937).

Charity Commissioners, *Digest of the Reports made by the Commissioners of Inquiry into Charities...* (London, 1843).

Chelmsford Chronicle, 11, 18 August, 16 November 1876; 2 July 1926.

Disused Burial Grounds Act 1884.

Emmison, F.G. (ed.), *Feet of Fines for Essex*, vol. vi (Oxford, 1993).

Evelyn, John, *The Diary of John Evelyn*, vol. iv (London, 1955).

Forbes, E.G., Murdin, L. and Willmoth, F. (eds), *The Correspondence of John Flamsteed, the First Astronomer Royal, Vol. 3, 1703–1719* (Bristol, 2002).

Gardiner, S.R. (ed.), *The Constitutional Documents of the Puritan Revolution 1625–1660* (3rd edn, Oxford, 1906).

Halliwell-Phillips, J.O. (ed.), *The Loyal Garland: A Collection of some Songs from the Seventeenth Century Reprinted from a Black Letter Copy supposed to be Unique* (London, 1850).

Hull, F. (ed.), *Dr John Warner's Visitations of the Diocese of Rochester, 1663 and 1670* (Kent Archaeological Society, new ser., Maidstone, 1991).

Journals of the House of Commons, vol. 23 (London, 1803).

Journal of the House of Lords, vol. 6, 1643 (London, 1767–1830) (https://www.british-history.ac.uk/lords-jrnl/vol6).

Kelly, F.R. (ed.), *The Post Office Directory of Essex* (London, 1874).

Local Government Act 1972.

London Gazette, 16 November 1714 and 10 September 1715.

McCulloch, J.R., *A Dictionary, Geographical, Statistical and Historical of the Various Countries, Places, and Principal Natural Objects in the World* (London, 1842).

The Public Catalogue Foundation, *Oil Paintings in Public Ownership in Essex* (London, 2006).

The Reports of the Commissioners appointed ... to enquire concerning charities in England and Wales relating to the County of Essex (London, 1819–37).

Royal Archaeological Institute of Great Britain & Ireland, *Colchester Meeting, August 1 to 8, 1876: Full Report of the Proceedings* (Colchester, 1876).

Sadler, M.E., *Report on Secondary and Higher Education in Essex* (Chelmsford, 1906).

White, W., *History, Gazetteer, and Directory of the County of Essex* (Sheffield, 1848).

Wright, C.E. and R.C. (eds), *The Diary of Humfrey Wanley, 1715–1726*, vol. 1 (London, 1966).

Early printed books (pre-1800)
Books extant in the Plume Library are given their standard numbers at the end of the relevant entry. Entries starting PP are replacements or additions to the library.

The Acts and Negotiations ... at Ryswick (1698); B01046.
Allestree, R., attrib., *The Art of Patience under all Afflictions* (1684); B01234.
Allestree, R., attrib., *The Causes of the Decay of Christian Piety* (1667).
Allestree, R., attrib., *The Lively Oracles Given to Us* (1679); B01228.
Allestree, R., attrib., *Whole Duty of Man* (1657).
Alsted, J.H., *Thesaurus Chronologiae* (1624); B02769.
Ames, W., *Bellarminus Enervatus* (1629); B05610.
Andrewes, L., *A summarie view of the government both of the old and new testament whereby the episcopall government of Christs church is vindicated out of the rude draughts of Lancelot Andrewes, late Bishop of Winchester: whereunto is prefixed (as a preamble to the whole) a discovery of the causes of the continuance of these contentions touching church-government out of the fragments of Richard Hooker* (Oxford, 1641).
Anon., *Account of Several Workhouses ... as also of Several Charity Schools* (2nd edn, 1732).
Aquinas, T., *Summa Totius Theologiae* (Paris, 1615); B04566.
Articles of Visitation and Inquiry Concerning Matters Ecclesiasticall according to the Laws and Canons of the Church of England Exhibited to the Ministers, Church-Wardens and Sidemen of every parish within the Diocese of Rochester, by the Right Reverend Father in God, John, Lord Bishop of Rochester (1662); B01701.
Arwaker, E., *Fons Perennis. A ... Poem on Making Sea-water Fresh* (1686); B02354.
Assheton, W.A., *Vindication of the Immortality of the Soul* (1703); B02791.
Bacon, F., *Baconiana, or, Certain genuine remains of Sr. Francis Bacon, Baron of Verulam, and Viscount of St. Albans in arguments civil and moral, natural, medical, theological, and bibliographical* (London, 1679); B03614.
Bacon, F., *The tvvoo bookes of Francis Bacon. Of the proficience and aduancement of learning, diuine and humane To the King* (London, 1605).
Bainbridge, J., *Astronomicall Description of the Late Comet* (1619); B07453.
Bayly, T., *The Royal Charter granted unto kings* (London, 1649); B00319.
Bayly, J., *Two sermons; The angell guardian. The light enlightening. Preached by Iohn Bayly ...* (Oxford, 1630); B03004.
Beck, C., *Universal Character* (1657); B01120.
Bernard, E., *Catalogi librorum manuscriptorum Angliae et Hiberniae in unum collecti; cum indice alphabetico* (Oxford, 1697); B04508.
Bishop, W., *A reformation of a Catholike deformed* (1604); B07423.
Bolton, R., *Last and Learned Works* (1632); B00417.
Book of Common Prayer (London, 1662).
Boothby, R., *Breife Discovery ... of Madagascar* (1646); B06088.

Boreman, R., *A Mirrour of Christianity, and a Miracle of Charity; or, A true and exact narrative of the life and death of the most virtuous Lady Alice Dutchess Duddeley. Published after the sermon in the church of St. Giles in the Fields by R.B. D.D. rector of the said church on Sunday the 14th of March, MDCLXIX* (London, 1669).

Boreman, R., *An Antidote against Swearing: to which is annexed an appendix concerning an assertory and promissory oath in reference to the statutes of the two now flourishing sister universities. Also a short catalogue of some remarkable judgments from God upon blasphemers, &c. By R Boreman, D.D. and Fellow of Trinity Colledge in Cambridge* (London, 1662); B03364.

Boreman, R., *Hypocrasie Unvailed and Jesuitisme Unmasked* (1662).

Boreman, R., *The Country-mans Catechisme: or, The Churches plea for tithes. Wherein is plainely discovered, the duty and dignity of Christs ministers, and the peoples duty to them. By R.B. B.D. Fellow of Trin. Col. Camb.* (London, 1651).

Boyle, R., *Some Considerations Touching the Usefulnesse of Experimental Naturall Philosophy* (Oxford, 1664); B01347.

Bray, T., *An Essay Towards Promoting all Useful Knowledge both Divine and Human, in all Parts of His Majesty's Dominions, Both at Home and Abroad* (London, 1697 [1698]).

Bray, T., *Bibliotheca Parochialis, or, A scheme of such theological heads both general and particular, as are more peculiarly requisite to be well studied by every pastor of a parish together with a catalogue of books which may be read upon each of those points* (London, 1697).

Bright, G., *A Treatise of Prayer* (1678); B01034.

Buck, M., *An Anniversary Sermon on the Martyrdom of King Charles the First, of Blessed memory. delivered on Jan. 30th 1701/2 by Maximilian Buck* (London, 1702); B05871.

Burton, R., *Anatomy of Melancholy* (1628); B01545.

Buxtorf, J., *Hebrew Dictionary* (Basle, 1607). There are other editions in TPL: B06283; B06453; B01622.

Calamy, E., *The Nonconformist's Memorial*, 2nd edition by S. Palmer, vol. I (London, 1778).

Cappel, J., *Historia Sacra* (1613); B06690.

Catalogus Variorum Librorum ... Amb. Atfield (1685).

Chamberlayne, E., *Angliae Notitia, or the Present State of England ... Time, Part 1* (London, 1671, 1687); PP1981 (1687 edn).

A Collection of Papers printed by Order of the Society for the Propagation of the Gospel in Foreign Parts (London, 1715).

Cox, T., *Magna Britannia, Antiqua & Nova: or, a new, exact, and comprehensive survey of the ancient and present state of Great-Britain*, vol. 1 (London, 1738 edn).

Cyprian, D., *Caecilii Cypriani ... Martyriis Opera* (Paris, 1616); B06548.

Cyprian, D., *Caecilii Episcopi ... Opera* (Antwerp, 1641); B04270.

Cyprian, D., Saint, bishop of Carthage, *Sancti Caecilii Cypriani Opera recognita & illustrata per Joannem Oxoniensem episcopum; accedunt Annales Cyprianici, sive,*

Tredecim annorum; quibus S. Cyprianus inter Christianos versatus est, brevis historia chronologice delineata per Joannem Cestriensem (Oxford, 1682); B00616.

Dallington, R., *Aphorismes* (1629); B05702.

Danes, J., *Paralipomena Orthographiae, Etymologiae, Prosodiae, ... Distributa* (London, 1638) [i.e. 1639]; B04640.

Davies, Sir John, *The true causes why Ireland was never entirely subdued ...* (London, 1612).

Descartes, R., *Meditationes de prima philosophia: in quibus dei existentia, & animae humanae à corpore distinctio, demonstrantur. His adjunctae sunt variae objectiones doctorum virorum in istas de Deo & anima demonstrationes; cum responsionibus authoris* (London, 1654); B04832.

Descartes, R., *Opera Philosophica* (Amsterdam, 1672); B04127.

Dugdale, W., *Monasticon Anglicanum* (1655–73); B00445.

Erasmus, *Adagia* (1500).

Evelyn, J., *Sylva* (1670); B00467.

Gassendi, P., *Institutio Astronomica* (n.d.); B06928 (missing in 2020).

Gassendi, P., *Tychonis Brahei ... vita* (Hague, 1655); B04678.

Godwyn, M., *The Negro's and Indians Advocate, Suing for their Admission to the Church* (1680), and *Supplement* (1681); B01800 and B01802.

Greenham, R., *The Workes* (1605); B02568.

Grotius, *De Jure Belli ac Pacis* (1650); B04013.

Hacket, J., *A Century of Sermons upon several remarkable subjects preached by the Right Reverend Father in God, John Hacket, late Lord Bishop of Lichfield and Coventry; published by Thomas Plume* (London, 1675); B01512.

Hacket, J., *Scrinia Reserata: a Memorial off'rd to the Great Deservings of John Williams, DD, who some time held the Places of Ld Keeper of the Great Seal of England, Ld Bishop of Lincoln, and Lord Archbishop of York. Containing a Series of the Most Remarkable Occurrences and Transactions of his Life, in Relation to both Church and State* (London, 1693); B00489.

Hale, M., *A Discourse touching Provision for the Poor* (London, 1683); B06032.

Hasted, E., *The History and Topographical Survey of the County of Kent*, 4 vols (Canterbury, 1778–99); PP0354.

Herle, C., *Davids song of three parts: delivered in a sermon preached before the right Honorable the House of Lords, at the Abby-Church in Westminster, upon the 15. day of June, 1643. Being the day appointed for publike thanksgiving for Gods great deliverance of the Parliament, citie and kingdome, from the late most mischievous conspiracy against all three* (London, 1643); B02961.

Heylen, P., *Cyprianus Anglicus ... till his death* (London, 1668); B04068.

Hobbes, T., *Leviathan* (London, 1651) (1670 edn in TPL, B06346).

Hodges, T., *A Treatise of Marriage with a defence of the 32th Article of Religion ... better to Godliness* (London, 1673); B05405.

Hooke, R., *Micrographia* (1665).

Huygens, C., *Kosmotheoros* (1698, 1699); B07053 (London, 1698); B06068 (Hague, 1699).

Hyde, E., *A Christian Vindication of Truth against Errour concerning ... 2. Of Priests Marriage ... by Edw Hide ... in Berks* (London, 1659); B03383.

Hyde, E., *The True Catholicks Tenure, or A good Christians certainty which he ought to have of his religion, and may have of his salvation. By Edvvard Hyde D.D. sometimes fellow of Trinity Colledge in Cambridge, and late rector resident of Brightwell in Berks.* (Cambridge, 1662); B06545.

Hyde, E., *History of the ... Civil Wars* (1702).

Jonson, B., *The Workes of Benjamin Jonson* (London, 1640); B06128.

Locke, J., *A Letter to the ... Bishop of Worcester* (1697); B04955.

Locke, J., *Essay Concerning Humane Understanding* (1694); PP0476.

Lubinus, E., *Clavis Graecae Linguae* (1640); B06444.

Lysons, D., 'Cheam', in *The Environs of London: volume 1: County of Surrey* (London, 1792), pp. 137–58 (online edition).

Lysons, D., 'Greenwich', in *The Environs of London: volume 4: Counties of Herts, Essex and Kent* (London, 1796), pp. 426–93 (online edition).

de Mariana, J., *Tractatus vii de Adventu B. Jacobi Apostoli in Hispaniam* (1609); B00152.

Marshall, S., *The song of Moses the servant of God, and the song of the Lambe: opened in a sermon preached to the Honorable House of Commons, at their late solemne day of thanksgiving, Iune 15. 1643. for the discovery of a dangerous, desperate, and bloudy designe, tending to the utter subversion of the Parliament, and of the famous city of London* (London, 1643); B02869.

Mayer, J., *Many Commentaries in One* (London, 1647); B04547.

Molina, L., *Liberi Arbitrii cum Gratiae Donis ... Concordia* (1595); B06004.

Morant, P., *The History and Antiquities of the County of Essex*, 2 vols (London, 1768); PP1221, PP1956.

de Mornay, P., *Fowre books* (1600); B05698.

Naudé, G., tr. J. Evelyn, *Instructions Concerning Erecting of a Library* (London, 1661).

Nektarios, *Nectarii ... Confutatio Imperii Papae in Ecclesiam*, trans. by P. Allix (London, 1702); B02626.

Newcourt, R., *Repertorium Ecclesiasticum Parochiale Londinense*, 2 vols (London, 1710); PP1982-3.

Newton, I., *Philosophiæ Naturalis Principia Mathematica*, 3 vols (1687); PP0464.

Oldenburger, P.A., *Notitia rerum illustrium imperii* (Geneva, 1669); B06356.

Ovid, *Metamorphoses* (1751); PP1535.

Pflacher, M., *Analysis Typica* (1587); B00789.

Randolph, T., *Cornelianum dolium; Comœdia lepidissima, optimorum judiciis approbata, & theatrali coryphœo, nec immeritò, donata, palma chorali apprimè digna. Auctore, T.R. ingeniosissimo hujus ævi heliconio* (London, 1638); B00694.

Salmon, N., *The History and Antiquities of Essex. From the Collections of Thomas Jekyll of Bocking, Esq.* (London, 1740–2).

Scaligero, G.C., *Iulii Caesaris Scaligeri Exotericarum exercitationum liber XV. De subtilitate, ad Hieronymum Cardanum: In fine duo sunt indices: prior breuiusculus, continens sententias nobiliores: alter opulentissimus, pene omnia complectens* (Hanover, 1620).

Scaliger, J.J., *Opus novum de Emendatione Temporum* (Paris, 1583).

Scaliger, J.J., *Thesaurus temporum, Eusebii Chronicorum Canonum omnimodae historae libri duo, interprete Hieronymo* (Leiden, 1606).

Shepherd, A., *Tables for Correcting the Apparent Distance of the Moon and a Star from the Effects of Refraction and Parallax* (Cambridge, 1772).

Sidway, J., *The Reasons of the Conversion of Mr John Sidway from the Romish to the Protestant Religion ...* (London, 1681).

Smith, R., *Complete System of Opticks* (1738).

Smith, R., *Harmonics, or the Philosophy of Musical Sounds* (1749).

The song of Moses the servant of God, and the song of the Lambe: opened in a sermon preached to the Honorable House of Commons, at their late solemne day of thanksgiving, Iune 15. 1643. for the discovery of a dangerous, desperate, and bloudy designe, tending to the utter subversion of the Parliament, and of the famous city of London (London, 1643); B02869.

Sprat, T., *The History of the Royal Society of London* (London, 1667); B01249.

Talbot, P., *Blakloanae Haeresis ... Historia et Confutatio* (Ghent (Gandavum), 1675); B01566.

Terence in English (1641); B00206.

Urrutigoyti, Michael Antonius Frances de, *De Ecclesiis Cathedralibus Erumque Privilegiis et Praerogativus Tractus ...* (Lyons, 1665); B00446.

Vince, S., *A Complete System of Astronomy*, 3 vols (1797–1808).

Vines, R., *Magnalia Dei ab Aquilone; set forth in a sermon preached before the right honourable the Lords and Commons, at St Margaret's Westminster, upon Thursday Iuly 18, 14644, being the day of publike thanksgiving for the great victory obtained against Prince Rupert and the Earle of Newcastles forces neere Yorke* (London, 1644); B04419.

Walsingham, F., *A Search made into Matters of Religion* (1609); B00421.

Williams, W.P., *Report of Cases Argued and Determined in the High Court of Chancery*, vol. 1 (London, 1740).

Zanchi, G., *Clariss. viri D. Hier. Zanchii Omnium operum theologicorum tomi octo [...]* (Geneva, 1619); B05690.

Zouch, R., *Elementa Jurisprudentiae* (1652); B04453.

Books and articles

Aslet, C., *The Story of Greenwich* (London, 1999).

Baker, R., 'On the Farming of Essex', *Journal of the Royal Agricultural Society of England*, 5 (1845), pp. 1–43.

Beadle, R., 'Medieval English Manuscripts at Auction', *The Book Collector*, 53 (2004), pp. 46–63.

Beal, P., *In Praise of Scribes: Manuscripts and their Makers in Seventeenth-Century England* (Lyell Lectures in Bibliography, Oxford, 1998).

Beal, P., 'My Books are the Great Joy of My Life', *The Book Collector*, 46 (1997), pp. 350–78.

Bennett, G.V., *The Tory Crisis in Church and State 1688-1730: The Career of Francis Atterbury Bishop of Rochester* (Oxford, 1975).

Bettley, J. and Pevsner, N., *The Buildings of England. Essex* (New Haven, CT, and London, 2007).

Bolt, B.A., Obituary of Harold Jeffreys, *Quarterly Journal of the Royal Astronomical Society*, 31 (1990), pp. 267–71.

Brown, J.H., *Elizabethan Schooldays* (Oxford, 1933).

Burbidge, M., Burbidge, G., Fowler, W. and Hoyle, F., 'Synthesis of the Elements in Stars', *Reviews of Modern Physics*, 29 (1957), pp. 547–650.

Burlinson, C., 'The Use and Re-Use of Early Seventeenth-Century Student Notebooks: Inside and Outside the University', in J. Daybell and P. Hinds (eds), *Material Readings of Early Modern Culture, 1580-1730: Texts and Social Practices* (Basingstoke, 2010), pp. 229–45.

Cannon, J., *Schooling in England 1660 to 1850, Part I – 'A Noiseless Revolution'* and *Part II – The Gazetteer of English Schools* (List and Index Soc., Special Series 55, Kew, 2016).

Carter, J. and Muir, P., *Printing and the Mind of Man: a Descriptive Catalogue Illustrating the Impact of Print* (London, 1967).

Chalklin, C., *Seventeenth Century Kent* (London, 1965).

Chapman, A., 'Private Research and Public Duty – Airy, George and the Search for Neptune', *Journal for the History of Astronomy*, 19 (1988), pp. 121–39.

Chaudhuri, K.N., *The English East India Company: the Study of an Early Joint-Stock Company 1600-1640* (London, 1965).

Cheney, C.R. (ed.), *Handbook of Dates for Students of English History* (1978 edn).

Christopher, A.J., 'Bishops, Dioceses and Cathedrals: the Changing Territorial Organisation of the Church of England', *Geojournal*, 67/2 (2006), pp. 123–36.

Churchill, W.A., *Watermarks in Paper in Holland, France, England etc. in the XVII and XVIII centuries and their interconnection* (Amsterdam, 1935).

Clark, A., 'Dr Plume as a Cambridge Undergraduate', *ER*, xiv (1905), pp. 147–8.

Clark, A., 'Dr Plume's Notebook', *ER*, xiv (1905), pp. 152–63, 213–20; xv (1906), pp. 8–24.

Clark, A., 'Dr Plume's Pocketbook', *ER*, xiv (1905), pp. 9–20, 65–72.

Clark, A., 'Plume MS Papers', *ER*, xiii (1904), pp. 30–3.

Clark, A., 'The Plume Pamphlets', *ER*, xii (1903), pp. 159–65.

Clark, J.W., *Endowments of the University of Cambridge* (Cambridge, 1904).

Clark, P. (ed.), *The Cambridge Urban History of Britain 1540-1840*, vol. 2 (Cambridge, 2000).

Clark, W.J.R., 'Excavations in St Peter's Tower, Maldon', *Essex Journal*, 36/1 (2001), pp. 7–11.

Clark, W.J.R., 'Maldon, St Peter. Excavation within the Tower, 1999', *Essex Archaeology and History*, 3rd series, 31 (2000), pp. 263–4.

Colclough, S., 'Readers: Books and Biography', in S. Eliot and J. Rose (eds), *A Companion to the History of the Book* (Oxford, 2007), pp. 50–62.

Collins, E.J.T., ed., *The Agricultural History of England and Wales, vol. vii, 1850–1914*, Part I (Cambridge, 2000).

Collinson, P., *Birthpangs of Protestant England: Religious and Cultural Change in the 16th and 17th Centuries* (Basingstoke, 1988).

Collinson, P., 'Lectures by Combination, Structures and Characteristics of Church Life in 17th-Century England', *Bulletin of the Institute of Historical Research*, 48/118 (1975), pp. 182–213.

Costello, W.T., *The Scholastic Curriculum at Early Seventeenth Century Cambridge* (Cambridge, MA, 1958).

Coward, B., *The Stuart Age, England, 1603–1714* (2nd edn, London and New York, 1994).

Cressy, D., *Literacy and the Social Order: Reading and Writing in Tudor and Stuart England* (Cambridge, 1980).

Cross, F.L., *The Oxford Dictionary of the Christian Church* (London, 1975).

Darwin, G.H., *The Tides: and Kindred Phenomena in the Solar System* (London, 1898).

Davids, T.W., *Annals of Evangelical Nonconformity in the County of Essex* (London, 1863).

Deed, S.G. and Francis, J., *Catalogue of the Plume Library at Maldon, Essex* (Maldon, 1959).

Deedes, C. and Walters, H.B., *The Church Bells of Essex* (n.p., 1909).

Dent, J., *The Quest for Nonsuch* (Sutton, 1970, reprinted 1981).

Doe, R.A., 'Exit Ussher, enter Brownrig: the Tale of a Portrait in the Plume Library, Maldon', *Essex Journal*, 45/1 (2010), pp. 5–7.

Doe, T. (R.A.), 'Thomas Plume was the Author of Two Bishops' Biographies', *Essex Journal*, 54/2 (2019), p. 66.

Doran, S. and Durston, C., *Princes, Pastors and People, The Church and Religion in England, 1500–1700* (2nd edn, Abingdon, 2003).

Doyle, A.I., 'John Cosin (1595–1672) as a Library Maker', *The Book Collector*, 40 (1991), pp. 335–57.

Earnshaw, M.G.L., 'The Church on Market Hill' (privately published, 1988).

Eckhardt, J. and Smith, D.S. (eds), *Manuscript Miscellanies in Early Modern England* (Abingdon, 2014).

Eddington, A.S., *The Internal Constitution of the Stars* (Cambridge, 1926).

Eddington, A.S., *The Mathematical Theory of Relativity* (Cambridge, 1923).

Eddington, A.S., *Report on the Relativity Theory of Gravitation* (London, 1918).

Edmond, P., *Maldon Workhouse 1719–1875* (Maldon, 1999).

Emmison, F.G., *Elizabethan Life: Morals and the Church Courts* (Chelmsford, 1973).

Fielding, C.H., *The Records of Rochester Diocese* (Dartford, 1910).

Fincham, K. and Tyacke, N., *Altars Restored. The Changing Face of English Religious Worship, 1547–c.1700* (Oxford, 2007).

Fitch, E.A., *Maldon and the River Blackwater* (Maldon, n.d.).

Foot, M., 'John Evelyn's Bookbindings', in F. Harris and M. Hunter (eds), *John Evelyn and his Milieu* (London, 2003), pp. 61–70.

Foster, J. (ed.), *Alumni Oxonienses 1500-1714* (Oxford, 1891).

Fox, A., 'Words, Words, Words: Education, Literacy and Print', in K. Wrightson (ed.), *A Social History of England* (Cambridge, 2017), pp. 129–51.

Frampton, T.S., 'List of Forty-Five Vicars of Tilmanstone. Compiled with Notes', *Archaeologia Cantiana*, 20 (1893), pp. 104–18.

Francis, F.C., 'Foreword', in S.G. Deed and J. Francis, *Catalogue of the Plume Library* (Maldon, 1959), pp. vii–ix.

Freeman, C., *The History, Antiquities, Improvements … of the Parish of Bromley, Kent* (Greenwich, 1832).

French, H., '"Gentlemen": Remaking the English Ruling Class', in K. Wrightson (ed.), *A Social History of England* (Cambridge, 2017), pp. 269–89.

Gascoigne, J., *Cambridge in the Age of the Enlightenment: Science, Religion and Politics from the Restoration to the French Revolution* (Cambridge, 1989).

Gerhold, D., 'Wandsworth's Industrial Transformation c.1634-90', *Surrey Archaeological Collections*, 95 (2010), pp. 169–91.

Gilbert, R., *The Clerical Guide and Ecclesiastical Directory* (London, 1836).

Glaisyer, N., *The Culture of Commerce in England 1660-1720* (Woodbridge, 2006).

Goose, N. and Evans, N., 'Wills as an Historical Source', in T. Arkell, N. Evans and N. Goose (eds), *When Death Do Us Part: Understanding and Interpreting the Probate Records of Early Modern England* (Oxford, 2000), pp. 38–71.

Gowing, R., *Roger Cotes – Natural Philosopher* (Cambridge, 1983).

Gregory, J. (ed.), *The Speculum of Archbishop Thomas Secker* (Woodbridge, 1995).

Gregory, J. and Chamberlain, J.S. (eds), *The National Church in Local Perspective: The Church of England and its Regions, 1660-1800* (Woodbridge, 2003).

Grieve, H., *The Sleepers and the Shadows*, vol. 2 (Chelmsford, 1994).

Griffiths, P., Landers, J., Pelling, M. and Tyson, R., 'Population and Disease, Estrangement and Belonging', in P. Clark (ed.), *The Cambridge Urban History of Britain 1540-1840*, vol. 2 (Cambridge, 2000), pp. 195–233.

Hammer, P.E.J., 'The Use of Scholarship: The Secretariat of Robert Devereux, Second Earl of Essex, c.1585-1601', *The English Historical Review*, 109 (1994), pp. 26–51.

Hartwell, C., *The History and Architecture of Chetham's School and Library* (New Haven, CT, 2004).

Helms, M.W. and Hampson, G., 'BRAMSTON, John (1611–1700), of Skreens, Roxwell, Essex', in B.D. Henning (ed.), *The History of Parliament: the House of Commons 1660-1690* (London, 1983; online edition www.historyofparliamentonline.org).

Herrmann, F., 'The Plume Library, Maldon: A New Chapter', in K. Neale (ed.), *Essex 'full of profitable things'* (Oxford, 1996), pp. 245–52.

Hindle, S., *On the Parish? The Micro-politics of Poor Relief in Rural England c.1550–1750* (Oxford, 2004).

Hiscock, W., *A Christ Church Miscellany* (Oxford, 1946).

Hobson, G.D., 'Et Amicorum', *The Library*, 5th ser., 4 (1949), pp. 87–99.

Hoyle, F., *The Black Cloud* (1957).

Hoyle, F., 'A New Model for the Expanding Universe', *Monthly Notices of the Royal Astronomical Society*, 108 (1948), pp. 372–82.

Hoyle, F. and Elliot, J., *A for Andromeda* (1962).

Howse, D., *Greenwich Time and the Discovery of the Longitude* (Oxford, 1980).

Hughes, L., *A Guide to the Church of All Saints, Maldon* (Maldon and London, 1909, reprinted 2006).

Hunt, E.H. and Pam, S.J., 'Responding to Agricultural Depression, 1873–96: Managerial Success, Entrepreneurial Failure?', *Agricultural History Review*, 50/2 (2002), pp. 225–52.

Isaacs, T., 'The Anglican Hierarchy and the Reformation of Manners 1688–1738', *Journal of Ecclesiastical History*, 33/3 (1982), pp. 391–411.

Jacob, W.M., 'Libraries for the Parish: Individual Donors and Charitable Societies', in G. Mandelbrote and K.A. Manley (eds), *The Cambridge History of Libraries in Britain and Ireland, Volume II 1640–1850* (Cambridge, 2006), pp. 66–82.

Jeffreys, H., *Theory of Probability* (1939).

Jeffreys, H., *The Earth* (1923).

Johnston, W., 'The Anglican Apocalypse in Restoration England', *The Journal of Ecclesiastical History*, 55/3 (2004), pp. 467–501.

Jordan, W.K., *Philanthropy in England 1480–1660* (London, 1959).

Kelly, T., *Early Public Libraries: A History of Public Libraries in Great Britain before 1850* (The Library Association, London, 1966).

Ker, N. (ed.), rev. M. Perkin, *A Directory of the Parochial Libraries of the Church of England and the Church of Wales* (Bibliographical Society, London, 2004).

Kimbell, J., *An Account of the Legacies, Gifts, Rents, Fees & appertaining to the Church and Poor of the Parish of St Alphege Greenwich, in the County of Kent* (Greenwich, 1816).

King, P., 'The Episcopate during the Civil Wars 1642–1649', *English Historical Review*, 83/328 (1968), pp. 523–37.

Kirby, J.W., *History of the Roan School (The Greycoat School) and its Founder* (London, 1929).

Lacey, A., 'The Office for King Charles the Martyr in the Book of Common Prayer, 1662–1685', *Journal of Ecclesiastical History*, 53/3 (2002), pp. 510–26.

Levene, J.R., 'Sir George Biddell Airy F.R.S. (1801–1892) and the Discovery and Correction of Astigmatism', *Notes and Records of the Royal Society of London*, 21/2 (1966), pp. 180–99.

Lloyd, A.H., 'The Benefactors to Fellows' Building', *Christ's College Magazine*, 38/119 (1929), pp. 26–37.

Love, H., *The Culture and Commerce of Texts: Scribal Publication in Seventeenth-Century England* (Amherst, MA, 1998).
McCarthy, M., *All Graduates and Gentlemen* (Dublin, 1980).
McGinley, M., 'Palmer's School and the Changing Educational Needs of the Nineteenth Century', *Panorama. The Journal of the Thurrock Local History Society*, 20 (1976/7), pp. 11–21.
McKerrow, R.B., 'The Relationship of English Printed Books to Authors' Manuscripts during the Sixteenth and Seventeenth Centuries: The 1928 Sandars Lectures', in C.M. Bajetta (ed.), *Studies in Bibliography* (2000), pp. 1–65.
McKitterick, D., *Print, Manuscript and the Search for Order, 1450-1830* (Cambridge, 2003).
Mandelbrote, G., 'John Evelyn and his Books', in F. Harris and M. Hunter (eds), *John Evelyn and his Milieu* (London, 2003), pp. 71–94.
Mandelbrote, G. and Manley, K.A. (eds), *The Cambridge History of Libraries in Britain and Ireland, Volume II 1640-1850* (Cambridge, 2006).
Manley, K.A., 'Thomas Plume', in W. Baker and K. Womack (eds), *Dictionary of Literary Biography: volume 213: Pre-Nineteenth-Century British Book Collectors and Bibliographers* (Farmington Hills, 1999), pp. 274–8.
Manross, W.W., *S.P.G. papers in the Lambeth Palace Library* (Oxford, 1974).
Michie, R.C., *The London Stock Exchange: a History* (Oxford, 1999).
Miller, A.I., *Empire of the Stars: Friendship, Obsession & Betrayal in the Quest for Black Holes* (London, 2005).
Mingay, G., *The Gentry: The Rise and Fall of a Ruling Class* (London, 1976).
Mitton, S., *Fred Hoyle: A Life in Science* (London, 2005).
Morgan, V., *A History of the University of Cambridge*, vol. 2 (Cambridge, 2004).
Morrill, J., 'The Church in England 1642-9', in J. Morrill (ed.), *Reactions to the English Civil War* (London, 1982), pp. 89–114.
Morrison, K., *The Workhouse. A Study of Poor-Law Buildings in England* (London, 1999).
Muldrew, C., 'The "Middling Sort": An Emergent Cultural Identity', in K. Wrightson (ed.), *A Social History of England* (Cambridge, 2017), pp. 291–309.
Narveson, K., *Bible Readers and Lay Writers in Early Modern England: Gender and Self-Definition* (Abingdon, 2012).
Nelles, P.A., 'Libraries, Books and Learning, from Bacon to the Enlightenment', in G. Mandelbrote and K.A. Manley (eds), *The Cambridge History of Libraries in Britain and Ireland, Volume II 1640-1850* (Cambridge, 2006), pp. 23–35.
Nixon, H.M., *Catalogue of the Pepys Library at Magdalene College ... Vol. VI, bindings* (Woodbridge, 1984).
Nunn, S.P., *Maldon and the Handshake of History* (*Maldon and Burnham Standard*, 17 March 1988).
Nunn, S.P., *Maldon: the Plume School – Four Centuries of Education (1608-2008)* (Maldon, 2008).

Nunn, S.P., 'The Origins, Development and Continuing Success of the Plume School', in *Maldon The Plume School – Four Centuries of Education (1608–2008)* (Maldon, 2008), pp. 5–28.

Nunn, S.P. (ed.), *St. Peter's, Maldon's Redundant 'Middle Church'* (revised edn, Maldon, 1984).

O'Day, R., *The Professions in Early Modern England: 1450–1800: Servants of the Commonweal* (London, 2000).

Ollard, S. (ed.), assisted by Crosse, G., *A Dictionary of English Church History* (London, 1912).

Osler, M. (ed.), *Rethinking the Scientific Revolution* (Cambridge, 2000).

Page, W. and Round, J.H. (eds), *VCH Essex*, vol. ii (London, 1907).

Pearman, A.I., *Diocesan Histories: Rochester* (London, 1897).

Pearson, D., *English Bookbinding Styles 1450–1800* (New Castle, DE, 2014).

Pearson, D., 'The English Private Library in the Seventeenth Century', *The Library*, 7th ser., 13 (2012), pp. 379–99.

Pearson, D., 'Patterns of Book Ownership in Late Seventeenth-Century England', *The Library*, 7th ser., 11 (2010), pp. 139–67.

Pearson, D., 'The Libraries of English Bishops, 1600–40', *The Library*, 6th ser., 14 (1992), pp. 221–57.

Peile, J., *Biographical Register of Christ's College, 1505–1905*, vol. i (Cambridge, 1910).

Peile, J., *Christ's College* (Cambridge, 1900).

Perkin, M. (ed.), *A Directory of the Parochial Libraries of the Church of England and the Church in Wales* (London, 2004).

Perry, P.J., *British Agriculture, 1875–1914* (Abingdon, 2006).

Petchey, W.J., *The Intentions of Thomas Plume* (Maldon, 1985; tercentenary edition, 2004).

Petchey, W.J., *A Prospect of Maldon 1500–1689* (Chelmsford, 1991).

Petchey, W.J., 'The History of the Church before c.1650: the Vanished Church of St Peter, Maldon', in S.P. Nunn (ed.), *St. Peter's, Maldon's Redundant 'Middle Church'* (revised edn, Maldon, 1984), pp. 2–5.

Petchey, W.J., *Maldon Grammar School 1608–1958* (Maldon, 1958).

Pevsner, N., *Essex* (Harmondsworth, 1954).

Poole, W., 'William Barlow's Books at Queen's', *Insight* (Michaelmas, 2013), pp. 3–7.

Powell, M., 'Endowed Libraries for Towns', in G. Mandelbrote and K.A. Manley (eds), *The Cambridge History of Libraries in Britain and Ireland, Volume II 1640–1850* (Cambridge, 2006), pp. 83–101.

Price, K., *Loving Faster than Light: Romance and Readers in Einstein's Universe* (Chicago, IL, 2012).

Ramsay, N., 'The Library and Archives to 1897', in D. Keene, A. Burns and A. Saint (eds), *St. Paul's. The Cathedral Church of London 604–2004* (New Haven, CT, 2004), pp. 413–29.

Raven, J., *The Business of Books* (New Haven, CT, and London, 2007).

Raverat, G., *Period Piece* (London, 1952).

Reaney, P.H., *The Place-Names of Essex* (Cambridge, 1935).

Rees, M., *Our Final Century: the Scientist's Warning: How Terror, Error, and Environmental Disaster threaten Humankind's Future in this Century – on Earth and Beyond* (London, 2003).

Reynolds, D., *Christ's: A Cambridge College Over Five Centuries* (Basingstoke, 2005).

Ringrose, J., 'John Moore and his Books', in P. Fox (ed.), *Cambridge University Library: the Great Collections* (Cambridge, 1986), pp. 78–89.

Royal Commission on Historical Monuments (England), *An Inventory of the Historical Monuments in Essex*, vol. ii (London, 1921).

Runcorn, K., 'Sir Harold Jeffreys (1891–1989)', *Nature*, 339/6220 (1989), p. 102.

Ryrie, A., 'Reformations', in K. Wrightson (ed.), *A Social History of England* (Cambridge, 2017), pp. 107–28.

Scantlebury, H., *Robert Nightingale: the Life and Times of an Essex Artist* (n.p., 2007).

Sell, R.D. and Johnson, A.W., *Writing and Religion in England 1558–1689: Studies in Community-Making and Cultural Memory* (Abingdon, 2009).

Sharpe, K., *Reading Revolutions: The Politics of Reading in Early Modern England* (New Haven, CT, 2000).

Shepherd, S.R., *The Bromley Magazine* (Bromley, 1845), issues 1–9.

Shoemaker, R.B., 'Reforming the City: The Reformation of Manners Campaign in London 1690–1738', in L. Davison, T. Hitchcock, T. Keirn and R.B. Shoemaker (eds), *Stilling the Grumbling Hive* (Stroud, 1992), pp. 99–120.

Slack, P.A., *The English Poor Law 1531–1782* (Cambridge, 1995).

Slack, P.A., *Poverty and Policy in Tudor and Stuart England* (London, 1988).

Sloman, D. and Watkin, E., *English Heritage Bell Frame Survey for Essex* (n.p., 1993).

Smith, J.R., 'Maldon's Old Moot Hall and Market Place: a Reinterpretation', *Essex Archaeology and History*, 4th ser., 7 (2017), pp. 104–13.

Smith, J.R., *The Borough of Maldon 1688–1800: a Golden Age* (Studley, 2013).

Smith, J.R., *Pilgrims and Adventurers: Essex (England) and the Making of the United States of America* (Chelmsford, 1992).

Spaeth, D.A., 'Common Prayer? Popular Observance of the Anglican Liturgy in Restoration Wiltshire', in S.J. Wright (ed.), *Parish, Church and People Local Studies in Lay Religion 1350–1750* (London, 1988), pp. 125–46.

Spencer, C., *Killers of the King: The Men Who Dared to Execute Charles I* (London, 2014).

Spurr, J., *The Restoration Church of England* (New Haven, CT, and London, 1991).

Standage, T., *The Neptune File: Planet Detectives and the Discovery of Worlds Unseen* (London, 2000).

Stanley, M., 'An Expedition to Heal the Wounds of War. The 1919 Eclipse and Eddington as Quaker Adventurer', *Isis. Journal of the History of Science Society*, 94 (2003), pp. 57–89.

Suckling, A., 'Weston', *The History and Antiquities of the County of Suffolk*, vol. i (Ipswich, 1846) (online edition), pp. 97–101.

Tarver, A., *Church Court Records* (Chichester, 1995).
Thrush, A., 'MILDMAY, Sir Henry (c.1594–1668), of Wanstead, Essex and Twyford, Hants.', in A. Thrush and J.P. Ferris (eds), *The History of Parliament: the House of Commons 1604–1629* (Cambridge, 2010; online edition www.historyofparliamentonline.org).
Todd, M., 'England after 1558', in A. Pettegree (ed.), *The Reformation World* (London and New York, 2000), pp. 365–86.
Tomalin, C., *Samuel Pepys: The Unequalled Self* (London, 2002).
Tuckwell, A., *That Honourable and Gentlemanlike House* (n.p., 2001).
Twigg, J., *The University of Cambridge and the English Revolution 1625–1688* (Woodbridge, 1990).
Venn, J. and Venn, J.A. (eds), *Alumni Cantabrigiensis*, Part 1 to 1751, 4 vols (Cambridge, 1922–7).
Walter, J., '"Abolishing Superstition with Sedition"? The Politics of Popular Iconoclasm in England 1640–1642', *Past and Present*, 183 (2004), pp. 79–123.
Willis, R., *The Architectural History of the University of Cambridge, and of the Colleges of Cambridge and Eton*, ed. J.W. Clark (Cambridge, 1886).
Wormell, P., *Essex Farming 1900–2000* (Colchester, 1999).
Woudhuysen, H., *Sir Phillip Sydney and the Circulation of Manuscripts 1558–1640: The Procreative Pen* (Oxford, 1996).
Wright, C.J. (ed.), *Sir Robert Cotton as Collector. Essays on an Early Stuart Courtier and his Legacy* (London, 1997).
Wright, T., *The History and Topography of the County of Essex* (London, 1833).
Wrightson, K. (ed.), *A Social History of England* (Cambridge, 2017).
Young, A., *General View of the Agriculture of the County of Essex*, vol. 1 (London, 1813).

Theses and unpublished papers

Austin, R. and Seary, P., 'The Old Archdeaconry. The Precincts, Rochester, Kent', unpublished historic buildings appraisal, Canterbury Archaeological Trust (Canterbury, 2011).
Best, G., 'Books and Readers in Certain Eighteenth-Century Parish Libraries', PhD thesis (Loughborough University of Technology, 1985).
Doe, R.A., 'The Churchmanship of Thomas Plume (1630–1704): A Study of a Career in the Restoration Church of England', MA dissertation (University of Essex, 2005).
Earnshaw, M.G.L., '"Always with you": public and private charity in Maldon and district', paper for the University of Essex Course EFW 9002 – The Origins and Development of English Towns.
Herrmann, F., 'The Importance of Books to Dr Plume', Plume Lecture, 1990.
Ignajatijevie, G.L., 'The Parish Clergy in the Diocese of Canterbury and the Archdeaconry of Bedford in the Reign of Charles I and under the Commonwealth', PhD thesis (University of Sheffield, 1986).
Kemp, H., 'Collecting, Communicating, and Commemorating: the Significance of Thomas Plume's Manuscript Collection, Left to his Library in Maldon, est. 1704', PhD thesis (University of Essex, 2017).

McNeil O'Farrell, N., comp., 'Calendar of Essex Assize Files in the Public Record Office', vol. iv, 1660–1685 (ERO library).
Petchey, W.J., 'The Borough of Maldon, Essex, 1500–1688', PhD thesis (Leicester University, 1972).
Wyatt, H., 'Preserving the Plume: towards an Analytical Evaluation of the Building Fabric with Particular Focus on Site Context, Available Documentary Evidence, Morphology and Repair Strategies', submission for the Frank and Patricia Herrmann Award, TPL (2015).

Dictionary of National Biography
Compact Dictionary of National Biography (London, 1975).
Concise Dictionary of National Biography, 3 vols (Oxford, 1992).
Oxford Dictionary of National Biography (Oxford, 2004).

Internet sources
Personal web pages are excluded.
ACAD: A Cambridge Alumni Database http://venn.lib.cam.ac.uk/Documents/acad/
Ancestry https://www.ancestry.co.uk
The Charity Commission http://apps.charitycommission.gov.uk
Clergy of the Church of England Database http://db.theclergydatabase.org.uk/
Diocese of Rochester http://www.rochester.anglican.org/
Economic History Association, Measuring Worth https://eh.net/howmuchisthat/
History of Parliament http://www.historyofparliamentonline.org/
Kent Archaeological Society http://www.kentarchaeology.org.uk/
London Gardens online http://www.londongardensonline.org.uk/
Measuring Worth https://www.measuringworth.com/
Old Bailey Online http://www.oldbaileyonline.org
Oxford Dictionary of National Biography (2008) https://www.oxforddnb.com/
R.O. Bucholz, *The Database of Court Officers, 1660–1837* http://www.courtofficers.ctsdh.luc.edu
Sawston Village History Society http://www.sawstonhistory.org.uk/
Sermon: Revd R. Knight, 'The Word Made Flesh', Holy Trinity Dartford, Advent 2008 http://www.cuxtonandhalling.org.uk/teaching.htm
Survey of London https://www.british-history.ac.uk/survey-london/
Thomas Plume's Library http://www.thomasplumeslibrary.co.uk
Travel in Times: Historic journey planner https://www.travelintimes.org/

Index

Note: page references in **bold** are tables and those in *italics* are illustrations. The suffix 'n' refers to a note.

Acts of Parliament
   Act of Uniformity (1662) 2, 43, 72
   Ancient Monuments Acts 187
   Charitable Donations' Act (1812) 132
   Corporation Act (1661) 42–3
   Education Act (1902) 140
   Endowed Schools Act (1910) 144
   Poor Law Amendment Act (1834) 113
   Toleration Act (1688) 80
   Workhouse Test Act (1723) 111
Adams, John Couch (1819–92) 256
Airy, George Biddell (1801–92) **251**, 254–6, *255*
Aldrich, Henry (1647–1710) 157
Allestree, Richard (1621/2–81) 160
Allix, Peter (1641–1717) 73, 268
All Saints' and St Peter's parish, Maldon 40, 43, 44, 102, 132, 146, 176–8, 199, 212
All Saints' church/parish, Maldon 28, 29, *29*, *32*, 35, 41, 53, *54*, 56, 111–12, 132, 145, 176, 179, 187
   Plume's bequests for
     augmenting income of vicarage 12, 102–3, 281
     bell tolling **125**, 126, *127*, 271
     prayer readings 125, **125**, 273
     silver flagons for communion table *54*, 100, 271
almshouses 81, 115, 227, *227*
   see also Deptford, Kent
Ames, William 159
Andrew, Charles *141*

Andrewes, Lancelot (1555–1626) 159, 209–10
Annastacy Wentworth Charity 38, 120, 127, 128, 129, 134, 143, 144
apprenticeships for Maldon Grammar School boys 14, 15, 109, 113, 116, 120–1, 128, 132, 134, 136, **137**, 140–3, *141*, *142*, 148
Aquinas, Thomas 210
Aristotle 210
Armine, Lady Mary (1594–1676) 12, 81
Arminianism 1, 59, 65–6, 70, 77, 79, 226
Arminius, Jacobus (1560–1609) 1, 65, 70
Arwaker, Edmund 168
Asheldham, Essex (Hall Farm) 38
Assheton, William 162
astronomy 249
   books and notes in Plume Library 17, **159**, 160–1, 165–6, 210
   Cambridge observatory 14, 19, 102, 107, 113, 250, **251**, 252, 253–60, *254*, *257*, 276
   Royal Observatory at Greenwich 9, 17, *18*, 249, 250, 255
   see also individual topics
Ayerst, *alias* Eyerst, Eyers
   Elizabeth 233, 279
   John Gunsley 233, 279
   Thomas 233
   William 233, 279

Bacon, Francis 159, 211
Bainbridge, John 161

Balsham, Cambs 102, 250
Barker, Francis 180, 181, 183
Barker, William 180
Barlow, Thomas (1608/9–91) 157, 170
Barrington, Sir Charles **122**
Bartlet, James (bell-maker) 178
Bartlett, James (farmer) 124
Batteley, John (1646–1708) 170
Baxter, Richard 81
Bayly, Dr 208, 217, 218
Bayly, Dr John (1595–1633) 218
Bayly, Dr Lewis (1575–1631) 218
Bayly, Dr Thomas (d. 1657) 218
Beale, Audrey (Anne?) 12, 20, 81–2, 98, 104–5, *105*, 272
Beale, James 181
Beaumont, P.M. 186
Beck, Cave 168
Beeleigh Abbey 176
Belchamp Otten, Essex 26
Belchamp St Paul, Essex 26
Belchamp Walter, Essex 26
Bellarmine, Robert 159
Belsham, Susan **130**, 147
Bentley, John 34
Bentley, Dr Richard (1662–1742) 19, 250, 277
bequests of Plume 3–5, **8**, 12–15, 73, 95–116, 120–1, 148–9
  church and religious causes 12, 96, 100, 106–9, 171, 234–5
    Corporation of the Sons of the Clergy 100, 107, 108, 115
    Dengie Hundred, poor clergy of 17, 108, 132, 138, 148, 272
    French Protestant ministers 107, 108
    Longfield rector, income for 103, 229, 234–5, 237, 238–9, 275, 280
    Rochester Cathedral 101, 234
    Rochester Diocese, poor clergy in 3, 12, 107–8, 109, 116, 225, 233, 234, 235, 241–3, 244, 245, 267–8, 274, 275
    Society for the Propagation of the Gospel in Foreign Parts (SPG) 80, 107, 268
    St Alfege's churchyard, charnel house 115, 235, 266
    St Alfege's vicars 101–2, 107, 234, 275
    Tonbridge and Malling deaneries 100, 234, 235, 281
    see also All Saints' church/parish, Maldon: Plume's bequests for
  education provision 12, 14, 96, 106–7, 113–14, 120, 138–40, 232–3, 244
    to Chelmsford School 113, 271
    to Christ's College, Cambridge 113, 116, 272
    Isle of Grain, education of poor schoolchildren 113, 116, 232, 275
    John Roan (Grey Coat) School, Greenwich 14, 97, 113, 232, 281
    Maldon grammar school, boys maintained at 3, 14, 15, 17, 38, 113, 114, 116, 120, 121, **125**, 128, 135, 136, **137**, 140, 148, 271
    observatory at Cambridge 14, 19, 102, 107, 113, 250, 251, 252, 253–60, *254*, *257*
    Plumian Professorship of Astronomy at Cambridge University 3, 6, 14, 17, 18–19, 107, 113, 114, 116, 146, 155, 249–62, **251**, 276–7
    public lectures 12, 14, 97, 108, 113, 116, 120, 124–6, **125**, *126*, *127*, 132, 136, **137**, 138, *139*, 146, 148, 149, 232–3, 270–1, 272, 273–4
    see also Plume Library
  family, friends and servants 3, 97, 100, 104, 106, 267
    Audrey (Anne?) Beale 104–5, *105*, 272
    Edward Brooke 30, 269
    James Plume (executor) 97, 105, 106, 278
    Nathaniel Plume (cousin) 33–4, 104, 106, 268
  poverty relief 12–14, 96, 100, 106–7, 109–13, 120, 226–31, 244, 266, 278–9
    almshouses (not achieved) 3, 14, 107, 109, 115, 227–8, 266
    apprenticeships for grammar school boys 14, 15, 109, 113, 116, 120–1, 128, 132, 134, 136, **137**, 140–3, *141*, *142*, 148
    Bromley College, widows of 108, 115, 226–7, *227*, 281

East Greenwich, poor of 226, 266
maids in marriage 109, 231, 267
Maldon poor, coal for *126*, 131–2, **137**
Maldon workhouse 3, 14, 33, 99, 103, 106, 109–13, *110*, *112*, 116, 120, 122, 138, 149, 269, 273, 278
Rochester, poor tradesmen in 109, 229–30
Sir John Hawkins Knight Hospital 230–1, 280, 281
Stone parish, Dartford, Kent, poor of 228–9, 281
Bernard, Edward 170
Bernard, Francis (1627–98) 157
Big Bang theory 259
Bigoss, Abraham 121, **122**, *123*
Billingsley, Nicholas 205
Bishop's War (1638) 55
black holes 258, 259, 260
Black Notley, Essex *8*
book collection in Plume Library
  bindings 20, 167–9
  book purchases in London 12, 69, 82–4, *82*, 161–2
  contents 17–18, 157–61, **159**, 294–8
    astronomy texts 17, **159**, 160–1, 165–6, 210
    law texts **159**, 161
    literature 160, 171
    medical texts **159**, 161
    philosophy texts 60, 67, **159**, 210, 216
    rarity of 169–70, 171, 172
    scientific texts 17, **159**, 160–1
    theological texts 157, 158, **159**, **159**, 161
  inscriptions and annotations 162, *165*, 200, 206, 211, 216
    of Plume 161, 162, 163–4, *163*, *164*
    Plume's monogram 20–1, *163*, 166–7
  prices 60, 162–3, 206, 216
  size of 3, 82, 106, 129, 135, 156–7
Book of Common Prayer 2, 57, 70–1, 72, 77, 87
Boothby, Richard 168
Boothby, Sir William (1638?–1707) 157
Boreman, Dulcibella 82

Boreman, John 216
Boreman, Robert (d. 1675) 10, 68, 81, 82, 210, 214–15
  manuscripts of 10, 67, 162, 200, 202–4, *203*, 208, 211–12, *215*
Boreman, William (1564–1646) 82
Boreman, Sir William (1614–86) 10, 82, 214, 216
Borough English custom 30, 87–8
Bowle, John (d. 1637) 170
Boyle, Robert 160, 210
Bramston, Sir John (1611–1700) 42
Bray, Thomas 16–17, 156, 170–1
Breeder and Plume Educational Trust 144, 147, 149
Breeder, Ralph 37–8, 114, 124, 127, 131, 178
  grammar school benefaction 37–8, 114, 120, 127, 128, 129, 134, 135, 143, 144, 147, 149, 178
Brickwood, Benjamin 129
Brickwood, John 121, 129, 271, 272
Bright, Edward 179
Bristol 156
Brome, Edward 170
Bromley College 108, 115, 226–7, *227*, 281
Bromley, Kent *8*, 77
Brooke, Edward 30, 269
Brooke, Robert 30
Browne, John 34, 268
Browne, Richard 81
Browne, Robert 204, *205*, 207, 211–12
Brown, George 181
Brownrig, Ralph 65, 184
Buchanan, George 159
Buck, Maximillian 53, 87, 226
Bugg, William 134
Burton, John 190
Burton, Robert 158
Buxtorf, Johannes 159

Calamy, Edmund 43
Calvinism 1, 65, 66, 73, 79, 85, 87, 226
Cambridge University 35, 53, 54, 58–9, 100
  Christ's College 1, 6, 26–7, 40, *58*, 209, 218, 250, 277
    Plume at 26–7, 45, 46, 57–63, 209

Plume's bequest to 113, 116, 272
observatory 14, 19, 102, 107, 113, 250, 251, 252, 253–60, *254*, *257*, 276
Plumian Professorship of Astronomy 3, 6, 14, 17, 18–19, 107, 113, 114, 116, 146, 155, 249–62, **251**, 276–7
Trinity College 19, 63, 202, 210–11, 250, 251, 252, 253
Campanella, Tomasso 210
Canterbury, diocese of 10–11
　Archbishop of 1, 115, 184, 243
　Archdeacon of 170, 205–6
　Dean of 73
　Prerogative Court of 105, 114, 115
Canterbury, Kent *8*, 11
Capell, Moses 205
Carey, William 184
Carr, William 33, 34, 44, 46, 268
Carte, Joseph (1636–1707) 201
Catholicism 1–2, 63, 66, 67, 70, 73, 159
Challis, James (1803–82) **251**, 255–6, *256*
Chancellor, F. Wykeham 176, 187, 189
Chancery Court 31, 126, 131, 136, 143, 148, 181, 238
　cases brought by James Plume 101–2, 104–5, 226, 228, 232, 235
　cases defended by James Plume 102–3, 106, 111, 226, 236
　and Stone Castle Charity 236–7, 239–41
Chandrasekhar, Subrahmanyan 258
charity commission 135, 136, 143–4, 148, 229, 232, 239, 240, 242, 243, 245
Charles I 1, 2, 35, 42, 53, 57, 58, 62, 66, 67, 68, 69, 80, 82, 87
　Plume's devotion to 53, 59, 61, 68, 87, 184
Charles II 2, 9, 17, 42, *72*, 74–5, 76, 84, 86, 184
　Plume chaplain in ordinary to 12, 76
Chatham Chest 107, 230, *230*
Chatham, Kent *8*, 11, 227, 229, 231, 266, 267, 274
　Sir John Hawkins Knight Hospital for poor seamen 9, 230–1, 280, 281
Cheam, Surrey 2, *8*, 63, 64, 69, 70, 201, 202, *213*
Cheese, Thomas 34

Chelmsford, Essex 2, *8*, 55, 57, 111, 141, 177, 187
　St Mary's church 55, *56*, 57
Chelmsford School
　Plume at 1, 53–7, 59, 114, 127, 199–200, 218
　Plume's bequest to 113, 271, 272
Chetham, Humphrey 16, 156
Christian, Ewan 185, 190
Christie, J. 242–3
Christ's College, Cambridge 1, 6, 26–7, 40, *58*, 209, 218, 250, 277
　Plume at 26–7, 45, 46, 57–63, 209
　Plume's bequest to 113, 116, 272
Chrysostom 210
Church of England 1, 2, 10, 16, 18, 54, 63, 68, 70–1, 73, 80, 81, 87, 136
　Plume's support for 2, 12, 57, 62, 71, 85, 108, 184, 235, 271, 274
Cicero 210
Civil Wars (1642–51) 2, 9, 10, 35, 36, 42, 46, 55, 57, 58, 66, 70, 77, 108, 198, 219
　and Plume's manuscript collection 204–5, 206, 208–9
Clark, Andrew (1856–1922) 5, 67, 197–8, 201, 204, 207
Clark, Duncan 187, 191
Clarke, A.L. (mayor of Maldon) 190
coal trade 11, 39, 40, 45
Cobham, Kent *8*, 274
Coe, John 191
Coke, Sir Edward (1552–1634) 161
Colchester, Essex *8*, 9, 11, 168, 187, 268
　Grammar School 157
　siege of (1648) 61
　St John's Abbey 124
　town libraries 156, 171
Collins, John 96
Compton, Henry 157
Comyns, Sir John 33, *110*, 111, **122**
Cook, Captain James 252
Cook, John 180, 181, 183
Cornwall, gentry wills 85
Corporation of the Sons of the Clergy 100, 107, 108, 115
cosmology 210, 259
Cotes, Roger (1682–1716) 19, **251**, 252
Cottle, Mark 235, 266
Cox, Thomas 5

INDEX

Crane, Robert P. **130**, 136, 138, 143, 184
Cranmer, Thomas *165*
Crayford, Kent *8*, 274
Cromwell, Oliver 35, 36–7, 67, 68, 69
Cromwell, Richard 68, 69
Cyprian of Carthage 86–7

Danes, John 28, 38, *45*, 46, 53, 127
dark matter 259
Dartford, Kent 206–7, 232–3, 273
   see also Stone Castle estate, Stone, Dartford, Kent
Darwin, George Howard (1845–1912) **251**, 256–7
Davies, Sir John 148
Davis, William 239
Dawes, William 95, 228, 234, 266, 275, 279, 282
Declarations of Indulgence (1687/1688) 80, 81
Dedham, Essex *8*, 40
Deed, Sidney **130**, 147
de Mariana, Juan 163–4, *163*
Dengie Hundred, Essex *8*, 106, 108, 121, 122, 124–5, 126
   Classis 41, 42, 48n33, 50n84, 66, 87
   Plume's bequest to support poor clergy of 17, 108, 132, 138, 148, 272
   see also Iltney Farm, Mundon
Dennis, M.G. 185
Deptford, Kent *8*, 72, 81, 113, 225, 235
   Dog Kennel Row almshouses 3, 14, 107, 109, 115, 227–8, 244, 266, 281
Descartes, René 160, 210, 216, 217
de Vere family 6, 25
Dewes, Paul 31
Dewes, Sir Simonds 31
Digby, Sir Kenelm 159
Directory of Public Worship (1644) 2, 72
Dolben, John (1625–86) 77, 80
Dorislaus, Isaac (1595–1649) 35
Dorrell, Thomas 104
Downes, Daniel W. **130**, 147
Dowsing, William 58
drama, theatrical 210–11
Draper, William 183
Dr Plumes Trust 3, 243, 244
   see also Stone Castle Charity (later Dr Plumes Trust)

Dudley, Lady Alice (1579–1669) 202
Duffin, Anne 85
Dugdale, Sir William *78*, 166, 170, 210
Dunlop, Arthur 146
Dunn, Salisbury 135, 140
Duppa, Brian 69, 184
Dycker, Thomas 232

Earnshaw, Olive **130**, 147
East India Company 14, 84, 99, 103, 109, 278
ecclesiastical courts 77, 79–80, 101–2
Eddington, Sir Arthur Stanley (1882–1944) **251**, 257–8, *257*
Edmond, Peggy 112
Edward VI 1, 184
E.H. Bentall Ltd of Heybridge 142
Einstein, Albert 256, 257–8, *257*
Eliot, Laurence **130**
Elizabeth I 1, 40, 82, 127
Elliot, John 259
Elliott, Thomas 227
Ellis, Richard (1950–) **251**, 259
Eltham, Kent *8*, 274
Ely, bishops of 69, 80
   book collection of 162–3, 206
Endeavour (ship) 141
episcopacy 2, 41, 57, 63, 65, 66, 69, 86–7, 208–9
   and Plume 2, 72, 87
Erasmus 159
Erpenius, Thomas 159
Essex 5, *8*, 9, 11, 14, 28, 39, 42, 43, 128
   Plume family in 5, 6, 7, 25
   Plume's bequests for 3, 97, 107, 108
   see also Dengie Hundred, Essex; Maldon, Essex; Maldon Trust (later Thomas Plume's Library); Thomas Plume's Library (charity); *individual towns and parishes*
Essex County Council (ECC) 144, 145, 146, 149
Essex County Library 145, 190
Essex Review 5, 67, 197
Evelyn, John (1620–1706) 16, 72–3, 157, 166, 167, 168
Eyerst or Eyers *see* Ayerst, *alias* Eyerst, Eyers
Eythorne, Kent 204–6, *213*

313

Faversham Grammar School, Kent 205
Fell Smith, Charlotte 5
Fincham, K. 66, 77–8
Finch, John 141
First World War 258
Fitzwilliam, John (d. 1699) 162
Flamsteed House, Greenwich *18-19*, 255
Flamsteed, John (1646–1719) 14, 17, 18, *18*, 249–50, 251–2, 277
Fleet Street, London 11, 12, 84
Foulgier, William *32*, 34, 268
France, Protestant refugees and ministers from 73, 107, 108, 115, 268
Francis, Sir Frank 157–8, 171, 172
Francis, Jane 147
Francis, Thomas 36
Frank, Richard 40
freemasonry *184*, 185
French, Professor Henry 5
Friends of Thomas Plume's Library 147, 148, 149
Fuller, Thomas 16

Garrington, widow Alice 27
Gassendi, Pierre 159, 161, 165–6, *166*, 210
Gateway to Early Modern Manuscript Sermons (GEMMS) 21
Gessner, Conrad 216
G.H. Tunmer & Son of Maldon 182
Gibbs, John H. 190
Gibson, Thomas **122**
Gifford, George (1547/8–1600, curate) 97, 212
Gifford, George (headburgess in 1643) 36, 42
Gifford, George (d. 1686, professor of divinity) 212
Gillett, Francis 95, 279, 279n14(2), 280n16
Godwyn, Morgan 158
Gosfield, Essex *8*
Gower, Humphrey (1638–1711) 170
grammar school, Maldon *see* Maldon Grammar School (now Plume School)
Gravesend, Kent *8*, 12, 108, 232–3, 237, *238*, 273, 274
Gray, George 121, **122**, *123*

Gray, Stephen 252
Gray, Victor 148
Great Yeldham, Essex 6, 7, *8*, 25, 26, *26*, 27–8, *27*, 31, 33, 99, 104, **122**, 215, 268, 280
Green, John 44
Greenwich, East (parish) 95, 99, 226, 228, 234, 235, 245, 274
 Plume as vicar of 2, 9, 10, 30, 69–74, 76, 77, 78–9, 81, 249, 265
 Plume's bequests for 97, 100, 101, 109, 225, 227–8, 231, 245, 266
 charnel house 115, 235, 266
 Church Street house 101–2, 107, 234, 275
 Deptford almshouses (not achieved) 3, 14, 109, 115, 227–8, 266, 281
 John Roan (Grey Coat) School 14, 97, 113, 232, 281
 maids in marriage 109, 231, 267
 poor of 226, 266
 see also St Alfege's church, Greenwich
Greenwich, Kent *8*, 9–10, 11, 12, 14, 17, 72, *72*, 84, 95, 178, 230, 265
 Boreman family in 10, 12, 82, 202
 Church Street house 101–2, 107, 234
 Flamsteed House *18-19*, 255
 Greenwich Park 9, 17, *18-19*, *71*, 249
 John Roan (Grey Coat) School 10, 14, 73, 82, 97, 113, 232, 281
 Placentia (Greenwich Palace) 9
 Plume's books in 128, 155, 167, 269
 as prime meridian 255
 Royal Observatory 9, 17, *18-19*, 249, 250, 255, *255*
 royal yachts moored at 74–5, *75*
 Sir John Hawkins Knight Hospital for poor seamen 9, 230–1, 280, 281
Grey, Enoch 41
Grey, Lady Jane *165*
Grieve, Hilda 55
Grotius 159, 161
Gunning, Peter (1614–84) 162–3

Hacket, John (1592–1670) 2, 63–4, *64*, 65, 67, 68, 69–71, 77, 81, 82, 86, 87, 161, 198, 201, 202, 208, 211, 218
 Plume's memoir of 63, 70, 86, 87, 202

Hackett, Francis and Vere 129
Hadlow, Kent 30, 269, 274
Hale, Sir Matthew 111, 112
Hale, William (d. 1582) 29
Halley, Edmond 161, 249–50
Hall, William 101
Halton, Timothy (d. 1704) 114–15
Hammond, Henry 159
Hamond, Mary (wife of Thomas Plume, d. 1615) 25, 26, *27*
Hancorn, Richard 232
Harker, Rev George 242
Harley, Robert 170
Harries, David 239
Harrison, John 43
Hart, John 44
Harvey, Thomas 132
Harvey, William 161
Hasted, Edward 10, 76–7, 236
Hatfield Broad Oak, Essex *8*, 40
Hatfield Peverel, Essex 141, 144
Hay, Robert 128, 129, 130, **130**, 135
Hayward, John Michael **130**
Hazeleigh, Essex *8*, 28, 30, 44, 138
Head, Elizabeth 44
Head, John *27*, 43, 44
Hearn, Francis H. 181
Hearn, William 183
Hearth Tax of 1671 9
Heasman, Arthur 187
Heinsius, Daniel 159
Henrietta Maria, Queen 10, 68
Henry V 127
Henry VII 9
Henry VIII 1, 9, 10–11, 25, 108, 179, 270
Herrmann, Frank 148
Hewitt, Israel 40–1, 45, 46, 55, 56, 199
Heybridge, Essex 33, 39–40, **122**, **130**, 132, 134, 136, 138, 142, 146, 178, 271
Heylyn, Peter 86
Hills, Joseph 35
Hoare's (C. Hoare and Co., Plume's bank) 11, 84, 99
Hobart, Sir Henry (1560–1625) 161
Hobbes, Thomas 67, 160, 210
Hody, Humphrey (d. 1707) 114–15
Holdsworth, Richard (1590–1649) 60, 203
Honywood, Sir Thomas 43

Hooker, Richard 159
Hooker, Thomas (1586?–1647) 55
Horrocks, Thomas 41, 43–4
Horsmanden, Daniel **122**
Horwood, Edward Russell (d. 1901) **130**, 136–8, 147, 185
Howell, Michael 104
Hoyle, Fred (1915–2001) **251**, 258–9
Hudson, Edward 205–6
Huggett, Charles 33, 269
Hughes, Leonard **130**
Hurrell, Henry 141
Hutchinson, William 130, **130**
Huygens, Christiaan 250
Hyde, Alexander (*c.*1596–1667) 204
Hyde, Lady Barbara 199
Hyde, Dr Edward (1607–59) and his manuscripts 67–8, 162, 198, 202, 204, 207–8, 210–11, 214–15, *215*, 216
Hyde, Edward, earl of Clarendon (1609–74) 204, 210
Hyde, Thomas 211, 216

Iltney Farm, Mundon 12, 103, 106, 107, 108, 113, 120, 122–4, *123*, **125**, *126*, 128, 129, 131–3, *133*, 135, **137**, 138, 143, 270–1, 272
  sale of 144, 149
Ingram, Richard 41
Institute of Astronomy, Cambridge 259, 260
Institute of Theoretical Astronomy (IOTA), Cambridge 259
Interregnum (1649–60) 2, 10–11, 35, 68–9, 70, 79–80, 161
Ipswich, Suffolk 39, 156, 171
Isaacs, T. 80
Isle of Grain, Kent *8*, 106, 107–8, 113, 116, 225–6, 232, 238, 239, 275

James I 1, 42, 62, 82, 184
James II 80–1
Jarman, William *27*
Jeffreys, Harold (1891–1989) **251**, 258
Jennings, John 36, 38, 41, 42, 43
John Roan (Grey Coat) School, Greenwich 10, 14, 73, 82, 97, 113, 232, 281

John Sadd and Sons Ltd of Maldon 142
Johnston, Warren 208
Jonson, Ben 160, 210–11
Jordan, W.K. 108, 109

Keck, Samuel 236
Kegworth, Leicestershire 63
Kelly, T. 156
Kennicutt, Robert C., Jnr (1951–) **251**, 260, *260*
Kent 3, *8*, 11, 61
　bequests of Plume 3, 6, *8*, 14, 97, 107–8, 225–48
　see also Stone Castle Charity (later Dr Plumes Trust); *individual towns and parishes*
Kevill-Davies, E.L.B. 144–5
Kimbell, John 228
King, Benjamin 38
King's Lynn, Norfolk 156
Kishlansky, M.A. 87
Knight, Edward 183
Knight, Roger 233
Knight, Thomas 216
Knipe, Thomas **130**

Lambert, Major-General John 68
Langdell (*alias* Langdale), Thomas 36, 41
Laudianism 1–2, 55, 56, 58, 65–6, 77, 79, 80
　of Plume 2–3, 79, 86, 87
Laud, William (1573–1645) 1, 2, 56, 65, 67, 86–7, 181, 184
Lawe, Thomas 31
Layer Breton, Essex *8*, 268n6
lectures, public 12, 14, 97, 108, 113, 116, 120, 124–6, **125**, *126*, *127*, 132, 136, **137**, 138, *139*, 146, 148, 149, 232–3, 270–1, 272, 273–4
legacies of Plume *see* bequests of Plume
Leicester 156
L'Estrange, Sir Roger (1616–1704) 61
Lewis, John R. 191
libraries
　Essex County Library 145, 190
　Marsh's Library, Dublin 157, 162, 174n50
　parochial (parish) libraries 156, 170
　in seventeenth and eighteenth centuries 15–17, 155–7, 159, 160, 162, 167, 168–9, 170, 171
　Tenison's Library, London 16, 174n50
　town libraries 15–17, 155–6, 170, 171
　Tudor libraries 155–6
　see also Plume Library; Sion College, London
Limner, Thomas 179–80
Lindsey, Alexander 121, *123*
Lipsius, Justus 159
Little Easton, Essex 74
Little Holland, Essex *8*, 28
Little Totham, Essex *8*, 33
London
　book purchases in 12, 69, 82–4, *82*, 161–2
　Fleet Street 11, 12, 84
　Great Fire of (1666) 10, *72*, *82*, *83*, 100
　Great Plague of (1665–66) 72
　Moorfields, market 12, *13*
　Royal Exchange 11, *83*, 84
　Sion College 100, **122**, **125**, 148, 157, 212, 270
　Smithfield *alias* Smithfields *32*, 34, 106, 268
　St Giles-in-the-Fields 202, *213*, 214
　St Paul's Cathedral 12, *82*, 84, 157, 170
　see also Westminster, London
Longfield, Kent (parish) *8*
　Plume's bequest to rector 103, 229, 234–5, 237, 238–9, 275, 280
　Plume's grave 98, *98*, 229, 234, 244, 265
　Plume's memorial 229, 244–5
　Plume's official residence 10, 76–7, 229, 234
Loton, John 227, 230–1, 265, 266, 267, 274
Lovelace, Robert 217–18, 224n139
Lowth, William 178

Malcholm, A. 182
Malden, Jonas 134
Malden, Massachusetts 35
Malden, Surrey 63, 65
Maldon, Essex 1, *8*, *15*, 25–52, *32*, *213*
　Blue Boar 122, 126
　Borough Council (becomes Town Council) 136, 138, 145, 146, 149, 190

INDEX

Clover Field 33
economy 9, 11, 39–40, 45, 109–11, 141–3
Fambridge Road *32*, 33, 34, 146–7
Fullbridge Street 31, 33, 111
Hawksdown Hills 33
High Street *15*, 31, *32*
  property owned by Plume family 29–30, *32*, 33–4, 44, 144
King's Head 31, 122
London Road 140, 190
Maeldune Heritage Centre 116, 190
Market Hill *15*, 33, 129, 185, 190–1
Masonic Hall *184*, 185
Molehills (then Longfield, 'Norton's land') 33, 122, 132, 135, 136, **137**, 138, 145, 146
Moot Hall 3, *4*, 29, *32*, 35, 36, *37*, 184
Mrs Melsop's house *32*, 33, 107, 109, 269
National School 15, 134–5, 138–40, 142, 180–1
population 9, 111
Pound Mead (then Fairfield, 'Norton's land') 33, 122, 132, 135, 136, **137**, 138, 144, 146–7
Spread Eagle 31
Town Council (formerly Borough Council) 145, 146
Ware Pond 30, 31, *32*
see also All Saints' church/parish, Maldon; Maldon Grammar School (now Plume School); St Mary's church/parish, Maldon; St Peter's church, Maldon
Maldon, bequests of Plume 3–5, 97, 99, 107, 120–54, **125**, 269–70
  coal for the poor *126*, 131–2, **137**
  public lectures 12, 14, 97, 108, 113, 116, 120, 124–6, **125**, *126*, *127*, 132, 136, **137**, 138, *139*, 146, 148, 149, 232–3, 270–1
  workhouse 3, 14, 33, 99, 103, 106, 109–13, *110*, *112*, 116, 120, 122, 138, 149, 269, 273, 278
  see also All Saints' church/parish, Maldon; Maldon Grammar School (now Plume School); Plume Library

Maldon Corporation 9, *37*, 99, 102, 109–11, 121, 128, 131, 180, 190, 191
  and religious strife 40–1, 42–3
  and Samuel Plume (Dr Plume's brother) 42–4
  and Dr Thomas Plume 82–4
  and Thomas Plume, snr 1, 5, 30–1, 34–7, 39–41
Maldon Grammar School (now Plume School) 3, 15, 28, 106, 121–2, **130**, 134–5, 143–4, 146, 147, 184–5
  Breeder and Wentworth benefactions 37–8, 114, 120, 124, 127, 128, 129, 134, 135, 143, 144, 147, 178
  maintenance for boys at 3, 14, 15, 38, 113, 114, 116, 120, 121, **125**, 128, 135, 136, **137**, 140, 148, 271
  and the Maldon Trust 127, 128, 131, 144, 146–7
  Plume rebuilds 17, 114, 127–8
  schoolmasters 28, 33, 38, 46, 100, 121, 124, 127, 128, **130**, 134–5, 136, 138, 140
  schoolmaster's salary 124, 127, 128, 129, 134, 136, **137**, 140
  see also apprenticeships for Maldon Grammar School boys; Plume Building
Maldon Iron Works Co. 142
Maldon Trust (later Thomas Plume's Library) 3, 6, 12, 15, 102–3, 105–6, 108, 116, 120–54, **122**
  accounts 120–1, 122, 124, **125**, 131, 136–8, **137**, 144–5
  and the grammar school 127, 128, 131, 144, 146–7
  minutes 105–6, 111, 120–1, *123*, 124, 131–2, 134, 136
  and the Plume Library 3, 6, 12, 99, 101, 102–3, 105, 108, 111, 116, 120–49
  trust deed of 1843 136, 140–1, 143
  trustees 99, 101, 102–4, 105–6, 120, 121, 122, **122**, *123*, 125, 131–2, 136, 137–8, **137**
Maldon Union Board of Guardians 113
Malling deanery, diocese of Rochester 79, 100, 234, 281

Malling, Town (parish), Kent *8*, 79, 235, 274
Manley, Keith 158
manuscripts/notebooks 3, 5, 6, 20, 21, 54, 60–3, 65–7, 135, 148, 164–6, *166*, 169–70, 196–224
  accounts in 58, 59, 60, 76, **137**, 198–9
  acquisition of 70, 162, 212–18, *213*
  bindings 197, 203, 204, 205
  of Boreman (Robert) 10, 67, 162, 200, 202–4, *203*, 208, 211–12, *215*
  cataloguing 147–8, 149, 197
  the Civil Wars in 204–5, 206, 208–9
  common-placing 166, 207, 211
  correspondence 198–9, 207, 211–12
  'Dr Plume's Pocket-book' 5, 67
  of 'the Eythorne preacher' 200, 204–6, 208, 210
  of Hyde (Dr Edward) 67–8, 162, 198, 202, 204, 207–8, 210–11, 214–15, *215*, 216
  John Plume's exercise book 28
  Latin phrasebook 54, 58, 59
  Plume bequeaths to library 100, 121, 128, 147–8, 196
  Plume's writings 5, 54, 58–63, 66–7, 100, 164–6, *165*, *166*, 196, 198, 199–202
  prices 206, 216, 217, *217*
  reading notes 166, *166*, 200–1, 204, 206, 207, 210–11
  scraps *200*, 201
  sermon notes 21, 54–5, 63, 70, 73, 164, 198, 199–200, 203, 204–6, 207–8, 211, 212, 218
  treatises 198, 207, 208–10, *209*
Marine, John **122**
Marriage, James 133
marriage, Plume on 67–8, 231, 267
Marsh's Library, Dublin 157, 162, 174n50
Mary I 1, 184
Mary II *72*, 80, 81
Matthew, Charles **130**, 132, 134, 135, 136, 181
Mede, Joseph 159
Melsop, Mrs, her house in Maldon *32*, 33, 107, 109, 269
Merston, Kent *8*, 74
Michaelson, John 55, 57

Mildmay, Sir Henry (*c.*1594–1668) 42
Milton, John 159
Milton, Kent *8*, 274
Mitchell, Francis 29–30
Monyns, John (1609–1707) 205
Moore, John (1646–1714) 157
Moorfields, market, London 12, *13*
Moot Hall, Maldon 3, *4*, 29, *32*, 35, 36, *37*, 184
Morant, Philip 5, 25, 135, 178
More, Henry (1614–87) 209
More, Thomas 159
More *alias* Moore, William 58, 59, 63
Morrill, J. 72, 87
Morris, John 177
Mott, Mark 55, 57
Moundeford, John 170
Mundon, Essex 3, *8*, 14, 46, 113, **122**, 128, 132, 136, 138, 146, 271, 278
  see also Iltney Farm, Mundon

Napoleonic Wars 132, 149
National School, Maldon 15, 134–5, 138–40, 142, 180–1
Naudé, Gabriel 167
Nektarios (*alias* Nectarius) (1605–*c.*1680) 73, 268
Neptune (planet) 255–6
Newcourt, R. 74
Newton, Isaac 17–19, 160, 249–50, 251, 252, 254, 256, 277
Nightingale, Robert *29*, 181, *182*, 184
Nonsuch, Surrey 63, 65, 68, 201
Northumberland Refractor, telescope 255–6
Norton, John and Mary 33, 122, 132, 272
Norwich, Norfolk 156
notebooks *see* manuscripts/notebooks
Nye, David E. 189, 190

observatory at Cambridge 14, 102, 107, 113, 250, 251, 253, 276
  in Madingley Road 253–60, *254*, *257*
  in Trinity College 19, 250, 252, 253
Oley, Barnabas 156, 170–1
Osler, Margaret 17
Ostriker, Jeremiah (1937–) **251**, 259
Owen, John 159

INDEX

Palmer, Samuel (d. 1724) *123*, 125
Palmer, William 14–15
pamphlets in Plume Library 5, 20, 63, 106, 129, 147–8, 156, 168–9, *169*, 197
  see also manuscripts/notebooks
paper, sources of 206–7
Payne, Edward 132, 133
Peake, Daniell 54, 57
Peile, J. 58
Pemble, William 159
Pepys, Samuel 72, 81, 167, 168, 172
Petchey, Dr W.J. 5, 17, 19, 36, 58, 63, 67, 69, 72, 85, 96, 109–11, **130**, 147, 148, 157–8, 161–2, 163, 178, 179, 198, 202
Peter/Peters, Hugh (1598–1660) 62–3
Pevsner, Sir Nikolaus 179, 191
philanthropy 15–16, 155, 244–5
  see also Bequests of Plume
Pilgrim Trust 145
Pindar, Thomas 206, 210
Placentia (Greenwich Palace) 9
Plaxtol, Kent 241
Plume, Ann (d. 1629, Plume's sister) *27*, 28
Plume, Bennony (bap. 1624, Plume's half-sister) *27*, 28
Plume Building 176–95, *177*, *180*, *183*, *186*, *188*, *189*
  see also Maldon Grammar School (now Plume School); Plume Library
Plume, Deborah (d. 1624, wife of Thomas Plume, snr) *27*, 28
Plume Educational Trust 15, 116, 144, 147, 149
Plume, Elinor (*d.* 1647, Plume's mother) *27*, 28, 34
Plume, Elizabeth (*née* Purchas) 25, *27*
Plume, Elizabeth (married Richard Symonds in 1580) 31
Plume, Elizabeth (d. 1665, married John Head) *27*, 28, 30, 34, 44
Plume, James (Plume's executor) 20, 74, 76, 81, 84, 97–106, 115, 124, 128, 225–6, 227, 231, 233, 234–5, 245, 265, 275, 277–8
  Chancery cases brought 101–2, 104–5, 226, 228, 232, 235

Chancery cases defended 102–3, 106, 226, 236
Church Street house, Greenwich 101–2, 107, 234
  Plume's bequests to 97, 105, 106, 278
Plume, John (d. 1636, Plume's half-brother) *27*, 28, 34, 215–16
Plume Library 5, 6, 15–17, *15*, 20–1, 108, 136, 143–9, 155–75, 181, *182*, 189–90
  building of 6, 14, 82–4, 85, 86, 107, 113, 114, 128
  catalogues 21, 121, 129, 135, 143, 147–8, 149, 158, 161, 171, 181, 197, 201, 212
  interior 181–4, *183*
  library keepers 33, 100, 105–6, 121, 128, 129–30, **130**, 132, 135, 136, 147, 184, 185
  mahogany box 129, 143, 197
  and the Maldon Trust 3, 6, 12, 99, 101, 102–3, 105, 108, 111, 116, 120–49
  Plume's bequests 3, 97, 102, 107, 113, 120, 148, 269–70
    book purchases **125**, 270
    library keeper's salary 33, **125**, 129, 132, 135, 136, **137**, 144, 148, 272
    repairs 122, 124, **125**, 128, 131, 132, 144, 178–9, 185–90, 234, 240
    Sion College oversight 100, **125**, 148, 270
    see also St Peter's church, Maldon
  portraits in 2, 3, 69, 81, 85, 86, 181, 183–4
  St Peter's tower, relationship with 178, 179, 191
  twentieth century restoration 145–6, 187, 189, 190
  see also book collection in Plume Library; manuscripts/notebooks; pamphlets in Plume Library; Plume Building
Plume, Nathaniel (Plume's cousin) 33–4, 104, 106, **122**, 268, 280
Plume, Robert (*temp.* Henry VIII) 6, 25, *26*, *27*
Plume, Robert (*fl.* 1584) 25, *26*, *27*
Plume, Robert (b. prob. *post* 1600) 25, *26*, *27*

Plume, Samuel (son of Robert Plume, *fl.* 1584) 7, 25, *27*
Plume, Samuel (bap. 1589) 7, 25–6, *27*, 45
Plume, Samuel (d. 1670, Dr Thomas Plume's brother) 7, 9, 25, *27*, 28, 30, 42–5, 46, 216
Plume School (was Maldon Grammar School) 3, 15, 33, 114, 127, 146, 147, 149
Plume, Thomas (d. 1615, Plume's grandfather) 7, 25–6, *26*, 27
Plume, Thomas, snr (d. by 1658, Plume's father) 7–9, 25, 26, 27–31, *27*, 34–41, 42, 45–6, 87–8, 215
  and Christ's College, Cambridge 26, 45, 46
  friendship with John Danes 38, *45*, 46, 53
  and Isaac Hewitt 40–1, 45, 46, 56
Plume, Dr Thomas (1630–1704) 1–21, *4*, *27*, 28, 30, 46, 53–94
  character 63, 171, 172, 234, 244
  Charles I, devotion to 53, 59, 61, 68, 87, 184
  church career 2–3, 5
    chaplain in ordinary to Charles II 12, 76
    income from church 74–6
    Little Easton living 74
    Merston sinecure living 74
    ordination 2, 69
    Rochester, archdeacon of 2, 3, 10, 30, 74, 75, 76–81
    Rochester Cathedral, prebendary of 2, 10, 74, 76
    St Alfege's church, Greenwich, vicar of 2, 9, 10, 30, 69–74, 77, 78–9, 99
  coat of arms 7, 181, *182*
  education 2, 26–7, 53–63
    Chelmsford School 53–7, 127, 199–200
    Christ's College, Cambridge 26–7, 45, 46, 57–63, 209
  family tree *27*
  life
    attempted poisoning 20, 96
    baptism 28, 53, *54*, 271
    birth 28
    death and burial 20, 84, 97–8, *98*, 104, 234, 244, 265
  on marriage 67–8, 231, 267
  monogram 21, *163*, 166–7
  poetry by 59, 60–2, 67
  portrait of 3, *4*, 184, 269
  publications by
    A Century of Sermons (including Plume's memoir of Hacket) 63, *64*, 70, 86, 87, 202, 208
    Hacket's biography of John Williams 70
  reading notes of 166, *166*, 200–1, 210–11
  religious practice and belief 2, 66–7, 85, 87
    and Arminianism 66, 79, 226
    and Calvinism 66, 79, 85, 87, 226
    Church of England, support for 2, 12, 57, 62, 71, 85, 108, 184, 235, 271, 274
    and episcopacy 72, 86–7
    Laudian ('High Church') view 2–3, 79, 81, 85, 86, 87
    and Presbyterianism 2–3, 56, 66, 67, 69, 87
    and Puritanism 79, 85, 113–14
    on Roman Catholicism 66, 67
    on salvation 66, 226
    on sin 72–3, 80, 85
  royalism 2, 59, 60–1, 62, 67, 72, 80–1, 87, 184, 204–5, 206
  sources of wealth 20, 30, 87–8
    allowance from father 64–5
    business interests 20, 84, 88
    church income 74–6
    inheritances 20, 30, 87–8
  see also bequests of Plume; will of Plume
Plume Trust (Essex) *see* Maldon Trust (later Thomas Plume's Library)
Plume Trust (Kent) *see* Stone Castle Charity (later Dr Plumes Trust)
Plumian Farm, Balsham, Cambs 102, 250
Plumian Professorship of Astronomy at Cambridge University 3, 6, 14, 17, 18–19, 107, 113, 114, 116, 146, 155, 249–62, **251**, 276–7

INDEX

Plumstead, Kent *8*, 274
Pond, Samuel 121, **122**, *123*, 271
Pope, Elizabeth 35
Powell, John 241
Powell, Michael 171
Power, Thomas 95, 96, 101, 103, 231, 265, 278, 279
Powys, A.R. 187, 189
Pratt, Elinor *see* Plume, Elinor (*d.* 1647, Plume's mother)
Pratt, Jeremy (*alias* Jeremiah) 28, 34
Pratt, Joseph 34
Presbyterianism 2, 41, 42–3, 56, 59, 66, 69
    Dengie Hundred Classis 41, 42, 48n33, 50n84, 66, 87
    Plume's attitude to 2–3, 56, 66, 67, 69, 87
Pride, Colonel Thomas 36, 68
Protectorate (Cromwellian) 2, 9, 35, 36–7
Punch, magazine 255, *255*
Purcell Miller Tritton & Partners 190
Purchas, Elizabeth 25, *27*
Puritanism 2, 40, 55, 58, 62–3, 65, 66, 67, 70, 77, 79, 85, 113–14, 232
Purleigh, Essex *8*, **122**, 132, 136, 138, 146

quantum physics 256
Queen's College, Oxford 114, 157, 170
Queen's House, Greenwich 9, 10

Randolph, Thomas 210–11
Raverat, Gwen 257
Rawson, Joseph 99–100, 101, 265
Rees, Martin (1942–) **251**, 259
reformation of manners 80, 108
Relativity, Einstein's theory of 256, 257–8
Restoration, the (1660) 2, 10, 42, 46, 64, 68, 78, 79–80, 86, 156, 172, 202, 208–9
Reynolds, Anna 20
Reynolds, Christopher S. (1971–) **251**, 260
Rice, Damarys 31
Richard III 184
Ridley estate, Kent 235, 237
Roan (Grey Coat) School, Greenwich *see* John Roan (Grey Coat) School, Greenwich

Robinson, Reuben 44
Robject, Isaac 36
Rochester, Kent *8*, 10, 265
    Corporation 230
    Plume's bequests for
        minor legacies 12, 109, 229, 266
        poor tradesmen 109, 229–30, 266
    see also Longfield, Kent (parish)
Rochester, Kent, cathedral and diocese 10–11, 77
    bishops of 67, 77, 80–1, 86, 170, 226
    cathedral 77, *78*, 79, 101, 234
    deaneries 79
    Plume archdeacon of 2, 3, 10, 30, 74, 75, 76–81
    Plume as prebendary of cathedral 2, 10, 74, 76
    Plume's bequests for
        cathedral 101, 234
        poor clergy of 3, 12, 107–8, 109, 116, 225, 233, 234, 235, 241–3, 244, 245, 267–8, 274, 275
Rogers, John 40
Root and Branch Petition (1640) 2
Roxwell, Essex *8*, 42
Royal Commission on Historical Monuments (England) 187
royalism 35, 36, 58, 77, 205, 208–9, 250
    of Plume 2, 59, 60–1, 62, 67, 72, 80–1, 87, 184, 204–5, 206
Royal Observatory, Greenwich 9, 17, *18*, 249, 250, 255
Ruck, Thomas 35
Rustat, Tobias (1608–94) 250
Rutter, Elizabeth 231
Ryland, R.L. 140

Sackrey, Thomas *127*
Salisbury, Wiltshire 115, 204
    bishop of 69, 115, 204
Salmon, Nathaniel 5
Salter, J.H. (d. 1932) 147
Saltmarsh, John 66
salvation and Plume 65, 66, 226
Samms, W.J. 184–5
Saunders, Ebenezer 185
Scaliger, Joseph Justus (1540–1609) 159, 210
Scaliger, Julius Caesar (1484–1558) 210

Scarrow, William 121, 128, **130**
schools 180–1
　Chelmsford School
　　Plume at 1, 53–7, 59, 114, 127, 199–200, 218
　　Plume's bequest to 113, 271, 272
　Faversham Grammar School, Kent 205
　John Roan (Grey Coat) School, Greenwich 10, 14, 73, 82, 97, 113, 232, 281
　National School, Maldon 15, 134–5, 138–40, 142, 180–1
　Westminster School 63, 90n84, 90n85, 202, 204, 210
　see also Maldon Grammar School (now Plume School)
science and Plume 17–21
　Plumian Professorship of Astronomy at Cambridge University 3, 6, 14, 17, 18–19, 107, 113, 114, 116, 146, 155, 249–62, **251**
　scientific works in Plume Library 17, **159**, 160–1
Secker, Thomas 232
Selling alias Sellynge, Kent 204, *213*
Seymour, Isaac 129, **130**, 191
Seymour, Jane (Queen) 179
Seymour, William (Marquis of Hertford) 214
Shacklock, Gwyneth **130**, 147
Shepherd, Anthony (1721–96) **251**, 252–3
Sherling & Son of Maldon 189
Shinglewood, Joseph 134
Sidway, John 73–4
Simonds (*alias* Symonds), Richard (*fl.* 1580, marries Elizabeth Plume) 31
Simonds (*alias* Symonds), Richard (Middle Temple lawyer) 31
Simonds (*alias* Symonds), Richard (antiquary) 178
Simonds, Sissilia 31
Simpson, John 209–10
Sion College, London 100, **122**, **125**, 148, 157, 212, 270
Sir John Hawkins Knight Hospital for poor seamen, Chatham 9, 230–1, 280, 281
Slack, P.A. 108–9

Slater, William 40
slavery 158
Smart, William 124
Smith, Robert (1689–1768) 250, **251**, 252
Soan, John (d. 1636) 35, 38
Social Sciences and Humanities Research Council of Canada 21
Society for Promoting Christian Knowledge (SPCK) 14, 16, 80, 111, 114, 156
Society for the Propagation of the Gospel in Foreign Parts (SPG) 80, 107, 111
Society for the Protection of Ancient Buildings (SPAB) 145, 187, 189
Spaeth, D.A. 72
Spelman, Henry 159
Spitzer Space telescope 260
Sprat, Thomas (bap. 1635–1713) 81, 86
Spurr, J. 86, 87
Stace *alias* Stacey, Thomas 32–3, 121, **122**, 271
St Alfege's church, Greenwich 9, 10, 69, *71*, 72, 74, 99, 101, 202, 228
　Plume's bequests for
　　charnel house 115, 235, 266
　　Church Street house 101–2, 107, 234, 275
Standish, Richard 131
Stapleford Tawney, Essex 41
stars 252, 257, 258–9, 260
Steeple, Essex 33, **130**, 141
Stevens, John 48n33, 48n34, 121, **122**, 271
Stillingfleet, Edward (1635–99) 157, 162
St Mary's church/parish, Maldon 32–3, 43, 111–12, 121, **122**, 125, **130**, 131, 132, 136, 138, 141, 142, 146, 178, 210, 271
Stone Castle Charity (later Dr Plumes Trust) 3, 116, 225–6, 228–9, 232–45, 268
　establishment of 106, 116, 235–7, 245, 274–5
　trustees 99, 101–2, 231, 233, 235–7, 239–40, 241–2, 243, 245
　Tudeley Farm estate, Tudeley 239, 245
Stone Castle estate, Stone, Dartford, Kent 3, 9, 106, 107–8, 225, 228, 235, 237–8, *238*, 240–1, 243, 245, 268, 273–4
Stone, Kent 109, 228, 273, 274, 281

INDEX

Stow, Louisa 142
St Peter's church, Maldon *15*, *32*, 145, 176–8, *177*, 179
  bells of 177, 178
  Breeder's grammar school in 38, 127, 178
  churchyard 179, 190–1
  Guild of the Assumption of Our Lady 176, 177, 178
  Lowth's school in 178
  medieval period 176, 177, 178, 179
  Plume Library in 3, 14, *15*, 106, 114, 120, 127–8, 156, 176
  Plume rebuilds 3, 14, 38, 114, 120, 127–8, 156, 178, 179
  Plume's grammar school in 14, 38, 106, 114, 120, 127–8
  tower *15*, 140, 145, 176–7, 178–9, *180*, 185–9, *186*, *188*, *189*, 190, 191
  see also Maldon Grammar School (now Plume School); Plume Building; Plume Library
St Peter's Lodge of Freemasons, Maldon *184*, 185
Straight, John 121, **122**
Strood, Kent *8*, 229, 231
Supernova Cosmology Project 259
Symond, Henry 43
Symonds (*alias* Simonds), Richard (Middle Temple lawyer) *see* Simonds (*alias* Symonds), Richard

Talbot, John 238
Talbot, Peter 168
Tarver, A. 79
Taverner, James 33–4
Tendring, Essex *8*, 41
Tenison, Thomas (d. 1715) 16, 69, 115, 174n50
Terling, John 183
Theydon Garnon, Essex *8*, 29
Thomas Plume's Library (charity) 3, 146, 149
Thomas, R.E. 147
Thompson, Dr Francis (*c.*1640–1715) 33, 98, 99–100, 101, 106, 121, 196, 235–6, 250, 265, 269, 274, 277
Thompson, Francis (Plume Librarian, d. 1743) 33, 100, 105–6, **122**, *123*, 129, **130**, 135, 267
Thomson, Paula **130**
Thurloe, John (1616–68) 69
Tilmanstone, Kent 204–6
Tonbridge deanery, diocese of Rochester 100, 234, 281
Tonbridge, Kent 239, 245
Tories 86, 128
Trinity College, Cambridge 19, 63, 202, 210–11, 250, 251, 252, 253
Tudeley, Kent 239, 245
Turner, Francis 80–1
Turner, Dr John 101–2, 234
Twigg, John 59
Tyacke, N. 66, 77–8

Vince, Samuel (1749–1821) **251**, 253, *253*
Voss, Gerhard 159

Waight, John 33
Walter, John 55–6
Wanstead, Essex *8*, 42
Waple, Edward (d. 1712) 114–15
Ward, Seth (d. 1689) 115
Waring, Francis 134
Warner, John (bishop of Rochester) 67, 77, 78, 80, 226
Warner, John Lee (archdeacon of Rochester) 78, 234, 244
Warwick, earl of 43
Wasse, John 34
Watling Street (the Dover Road) 11, 81
Wells, Thomas 39
Wentworth, Annastacy (d. 1634) 29, 30, 38, 127
Wentworth, Henry 29
Westminster, London 12, 43, 81–2, *105*, 221n64
  St Margaret's 81, 221n64
  Westminster Abbey 202, 221n64
  Westminster School 63, 90n84, 90n85, 202, 204, 210
Whigs 128
Whiston, William 251, 252
White Notley, Essex *8*
Whitgift, John 184
Whitter, Justinian (d. 1649) 162, 200, 210, 214, 215

Wickham Bishops, Essex *8*, 41
Wilkins, John 159
Willet, Andrew 159
William III 80, 81
Williams, John (1582–1650) 63, 70, 77, 86, 87
Williams, William **130**
Willis, N. 243
will of Plume 3, *4*, 5–6, 18–19, 33, 67, 79, 84–8, 95–119, *95*, 196, 201, 225–6, 263–82
  attempted forgery 20, 96, 104–5
  codicils 95, 97, 104, 113, 232, 234
Wilson, Alfred **130**
Wisbech, Cambs 69
Witty, John 252
Wood, Anthony 68
Woodham Water parish, Essex *8*, 30, **122**, 130, 132, 136, 138, 141, 146, 269, 271
Woodhouse, Robert (1773–1821) **251**, 254
workhouses 111, 115
  Maldon 3, 14, 33, 99, 103, 106, 109–13, *110*, *112*, 116, 120, 122, 138, 149, 269, 273, 278
Wren, Sir Christopher *18*, 100
Wren, Matthew 35
Wright, John 229
Wyldes/Wildes, John 124, 131
Wylie, Erica **130**, 147

Young, Arthur 122–4

Zanchi, Girolamo (1516–90) 210
Zouch, Richard 159, 161